Travels into Muscovy, Persia, and part of the East-Indies. Containing, an accurate description of whatever is most remarkable in those countries. And embelished with above 320 copper plates, In two volumes. Volume 2 of 2

Cornelis de Bruyn

Travels into Muscovy, Persia, and part of the East-Indies. Containing, an accurate description of whatever is most remarkable in those countries. And embelished with above 320 copper plates, ... To which is added, an account of the journey of Mr. Isbrants Volume 2 of 2

Bruyn, Cornelis de

ESTCID: T110676

Reproduction from British Library

In vol. I the numbering of pp.225-228 is repeated; pp.236-240 misnumbered 363, 263-266.

London : printed for A. Bettesworth and C. Hitch, S. Birt, C. Davis, J. Clarke, S. Harding [and 4 others in London], 1737.

2v.,plates : ill.,maps ; 2°

Eighteenth Century
Collections Online
Print Editions

Gale ECCO Print Editions

Relive history with *Eighteenth Century Collections Online*, now available in print for the independent historian and collector. This series includes the most significant English-language and foreign-language works printed in Great Britain during the eighteenth century, and is organized in seven different subject areas including literature and language; medicine, science, and technology; and religion and philosophy. The collection also includes thousands of important works from the Americas.

The eighteenth century has been called "The Age of Enlightenment." It was a period of rapid advance in print culture and publishing, in world exploration, and in the rapid growth of science and technology – all of which had a profound impact on the political and cultural landscape. At the end of the century the American Revolution, French Revolution and Industrial Revolution, perhaps three of the most significant events in modern history, set in motion developments that eventually dominated world political, economic, and social life.

In a groundbreaking effort, Gale initiated a revolution of its own: digitization of epic proportions to preserve these invaluable works in the largest online archive of its kind. Contributions from major world libraries constitute over 175,000 original printed works. Scanned images of the actual pages, rather than transcriptions, recreate the works *as they first appeared.*

Now for the first time, these high-quality digital scans of original works are available via print-on-demand, making them readily accessible to libraries, students, independent scholars, and readers of all ages.

For our initial release we have created seven robust collections to form one the world's most comprehensive catalogs of 18th century works.

Initial Gale ECCO Print Editions collections include:

History and Geography
Rich in titles on English life and social history, this collection spans the world as it was known to eighteenth-century historians and explorers. Titles include a wealth of travel accounts and diaries, histories of nations from throughout the world, and maps and charts of a world that was still being discovered. Students of the War of American Independence will find fascinating accounts from the British side of conflict.

Social Science
Delve into what it was like to live during the eighteenth century by reading the first-hand accounts of everyday people, including city dwellers and farmers, businessmen and bankers, artisans and merchants, artists and their patrons, politicians and their constituents. Original texts make the American, French, and Industrial revolutions vividly contemporary.

Medicine, Science and Technology
Medical theory and practice of the 1700s developed rapidly, as is evidenced by the extensive collection, which includes descriptions of diseases, their conditions, and treatments. Books on science and technology, agriculture, military technology, natural philosophy, even cookbooks, are all contained here.

Literature and Language
Western literary study flows out of eighteenth-century works by Alexander Pope, Daniel Defoe, Henry Fielding, Frances Burney, Denis Diderot, Johann Gottfried Herder, Johann Wolfgang von Goethe, and others. Experience the birth of the modern novel, or compare the development of language using dictionaries and grammar discourses.

Religion and Philosophy
The Age of Enlightenment profoundly enriched religious and philosophical understanding and continues to influence present-day thinking. Works collected here include masterpieces by David Hume, Immanuel Kant, and Jean-Jacques Rousseau, as well as religious sermons and moral debates on the issues of the day, such as the slave trade. The Age of Reason saw conflict between Protestantism and Catholicism transformed into one between faith and logic -- a debate that continues in the twenty-first century.

Law and Reference
This collection reveals the history of English common law and Empire law in a vastly changing world of British expansion. Dominating the legal field is the *Commentaries of the Law of England* by Sir William Blackstone, which first appeared in 1765. Reference works such as almanacs and catalogues continue to educate us by revealing the day-to-day workings of society.

Fine Arts
The eighteenth-century fascination with Greek and Roman antiquity followed the systematic excavation of the ruins at Pompeii and Herculaneum in southern Italy; and after 1750 a neoclassical style dominated all artistic fields. The titles here trace developments in mostly English-language works on painting, sculpture, architecture, music, theater, and other disciplines. Instructional works on musical instruments, catalogs of art objects, comic operas, and more are also included.

The BiblioLife Network

This project was made possible in part by the BiblioLife Network (BLN), a project aimed at addressing some of the huge challenges facing book preservationists around the world. The BLN includes libraries, library networks, archives, subject matter experts, online communities and library service providers. We believe every book ever published should be available as a high-quality print reproduction; printed on-demand anywhere in the world. This insures the ongoing accessibility of the content and helps generate sustainable revenue for the libraries and organizations that work to preserve these important materials.

The following book is in the "public domain" and represents an authentic reproduction of the text as printed by the original publisher. While we have attempted to accurately maintain the integrity of the original work, there are sometimes problems with the original work or the micro-film from which the books were digitized. This can result in minor errors in reproduction. Possible imperfections include missing and blurred pages, poor pictures, markings and other reproduction issues beyond our control. Because this work is culturally important, we have made it available as part of our commitment to protecting, preserving, and promoting the world's literature.

GUIDE TO FOLD-OUTS MAPS and OVERSIZED IMAGES

The book you are reading was digitized from microfilm captured over the past thirty to forty years. Years after the creation of the original microfilm, the book was converted to digital files and made available in an online database.

In an online database, page images do not need to conform to the size restrictions found in a printed book. When converting these images back into a printed bound book, the page sizes are standardized in ways that maintain the detail of the original. For large images, such as fold-out maps, the original page image is split into two or more pages

Guidelines used to determine how to split the page image follows:

• Some images are split vertically; large images require vertical and horizontal splits.
• For horizontal splits, the content is split left to right.
• For vertical splits, the content is split from top to bottom.
• For both vertical and horizontal splits, the image is processed from top left to bottom right.

TRAVELS

INTO

MUSCOVY,

PERSIA,

And PART of the

EAST-INDIES.

CONTAINING,

An Accurate DESCRIPTION of whatever is moſt remarkable in thoſe COUNTRIES.

AND EMBELISHED

With above 320 Copper Plates, repreſenting the fineſt Proſpects, and moſt conſiderable Cities in thoſe Parts ; the different Habits of the People ; the ſingular and extraordinary Birds, Fiſhes, and Plants which are there to be found: As likewiſe the Antiquities of thoſe Countries, and particularly the noble Ruins of the famous Palace of PERSEPOLIS, called *Chelminar* by the *Perſians*. The whole being delineated on the Spot, from the reſpective Objects.

To which is added,

An Account of the Journey of Mr *ISBRANTS*, Ambaſſador from *Muſcovy*, through *Ruſſia* and *Tartary*, to *China* , together with Remarks on the Travels of Sir *John Chardin*, and Mr *Kempfer*, and a Letter written to the AUTHOR on that Subject

In Two VOLUMES.

By M *CORNELIUS LE BRUYN*.

Tranſlated from the Original *FRENCH*.

VOL. II.

LONDON.

Printed for A BETTESWORTH and C HITCH, S BIRT, C DAVIS, J. CLARKE, S HARDING D BROWNE, A. MILLAR, J SHUCKBURGH, and T. OSBORNE

M DCC XXXVII.

KARWANSERA MALAER

THE
TRAVELS
OF
CORNELIUS LE BRUYN.

Through Muscovy and Persia, to the East-
Indies, the coaſt of Malabar, the iſland
of Ceylon, Batavia, Bantam, and other
places.

CHAP. L.

*The Author's departure from Iſpahan   An account of the
Perſian couriers, and the bearers of Caljan.   A fine
Caravanſerai   A deſcription of Jedagaes.   Excellent
bread   Dangerous roads   The manner in which the
Arabians live*

T HE preparations for our
journey being complet-
ed, we waited till twen-
ty beaſts of carriage,
that were loaded with
commodities which be-
longed to the *India* company, had
ſet out before us, and we departed
from *Iſpahan* the 26th of *October*,
1704, about two in the afternoon.
The *Engliſh* merchants, together
with father *Antonio Deſturo*, and all

our friends, accompanied us out of
the city on horſeback, and were followed by all their domeſtics and couriers   We took a ſhort repaſt in the
King's gardens, at the diſtance of a
league from the city, and continued
there till four of the clock.   We then
proceeded on our journey, after we
had taken leave of our friends, and
arrived, about ſeven, at the Caravanſerai of *Spahancc*, three leagues from
Iſpahan, where we found thoſe

Vol II   B   who

1704 who had set out before us, and we all passed the night in that place We had several couriers, whose dress is very different from those who live in *Ispahan* The reader will find a representation of them in plate 110 The plumes which they wear on their turbans, and the ornaments that accompany them, are of various colours Their vests are usually of scarlet, and little bells are fastened to their girdles, with tufts of black silk The sound of these bells is heard at a considerable distance, when the couriers are in motion Those who hire them, are obliged to furnish them with their habit, which becomes their own at the end of the journey, over and above the wages they receive It is usual to hire as many of these couriers as are judged necessary, with a bearer of *Caluci*, or a bottle of tobacco, who is mounted on a mule, that likewise carries two portmanteaus, or leathern cases, filled with coffee, rose-water, tobacco, and such like accommodations We have represented one of these persons, with his equipage in plate 111 The *Persi* are always attended by some of these servants in their travels, and are imitated by all *Lords* of any rank The little machine, which hangs on one side of the mule, is filled with fire

We proceeded on our journey at once in the morning, and arrived, in the space of two hours and an half, at the Caravansera of *Mina L'rasa*, and, within another hour, at a place, where part of the customs exacted for mercantile goods, is paid We arrived, about the twenty eighth, at the

Free Caravansera village of *Maier*, where a fine Caravanserai is built of stone, and was founded by King *Sulimaan*, the father of the Prince who now reigns A range of fine stables runs all round the inside of the court, and the outside of this building has more the air of a palace, than of a publick house for travellers There are two kinds of wings on the sides of the fore-gate, and a large entrance, that appears beautiful, and opens into exceeding fine walks of

trees to the right and left, and 1704. of which that in the middle is the largest It likewise fronts the edifice, and extends very far towards the mountains No situation can be more amiable than that of this Caravansei, which we have delineated in plate 112 The principal customs are paid there The village, on one side of it, is large, and surrounded with trees, and the officers of the customs sent from thence refreshments of melons, and grapes, to Mr. *Bakker*, my companion in this journey

We left this place on the twenty eighth, about three in the morning, and passed by a water mill, on a little river, which we crossed twice, on two small bridges of stone, and arrived, about ten that morning, at a large town, called *Kemmnya*, which is filled with gardens, and little towers that serve for pigeon-houses On one side of this town, we observed the tomb of a saint named *Zja-resa*.

The Tomb of a Saint

It is enclosed with a wall, whose inward space is ornamented with several trees, and two fountains filled with fish, which the *Persian* superstition will not permit any one to touch We saw carps in the smallest, and large fish in the other. This tomb has a lofty situation on the slope of a mountain We passed the night in the Caravanserai built of earth, in the town, and pursued our journey on the twenty ninth, about five in the morning We were informed, that some other travellers had been robbed, as they left the town, of two beasts loaded with goods, and as the inhabitants of that place have the reputation of being great thieves, we had reason to suspect they had given this instance of their abilities in that profession, we, therefore, judged it expedient to be upon our guard, especially as we were well provided with fire arms Robberies of this nature are very frequent in that quarter, but if one has any friend to make proper complaints at court, the lord of the town is obliged to be responsible for what is lost, but if a person has not such an

in-

JESDAGAES

1704 interest as I have mentioned, he must not expect any restitution This regulation obliges the officers of the place to be very attentive to the conduct of the inhabitants, and yet robberies are frequently repeated

The road, without the town, contracts itself into a narrow pass, between two ranges of mountains, and which is rendered very dangerous by the torrents that are continually rolling from the summit, but it opens, at the distance of half a league, into a plain, which is encompassed by these mountains Several villages, full of gardens, present themselves to the view on the right, but the mountains are all barren and rocky, and the land upon them lies wild and uncultivated We came, about eleven, to the Caravanserai of *Megsee-bigie*, without having met any game in our way. We there found several pigeons, woodcocks, mallards, and larks, along the edges of a little canal We left this place, at one in the morning, and arrived, about five, at the village of *Amanabaet*, which is said to separate *Persia* from *Parthia*

Jesdagies We arrived, about eleven in the forenoon, at the Caravanserai of *Jesdagas*, which is a village seated among the mountains, and part of it on rocks The houses rise one above another, and form a very fine prospect by that disposition Below the village is a large valley, watered by a small river abounding with fish, and which must be crossed over a stone bridge, in order to arrive at the Caravanserai, which is likewise built of stone The prospect, a little below this building, is diversified with large plantations of trees, and a variety of gardens, which extend three or four leagues This village appears from the Caravanserai in the manner represented in plate 113 It rises very high on each side, with a steep declivity. On one side of the great road, we saw a building that resembled a fortress, the foundations of which are of stone, and the superstructure of earth and clay You enter it by a little bridge, and the adjoining

houses rise, some four, others five, 1704. six, or seven feet one above another, and with such small apertures for the admission of light, that one would rather take them for pigeon-holes than windows. The buildings in the highest range enjoy a sufficiency of light and air, which the second row receives only on one side, but the lowest are so extremely dark, that the inhabitants are obliged to burn candles night and day, even in the stables and folds, where they lodge their cattle This place is, however, said to have been once a city, founded several ages ago, which may be very probable, since there is not such another form of buildings in all *Persia* I had the curiosity to enter the place, but did not continue there long, for fear of engaging myself too far among a people with whose aspect I was not greatly pleased, and, indeed, there was nothing remarkable to excite my attention These poor people are real objects of compassion, and one cannot easily conceive what inducements they can possibly have to continue in so disagreeable a place, in one of the finest countries of the world, unless it be mere habitude, which may be considered as a kind of second nature I was informed, that there was a well in this place, cut twenty fathoms deep, and ten feet in diameter, through the rock, and which serves as a bason, into which there is a passage on one side, through a small fortress, and an ascent out of it, on the other, by a flight of stairs; but those who visit it are always obliged to have candles in their hands

We were presented, at the Caravanserai where we lodged, with little hot loaves of white bread, made in the manner of our country, for the *Europeans* who travel in these parts, and altogether as good as the small loaves of *Amsterdam* This part of the country produces the best corn in all *Persia*, which the governor of *Zjie-raas* preserves for the King and court This proceeding occasioned the *Persian* proverb, *Chiraup Zjie-raas, noen Jesgadaes, Jen de Jes*;
that

1704. that is, *Zjie-raas for wine, Jesdagaes for bread, and Jes for women,* all which are in perfection in those places. Ovens are very numerous through the whole kingdom, and they are made in the form of wells, in each of which the paste is rolled into thin cakes, which are baked in a moment, and when they are taken out, others are immediately placed in the room. Large bread is likewise baked in these ovens, as among us, and they make Biscuits at *Ispahan,* which are altogether as good as those in *France.*

I took the draught of the south side of this place, from the great road, where I had a full prospect of the mountain, with the houses built upon it one above another, as may be seen in plate 114 with a view of some gardens and other scattered places, that are comprehended under the same name, and give a large extent to this village.

We renewed our journey, at two in the morning, through a very incommodious narrow way, which gradually enlarged as we advanced forwards. And we found, at the distance of some leagues from thence, a small house, which usually serves as a retreat to the robbers who infest that road and the adjacent parts, and who never fail to attack those travellers who are not in a condition to defend themselves, and are frequently murdered as well as robbed.

We arrived, about ten in the morning of the thirty first of this month, at *Dedergoe,* a village eight leagues from *Jesdagaes,* where we were surprised with a great tempest, which involved us in so thick a cloud of dust, as made us almost incapable of opening our eyes, and the cold was very violent at the same time. The clouds, towards noon, discharged a greater quantity of rain than had fallen in the space of all that summer. But these inconveniences did not prevent us from proceeding on our journey, and our company was increased on the way, by several travellers, who joined us for their greater security. Two of our cou-

riers were here taken ill, and we 1704 were obliged to leave one of them behind us, till he could be capable either of returning to *Ispahan,* or following us. The other, whom I had hired, finding his indisposition a little abated, was determined to continue with us.

The weather grew fine again, on the first day of *November,* and we advanced through a village that was chiefly inhabited by robbers, and had hardly left it before we mist an ass that belonged to the conductor of our caravan. Upon which, we immediately dispatched two of our men to the village, where they had the good fortune to find the beast, in the hands of an honest man, who desired them to search the packs of goods, in order to see whether any thing had been taken away, and when they had satisfied themselves as to this particular, they rejoined us in a short time.

We then advanced into a plain, and arrived at a stone bridge with five arches, which we did not care to pass over, because it seemed in a ruinous condition on one side, for which reason we rather chose to ford the river, which was but shallow. It likewise abounded with fish, but we were incapable of receiving any benefit from them, because the day was far advanced, and we had a long way to travel.

We met a small body of *Arabs,* Arabs who had lately decamped, and were in quest of a new settlement. Their wives and daughters had rings, with a mixture of pearl, and common stones, at the tip of their noses, and which hung down, in the form of a cross, to their mouths, their hair was set off with other ornaments, and a piece of linnen wound over their heads, but their faces were uncovered. Their upper vest descended no lower than their hips, their under one fell down to the middle of their legs, their shifts came something lower, and flowed over their drawers and stockings. The generality of these women rob with as much intrepidity as the men, and are almost

as

as ftrong Thefe people are fcatter-ed through the whole Kingdom, their complexion is tawny, and the men are habited like the common people of the country

We arrived, in the fpace of two hours, at the village of *Kouskiefar*, which is a good *Caravanferai* built of ftone, where we ftopped a while, the weather being very bad, but this did not prevent us from continuing our journey at five in the morning, through lovely plains, and afterwards through ways that opened between rocks and mountains, and were very in-commodious We then paffed by a ruinous *Caravanferai*, in a tract that was filled with robbers, and where travellers ought to be always upon their guard From thence we ad-vanced into a plain that was covered with water and reeds, and likewife with feveral forts of birds, among whom there was one of an extraor-dinary fize, and which I took for a bird of prey We alfo faw feveral *Arabs* under tents, and when we had fufficiently traverfed the mountains, we came, at twelve, to the town of *Anapas*, feated in a fertile plain, where the Lands are all arable, and well watered, and a *Caravanferai* of ftone is likewife built there

We continued here till midnight, and arrived, the third of this month, at the town of *Ooesjorn*, where there is another *Caravanferai* of ftone, on the edge of a running ftream This fituation is equally agreeable and com-modious, and it lies in the neigh-bourhood of feveral other villages. The land affords pafture for a prodi-gious number of fheep and goats. The grafs is entirely parched by the Sun, and yet proves very nourifh-ing to the cattle This is a furprifing circumftance, confidering the drought that reigns in *Perfia*, and the fterili-ty of the mountains, which are co-vered with rocks, and there are like-wife but few trees to fhade the land.

A Tomb On one fide of this *Caravanferai* we faw a tomb, cover'd with a fmall rifing dome, and furrounded with a wall The inhabitants pretend that it is the fepulchre of a brother of King *Sefi*, who endeavour'd to make himfelf mafter of this part of the Kingdom, but broke his leg on this mountain, which occafioned his death The revenues arifing from the village are ftill appropriated to this monument, in conjunction with thofe to whofe care it is configned

As this tract abounds with fifh, we *Great plen-* caufed fome nets to be caft, and drew *ty of Fifh* out four great fifh, the two largeft of *and Game.* which much refembled carps, the others had broad fcales and yellow bellies, and they are excellent food, tho' their fkin be very thick This part of the country is likewife ftock-ed with partridges, woodcocks, and cranes, which fpring to a great height in the air

We proceeded on our journey af-ter fun-fet, and by break of day ftruck into a road between the moun-tains that are very lofty and rocky; and the ways are fo narrow, that they are hardly paffable by horfes, and other beafts of burden They are likewife fo fteep and flippery in feve-ral places, that the poor animals are frequently overthrown with all their load, and they are altogether as fatiguing to travellers, who are not able to fit their horfes, and are continually obliged to alight and re-mount This place called to my re-membrance thofe defiles, which *Quintus Curtius* fays *Alexander* paf-fed in this tract On the very top of this mountain we found a delight-ful fpring, covered over with ftone. It was ten when we had croffed to the other fide of the mountain, where we found a ruinous *Caravanferai*.

We arrived, about two in the af-ternoon, at a fmall canal of running water; after paffing feveral rocks which occafion'd very bad ways. I there ftopped with fome others, and we dined in the fhade of a growth of trees, while the reft of the com-pany purfued their journey This plantation, which extends as far as the rocks, is compofed of wild Al-mond-trees, and Sackas. We after-wards travelled, by the fide of this canal, through arable lands, and ar-rived about three, at the *Caravan-ferai* of *Majien*, where we difconti-nued our journey

VOL II   C   CHAP.

CHAP LI.

Wild Almond, and other Trees   Mountains, on which Fortresses were antiently erected   The River of Bendemir. *The Author's Arrival at* Perfepolis

I DREW, in this place, a branch of a wild Almond-tree, and another of a Sackas   The former was long and pliant, as appears in plate 115 *A* and had only one almond on it, the feafon for that fruit being over   *L* The branch of the Sackas bears a fmall reddifh fruit, that much refembles the feeds of a pomegranate, a large clufter of berries grow on one ftalk, which is reprefented with its foliage, at the letter *B*   This firft affumes a green complection, when it begins to ripen   The fkin muft be peeled off, and the fhell broken, to come at the kernel, which, like wild almonds, has an excellent relifh when pickled

Perfia produces another tree called *Afrag*, which bears a profufion of flowers and leaves, that are thick fet, but eafily feparable from one another, and they refemble the kernels of white melons, when viewed at a diftance   This tree is not productive of any fruit, but its thick, fpreading and leafy branches, diffufe a deep and pleafing fhade   The reprefentation of one of thefe plants, may be feen in plate 116   This country likewife produces another tree, which is called *Naer-wend*, and bears a fruit with a fmooth fkin, fome growths of which are as large as ones fift, others fmaller   This fruit is white, and refembles a bladder, it is likewife impregnated with a water, which converts itfelf into a gum, that proves falutary in the cure of a cough.   This fruit is exhibited to view at the letter *C*

The town of *Mayen*, where we then were, is very large, and full of fruit gardens and vines, and there are feveral of the latter that grow wild upon the mountains   The interjacent country is very agreeable, and well watered by a canal which flows through the town

We left it at five in the evening, and proceeded, to the diftance of a league, through a road much infefted by robbers, who frequently carry off beafts of carriage, with all their load, in the night, and drive them into the woods, where travellers never think it advifeable to purfue them

On the fifteenth of the month, we enter'd a plain, and faw, at about two leagues diftance on our right, a large and very lofty rock, on which a confiderable fortrefs had been erected in ancient times, and fome of its ruins are faid to be ftill remaining It is likewife pretended, that the fummit of this rock opens into a fpacious plain, which is cover'd with flocks of cattle in the proper feafon of the year

We proceeded on our journey, always keeping to the right, and arrived at the river *Bendemir*, which croffes the country, and we paft it, about eleven, at a fmall diftance from two other mountains very near each other, and which had formerly been crowned with fortreffes, tho' none of their ruins are now vifible   We obferved an opening on the upper part of each of thefe mountains, and which is continued through the rock that rifes upon them, and ferves as a paffage to the top, which ends in a round mafs of ftone, that, at a diftance, refembles a caftle   Some perfons pretend, that the remains of an ancient gate are vifible on the top of one of thefe mountains, but this is an uncertainty   It is likewife faid, that this place formerly afforded a retreat to rebels, and that after they had been diflodged from that fituation, all the remaining ruins were carried away, to prevent their being employed by others to the fame difloyal purpofe for the future   Travellers

BRANCHE D'AMAS ET MAER-WEND.

1704 ve'lers therefore, think thefe mountains not worth afcending, as well becaufe theie are no curioities any longer to be feen, as on the account of the danger to which they are expofed in fuch a folitary Situation

Roads to Perfepolis We found, in this place, two roads which led to Perfepolis, one to the left, on the fide of thefe two mountains, and the other to the right, at a fmall diftance from the former, where a ftone bridge of four arches is built over the river Bendemir, which the antients called by the name of Corus, Corius, or Cyrus, and to which they joined another, under the name of Araxis, which is mentioned in the life of Alexander the great, and they likewife called it Cyropolis, or Cyrefchatas This road is ufually chofen, leaving the river on the left, as thofe do, who go to Zyw-raes Near the bridge I obferved part of a column, which had formerly been join'd to it, like feveral others that are frequently to be feen at the end of bridges This river, which has likewife the appel-

lations of Aras, Kur, and Araxes, 1704 croffes the country, and after it has received into its channel the waters of feveral leffer ftreams, is faid to difcharge itfelf into the rivers of Medum and Medus, for which reafon it ought not to be confounded with the Cyrus, and Araxes, which we have formerly mentioned, and which empty themfelves into the Cafpian Sea

The fteep banks of this river, abound with the moft agreeable little trees in the world When we had pafs'd over the bridge, and advanced half a league beyond it, we left the Caravanferai of Aebgerm on our right, and arriv'd about noon, and after a journey of five leagues, at the village of Frograbaet, where there was no Caravanferai And we were furprifed with a great tempeft, which continued till night, after which the air clear'd up, and we had a fecond view of the mountains I was defirous to take a draught of them, and they are reprefented in the plate which is here inferted. I mean the

LES MONTAGNES LES TROIS FRERES

1704. two mountains which are nearest the bridge, for I could not see the third, tho' it rises higher than these The inhabitants call them the *Three Brothers*, from their resemblance to each other, those who advance in the usual road, stop at the *Caravanserai* of *Aebgerm*, from whence they proceed to *Assaf*, *Pehgorg*, or *Sergoon*, but we kept on by the plain and mountains, and came, about nine in the morning, to a very lofty stone bridge with five arches, three of which are very large, and the other two but small, and the river I have lately mentioned, runs with much rapidity under them, it is likewise very broad and deep there, and its banks are steep and extremely high This river is resorted to by various species of ducks, and it must be crossed before one can arrive at *Persepolis*, which lies at no greater distance from it than two leagues We came, about eleven, to a village called *Zargoen*, which is pleasantly situated among mountains, and is full of gardens, which abound with melons, grapes, and all sorts of fruits, some of which were presented to us by our *Muleteer*, who stopped there, and entertained us in a very agreeable manner, after he had ordered the inhabitants not to sell provisions to any of our train The generality of *Muleteers*, who convey mercantile goods from *Gomron* to *Ispahan*, have a dwelling in this place, and they take pleasure in regaling the *Europeans*, who belong to their *Caravan*

Arable lands, and large flocks of sheep and goats, are seen in this plain, which exceeds two leagues in breadth, and extends in length beyond the reach of the eye It is likewise full of villages, but the rains frequently deluge it in the winter

A few days before our arrival in this place, some of the King's officers, who come to collect his Majesty's revenues, and had received sums to the amount of 33000 livres, were robbed and rifled at the bridge I lately mentioned Robberies are very frequent in these parts, and are committed by the rebbels, who live un-

The King's Officers robbed.

der tents on this plain, and march with fifty, sixty, and even a hundred in company, and yet such is the weakness of the government, that they are permitted to rob with impunity, and no precautions are taken to suppress these injurious proceedings.

The rain surprised us this day, and continued for the whole night, accompanied with hail, lightning, and thunder, till eleven in the morning, when the sky began to clear up We were willing to improve this opportunity, but it began to rain anew, before we came to the end of the village, and with so much violence, that we were obliged to have recourse to shelter We renewed our journey the eighth day of the month, at the first break of dawn, and favour'd with a very serene sky, but we found all the country on this side of the bridge floated with water, which obliged us to proceed very leasurely, otherwise our couriers would have been incapable of following us, the ways were so extremely slippery We however arriv'd about, eleven, at the town of *Mier-chas-koen*, which lies at a little distance from the ruins of *Persepolis*, and we alighted at the house of the chief magistrate of place, to whom Mr. *Bakker* had the goodness to recommend me on the part of Mr. *Kastelkin*, for whose arrival I was to wait in this Town This magistrate favoured me with a most obliging reception, and desired me to accept of one of his servants, to conduct me to the *Caravanserai* of the place, and procure me a commodious Lodging. I no sooner came thither, but I was seized with impatience to behold those famous ruins which were then very near, and I went thither with one of the Inhabitants, whom I had taken into my service as a guide, but I could not take the liberty to make any stay there, because my friend was obliged to return to *Zaergoen*, where he had left effects in merchandize, and all his domesticks, except one valet, and two couriers, who attended him, and the way to

1704.

pro-

1704 proceed, the following night, to *Zyte-raes* I had left my baggage with his, and had only taken out a few neceffaries, having requefted him to leave all my other parcels at *Zyte-raes*, where I was to arrive, in order to proceed to *Gomron*, and from thence to *Batavia*, with Mr. *Kaftelein*, by the firft Opportunity that fhould offer I continued alone after the departure of my friend, with whom I had maintained a very good intelligence at *Ifpahan*, as well as through the whole courfe of our journey , and I was now entirely devoted to the fatisfaction of my curiofity, and the defire I had fo long conceived, of beholding the celebrated ruins of *Perfepolis*

But before I enter upon their defcription, I believe it will not be un-

neceffary to mention the principal 1704. bridges that are to be croffed in the way thither The firft, of which I have already taken notice, is called *Pol Jefnejoen*, from a neighbouring village. The fecond, which was the laft we had then croffed, is called *Pol Chanje*, from the *Cham* who erected it. The name of the third, which lies between the two former, is *Pol Noof*, or the new bridge The fourth, which is fome leagues diftant to the fouth from the laft, is called *Pol Bendemir*, from the river of that name, whofe fourfe, as I was affured, was in the mountains, and its outlet, to the fouth, in the fea of *Derja nemeck*, or the bracky fea, which is twelve leagues from *Perfepolis*, and four or five from *Zyte-raes*

CHAP. LII.

The ruins of the antient Perfepolis *defcribed The fituation of* Naxi-Ruftan.

The ruins of Perfepolis

ON the 9th of this month, I began to vifit thofe ftately remains, which are called *the Ruins of Perfepolis*, and are the moft famous antiquity in all the *Eaft*, in order to give the public the moft exact and circumftantial account of them, that my abilities will permit They are delightfully fituated in a lovely plain, which extends two leagues in breadth, from the fouth weft to the north eaft, computing from the bridge of *Pol Chanje*, on the river of *Bindemir*, beyond which it ftretches out three leagues more, to the foot of the mountains , and it comprehends near forty leagues in length, from the north-weft to the fouth-eaft It is ufually called *Mardayo*, and the inhabitants pretend, that it contains 880 villages, and above 1500, in the circumference that extends around thefe ruins to the diftance of twelve leagues, including thofe villages which are feated

among the mountains, fome of which are filled with beautiful gardens, fhaded with large growths of trees The greateft part of this plain is floated with water, in the winter feafon, which is a very advantageous circumftance to the rice which grows there at that time. Moft of the foil of this amiable plain is converted into arable land, watered with a variety of ftreams that render it exceeding fertile It likewife abounds with all forts of birds, particularly cranes, ftorks, ducks, and herons of feveral fpecies, partridges, fnipes, quails, pigeons, hawks, and efpecially crows, which fwarm through all *Perfia* The plain likewife affords a prodigious quantity of little birds that defcend from the mountains which furround it

The antient palace of the kings *The antient palace of the kings of Perfia* of *Perfia*, ufually called *the Houfe of Darius*, and, by the inhabitants, *Chel-perfia*

Vol II.

D

1704 *Chel-menar*, or *Chil-minar*, which signifies *the forty Pillars*, is situated to the west, at the foot of the mountain of *Kuhrag-met*, or *Compaffion*, antiently called *the Royal Mountain*, and which is entirely composed of free-stone. This superb edifice has all its walls still standing, on three of its sides, with the mountain to the east. The extent of the front comprehends six hundred paces, from north to south, and three hundred and ninety, from west to east, as far as the rock, and without any stair-case on that side, till you come to the mountain, where the ascent is formed between some scattered rocks, where the wall is lowest, and rises to the height of no more than eighteen feet, and seven inches, and the altitude is less in several other places. This curtain contains four hundred and ten paces in length to the north, and is twenty one feet high in some parts, it is likewise carried on thirty paces more to the mountain, where there is still to be seen part of a wall, with an entrance in the middle, through which you may ascend to the top, through several broken rocks. Before these remains of the wall on the western side, several others rise to the north, as high as the wall itself, and then extend eighty paces to the east, like a platform before the wall, at the place where you ascend. There seems to have been formerly a stair-case in this part of the structure, and some buildings beyond the curtain, the rocks appearing finely smoothed and polished in several places. The top of this edifice presents to the view a platform of four hundred paces, which extends from the middle of the front wall, to the mountain; and along three sides of this wall a pavement of two stones joined together, to the breadth of eight feet, is carried on. Some of these stones are from eight to ten feet in length, and six in breadth, but the others are smaller. The principal stair-case is not placed in the middle of the front, but near the northern end, which is but one hundred and sixty five paces beyond it, 1704. whereas the distance between the stair-case and the southern extremity of the wall, is six hundred paces. This stair-case is double, or consists of two flights of steps, which wind off from each other, to the distance of forty two feet at the bottom. It is twenty five feet and seven inches in depth, to the wall from whence the steps project, and the length of these equals the depth of the stair-case within five inches, which are inserted in the wall, on the right and left where the stairs are equal. They are only four inches high, and fourteen in depth, and I never saw any that were so commodious, except those of the Viceroy's palace in *Naples*, which, however, are something higher in my opinion. There are fifty five of these steps on the northern side, and fifty three to the south, but these last are not so entire as the others. I am likewise persuaded, that there are several under ground, and which have been covered over by a length of time, as well as part of the wall, which rises to the height of forty four feet and eleven inches, in the front; and I shall observe this method of computation for the future. When you arrive at this part of the stair-case, you find a perron, fifty one feet and four inches in breadth, proportionable to the width of the stairs, and the stones of this perron are extremely large. The two flights of this stair-case are separated by the front wall, which rises to the top, in consequence of which they are carried off from each other at the middle of the wall, and returned back at the centre at an equal distance from the two extreme parts on the top, which creates a very charming and singular effect, and corresponds with the magnificence of the rest of the building. The upper part of this stair-case has forty eight steps in each flight, some of which are impaired by time, notwithstanding they were cut out of the rock. At the top of the stair-case another perron presents
itself

itself to the view, between the two flights, this is seventy five feet in breadth, and has likewise a pavement of large stones, some of which are from thirteen to fourteen feet in length, and from seven to eight in breadth, like those of the facade; others are square, some long and narrow, and there is another sort smaller than these They are still entire, and joined together in a very masterly manner, to the extent of thirty two feet of the facade The rest of the perron is composed of cemented earth; and the wall which rises between the flights of the stair-case is thirty six feet in height.

This description corresponds, in a great measure, with the exterior plan of this edifice, of which some authors have treated in a very superficial manner, and without a sufficient inspection into particulars Some have confined themselves, to an explication of the remotest antiquities, without regarding the present state of these superb ruins, and content themselves with offering a set of uncertain, and difficult particulars, instead of representing them as they ought, in a natural manner This defect in their accounts proceeds from their not having observed those ruins with all the circumspection and exactness that are requisite. Others have attempted to please, by introducing pompous relations, to which they have added, a set of fables, or voluntary errors one of which is, that the storks never remove to any distance from this plain, which is so far from being true, that it is very certain, they continue there only for a certain season, as they do in other places, and disappear, when they have completed their nests, and reared their young on several columns of these ruins.

The inside of the edifice
It will now be necessary to open the scene, and present the interior part of these celebrated antiquities to view. The spectator first sees, in a right line, and at the distance of forty two feet from the facade, or front wall of the stair-case, which has been already described, two grand portals, and as many columns. The first is paved with two tables of stone, which fill up two thirds of the space; but time has destroyed the third. The second is sunk into the earth, five feet lower than the other These portals are twenty two feet and four inches in depth, and thirteen feet four inches in breadth. In the inside, and on each pilaster, is seen a large figure in low relief, and almost as long as the pilaster; with a distance of twenty two feet from the fore to the hinder legs, and a height of fourteen feet and a half. The heads of these animals are entirely destroyed, and their breasts and forefeet project from the pilaster Their bodies are likewise greatly damaged. Those of the first portal are turned towards the stair-case, and those of the second, each of which has a wing on the body, face the mountain. On the upper part of these pilasters, within the portal, are a set of characters, which it is impossible to distinguish, by reason of their smallness and elevation. The height of the first portal is thirty nine feet, and that of the second, twenty eight. The base of the pilasters is five feet and two inches high, with a projection within, and those on which the figures rest, are a foot and two inches. These animals are not cut out of one stone, but out of three, joined together, and which project without the portal. The wall is five feet and two inches thick The first portal has likewise eight stones in its elevation, and the second, seven

1704.

Figures of animals
With respect to the animals I have mentioned, it would be difficult to determine what they represent, unless it may be said, that they have some similitude to a sphinx, with the body of a horse, and the paws thick and short, like those of a lion But all this is rendered the more uncertain, because the heads are broken into shatters Some persons have pretended, that they represented human heads, and, it must be owned, there is some appearance

ance, on the hinder part of the neck of one of those monsters, which may seem to justify that conjecture It is a kind of a contour, or crowned bonnet, which greatly resembles those towers which the antients placed upon elephants, in order to shoot their arrows in a shelter from the enemy But whatever it be, those figures seem to have been extremely curious, and we meet with some that resemble them, on antient medals. One might even say, that they are covered with arms, adorned with a good number of round studs

The two columns that appear between the two portals, are the least damaged of all, especially with respect to their capitals, and the other ornaments of their upper parts, but the bases are almost entirely covered over with earth They are twenty six feet from the first portal, and fifty six from the second, are fourteen feet in circumference, and rise to the height of fifty four There were formerly two others, between these and the last portal, and the cavities in which they stood are still to be seen in the earth, several pieces of them likewise appear overthrown, and half buried in the ground At the distance likewise of fifty two feet south from the same portal, is seen a large watering bason, cut out of a single stone, twenty feet long, and seventeen feet five inches in breadth, and raised three feet and a half above the surface of the earth From this bason to the northern wall, is an extent of ground comprehending a hundred and fifty paces in length, and where nothing is to be seen but fragments of large stones, and part of the shaft of a column, which is not fluted like the rest It is twenty feet in circumference, and twelve feet four inches long, beyond this tract of ground, and as far as the mountain, the earth is covered with several heaps of stones

Proceeding southward from the portal, I have described, and opposite to the last, on the right, and at the distance of a hundred and seven-

ty two feet, is seen another staircase, with two flights of steps like the former, the one to the east, and the other to the west The facade, or wall, which belongs to it, is six feet and seven inches high, but the middle part is almost entirely in ruins It extends, however, eighty three feet to the east, and the lower stones make it evident, that it was adorned with figures in low relief. The upper part of the flight is embellished with foliage, and the representation of a lion rending a bull, much larger than the life, and likewise in low relief This staircase is half buried under the earth There are also little figures on the two sides of the middle wall, which extends to the end of the staircase. The western flight has twenty eight steps, and the other, where the ground rises higher, has only eighteen. These are seventeen feet in length, and three inches high, their breadth is fourteen inches and an half several of these steps are damaged towards the top, and two or three of them are entirely destroyed, tho' they are cut out of the rock The perron of this staircase ends in another facade, on which are three ranges of small figures, one above another, and of which those in the upper row are only visible from the waist downwards, the other part of the body being greatly defaced, and the middle range, which is preserved the best of the three, is, however, much damaged But as to the lower rank, the heads of the figures are only visible, all the rest being buried under the earth These figures are two feet and nine inches high, and the wall, which rises to the elevation of five feet and three inches, has an extent of ninety eight feet, from the first step to the end of the left angle, which is contiguous to another staircase, of which thirteen steps are still remaining, and whose dimensions correspond with those I described last There is likewise to be seen, on the remains of the inner wall along the side of the staircase, another range of figures, of which only and only h If of the bodies are now vifible, and at the end of this ftair-cafe, appears ar other wall which extends ninety feet beyond the perion. The angle of it declines a little to the fouth, and is there difcontinued, becaufe the rifing ground in that part is as high as the wall itfelf This extremity is carried off in a right line, a little beyond the laft columns, which are extended towards the mountains

In returning to the weftern flight of the ftair-cafe, one finds a wall of forty five feet in length, beyond the lower part of the ftair-cafe, and then an interval of fixty feven feet, extending to the weftern facade This fide correfponds with the preceding, and has three ranges of figures in the fame tafte, with a lion tearing a bull, or an afs, that has a horn projecting from the forehead, and between thefe animals and rows of figures, is a fquare filled with characters, the uppermoft of which are defaced, the reft will be found in the draught I made of this ftaircafe But the characters are entirely defaced on the other fide The figures are alfo lefs damaged in this part of the ftructure, where the ground is lower, and this place has an extent of twenty five paces The wall, which is carried on from the perron to the weft, extends to the facade, and has not any figures beyond the ftair-cafe

On the top of this ftair-cafe, and between the two flights of fteps, is an entrance into an open place, paved with large tables of ftone, whofe breadth is equal to the diftance from the ftair-cafe to the firft columns, and which comprehends a fpace of twenty two feet and two inches Thefe columns are difpofed into two ranges, each of which contains fix pillars, but none entire, eight bafes, or pedeftals, and the ruins of fome others They are continued along the wall of the ftair-cafe, with as many intervals of diftance between each other, as there are fteps in this There are likewife fix rows of other pillars, at the diftance of feventy feet

and eight inches from the laft, and each row confifts of fix pillars Thefe thirty fix columns, are alfo twenty two feet and two inches diftant from each other, like the preceding, and only feven of them are now entire; but all the bafes of the others are ftill in their places, tho' moft of them are damaged Among thofe that are ftill fubfifting, there is one in the firft and fecond ranges, two in the third, and one in each of the others. Between thefe columns and the firft, which have been already defcribed, feveral large ftones of a fubterranean edifice are ftill to be feen At the diftance of feventy feet and eight inches from thefe rows of columns, on the weft, and towards the facade of the ftair-cafe, were twelve other columes in two ranges, each of which contained fix, but there are only five now remaining, three in the firft, which is fifty five feet from the facade, and two in the fecond, at the fame diftance from each other as the preceding. The bafes of the other feven are no longer vifible, and thofe which ftill fubfift, are partly in ruins. The ground, in this place, is covered with feveral fragments of columns, and the ornaments that crowned them, between which are pieces of fculpture reprefenting camels on their knees A compartment is ftill to be feen, on the top of one of the columns, exhibiting the reprefentation of one of thefe animals in this pofture, and the figure is altogether as entire, as our delineation of it in the plate. South of thefe columns is to be feen an edifice which rifes higher than any other part of thefe ruins, but before I enter upon its defcription, it will be proper to obferve, that on the eaft quarter, to the left, and towards the mountains, were formerly two other ranges of pillars, with fix in each, and of which only four or five pedeftals now appear a little above the furface of the earth, and the place where the others were fixed, has been formed by time into a fmall hill Several pieces of columns and fragments of ftone are likewife vifible

1704. on this spot, and there is reasons to conjecture that these columns fronted those which extend along the facade.

As we advance towards the east, we are presented with a view of several ruins, which consist of portals, passages, and windows The insides of the portals are ornamented with figures, and these ruins extend ninety paces from east to west, and 125 from north to south They are likewise sixty paces from the columns and the mountains The earth, in the middle of these ruins, is covered with broken columns, and other stones, which shall be taken notice of in the sequel of this description, as well as two sepulchres which are hollowed in the rock One of these is adorned with figures, and it fronts those ruins The columns I last mentioned are seventy six in number, and nineteen of them have still their entablature Their shafts are formed by a conjunction of four pieces, without comprehending either the base, or the capital. But we will now proceed to the lofty building, which rises on a hill to the south.

The loftiest part of these ruins

The distance of this structure from the columns is 118 feet, and the front wall, which is five feet and seven inches high, on that side, is composed of a single range of stones, some of which are eight feet in width, and the wall itself extends 113 feet from east to west Opposite to the middle of this edifice are seen some foundations of stone, which constitute a part of it, though it is impossible to comprehend their original use, since not the least appearance of any stair-case is now discoverable Several stones are likewise found on the same level with the columns, and they extend as far as this place There is likewise a canal which formerly served as an aqueduct, with a heap of large stones, that once formed some edifice. Beyond the wall are several other pieces ranged at the distance of three

feet and two inches from the II side of it, they are likewise five feet high, and some are broken to the left This wall has neither figures, nor any other ornaments At the distance of fifty three feet from the facade of this structure, the entrance into which is hardly distinguishable, because the ruins of it are partly covered with earth, a stair-case appears on the right hand, six of the steps of which are still entire, but the uppermost are all entirely destroyed These steps are six feet and one inch in length, four in height, and a foot and a half in breadth Several figures are seen to the right and left, on the little wings of this stair-case, and likewise on the adjoining stones, and over the perron on the top of these steps lies a stone five feet in length, and seven in breadth There was likewise another flight on the contrary side, which corresponded with this, and where two ranges of steps are raised opposite to each other The first of these flights is to the north, and the second to the south, and on the perron which lies between them, were two pilasters of a portal, which have apparently been shaken down by an earthquake All the rest of the building, which was chiefly composed of large and small portals, is entirely destroyed They were built of large stones, of which some are opened like windows, and the portals themselves were filled with figures in low relief The tract of ground on which these ruins stand, contains 147 feet in length, and is almost square There was likewise a stair-case with two flights of steps to the south, whose dimensions and form corresponded with those of the other, and of which the four last steps are still visible on each side Between the two flights, one of which is to the east, and the other to the west, a facade is yet to be seen, and it extends fifty five feet in length, without including the sides of the stair-case, where the wall is lowest, and only rises two feet and seven inches above

1704 above the level of the pavement The ground to the eaſt is more lofty than the ſide walls, and its inward area is almoſt ſquare, ſince it extends fifty five feet on one ſide, and fifty three and a half on the other, with a large hill of ſand in the middle The largeſt of theſe portals are five feet wide, and five feet and two inches deep The wall is three feet in thickneſs, and its height to the cornice is about twenty three feet It is impoſſible to conceive how the ſide-ſtones were originally joined in that part with the ſmalleſt, nor how this part of the fabric was aſcended, becauſe there is not the leaſt trace of a ſtair-caſe to be ſeen, nor can it be determined whether there was any arch above It is, therefore, difficult to imagine for what uſe this ſtructure was intended It may poſſibly have been ſome royal apartment

Two portals appear on the north ſide, with three niches, or windows walled up, and to the ſouth, a portal and four open windows, each of which are five feet and nine inches wide, eleven in height, including the cornice, and their depth is equal to that of the grand portals. There are two other portals to the weſt, which are not covered, together with two openings, and a third to the eaſt, with three niches, or windows walled up. Six of theſe openings are without any cornice, and there is only the half of one to the eaſt Under the portals, which are erected to the north, are the figures of a man and two women viſible down to the knees, the legs being covered with earth, and under one of thoſe which are to the weſt, is the figure of a man hunting a bull, who has one horn in his forehead, which is graſped by the man's left hand, while his right plunges a large dagger into the belly of the bull On the other ſide the figure of another man claſps the horn with his right hand, and ſtabs the beaſt with his left The ſecond portal diſcovers the figure of a man carved in the ſame manner, with a deer that greatly reſembles a lion, having a

horn in its forehead, and Wings on 1704 the body. The ſame repreſentations are to be ſeen under the portal to the north, with this exception, that inſtead of the deer, there is a great lion, whom a man holds by the mane. Theſe two figures are covered with earth to the middle of their legs. The two ſides of the portal to the ſouth are carved with the figure of a man with an ornament on his head, like a crown, he is accompanied by two women, one of whom holds a paraſol over his head, the other has a certain ornament in her hand And above this portal, on the inſide, three different niches are filled with characters. On the pilaſters of the firſt portal, which have ſtarted out of their place, and appear on the ſide of the ſtair-caſe, that has been mentioned before, are the figures of two men, each of whom is graſping a lance; one with both his hands, and the other with his left, but only one of theſe figures is entire Behind this edifice is another ſtructure, which reſembles it in ſome meaſure, but exceeds it in length by thirty eight feet It has likewiſe a niche or cloſed window, and another that is open, with two ſtones raiſed on the right and left, and of which that to the eaſt is broken, the other, on the weſt, is twenty eight feet high, and ſeems to be all of a piece. It is three feet and ſeven inches in breadth, and five feet four inches thick The upper part of this ſtone is hollowed into three niches, or ſeparate compartments, filled with characters, below which is a fourth that ſeems to have been cut after the others Several characters of the ſame nature appear in the other niches or windows, already mentioned, as well as all around them; and likewiſe on the raiſed ſtone, and ſome of the portals, whoſe pilaſters are of one piece, as are alſo the cornices. The niches, or cloſed windows, are alſo cut out of one ſtone, and to the ſouth of theſe are two flights of a ſtair-caſe; one to the eaſt, and the other to the weſt; and of which five of the uppermoſt

1704. permoſt ſteps are ſtill remaining, like thoſe in the preceding ſtair-caſe The wings, as well as the walls which ſeparate them, exhibit the repreſentation of little figures and foilage, which are partly covered with earth At the diſtance of a hundred feet from this place, to the ſouth, the laſt ruins of theſe famous ſtructures appear, and the greateſt part of theſe likewiſe conſiſt of portals and inclosures Between theſe ruins and thoſe which have been deſcribed laſt, is a demoliſhed ſtair-caſe, with two flights of ſteps, to the north and ſouth, but there are only ſeven of the uppermoſt now remaining It is likewiſe ornamented with figures and ſpreading leaves To the eaſt of this ſtair-caſe are ſubterranean paſſages, into which no one preſumes to enter, though they are ſaid to contain great treaſures, becauſe there is a general perſuaſion, that the lights which perſons may happen to carry into theſe places, will be extinguiſhed of themſelves, after they have advanced a few paces. This opinion, however, did not intimidate me from making the the experiment, in the company of a *Perſian* of reſolution

We deſcended between the rocks, and entered upon two ways, but we ſtruck into that which runs to the eaſt. The height of this we found to be ſix feet, and the width two feet and four inches, at the entrance, but this was contracted into the ſpace of one foot, and about eight inches, as we advanced forward . And when we had proceeded to the length of twenty paces, we found the roof ſo low, that we were obliged to creep forwards on our bellies, ten paces farther, after which we found the paſſage as high as it was at our firſt entrance · But when we had advanced a few paces more, we were ſtopped by the occurſion of the rock, and I found that there was only a narrow track, which extended to a great length, and had all the appearance of being originally contrived for an aqueduct,

Subterra-nean paſſages.

but the ſtraitneſs of it rendered it 1704 impoſſible to be paſſed We then returned to the place from whence we deſcended, and I entered the paſſage on the weſt, and found a way which ſtruck to the north, but it was too low to be paſſed even on the breaſt, and had it been higher, the humidity of the earth would have made it impracticable for me to have proceeded farther We were therefore obliged to return, but without having our lights extinguiſhed, or finding the treaſure which the people of the country pretend is concealed in theſe ſubterranean paſſages, which in all probability were never intended for any other uſe than the conveyance of water, as well on account of their inconſiderable height, as becauſe there are no cells to be ſeen, nor any traces of little altars, or other objects of that nature, which could induce one to believe they were ever conſecrated to devotion, like ſeveral ſubterranean paſſages in *Italy*, and a variety of other places

The other edifice, already mentioned, extends a hundred and ſixty feet, from north to ſouth, and a hundred and ninety one from eaſt to weſt Ten portals belonging to it, are ſtill to be ſeen, together with ſeven windows, and forty encloſures, that have formerly been covered with buildings, whoſe foundations are viſible to this day, as are likewiſe ſeveral round baſes in the middle, and on which have been erected thirty ſix columns, in ſix ranges Theſe ſtones are three feet and five inches in their diameter, and all the ground is covered with large fragments, under which were aqueducts in former times The entrance into this building, is likewiſe diſtinguiſhed by two raiſed ſtones, like that which has been already deſcribed, and ſeveral characters that are ſtill viſible are impreſſed upon them

There was formerly another ſtructure, weſtward from the front of this, but it is now entirely deſtroyed,

A ſtructure to the ſouth

ed, and nothing is to be seen but a square place fronting the portals lately mentioned. The wall of this place is still near two foot in height above the pavement, and one sees along this wall the upper part of some figures, with which it was embellished, each of which is represented with a lance, and they were almost as large as the life The ground enclosed by this wall contains nothing more than a number of round stones, which were formerly bases to columns, whose demensions corresponded with those of the preceding. These stones are placed at the distance of eleven feet from one another, and I think there are thirty six of them still remaining. There is likewise a large hill of sand, before this last edifice, which extends along the portals, with several fragments of stone. On the east side of these last ruins, are the remains of a beautiful stair-case, which resembles that of the front wall, and is sixty feet in length. The lower part of it has twelve steps still remaining, and there are fifteen above the perron The breadth of each of them is six feet and two inches, and the wings of this stair-case are beautified with little figures The wall which separates the two flights of steps, and is still eight feet in height, is likewise adorned with figures almost as big as the life, but the stones on which they are carved, are greatly damaged. The front contains the representation of a lion encountring a bull, together with some broken stones, on which several characters are impressed. There are also lions of the same workmanship on the wings of the stair-case, but they are smaller than the other; and are likewise accompanied with characters and figures, almost as large as the life. The same is also to be seen on the other side of the walls, together with the figures of women which are all defaced in a great measure The principal stair-case of this building, was situated to the west, not of the front wall, but of the most lofty part of

Vol. II.

the pile, and fronting the great edifice · It likewise differs from the others, by being placed directly before the wall, with the additional circumstance of its shooting out into a great breadth below, and gradually contracting itself in the ascent. There are two flights of steps, as in the others, one to the west, and the other to the east, and the latter still ascends by twenty seven steps. The western flight has twenty three steps, but time has destroyed eight of them, notwithstanding they were cut out of the rock When one has arrived at the perron of the first flight, a second division of the staircase on the side of the wall, from west to east, presents itself to the view, and contains thirty steps, the greatest part of which are still entire, and are four feet and three inches in breadth, and one foot three inches in depth The eastern flight corresponds with the other, but is destroyed in a very great measure, and nothing now remains of it, but a part of the wall, with two or three steps. These two flights are separated by an extent of 117 feet, including the wall of the perron, along which the buildings are carried to the distance of eight feet. Columns were formerly disposed between this lofty edifice, and the portals already mentioned : But there are only four to be seen at present, with two fragments of bases, which still rise a little above the surface of the ground. Four portals are likewise to be seen among these last ruins, and on each of their pilasters within, the figure of a man is represented, with two women holding a parasol over his head, in the same disposition, as the others which have been already described. There were figures of the same nature, on the pilasters to the west, and they held something in their hand, like those on the east. There was likewise the representation of two men armed with lances, under the two other sculptures, in the same manner as those under the preceding, together with three women holding something that

is

1704 is now broken in their hands, but these laſt figures are extremely damaged There are alſo two other figures on each ſide, in the two niches to the ſouth, one of which graſps the horn of a goat with one hand, while the other reſts on the neck of that animal The ſecond figure had likewiſe ſomething in its hand, but time has entirely deſtroyed it

Between thoſe ruins, and the laſt ſtructures, which are toward the mountain, we obſerved ſome pilaſters which were orramented with figures reſembling the others But with this difference, that one of the women holds a crooked machine over the head of the man, who had alſo ſomething in his hand, but it is now broken Other machines like this are to be ſeen in the hands of ſeveral other figures, that ſeem to be diſpoſed on the ſide of ſome great perſonages, and they may poſſibly be the tails of ſome Sea-horſes, which are uſed even now by perſons of quality in this country, to chaſe away the flies They ſometimes coſt a hundred rix-dollars a piece, and are inſerted into golden handles, which are frequently garniſhed with jewels The King, and the great lords likewiſe carry them faſtened to the head of their horſes, from whence they fall down over their breaſts

Near theſe two edifices are two very lofty ſtones, but the greateſt part of the other ſtructures are under the earth Two portals, with their pilaſters, are, however, to be ſeen at a little diſtance to the north, and one of theſe laſt ſupports the figures of a man and two women, one of which holds a paraſol over his head Above theſe women, we obſerved a figure with wings, which are expanded to the ſides of the portal. The lower part of the buſt of this little figure ſeems to terminate on the two ſides with a ſpread of foilage, and a kind of freeze Over the ſecond figure, a man is ſeated in a chair, with a ſtaff in his hand; and another ſtands behind

him, with his right hand upon the 1704 chair, and holding in his left ſomething that is not to be diſtinguiſhed The little figure which appears above, holds a kind of circle in its left hand, and points to ſomething with its right Under this portal are three ranges of figures, all of which have their hands lifted up, and over the third pilaſter, which ſtill remains, two women hold a paraſol above the head of a man The earth is alſo covered with fragments of columns, and other antiquities, between which three baſes are viſible. Theſe portals are nine feet in depth, with a breadth of the ſame dimenſion, and they are ſunk into the earth to the depth of ſome feet

We proceeded from hence to the laſt ruins of the ſtructures that are on the ſide of the mountain, and whoſe circumference has been marked out They are repreſented on the ſouth ſide, where are two portals, under each of which a man is ſeated in a chair, with a ſtaff in his right hand, and in his left a kind of vaſe. Behind him is another figure, which holds over his head a machine, like the tail of a ſea-horſe, and has a linen cloth in his right hand Below there are three rows of other figures with lifted hands, four in the firſt, and five in each of the other two rows They are three feet and four inches high, but the ſeated figure is much larger than the life Above this are ſeveral ornamental ranges of foliage, the loweſt of which is intermixed with ſmall lions, and the higheſt with Oxen Over thoſe ornaments is a little winged figure, which holds in its left hand ſomething which reſembles a ſmall glaſs, and makes a ſignal with its right. The reſt of the figures reſemble thoſe others that have been already deſcribed

Theſe portals are twelve feet and five inches in breadth, and ten feet four inches deep Their pilaſters are compoſed of ſeven ſtones, and are about ſix feet in thickneſs The higheſt are from twenty eight to thirty feet On the two which are

to-

1704 wards the north, a man is seated, with a person behind him like the preceding figures, and behind this are two other men holding in their hands something which is broken there are likewise two other figures, before him that is seated, one of which places his hands on his lips with an air of salutation, and the other holds a small vessel. Above these figures is a stone filled with ornaments, but it is not so high as the others that have been already described Below the person who is represented sitting, are five ranges of figures, three feet in height, these are a band of soldiers armed in different manners

In one of these portals to the east, we observed the figure of a man encountring a lion, and in another compartment, a man fighting with a bull We likewise beheld, under the two portals to the weft, several figures of lions, one of which is represented with wings Those to the east and weft, are much lower than those to the north and south, and the figures are sunk up to the knees in the earth The other portals are likewise sunk in the manner represented in one of the plates of these ruins Each of them had nine niches or windows on every side, but they are all destroyed, in a great measure It is evident, however, that none of them were open, except those that front the north, three of which, that were disposed in the middle, are still entire, and open so as to shew a prospect through them The pilasters, as well as the architrave, are composed almost of one stone, but their cornices are broken. These portals are eleven feet and five inches deep, and four feet ten inches wide Several pieces of columns, bases, and ornaments, lie scattered between these structures, and their number may amount to about thirty or forty All the last that have been mentioned, amount to 119. which being added to the seventy six that were first specified, compleat the number of 195.

The first large stones of the rock, 1704 that appear on the side of these structures to the north, are the pilasters of two grand portals, one of which resembled the two that were erected at the stair-case of the front wall, the other is adorned with two vast figures of men armed with lances, and likewise holds a machine which corresponds with those that have been formerly mentioned There were also two others, disposed in the same manner, a little further to the weft, and fronting the former, as appears by the little which now remains of them There are likewise two other portals to the north, like those of the stair-case of the facade, and though they are now in ruins, the animals with which they were ornamented, are still distinguishable There is also a vast fragment of stone resembling a horse's head, but it is now sunk into the earth This figure induces me to conclude, that the other pilasters were embellished with heads of the same nature, and several figures of beasts, fragments of columns, and other broken stones, are scattered about in great numbers, on the side of these ruins, but nothing is to be distinguished among those that lie to the north.

After this general description of these famous ruins, it will be proper to offer a particular account of them, as they are represented in four general plates, and four different points of sight, and where the principal fragments, and even the separate pieces, are exhibited to view. The first plate is marked N° 117 and represents the facade to the weft, the particular members of which are distinguished by letters A marks out the grand stair-case in the front of the edifice B the two grand portals with two columns C the only remaining column of twelve D the seven which are left out of thirty six E. the five columns, which are all that are now standing of the twelve, that were disposed along the wall of the facade. F. the four which

A more particular description of these ruins

1704 which remain of the twelve that were placed towards the mountains. The other ruins could not be represented in this plate, the hill from whence the design was taken, not being high enough for that purpose. G represents one of the tombs on the mountain H the highest structure on a hill I the last ruins to the south K the other tomb on the mountain L the portal to the north, placed without the structures

The second view The second view was taken at the foot of the mountain to the south, and is represented in plate 118 which exhibits a direct prospect of the ruins to the east, with the highest edifice at the western entrance, at the wall of which were the two grand ascents of stairs, already described That to the left is distinguished by the letter A, but the ruins of the other are not visible on this side any more than the column, which rises to the left, without the edifice. The two mountains on which the fortresses were erected, are marked by B, and the town of *Mier-chas-koen*, with the gardens before it, by C Two villages are represented a little beyond it, in a distant prospect

The third view The third view, exhibited in plate 119, was designed from the east, and under the first tomb on the mountain, before which are two hills of sand. From this situation the prospect opens upon all the ruins separated from one another, and I chose this point of sight, and the eminence which commands it, for the satisfaction of those who shall have the curiosity to consult this work That particular portion of them, which is situated towards the mountains, as I have already intimated, is visible at the east entrance into the ruins, and is distinguished by the letter A The columns behind are marked out by B, and on the right of these, the two portals which are near the staircase of the facade, are represented at the letter C Several fragments of stone on the same side, together

with other columns on the left, and 1704 which stand on an emicence beyond the two portals, already described, are exhibited at D After which those of the lofty edifice to the south, before which is a stair-case to the east, appear at the letter E. The other portals are expressed at F And the last part, to the south, by G The column, which stands alone, in the fields, is likewise represented, and beyond this, the villages and mountains, together with the town of *Mier-chas-koen*, are to be seen at H.

The fourth view The fourth view, represented in plate 120, was designed on the northern quarter, above the edifice, and at an angle of the highest wall, which has the greatest projection, in form of a stair-case, as well on this side as on the other This situation presents to the view part of the stair case of the facade, before which are the two grand portals, and the two columns. The wall, and likewise the stair-case, adorned with figures up the ascent to the place where the columns stand, are marked by the letter A. Beyond these, several other ruins, with those on the side of the mountain, and likewise the two tombs, are represented at B and C; and on the other side, the column appears alone in the fields

A particular description of the several pieces We will now proceed to a description of each particular piece, and begin with the two portals, and the two columns, which are represented in plate 121 The design of these was drawn on a quarter to the south, by which means, part of the staircase of the facade, and the end of the wall to the north, are rendered visible One of the Sphinxes of the first portal, adorned with broken ornaments, is delineated in the plate 122. And in plate 123, is to be seen a winged animal, under the second portal. The stair-case of the facade, designed from a northern situation, is exhibited in plate 124. We have likewise added in plate 125, the steps of the wall, which ascend to the columns. This view was drawn to the west, on the front

wall

QUATRIEME VÙE DE PERSEPOLIS

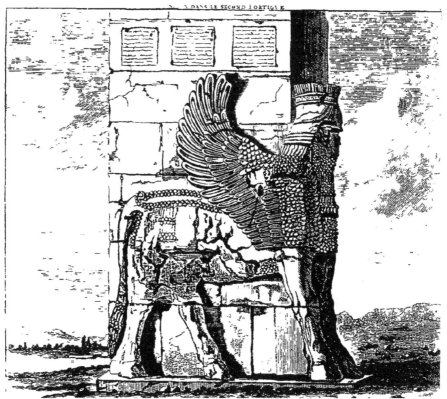

DANS LE SECOND PORTIQUE

DEGRÉ QUI CONDUIT AUX COLOMNES.

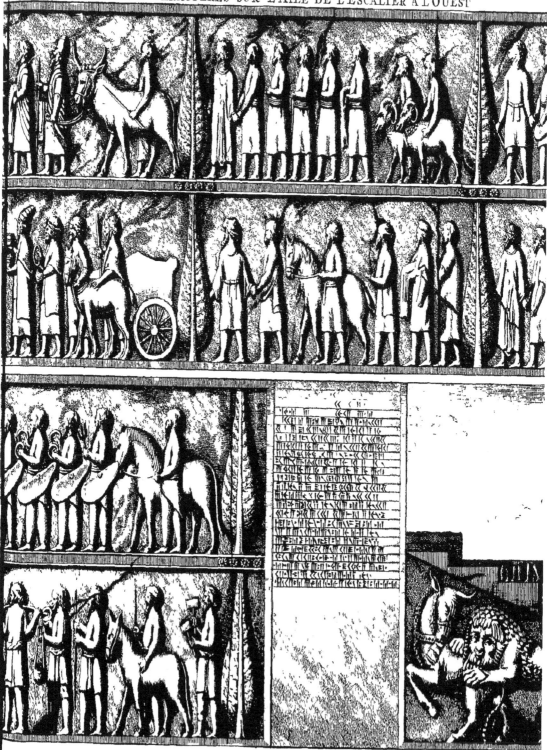

A

A

B

1704 wil' of the edifice, from whence part of the ſtair-caſe of the facade is ſeen, together with the two portals, and the two columns, and likewiſe ſome other columns, with the mountain, all which are repreſented in this plate. In the 126th are exhibited the figures which appear on the wings of this ſtair-caſe to the weſt, with ſeveral characters; and the 127th plate repreſents the figures that are ſtill remaining on the eaſt ſide of the ſame ſtair-caſe.

The firſt ſix figures which appear at the entrance of the ſtair-caſe to the eaſt, are ſmaller than the reſt, and have large veſtments, with great plaited ſleeves, and a round bonnet riſing in plaits, and larger in the upper than the lower part. They are likewiſe repreſented with hair and long beards. Each of them holds a lance in the right hand, and a quiver of arrows is faſtened to the back, with a ſtrap carried over the ſhoulder. The figure which precedes all the others, holds the next by the left hand, and graſps a fork with its right. It ſeems to repreſent an eccleſiaſtic at the head of a proceſſion of others; it is likewiſe arrayed with a large robe, with a girdle hanging down very low.

The three figures by which theſe are ſucceeded, have ſhorter robes and ſleeves, with upper, and under veſts, and pointed bonnets formed into five plaits. Theſe laſt are properly the *Tiaras*, which are alſo called *Reflexa*, becauſe they are ſloped into a curve behind, as the *Tiara Phrygia* are thoſe which are bent before. One of theſe appears on the head of *Ulyſſes* on antient medals. Two of theſe figures hold a little bucket in each hand, and the third has two hoops. This laſt is followed by two horſes, drawing a chariot, and by two other figures that place their left arms, one on the back, and the other on the neck of the horſes. They are all repreſented with hair and beards; ſome are likewiſe bare-headed, others have a bandage, or a kind of diadem, folded round their

heads. Between each compartment 1704 of ſix or ſeven figures, a kind of vite appears, and the two firſt figures always hold each other by the hand. An horſe, led by the bridle, is repreſented in the ſecond diviſion, and two figures bear ſomething that reſembles a veſtment. There are five of theſe figures in the third compartment with little buckets, and two others with large bowls. Thoſe in the fourth are not habited ſo well as the others, ſince they have only a ſhort and very ſtrait veſt, together with a cincture and long drawers, which are likewiſe ſtrait and plaited. Three of theſe figures have alſo little buckets in their hands, and are followed by a camel, that has two bunches riſing on his back, with a halter, and a little bell hung about his neck, after the manner of the eaſtern caravans, that the ſound may be heard at a diſtance, eſpecially when they paſs through narrow defiles or bad ways, where ſome of the company ought to ſtop, to give the others an opportunity of paſſing on. Theſe bells likewiſe give notice in the night to the inhabitants, of the caravans arrival at thoſe places where the company are to lodge; it is likewiſe a ſignal to thoſe who have loſt their way, and enables them to rejoin their companions.

The laſt compartment is diſtinguiſhed by a figure bearing a pole before him on his ſhoulders, with a pot ſuſpended at each extremity, and in each of theſe pots are ſeen little water veſſels in an upright poſition. The habit of this figure is likewiſe but indifferent. A mule or an aſs is repreſented next, with two men armed with poles, and theſe are followed by another figure bearing two mallets. Several other characters appear next, and laſt of all a great lion encountring a bull or ſome other animal, from whoſe forehead a horn is extended. The ſtair-caſe, around which ſeveral broken figures appear, preſents itſelf to view in this place. We counted forty eight figures of men and beaſts in

Vol II   G   this

... the range and as many in that a-
bove. The first are nearly ha-
bred, and each of them has some
vestment in its hand. Those that
follow carry the same, and are ar-
ranged in a better manner, but most
of them are greatly impaired by
time. These are succeeded by an
ox led with halter. The only
difference between this and the third
compartment is, that in the latter
two rows are led, and each of them
has a large crooked horn denoted
towards the earth. After these appears a figure armed with a buckler,
and another, leading a horse by the
bridle, followed by a third with
two hoops. The other three are
habited like the preceding figures,
and they march before a led ox, that
is followed by a man armed with a
lance and shield, behind whom appears two other figures, each of
which has three lances, and their
sleeves are longer than their vests.
The last figures that follow, have very
short vests, with drawers that are long
and strait, and which fall down to
their feet. They are likewise armed with long bucklers hanging at the
girdles of their waists. Two of them
have hoops in their hands, and another a fork, and they are followed
by a horse led by the bridle. These
figures are represented in two divisions which follow the letter A.

The eastern range contains the first
twenty eight figures, including the
stair-case, each of which grasps a
lance with both hands. Their vests
are long and wide, and they are represented with hair and beards, and
seem to be bare-headed, unless
we may rather suppose them to wear
a plaited bandage, or a kind of diadem. These are succeeded by a set
of other figures, armed with long
bucklers, which are pointed and bent
at one end, together with a short
and broad dagger, hung at the girdle
of their waists, and their vests have
an inequality in their length. They
resemble the last figures in the attire
of their heads, they have likewise
some ornament in one hand, and

the other is placed upon their beard.
This range consists of sixty figures,
the last of which are entirely defaced. These three divisions follow
the letters A and B.

All these figures, ranged in the
disposition we have described, seem
to represent some triumph, or a procession of people bearing presents to
the king, which was very customary
under the antient Monarchs of *Persia*, and is practised to this day.
Presents of this nature are offered to the king on the twentieth of
March, which is the festival of the
new solar year, and I have been a
spectator of this solemnity, as has
been formerly intimated.

When we left these columns, we
proceeded to the first portal, which
stands to the south, the inward prospect of which I drew on a spot of
ground to the east. The last window on the right, is in the western
part of this pile, as may be seen in
plate 128 with the portals lateral
to each other, the back view of
which is here represented, together
with the ruined stair case already
mentioned, and which is disposed
between this, and the highest edifice.

The inward prospect of the
northern portal is exhibited in plate
129. and that of the western, in
plate 130. The three compartments of characters, which appear on the lofty pilaster to the
south, are delineated in plate 131.
and the three compartments of characters on the portal itself, in plate
132.

The seven divisions of characters,
which once appeared on the folds of
the large outward robe of the principal figure, have been broken off in
part, but I have replaced them in
the best manner I was able, and they
are represented in plate 133.

Those that were disposed round
the windows, are exhibited in plate
134. The first is the upper range;
the second filled the right side of the
window, and the third, that of the
left, in the manner they are carved

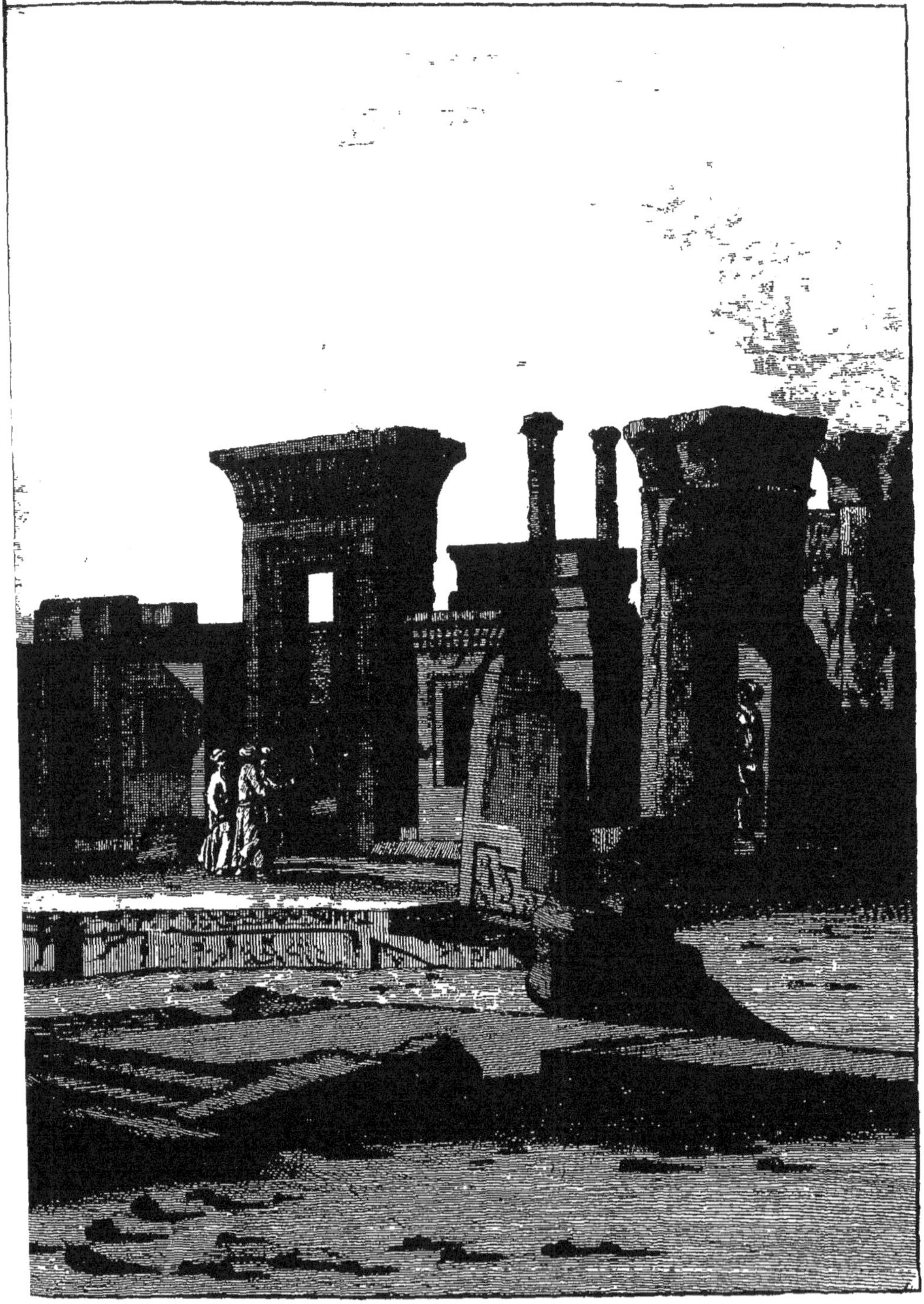

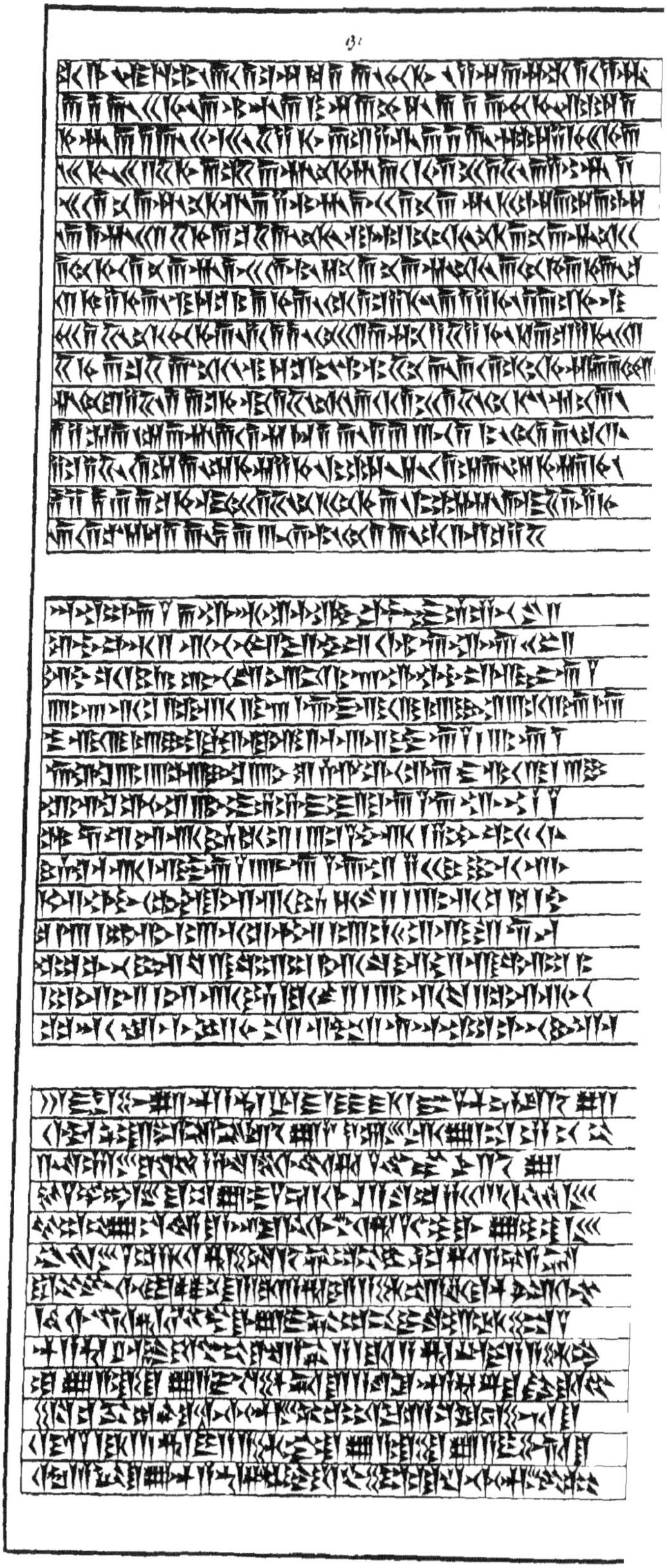

132

134

1 Il n'appartient qu'a Dieu de donner de la force

2 Il ne faut pas trop se fier a ses propres Lumières

3 C'est moi ...

4 Tout passera, mais Dieu subsistera éternellement
C'est moi Moushey ...

5 ...

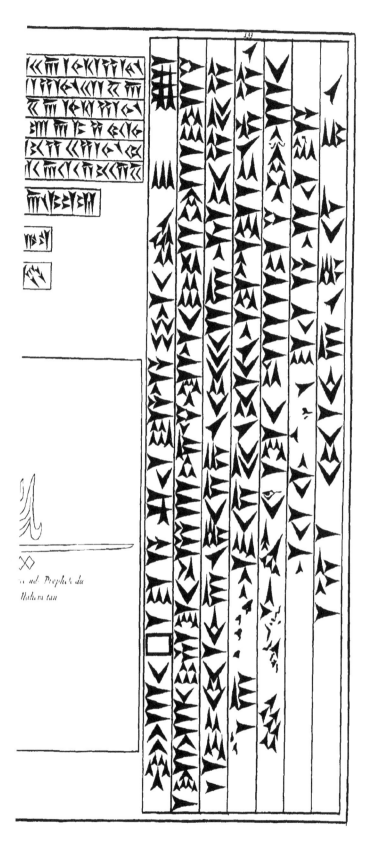

… ud: Prophet du
Nahem tan

PORTIQUES AU DEDANS

all the other windows The fculpture of them appears as perfect, as
if they were but newly carved, as
is evinced by thofe fragments of them,
which I brought away with me ,
and this circumftance may be a-
fcribed to the hardnefs of the ftone
on which they were impreffed

I found, within the opening of
one of thefe windows, feveral other
characters lefs antient than the o-
thers, and which have been carved
fince them   They are *Arabic* letters, and are exhibited on the left
fide of plate 135, and on the right
of plate 136, together with their
explication

The obfcu-
rity of the
antient
characters
As to the other characters of great
antiquity, they are no longer known,
and I made feveral ineffectual at-
tempts to obtain a difcovery of their
meaning, without being able to find
any perfon, who could decypher a
fingle letter This difappointment,
however, did not prevent me from

being at the pains to copy them exactly, in hopes of meeting with fome
prieft among the *Guebres*, who
could afford me fome light with relation to them, and the event fhall
be related at large in the fequel of
this work

My ardent defire to examine thefe
fuperb ruins with the greateft care,
and to render them more known to
the curious than they had been till
then, caufed me to fend for a ftone-
cutter of *Zie-raes*, or *Chiras*, whofe
affiftance I had occafion for in the
execution of my defign, the hardnefs of the rocks having blunted all
the chifels I had brought from *Ifpahan*, fo that they were no longer
ufeful to me   This perfon however
fucceeded no better than my felf,
and all his inftruments were foon reduced to the fame condition as mine,
though they were much larger and
ftronger   Notwithftanding which,
my earneft defire to convey fome of
thefe

these precious antiquities in my native country would not permit me to rest till I had cut off a fragment of a window, that was filled with characters, the representation of which will be seen in plate 137. I likewise brought away a little broken figure contained in plate 137, as large as the original, two pieces of heads, in plate 139 part of the body of another small figure, in plate 140, and a little piece of one of one of the smallest figures in a portal, exhibited in plate 141. I was very desirous to bring away some others, but found it impossible, because they flew off in shivers with the strokes of our tools.

The principal piece which I endeavoured to procure, was a figure cut on a stone detached from the rock that formed the grand staircase. As this stone was thick, I flattered myself that I should be able to separate the whole figure from it, by dint of time and patience, but it shivered into three pieces, in spite of all my precautions. I, however, rejoined them in the best manner I was able, and Monsieur *Kasteleyn* undertook to deliver it, as he passed by *Zie-raes*, into the hands of Monsieur *Hoorn*, governour-general of our *India* company, and that he would request him, at the same time, to transmit it to *Holland*, the first opportunity, to Monsieur *Witsen*, burgo-master of *Amsterdam*, to whom I intended to present it, as some acknowledgment of the obligations he had conferred upon me. This figure is represented in plate 142.

The 143d plate exhibits to view a pilaster of the lofty edifice to the north, and on which is seen the figure of a man of rank, with two women, one of whom holds a parasol over his head, the other drives away the flies with the tail of a sea horse, for I took all those figures for women, which held these tails and parasols that were much used in antient times.

On another piece of the high edifice to the west, and fronting a kind of window, may be seen three figures of men, greatly decayed. The foremost has a bonnet, which passes under his chin, like those which were worn by the antient Magi when they celebrated divine service. This fragment of the edifice is represented in plate 144.

The 145th plate represents another pilaster of the same edifice, on which may be seen two men armed with lances or pikes, to the east, and on the side of them is a fluted machine, which extends to the chin. There was another reversed on the side of the same edifice, which presents the appearance of a man combating a lion, and grasping a sword in his left hand, agreeably to the representation in plate 146.

In one of the niches, or windows, of this edifice to the south, are to be seen two figures of men, with a goat, that has a large bending horn, by which one of the figures holds him with his left hand, and lays the other on his neck. The first of these figures has likewise a bonnet, which is brought under his chin, and in his left hand, he holds something that was perhaps employed in oblations. These figures are exhibited in plate 147, and the 148th plate represents the pilaster of a portal, on one side of the edifice last mentioned, on which appears three figures half buried, one of which holds the tail of a sea horse above the head of a man of distinction, whose bonnet, hair, and beard, resemble those that appear on the bust of *Arsaces*, on medals.

All the rest of the edifice, which is to the south, had a flat cornice without any ornament, and which was continued through the whole length of the wall. There are still to be seen four openings that resemble windows, and are partly buried in the earth. The whole wall, except the uppermost stones, is cut out of the natural rock, the steps of the stair-case, which are likewise shaped out of the rock, are seven feet and seven inches long, and two inches and a half high. This stair-case be-

comes

FIGURE DE L'ESCALIER

FIGURES D'HOMMES.

PIECE D'UN PILASTRE

PROSPECT DE L'EDIFICE PAR DERRIERE

Restes de l'Escalier.

152   PILASTRE D'UN PORTIQUE, AVEC UN GRAND NOMBRE DE FIGURES

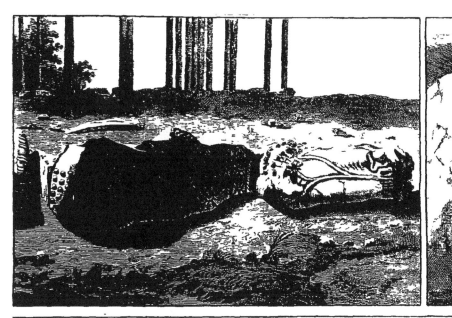

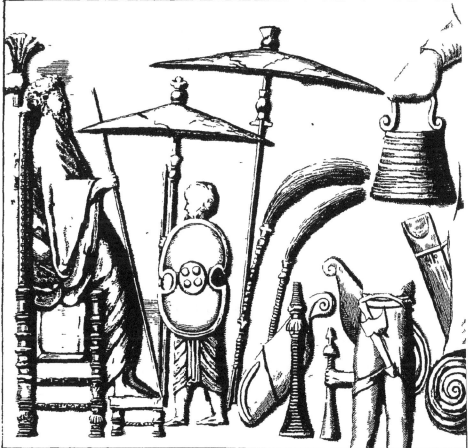

PLUSIEURS ORNEMENS & FIGURES DE PERSEPOLIS

1704 comes vifible at the opening to the left, and the other flight of its steps was at the end to the right The reprefentation of it appears in plate 149

There is likewife another ftaircafe to the eaft of this edifice, as I have already obferved, and which was formerly filled with figures, reprefented in plate 150, of which there are ftill very fine remains. The walls of it are likewife ornamented with figures

The 151ft plate reprefents the pedeftals of two pilaftars in the portal of the high edifice, towards the mountains, and a great number of figures ftill appear to the north, on one of the pilafters of the fame edifice, in plate 152 The feated figure on this pilafter is evidently that of a prince, receiving prefents, and the other figures are probably his guards, and retinue · the two vafes that have fome refemblance to ninepins, and are feen at the feet of the prince, may poffibly be intended for perfumes, and odoriferous herbs The tail of a fea horfe is likewife held above his head

The 153d plate reprefents another portal of fingular beauty, adorned with a variety of figures, and on the top is the little myfterious figure already mentioned, which is ftill entire

In the portal to the north, is feen the head of a horfe lying on the ground, and defigned in two different manners, with a profufion of ornaments. I frequented thefe ruins above three weeks, before I difcovered it, and indeed, it muft be carefully fearched for The two different defigns of this head are in plates 154 and 155

I have added, for the greater accuracy, to all thefe ruins, feveral pieces which I found on the earth, on the fide of fome figures, in one of the laft portals, namely, the tail of a fea horfe, a parafol, the two vafes like ninepins, a fine chair, a variety of things which are in the hands of the figures, and two forts

Vol II.

of round ornaments The whole 1704. is reprefented in plate 156

It is now time to give fome account of the architecture of thefe famous ruins, with refpect to which *The architecture of thefe ruins* it may be proper to obferve in general, that all the columns are fluted in the fame manner, and that the fhafts of fome confift of three, and others of four pieces, exclufive of the capital, which is compofed of five different pieces, and of an order which varies from the five known orders, as well as from all others which I have ever feen.

Some writers pretend that there are winged horfes of an uncommon magnitude on the two columns that are near the two portals, on the fide of the ftair-cafe, in the facade of the edifice, and one author in particular affirms, that he had feen them, tho' without mentioning in what year, but he takes no notice, at the fame time, of the camels that are placed on the others This however is a fact which I can take upon me to aver, and that they are ftill to be feen on their knees, on one of the nine columns, without capitals, and which are placed in a lateral pofition to each other. This camel is, indeed, greatly damaged, but, however, one part of the body is ftill vifible, with the two fore feet, and feveral ornaments that refemble thofe of the animals in the firft portals One cannot be deceived in this particular, if one examines the pieces which are fallen from the tops of thefe columns. The capital of that which is reprefented in plate 157, feems to have been fhaken by an earthquake, and to have ftarted out of its place, but it ftill preferves its equilibrium, tho' it hangs on the fide.

We have likewife been careful to mark, on two or three of the ten columns that have preferved their capitals, a fragment of fhapelefs ftone, which certainly reprefented fome animal, though the particular fpecies is not to be now diftinguifhed

H The

1704

The error of a certain author.

The writer already mentioned, declares, that he found fixteen columns, which being added to the two of the ftair-cafe in the facade, make eighteen in the whole This is what I am unable to comprehend, becaufe I found no more than nineteen, but this is not the only miftake that has been committed by him in his account I muft, however, acknowledge this in his praife, that he is the moft exact of all whom I have read on this fubject

As to any other particulars, I did not obferve any difference in thefe columns, unlefs that fome of them have capitals, and others not. With refpect to their elevation, they are all from feventy to feventy two feet in height, and feventeen feet feven inches in circumference, except thofe two that are near the firft portals, which have been already defcribed. The bafes are round, and twenty four feet five inches in circumference, and four feet three inches high the lower moulding is one foot and five inches thick. They have three forts of ornaments, but the cornice of the portals and windows are exactly the fame, as appears by the plate.

The caufe of this deftruction.

The miferable ftate to which thefe fine ruins are now reduced, is chiefly imputed to the governors of *Zje-raes*, and other places adjacent to *Perfepolis*, who, to avoid the expences to which they were expofed by the great lords who came to vifit thefe fuperb antiquities, have demolifhed whatever was then remaining entire, to prevent their having any curiofity to come there for the future

The royal tombs

We fhall now offer fome obfervations on the two antient tombs of the kings, that have been already mentioned, and which are to be feen on the mountain, one to the north, and the other to the fouth The facade of the firft, which is hewn out of the rock, is a noble fragment of antiquity, covered with figures and other ornaments The form of both is the fame, and they are about feventy feet wide at the bottom.

That part of the tomb on which the figures are carved, is forty feet wide, the height is almoft equal to the width below, and the rock extends on each fide to the diftance of fixty paces The wall of the facade comprehends half this extent, and is fix feet and a half in height The rock, by which one afcends to this tomb, on the corner of the left fide to the north, is broken There are three or four little trees near this facade, and four columns below the edifice, and above thefe are feveral heads of oxen reprefented as far as the breaft, with other ornaments. The gate, whofe architrave is likewife filled with ornaments, is placed in the middle, but fmall, and almoft clofed up, the aperture being but a foot wide, becaufe there is water within The wall is carried out into a projection of five feet on each fide, on which are feen two figures to the right and left, one above the other, and partly broken like the wall. they are five feet and feven inches high. Above the columns, is a cornice, which projects out to the extent of two feet and nine inches, and is about four feet high It refts upon four great beams, which appear above the columns, between the head of the oxen Above this cornice are eighteen fmall lions, nine on each fide, and advancing toward the middle, where is a little ornament like a vafe, and below a modillon. Above the lions are likewife two ranges of figures, almoft as large as the life, fourteen in each range, armed, and lifting up their hands, and on the fide is an ornament in form of a column, with the head of fome animal, who has only one horn Above this is another cornice ornamented with leaves On the left, where the wall projects out, are three kinds of niches, one above another, and each of them contains two figures, armed with lances, and three others, on the fide, armed in the fame manner There are likewife two on the right fide, in the aperture of a window, with their

left

1704

COLOMNE DEVANT LE BATIMENT   PORTIQUE DEVANT LE BATIMENT

1704 left hands placed upon their beards, and the right on their body, and on the side of these are three others, in the same disposition as those on the other side At some distance below, and between these figures and the ornament that resembles a column, is another figure very much impaired on each side Above this tomb, and on three steps, is likewise a large figure, which has the air of a king, pointing at something with his right hand, and holding a kind of bow in his left On the right side of this figure, is an altar, on which an offering is made, and from whence the flames are represented as ascending The moon appears above this altar, and it is said, that there was once a sun, on the left, and behind this figure, but nothing of that nature is now to be seen. In the middle, and above all this work, appears the little mystic figure, which has been so frequently mentioned, and it differs a little from the others

The uncertainty, as respect to the tomb of Darius It cannot be affirmed, that the body of *Darius* was deposited in one of these tombs, since authors have not taken any notice of that particular, and even *Quintus Curtius*, who wrote the life of *Alexander the Great*, in a very copious manner, only declares, that this prince sent the body of *Darius*, who was assassinated by *Bessus*, to queen *Sysigambis*, the mother of that monarch, to be buried in the tomb of his ancestors

Between these tombs, is seen a square pit, fifteen feet wide, and about twenty five deep This was undoubtedly hollowed in the rock, but there is only a single tree now to be seen near it

With respect to the tomb on the southern side, and which is in a very ruinous condition, I had the curiosity to enter it, by creeping on my breast, the water being evacuated at that time I found that the passage into it was two feet high, and the vault within, forty six feet in breadth, and twenty in depth This cave is divided into thre vaults, which begin at half the depth of the main cavity, and are carried up seven feet high. On the left side of the entrance, a breach appears in the rock or facade, and gives admission to a little light. There are several stones in these vaults, and especially in that to the left. They are said to contain two tombs covered with stones, in a demi round, and in all probability they have been wilfully broken, every person whatever being permitted to enter there, at several times, but at present there are no more than I have mentioned, and they seem to be 159 in number

The rock, or wall of this facade, advances thirty feet on one side, and forty on the other, and has no entrance like the other On each side of this facade, and in three separate compartments, are the figures of two men armed with lances, and it is said that six others are fallen down in the first of these monuments, tho' others declare there are but three, which was confirmed to me by the person whom I caused to enter therein, by creeping on his belly On the south side of this building, and at the distance of 215 paces from the corner of the facade, is the column already mentioned, part of which is now broken, in the manner it appears on its base in plate 160. and round it are eight other bases, one of which is to the north, and seven paces from this, a second is to the east, at an equal distance; and three to the north east, ten paces from the first; the corner to the west containing eighteen paces The two to the south possess a space of ground twenty two paces in extent, and are eight paces from each other. Around these bases are several large and globular stones, with three great fragments of the rock, which have evidently supported some edifice. The column lately mentioned is twelve feet and seven inches in diameter, and its base rises three feet and six inches above the surface of the causey On the side of the two bases to the south, are

1704

are two fragments of figures representing camels, which were placed, with other ornaments, on the columns.

At the distance of 650 paces from this edifice, to the north, is another portal, which is not one of the largest, and the pilasters on the two sides support the statue of a woman as large as the life. This is represented in plate 161.

As the tombs I have been describing are only exhibited in small in the plate, I thought it proper to trace out their fine ornaments on the sides, with the beautiful head above them, in plate 162 together with one of those on the southern side of the portal, in plate 163, as likewise the two heads of oxen on one of the columns under the cornice of the tomb, in plate 164, and lastly, a fragment of one of the columns, on which the forefeet of a kneeling camel are still distinguishable, in plate 165.

When I had travelled so far in search of these fine antiquities, I employed the remainder of the time I had to continue at *Chil menaer*, in reviewing what I had already seen, and numbering all the figures of men and beasts, which are yet to be distinguished, in order to give as perfect an idea as possible, of the grandeur and magnificence of these superb ruins.

The second survey of these antiquities. I began this second survey at the two first portals which are near the stair-cafe in the facade, where are the figures of four large beasts, with the ascent of steps which conduct one to the columns. The figures, which are there to be seen, amount to 520, beside which there are forty two below, and round the first portal, they are also as large as the life, but those of the men over whose heads a parasol is held, and likewise those which are represented as encountring lions, with the others that are armed with lances, are two feet taller. Eighteen figures armed with lances, are seen on the wall of the back facade, and they all as large as the life. There are likewise twenty five figures on the ruined staircafe, which, with the others, make eighty five in number. There are also twenty figures of women in the raised edifice, as big as the life, with thirty three more, that are something less, and five pilasters, on which the men, who are supported by them, are ten feet and seven inches high. There are two other portals, the figures of which are armed with lances, and are seven feet five inches in height. On the side of these portals, on the wall of the facade, and before a vacant space of ground, are eighteen demi figures, armed with lances like the preceding. They are opposite to each other, and with the rest amount to eighty two. Four figures of women are likewise to be seen on the wall of the facade of the stair-cafe belonging to the same edifice, to the east, a little larger than the life, but they are only visible as far as the neck, and there are eight others that resemble these, on each of the side walls. One may easily distinguish, on the wings of that stair cafe, thirty six figures, two feet high, and three lions, at the entrance, encountring with bulls. There are sixty three of these figures in the whole. On each of the three pilasters of the eastern portals, is a figure with a parasol, and in another portal, which is not far from the other, are six large figures on each side, and below these, are three ranges of little figures, a foot and six inches in height, nine in the upper range, as many in the lowest, and ten in the middle, which make fifty six, and seventy one in the whole. On the top of each of these two last portals, which are toward the mountain, are six large figures, below which are five ranges of small ones, each range containing ten, and one hundred and twelve in the whole. On the top of each of the four pilasters of the two portals to the south, are three large figures, which make twelve in all, and below these, are three rows of small figures, the uppermost contain

four,

1704 four, and the other two have five a piece, which amount, in the whole, to sixty eight. The two portals to the east, and the two others, which are opposite to the west, have sixteen figures encountering with lions. In the two northern portals, which are at a little distance, are several figures armed with lances, the head of each of these figures is two feet and seven inches high, and the hand which holds the lance, is ten inches in breadth. This piece was still entire, because it could not be approached by any who might be desirous of breaking it, the entrance being closed up with a large stone, so that those figures are only to be seen from one side. Had it not been for this impediment, I should have attempted to procure one of the hands. The rest of the body, as far as the stomach, is buried in the earth. I found three hundred distinguishable figures of this nature, in the edifice to the east, and the nearest of any to the mountain. Among the ruins to the south are twenty six large figures of men and beasts, on the pilasters of the portals. In each of the tombs on the mountain are fifty human figures, exclusive of the animals, and they amount to a hundred in the whole. So that when we add all the figures together, comprehending those which are still visible on the ruined staircases, and other places, I believe they will amount to near 1300 figures of men and beasts.

The *Persians* call the remains of these antient ruins, *Chil-minaer*, or *Chel-menaer*, which signifies the *forty columns*, as has been already observed, and they undoubtedly received this appellation, at a time when no more than that number were remaining. The word *Chil* signifies *forty*, and *menaer*, a *circumference*, and it is very usual for the *Persians* to bestow that name on any building which has about the same number of pillars, as was intimated in my description of the palace of *Ispahan*, which is called by the same name, tho' the number of columns in that structure do not exactly correspond with its appellation.

Other travellers, who have written before me, have confirmed this truth, but add, that the columns which were still remaining to the number of forty, were entirely decayed, but these gentlemen must certainly have surveyed these stately ruins with an unpardonable inattention, since I have found, as well by the bases which are still visible, as also by the cavities into which the columns were inserted, that their number was formerly 205.

I shall now make some remarks on the drapery of the figures, which entirely differs from all that I have ever seen before, and has no similitude to that of the *Greeks* and *Romans*, nor even to that of the antient *Persians*. The rules of art are not observed in the figures, since no muscles are visible in the naked parts and the figures in general have a motionless air. Nothing has been observed but the contours, and this neglect causes them to appear stiff and inelegant. The draperies have likewise the same defects, and the whole is a tasteless sameness, as is evident by the plates I have made without any addition or diminution.

The proportions, however, have been finely kept, both in the great and small figures, which is a demonstration that those who made them, were not destitute of capacity, but were possibly obliged to be too expeditious, to be capable of employing all the necessary attentions, and to finish them with the utmost perfection. But it must be confessed, that most of the ornaments are exceeding beautiful, as well as the chairs in which the figures are seated, notwithstanding they are much impaired. It is therefore reasonable to believe, that there were formerly some very fine fragments, which have since been destroyed by time, and I am persuaded that some figures have been found there completely rounded, and

The negligence of travellers

The Drapery of the figures

The irregularity of the antient architecture

The proportions well kept.

Vol II   I

1704 and that there were several things much more remarkable, and in greater perfection, in a place where such stately remains are still to be seen. They are now supposed to be the ruins of one structure, because no distinction appears among them. Several persons likewise imagine the stones of the rock which composed it, to be a white marble, and those of the stair-case black. For my part, I am persuaded, on the contrary, that the whole has been hewn from the rock, which is the natural product of the mountain, so that there was no necessity to go to a greater distance for those materials. It is even visible, that great part of this edifice has been cut out of the rock itself in the mountain, to which the structure joins, and any one will be sufficiently convinced of this truth, by examining ever so little the two tombs on that mountain, together with most of the stair-cases, the principal foundation of the walls, and the other rocky fragments that are to be found up and down, especially in the northern part of this edifice. What has contributed to the propagation of this error, is, that the generality of these stones are polished like a mirror, and particularly those within the portal, and those which compose the windows and pavements, that are still to be seen. Another reason which causes them to be taken for marble, is their appearing with different colours, such as yellow, white, grey, red, a deep blew, and even black in some places. But I impute this variety to time, and the rather, because it is to be seen in the rock of the mountain.

The greatest part, however, of this edifice, is a clear blue, and that a better judgment may be formed of the colours, I have been at the pains to copy them from the structure itself, in distemper.

The city of Persepolis destroyed. With respect to the city of Persepolis, there are not any traces of it now remaining, only the rocks that appear on each side, incline one to believe that there were buildings formerly, beyond the enclosure of the

edifice which has been described. 1704 The Persians say, and it likewise appears by their writings, that this city was once of great extent, situated in a plain, and that the ruins which are still to be seen, are those of the palace of the antient kings of Persia. According to the best of my judgment, it seemed to have extended along the mountain, and from thence a great way into the plain, but after all, these are only conjectures, since there are no traces of it now to be seen, except the column which stands to the south, and without the inclosure of the ruins of the palace, and likewise the portal to the north.

I had generally the good fortune to be favoured with very fine weather, during my continuance there. Rains and snow would indeed fall sometimes, and at other times it proved frosty, so that I was then obliged to confine my self to my house till the weather became more favourable. I, however, visited the ruins as frequently as possible, and made a kind of kitchen there, but if I had enjoyed the company of a friend as curious as my self, together with a good dog, I should have passed the night in a grot of the mountain, to save my self the labour of returning thither every day. This is generally practised by the Arabians who live in tents, and are followed by their cattle, with which they cultivate the earth, even under the walls of these ruins. They came frequently to visit me, while I was employed among these celebrated antiquities. The inhabitants of the circumjacent villages did the same, as well as their Kalantaer, or Bailiff. Several poor people likewise, induced by the curiosity to behold so noble a spectacle, came daily thither with their families, and camels, who ascended and came down the grand stair case, as easily as their conductors. I took notice that these people examined these famous ruins with more curiosity than Mr Tavernier, who assures us that twelve columns were standing forty eight years ago, and adds, that these ruins, which are

10

FIGURES ENTRE LES DEUX TOMBEAUX   FIGURES A DEMI ENTERRELS

DEUX CAVALIERS A CHEVAL 170   DEUX PETITS EDIFICES 171

so much talked of in the world, are not worth a traveller's going half a league out of his way to see them. They were likewise more curious than a *Dutchman*, who drew them by the order of the *India* company for King *Abbas* the second, and complained that he had lost so much time in that employment As to the first particular, I can hardly believe that Mr *Tavernier* was ever there There are nineteen columns now standing, and as to the other, a judgment may be formed of the merit of the ruins by the designs which I have exhibited.

The town of *Mier-chas-koen*, which is the nearest of any to these antiquities, is of a considerable extent, and accommodated with several *Bazars*, it likewise abounds with all sorts of provisions and fruits, especially melons, grapes, oranges, citrons, pomegranates, &c

Besides the birds I have already

Birds in he moun ains

mentioned, I likewise found four or five sorts of little birds that continually harbour among these ruins, and on the mountain, and entertain the ear with the most agreeable melody in the world The notes of the largest species have a near correspondence with those of the nightingale Some of them are almost entirely black, others are of the size of the swallow, and have their bodies spotted, a third class is smaller and variously coloured, some are yellow, others grey, and several entirely white, and shaped like a chafinch I should certainly have fired at some, in order to have drawn them afterwards, if I had not been prevented by impatience desire to take a careful survey of those other objects, which I was desirous of knowing as much as possible I sometimes saw foxes, but they never come within musket shot

Two leagues from these ruins is a place called *Naxi Ruftan*, but a large circuit must be taken in order to arrive there, because a river crosses the country, and is not to be passed, but over a certain bridge, which is at a considerable distance.

The plain is likewise cut into a variety of small channels, which are so many impediments to travellers in their way thither

I found, in this place, four tombs of persons of eminence among the antient *Persians*, and they much resemble those of *Persepolis*, only they are cut abundantly higher in the rock, and therefore are not to be approached, without the aid of cords This place receives its denomination from *Ruftan*, whose figure is there to be seen, and was carved to perpetuate his memory He is said to have been a potent prince, of an immense stature, being forty cubits high, and he lived, according to the same report, 1113 years

The tombs, which extend upward on a steep rock, have their bases eighteen feet above the surface of the causey, and rise four times as high, as near as one can judge by surveying them, and the rock is twice as high as the tombs, which are sixty feet wide in the middle Under each tomb is a separate table filled with large figures in low relief, on two of which tables some traces of men fighting on horseback are still to be seen Between these tombs are three other tables covered with figures, and among these, appears the figure of a man on horseback, preceded by two others, and followed by a third, which is almost entirely defaced. There are likewise some figures in the space between the two last works, and three under the third, two of which tender their hands to each other. One of these is a woman, and both of them are half buried in the earth. There is also a square edifice fronting the first tomb, each of whose sides has a width of 27 feet It rises higher than the tomb, and has an opening over against it, to the north, to which I climbed with great difficulty, and found nothing but a little square apartment, with four windows in two of its sides, and several long apertures. I seated myself on the southern side of this building, where I drew the design

of

crown of the whole work, as it is exhibited in plate 166, and one of the tombs in particular, as it appears in plate 167

These tombs possess an extent of 280 paces, and the little square edifice is sixty paces distant from the first of them. The figure of a man on horseback, between the two tombs, and in the middle of the fourth niche, has his hair shaped according to our mode, with a crown upon his head, and a pointed bonnet rising above it. He is habited after the *Roman* manner, and has a large sword at his side, with the hilt in his left hand. His legs hang down very low, and he presents his right hand to another on foot before him. The third figure has one knee buried in the earth, and opens the hands like a supplicant, and its dress is likewise in the *Roman* mode. There was formerly another figure behind the horse, but it is almost entirely destroyed by time. They are represented in plate 168.

The figures that were half buried, appear on the side of the third tomb, and two of them have their hands placed on a kind of circle. That in the middle represents *Ruftan*, in a *Roman* dress, he has likewise a bonnet, and an ornament like a crown, together with flowing hair, a large beard, and his left hand clapt upon the hilt of his sword. Before him is the figure of a woman, and perhaps one of his mistresses, her hair is represented floating over her shoulders, she likewise wears a crown, and above it another ornament which is not distinguishable. She is habited almost like a *Pria*, and supports part of her drapery with her left hand. The third figure represents a military man, with a tiara on his head, ornamented at the top, and his left hand grasps the hilt of his sword. What he once held in his right hand, is now broken, all that I could distinguish, with relation to these figures, is exhibited in plate 169.

The niche, or table which follows, represents two other broken

figures on horseback, that seem to be engaged in a combat with lances, one of them has a bonnet like that of *Ruftan*, and something was originally behind it. The fifth niche has nothing entire, but there is an imperfect appearance of figures fighting on horseback, as well as in the last, which is reduced to the same condition, and was, as I suppose, like the preceding niche. All these figures are carved in the rock, and the appearance they make, is odd enough.

On the western side of this mountain, and at the distance of two hundred paces from the tombs, are two tables with figures, that are likewise carved on the rock. That to the left represents two men on horseback, one of whom strongly grasps a circle, of which the other has quitted his hold. It is pretended by some, that the first is *Alexander*, and the other *Darius*, who resigns to him the empire by this action. Others say these figures represent two potent princes, or generals, who, after they had been engaged in a long war with each other, without obtaining any advantage, came to an agreement, that he who could wrest this circle out of the hand of his competitor, should triumph over him, and be acknowledged the victor. But there is no stress to be laid on these stories, nor in what is related of *Ruftan*, who, they pretend, was forty cubits high, and yet he is represented with the common stature of a man, and the horse is not larger than the usual size of those animals.

With respect to the two horsemen, who hold the circle, one has a round bonnet, out of which a set of plumes seem to flow, and he is habited in the antique manner, with a kind of general's staff in his left-hand. On the crupper of his horse is something that resembles a chain, at the end of which hangs a machine that is not to be distinguished. The other has something of the same nature, with a round bonnet, which rises higher than that of the preceding

ceding figure, and behind him is another figure holding something above his head, which might possibly have been the tail of a sea horse. The whole is represented in plate 170. On the right of these figures, and in the middle of another niche, is the figure of a man, who seems resolved to come out of it, and grasps his sword with both hands. The other figures, which are on the side of this, three to the right, and two on the left, are visible no farther than the breast, and they appear behind a wall, but there is another on this side of the wall, with his hands crossed upon his breast.

There are likewise two little square structures at the corner of the same mountain, and at the distance of 250 paces from that which has been already described. They have the air of little temples, and are near one another, being but six feet high, and five in width, on every side. There is also an ascent of three steps to the south, as may be seen in plate 171.

The inhabitants of the village having informed me, that there were several other tombs among the monuments of *Naxi Ruflan*, I resolved to visit them with a man strong enough to raise me up with a cord, that I might view every thing my self, but when I arrived at the place where the cord was to be employed, I became sensible that the enterprize would be dangerous, could not prevail upon my self to undertake it, by the assistance of only one man, with whom I was entirely unacquainted. I therefore caused another, whom I accidentally met, and who spoke *Dutch*, to attend in my place. The villager, who had frequently been there before, climbed up first, and then raised the other by the aid of the cord, which he wound about his body; this person, at the same time, exerted himself with his feet and hands on the side of the rock, by which means he soon attained to the place where the villager had fixed himself, and advanced to the first

tomb to the west, which was more 1704. accessible than the rest. I remained below to give him the necessary instructions, which I communicated to him with a loud voice. He then measured the height of the first platform of the steep rock, and found that its altitude was equal to eighteen feet after which he proceeded inward to the distance of six feet, and as far as the bottom of the second platform of the same perpendicula rock, which likewise rose to the height of eighteen feet, and had a depth of seven, with a facade of fifty three feet in extent. The entrance into that in the middle was three feet and a half in height, and the rock within, was two feet and three inches thick, and as much without. He there found, opposite to the entrance, a tomb disposed lengthwise, and on the sides of it were two others, one on the right, and the other on the left. Two of these tombs were eleven feet in length, and the third ten, with a breadth of six feet, and a height of five, and its distance from the others is no more than a foot and a half. The vault which contains these tombs, is entirely formed out of the rock, and they are joined to it at the end, but distant from it a foot at the other extremity. These tombs are hewn out of the same rock to which they are joined below, as is likewise their upper part, so that it is impossible to judge whether they have ever been opened. They are a foot thick, and no ornaments are to be seen upon them. The vault of this grot is ten feet high, twelve in depth, and forty in width. I have been assured that there have been nine tombs in the second monument, six in the third, and nine in the fourth, but I am not certain whether they are there now, being only able to answer for the first. At some distance to the east, near a village, half a league from this place, and in a plain surrounded with mountains, is a column, near which, it is said, that there is a portal still to be seen, like those

of

at P——, and the country people say, that there was formerly a large structure in that place.

It would be difficult to come to any certainty, with regard to the ruins of Persepolis, since there are not the least remains of any standing edifice, nor any building above the cornices of the portal, doors, or windows, by which any reasonable conjecture can be formed. It must, however, be granted, that they have a much greater resemblance to the members of a palace, than to those of a temple, of which there is not the least appearance. On the contrary, every thing corresponds with the grandeur and magnificence of a great king's palace, to which the images and figures which cover these ruins impart a surprising air of majesty. It is certain that there have been very stately portals and grand galleries to afford a communication with all the detached parts of that structure; and most of the columns, whose remains are still to be useful, were certainly intended to support those galleries, while others might, perhaps, be merely for ornament, like those of Susa, or Shushan, which is mentioned in the book of Esther. The lodgings of the men and women were separated from each other, according to all appearance, and there even seems to be still some remains of the royal apartments. In a word, the magnificence of these ruins can never be sufficiently admired, and this structure must undoubtedly have cost immense treasures. The same may be said of the ruins which are scattered thro' all Greece, of which so many noble antiques are still preferred, and of those of old Rome, whose remains still display such inexpressible grandeur. These last, however, have not been so entirely demolished as the seat of the first palace of the kings of Persia, which was the glory of all the East, and owed its destruction to the debaucheries and frenzy of Alexander the Great, who, after he had preserved it from the ravages of war, reduced it to ashes, 170 at the solicitations of Thais, a Grecian courtesan. He, indeed, repented of his rash action, but it proved too late. Quintus Curtius observes, that all the joinery work of this palace was made of cedar, but I should rather imagine it to be tenar, which is a wood that abounds in Persia, where no cedars are to be found. This last is a tree with which I am well acquainted, and have described it in the first volume of my travels, where I offer some account of mount Libanus. I may, however, be mistaken, and a length of time may have created a great change, with respect both to those trees, and the ruins I have been describing.

These latter are situated in the thirtieth degree, and fortieth minute of northern latitude, in the southern part of Asia, in the province of Fars, or Farsistan, to the south of Ispahan, and north east from Zjeeras, or Chiras, according to the computation I have made both by sea and land, and I have observed the same exactness through the whole course of my relation, where I have marked the true distances of places, by which means I have rectified the inaccuracies of several writers, and the generality of maps.

The Persians pretend, that the city of Persepolis, was formerly called Zjeeras, and afterward Ieus, from the province of that name, if this did not rather derive its name from the city. It is likewise called Libnas, in the first book of the Maccabees, where it is said that Antiochus advanced to this city with a powerful army, after the death of Alexander, to seize the treasures that were there deposited, but that he could not accomplish his purpose. The second book declares, that this prince was shamefully repelled by the inhabitants, which evidently proves that Persepolis is the very city which the Hebrews call Elmai. The antient annals of Persia declare, that it was founded by a king named Yemjcind, who

who reigned in that country, with the title of emperor, about 4000 years ago. They perhaps mean Coras, or Cyrus, the first founder of that empire, and the most illustrious of all its kings, who is mentioned in such an honourable manner by the prophet Daniel, and who delivered the Jews from the Babylonish captivity, after which he caused the temple of God to be rebuilt, as we find it recorded at the beginning of the book of Esdras. They even pretend, that Spemschid lived a thousand years, and comprehend in that period all the successors of that prince, who flourished to the time of Alexander, who is known among them by the name of Schandar, or Schandar Su-alcarnaim. This last name intimates that the king of Macedonia wore two sorts of horns, which were the emblems of his fortitude and power. There are some learned men among them, who distinguish him, as I have been since informed, by the name of Schandar-Ferrages, which signifies Alexander the Son of Philip, as he really was, and who take the wreathes of his horses mains for horns. Others apply to them a mystic sense, and maintain, that they adumbrate the two parts of the then known world, which were the east and west, and it must be acknowledged that it was customary for the orientals to give this name of Horns, to the verges or borders of any thing. We accordingly see Alexander represented in this manner, on some particular medals, where the tresses of his horses resemble horns.

C H A P. LIII.

Particular remarks, with respect to Persepolis, and the antient authors, who have written upon that subject.

The scripture of Persian authors, with relation to the founder of Persepolis

MODERN writers, as well Persians as Arabians, pretend that one of their kings, or heroes, called Giemschid, or Zjemschid, founded this capital of the kingdom of Persia, and gave it the name of Estchar, which signifies *hewn out of the rock*. They likewise add, that this city was of such a vast extent, that it comprehended the city of Chiras in its circuit: that Queen Homai, the daughter of Bahaman, built the palace of this city, called Gihil, or Chilminar, and that the tombs on the mountain owe their origin to prince Kitschtasb, the son of the fifth king of the race of the Cajanides, named Lohorasp. See Herbelot (a)

But as these relations are blended with so many fabulous accounts, as render them altogether incredible, and as they neither correspond with each other in any material particular, nor with the antient Greek historians, or the sacred records, we cannot repose any confidence on their authority.

The accounts of modern authors uncertain

These particulars being premised, I shall venture to affirm, with all due deference to the judgment of the learned, that the remaining ruins of Chilminar, their situation, the traces of the structure, the figures and their habits, together with the ornaments, and whatever else is now discoverable among them, correspond with the manners of the

The author's opinion

(a) Biblioth Orient at the word Estehar pag 5,-

ancient

antient *Persia*, and the description, which is still extant, of the
antient palace of *Perjepolis*

Diodorus Siculus, who is said to
have been contemporary with *Julius
Cæsar*, is the only ancient historian
who has transmitted to us a sketch
of the famous palace of *Perjepolis*,
destroyed by *Alexander the Great*,
and this he copied from the *Egyptian*
and *Greek* antiquities, which are
now lost in the ocean of time   This
author, after he had declared that
Alexander exposed all this capital * of the *Persian* kingdom, except the royal palace †, to the plun-
der of his *Macedonians*, describes
this palace, as an extraordinary
structure, in the following words
*This superb edifice, says he, or the pa-
lace royal, is surrounded with a triple
wall; the first, which is exceeding
magnificent, is sixteen cubits high,
and is furnished with towers and a parapet   The second resembles the first,
with respect to the fabrication, but
has twice its height   The third is
square, and hewn out of the rock; it
is likewise sixty cubits high   Its cur-
tains are fenced with palisades of copper,
and gates of the same metal, twenty
cubits high; the former of these were
intended to create terror, the latter
were designed for the security of the
palace, to the east of which is a tract
of land, containing two acres, and
beyond that, the royal mountain, where
the tombs of the* Persian *kings are e-
rected* [a]

We can hardly be surprized, if
the ruins of this antient Pile, which
was reduced to ashes by *Alexander
the Great*, two thousand years ago,
do not exactly correspond to the
description given of this palace by
Diodorus, if we only consider the
great changes which have happened
in *Persia* since that time   After
the death of that prince, for instance,
it fell to the share of one of his captains, who rendered it hereditary in
his family   It was afterwards conquered by the *Parthians*, but the

Persians, in process of time, regained it by the bravery of *Artaxerxes*, in
the time of *Alexander Severus*, and
governed it for a long space of time,
till at last the successors of *Mohammed* made themselves masters of it by
force of arms   I say, when all these
particulars are duly attended to, it
can never be thought surprizing,
that authors should have different
sentiments with respect to the subject
before us, and especially since it may
be presumed, that the devastations
of wars, tempests, and earthquakes,
have entirely destroyed a considerable part of this stately edifice, or
buried it, at least, in the bosom of
the earth   On the contrary, there
is reason to be astonished, that there
are now to be found several things,
according to the description of *Don
Garcias de Silva de Figueroa*, in his
embassy to *Persia*, [b] which correspond with *Diodorus Siculus*, and
several other antient writers, and as
my plates agree with those descriptions, I think we may conclude
that the ruins of *Chilminar* are those
of the famous palace of *Perjepolis*,
which was destroyed by *Alexander
the Great*

Diodorus Siculus declares, in the
Place before cited, that there was
a piece of ground, containing two
acres, between the palace and the
mountain, where the tombs of the
kings are to be seen   I have made
the same observation, as well as the
Spanish Ambassador already mentioned, who concurs with my account in his description of *Chilminar*,
the distance only excepted, in which
he differs a little from the *Greek*
historian   For though the *Latin*
version of that Author, to which I
had recourse, assigns no more than
an extent of 400 feet to four *plethra*,
or half acres of land, it is not to be
inferred from thence, that he means
the usual feet of the *Greeks* and
Romans   On the contrary, tho'
a certain unknown author, cited
by *Saumaises*, affirms, that the

*Other Re-
marks of
Diod Si-
culus*

[a] Vide lib xii p r Lat Her Seph 599 se & Wech p 54,
[b] Page 144 seq   In Exerc Plin

Greek

1704 Greek word πλεθρον signified, among the *Romans*, an extent of land, comprising a hundred square feet, it is still certain, that the royal foot, which the *Greeks* call *Plethaerius*, was sixteen inches long, and this is confirmed by the same (a) *Saumasius* The learned *Lipsius* judges likewise, that the πλεθρον almost corresponded with *jugerum agri Romani*, or half an acre of land, according to the *Roman* measure And in order to be convinced of this, we need only examine this treatise of the military art of the (b) *Romans* All these particulars being duly considered, I am of opinion, that my usual steps sufficiently agree with the relations of these antient writers, and this contributes to prove, that the ruins of *Chilminar* are those of the antient palace of *Persepolis* The illustrious *Isaac Vossius* thinks to the same effect in his remarks on *Pomponius* (c) *Mela*

Ptolemy (d) of *Alexandria*, an antient Geographer, likewise places *Persepolis* in the height of 33 degrees and 20 minutes of south latitude *Strabo*, *Stephanus*, *Ammianus Marcellinus*, and some others, likewise mention *Persepolis*, but without specifying its situation (e) *Saumasius* is of opinion, that *Ptolemy*, and his transcriber *Ammianus*, have taken notice of this city, as of a place which still subsisted, tho he is persuaded, that no traces of it were remaining in their time, and that *Alexander* reduced that city to ashes, as well as the palace *Quintus Curtius* seems also to have embraced the same (f) sentiment Whether the *Greeks*, therefore, and *Romans*, had travelled but little into *Persia*, after the death of *Alexander*, or that the writings of those among them, who gave any account of *Persepolis*, have been destroyed, like several other works, it appears, however, by the first book of the (g) *Maccabees*, and likewise by the

testimony of (h) *Josephus*, that the 1704 city of *Persepolis*, which was called *Elimais* by the antient *Persians*, subsisted, at least in part, in the time of *Antiochus Epiphanes*, whether it was, that *Alexander* had not entirely destroyed it, as I am inclined to think, or that part of it was rebuilt since that time (i) Nor can I see any reason why we should not pay as much regard to the apochryphal books of the sacred Scripture, and the history of *Josephus*, as we do to the pagan authors, and the rather, as we are sensible, that the *Jews* were dispersed through all parts, after the *Babylonish* captivity, and that several of them, after the time of *Alexander*, went to settle in *Persia*, where I am persuaded their descendants have continued to this day.

But if these particulars should *Proofs* not be thought decisive in this point, *arisen* yet it evidently appears, by the arms, *from the* habits, and ornaments of the figures, *figures and* as well as by the hieroglyphics that *ornaments* are still to be found at *Chilminar*, that it was an antient palace of the *Persian* kings, and must certainly be that of *Persepolis*. This I shall endeavour to prove, by the testimony of authors who have written on this subject.

The military habits of the figures *The milita-* no the stair-case, are partly agreeable *ry habits* to the mode of the *Persians*, and *of the Per-* partly to that of the *Medes* Those of *sians and* the antient *Persians* were of leather, *Medes* with a girdle of the same substance, according to (k) *Herodotus*, but they changed this fashion after the reign of *Cyrus*, and it is certain that those of the figures on the stair-case are the same that were worn in *Persia*, when *Xerxes* invaded *Greece* They used bonnets made in the form of *Tiaras*, their robes were covered with thin plates of iron, like the scales of a fish, and their drawers were fastened below, round the leg They likewise carried of bucklers, called *Gerra*, and made of interwoven cords, and the *Romans* after-

(a) Ad Sol p 582 seq & p 684 seq
(c) Ad melam de situ orbis lib 3 c 8 p m 379
(e) Vid exercit ad solin p m 1226 & 1228 A
(g) Chap vi ver 1 seq & chap ix ver 2
L 2 c 10 &c   (k) Lib 1 c 71

(b) l v Dial 2 sub finem.
(d) Vide lib 6 c 4 sub finem p m 1/4.
(f) Lib 5 c 23
(i) Lib 12   (i) Vide Bochart Geog sacr.

ward called the *Spanish* bucklers by the same name. Beside these, they also carried arrows, which hung down on their bodies, and short pikes, together with a large quiver, and javelins made of canes or reeds, with a poniard on the right him, and they used these arms in imitation of the *Medes*. The *Cyrians*, or *Kissians*, a people in *Persia*, wore at that time, mitres instead of Tiaras, according to (a) *Herodotus*. The long robes without plaits, were undoubtedly *Persian*, *Stola Persica*, and they are mentioned by *Cælius* (b) *Rhodiginus*. but *Cyrus* introduced the plaited robes, after he had conquered *Asia*, and he caused these habits to be distributed to the *Persians* at his first offering, after he taken *Babylon*, agreeable to the mode of *Media*, and the *Persians* had no such habits till that time, according to *Xenophon* (c).

An evident proof taken from the stair-case
The stair-case, where the figures appear, is a manifest proof that the ruins of *Chilminar* are those of the palace of *Persepolis*, because the habits and arms of the figures, which are entirely different from those which are now used by the modern *Persians*, make it evident, that this stair-case subsisted at the time of the kings of the first race, and even in that of *Xerxes the Great*. Don Garcias de Silva de Figueroa, ambassador of *Spain* to king *Abbas*, mentions this stair-case, as a piece of sculpture which represented a triumph, and yet it has no similitude to those which are now exhibited in *Persia*. For *Xenophon* expresly (d) declares, after he had described the offering made by *Cyrus* at *Babylon*, that all the kings of *Persia* who succeeded that prince, imitated his manner of habiting himself, when he appeared in public, and that no beasts were ever introduced, when oblations were not made. It is well known that the *Persians* sacrificed horses to the

sun, and oxen to the moon. The horses represented the rapidity of the sun's course, and the oxen were emblems of husbandry, over which the moon was said to preside. See (e) *Xenophon*, (f) *Herodotus*, and (g) *Cælius Rhodiginus*.

But as the figures of camels, asses, and goats, are to be seen upon this stair-case, as well as those of horses and oxen, I will venture to affirm, with all due submission to the learned, that the whole sculpture of this stair-case represents a festival at the birth of a king, with the offerings presented to him, and which is still practised on that occasion, when sheep, deer, and all manner of roasted provisions are brought to the king's tables as an offering. See (h) *Athenæus*.

These processions are preceded by some persons who wear a *Tiara*, or a kind of crown upon their heads, which was customary in the time of *Cyrus*, in whose reign the principal lords of his court, who were called *Æquals*, were obliged to assist at offerings and festivals, with crowns on their heads, because it was the general opinion, that the gods were delighted to behold the magnificence of those who made oblations to them, and that they received them more favourably on that account. See *Xenophon* (i).

The vases which are carried by these figures, were undoubtedly filled with odoriferous herbs, and particularly with myrrh, which were presents that the kings of *Persia* received with pleasure, even from their subjects, as *Athenæus* (k) declares.

The *Spanish* ambassador, who has been so often mentioned, is persuaded, that the animal attacked by the lion, on the stair-case, represents an ox, or a bull, but I rather think it intended for a horse or an ass. This particular piece of sculpture, is no more than a hieroglyphic,

(a) L. . . c. 61 & se. . . . (e) Lect. ar. q. Lib. 18 c. 9. . . . . C. ropæd. L. b. . . .
(d) L. . c. 25. . . . . (c. L. b. . . . . . (f. Anno. Lib. X. . . . . . (g. L. . . P. . d. 16. 9
(c) L. 4 p. 14. & I. 12 p. 514. see . . r. Cornelm. 159. . . . . . . (h. C. op. l. . 22 . . .
(k. L. 12 p. 514.

1704 reprefenting ſome ſe victorious over ſome, and every one knows, that the antient Perſians and Egyptians, concealed their greateſt myſteries under equivocal figures, as Herodotus obſerves (a).

As all theſe animals, therefore, are repreſented with horns, which are not natural to them, ſome myſtery muſt certainly be intended by that ſculpture, and this ſuppoſition ſeems the more reaſorable, becauſe it is well known that horns were antiently the emblem of ſtrength, and even of majeſty itſelf, and that they have been conſigned to the ſun and moon, as well as to Alexander the Great, who is called Dhulkarnam, or the horn d, by the Oriental people, becauſe he made himſelf king of the two horns of the ſun, namely the eaſt and weſt (b)

Juſtice repreſented by a balance

As to the ſcales, it is well known that juſtice was held in great veneration by the antient Perſians, as Xenophon has obſerved (c), for which reaſon balances were carried before the king and the grandees, to repreſent that juſtice to their view This cuſtom likewiſe prevailed among the antient Greeks, and afterward among the Romans

The figures in the two firſt portals very much reſemble a horſe, both before and behind, only the head ſeems to be like that of an ape, and indeed the tail has no great ſimilitude to that of a horſe, but this may be imputed to the ornaments which are faſtned to it, and were much uſed among the antient Per

The ſ x ſphinxes were repreſented with wings

ſians They had the name of ſphinx, becauſe they reſembled apes, and as the antients likewiſe gave this denomination to a certain bird, the Greeks, and undoubtedly the Perſians, repreſented them with wings Some naturaliſts pretend that they are alſo emblematical of the power of fixed and volatile ſalts

Paraſols uſed by the antient Perſians

The paraſol was antiently in uſe among the Perſians, and Xenophon (d)

ſeems to fix the invention of it to the time of Artaxerxes, the brother of Cyrus the Younger, and not to that of Cyrus the Great, in whoſe reign the Perſians imitated the habits, ornaments, and manners of the Medes, without having recourſe to any precautions againſt the heat of the ſun, or the violence of winds and ſeaſons. But this was changed in the reign of Artaxerxes, who addicted himſelf to wine and debaucheries, with his whole court, and ſunk into ſuch an effeminate ſoftneſs, that the ſhade of trees, and refreſhing coolneſs of caverns and grots, were no longer thought a ſufficient ſhelter from the heat of the ſun, paraſols therefore became neceſſary, and domeſtics to carry them

The plaited robes of the Medes

The two figures armed with lances, repreſent the Tunicæ manicatæ, or long plaited robes of the Medes, which were worn by the baſtati, or lance-men, as well Medes as Perſians, in the reigns of Cyrus, and ſeveral of his ſucceſſors What theſe figures have on their heads, is a kind of bonnet or mitre, mentioned by Herodotus (e) in his deſcription of the habits and arms of the forces of king Xerxes, and likewiſe of the Greeks Rhodiginus (f), in conjunction with this author, will ſufficiently clear up this point

The three figures that are partly broken, and one of which has a plaited robe, and a tiara, together with his chin wrapped up with linnen, repreſents a Perſian prieſt. Hyde gives a particular account of them in his hiſtory of the religion of the antient Perſians (g)

The figure which is repreſented as bearing ſome particular offerings, exhibits a Perſian ſoldier, of the claſs already mentioned, and I take the other figure, which encounters a lion, and is habited like a Mede, to be an Hieroglyphic, becauſe the Egyptians, from whom the Perſians borrowed ſeveral cuſtoms, repreſent

(a) Lib 10   (b) Vid Abul Pharai Dinaſt vi pr p m 96
(c) L 8 c 54 coll l 1 c 4 & 12   (d) Lib 8 c 53 & 55
(e) L vii c 61 & 62   (f) Lect ant L xviii c 21
(g) C 30 p 369 Fig 2

ſtrength

1704 strength and fortitude, by the figure of a lion. The reader may confult *Clemens Alexandrinus* (a) with relation to this particular. It may likewife be intended for a real combat, the *Medes* and *Perfians* having been very fond of encountring animals, as *Xenophon* obferves in his inftitution of *Cyrus* (b) Thofe who are verfed in antiquity may judge of thefe figures as they think proper

The figures of the pilafter, which is half buried in the earth, are alfo arrayed after the manner of the *Medes*, as was intimated in my obfervations on the figure that bears a parafol There is likewife a *Perfian* prieft habited in the fame mode, againft the window, and he is reprefented as conducting his offering, which is a goat with a bending horn The figure is very extraordinary, in the ftyle of the antients, who reprefent their oblations by ftrange figures, when any myfterious confecration was to be celebrated *Heliodorus* (c) treats of this fubject at large, as well as *Pignoriu*, in his defcription of the temple of *Ifis*

The pilafter which is covered with figures, reprefents a royal audience, where the king appears feated on his throne, with a foot-ftool, after the manner of the antient *Perfians* The book of *Efther* (d) makes mention of this folemn appearance of the king on his throne, and fo does *Xenophon* (e) The firft figure, which ftands behind the king, is habited in the *Median* mode, the fecond in the *Perfian*, and the third like the firft The lances compacted together reprefent the ftrength and concord of the kingdom, and the woman, habited in the *Perfian* manner, is the figure of a fupplicant The other figures, armed with lances and bucklers, are guards clothed like *Medes*, and they are ranged on each fide, in the hollow of the pilafter

The pilafter which is moft ornamented, exhibits the figure of ano-

ther king, or fome perfon of great 172 diftinction, who is likewife habited like a *Mede*, with a kind of crown on his head, which was an ornament ufually worn by thofe who were the king's favourites See *Xenophon* (f)

The figures below the Work feem intended as ornaments and fupporters, and they are habited after the *Perfian* manner The Pilafter, whofe pedeftal is ftill to be feen, reprefents fomething of the fame nature

The tomb, which is hewn out of *Tombs near Perfepolis* the rock near *Perfepolis*, exhibits the figure of a king before an altar, flaming with the facred fire, which was held in fuch great veneration among the *Perfians*, that they carried it into the army in times of war, upon a filver altar, as *Quintus Curtius* obferves (g) The care of this fire was committed to the *Magi*, and it was never fuffered to be extinguifhed, but at the death of the king See *Diodorus Siculus* (h)

The figure, that is fuppofed to be a king before the altar, is arrayed with a long robe, after the manner of the *Medes*, with a crown upon his head, and a deflected ferpent in his hand I am perfuaded that he is making fome oblation, and this is the more probable, becaufe it is well known, that *Cambyfes* and *Cyrus* were *Magi*, as well as kings, and confequently were obliged to prefent offerings in that quality For which reafon, when *Cyrus* accompanied his uncle *Cyaxares*, king of the *Medes*, in his expedition againft the *Affyrians*, *Cambyfes* prefented an offering for his fon and his army, and when *Cyrus* returned into *Perfia*, after the conqueft of the *Babylonian* kingdom, *Cambyfes* affembled the grandees of his empire, and iffued a decree, by which he enjoined *Cyrus* to make an offering in perfon, and in favour of his people, when he fhould afcend the throne of *Perfia*, after his death, and this ceremonial was to be performed by a prince of the blood, in

(a) 4 Hierogl   (f) Lib i   (b) Æthiop. 5 x
(d) Chap v ver 1   (e) Lib vii cap 25 feq
f Lib viii cap 12, 17, 22, 23, & 28   (g) Lib iii cap 7   (h) Lib x ii

the

1704 the abfence of the king Xenophon takes notice of thefe particulars in his inftitution of Cyrus (a)

As to the ferpent deflected into a half round, the antients intended to reprefent by this hierogliphic, a king whofe dominion was not very extenfive, but when they would exprefs a great monarch, they delineated a ferpent form'd into a circle, and holding his tail with his teeth, as may be found in Orus Apollo (b) From whence I judge, that this ferpent, if it be one, which the king has in his hand, adumbrates the king of Perfia, but if it fhould even be a bow, my conjecture would not be lefs reafonable, becaufe the Perfians affected to carry a bow and arrows, to diftinguifh themfelves from other nations, and this remark is confirmed by the figures on the ftair-cafe, which are reprefented with quivers on their fhoulders.

The little figure that appears in the air, and which Mr. Hyde takes for a king, in the act of flying, or for a foul that foars to the heavens, has the fame habit and ornaments for the head, as that of the king, below it Strabo declares (c), that the Perfians did not burn the offerings they prefented to the fun, but divided them among themfelves, through a perfuafion that the Gods were fatisfied with the fouls of thofe animals that were offered to them For my part, I think this figure may properly fignify an oracle, becaufe it is feated on a tripod, as was cuftomary at Delphos

The figures on each fide of the tomb, are alfo habited like Medes, and thofe that appear between the ornaments, with lifted hands, are dreffed after the Perfian manner.

The heads of animals, with a horn, are only ornaments expreffive

of the regal power, as I have already intimated

The fun, that appears above the altar, reprefents the antient divinity of the Perfians, as Strabo and Quintus Curtius have obferved.

In a word, one of the principal reafons by which we are inclined to believe, that Chilminar was the antient palace of Perfepolis, is becaufe we find that the tombs which are to the eaft, on the mountain, were antiently called the royal monuments

As to that of Naxi Ruflan, I am well perfuaded that it was built by Darius the fon of Hyflafpes, becaufe the exterior part of this tomb exactly correfponds with the defcription given of it by Ctefias in his hiftory of Perfia (d), after Herodotus, and with that of Diodorus Siculus, which has been already mentioned.

The words of this hiftorian are thefe· Darius ordered a tomb to be built for himfelf on a double mountain, where his friends, who had an inclination to fee him, caufed themfelves to be raifed up by a prieft, with the aid of a rope.

When all thefe particulars are duly confidered, it muft be granted that there is a great refemblance between Chilminar, and the palace of the antient city of Perfepolis But it would be difficult to affign the particular time when it was founded, becaufe when Xenophon (e) mentions the journey Cyrus took from Babylon to Perfia, to vifit the king his father, he only fays, that having left his troops by the way, he proceeded to the city, without naming it As to any other particulars, it is very probable, that the city of Elymais, which was the capital of the kingdom, was afterward called Perfepolis As to the figures and ornaments that are to be feen at Chilminar, they were made in after-times by feveral kings

1704 The fun an antient divinity of the Perfians

(a) Lib 1 cap 24 & lib viii cap 38 & alibi   (b) Nicolai hieroglyph No 56, 58, 60, 61.
(c) Georg lib xv p 732 feq Edit Cafaub
(d) Vide Exerp Phot. Segm 15 feu p 642. Op Herodot Ed Francof
(e) Lib viii cap 37

C H A P. LIV.

Obfervations concerning the founder of the royal palace of Perfepolis, *which was deftroyed by* Alexander the Great, *and is known at this time by the name of* Chilminar

The Macedonians mafters of Perfia

WHEN *Alexander the Great* had conquered king *Darius*, and feized his empire, agreeably to the prophecy of *Daniel (a)*, that prince gave up, to the pillage of his foldiers, the famous city of *Perfepolis*, which was fituated on the *Araxes*, that flows on one fide of *Chilminar*, at a fmall diftance, according to the learned *Ifaac Voffius (b)* He afterward made himfelf mafter of the treafures which had been amaffed in the palace of that capital, from the time of *Cyrus* the founder of the *Perfian* empire Thofe treafures, according to antient authors, amounted to a hundred and twenty thoufand talents *(c)* To thefe muft be added fix thoufand talents which were found at *Pafagarda*, 50000 at *Sufa*, and 26000 at *Ecbatane*, which amount in the whole to 202000 talents, exclufive of the money that was at *Damafcus*, *Arbela*, and *Babylon (d)* Tho' *Diodorus* and *Plutarch*, as well as *Juftin*, fay there are no more than 40000 talents at *Sufa*

Its treafures

Nothing can give a better idea of the ill ufe *Alexander* made of his fortunate conquefts, than the exceffes he committed on the day when he celebrated their feftival He invited all his friends on that occafion, and feveral courtifans, among whom was a *Grecian* woman, named *Thais*, who, feeing him heated with wine, perfuaded him to fire the ftately palace of that city, and, at the fame time, fpirited up all the guefts, to imitate the example of that prince His troops, who were then encamp-

ed at a very fmall diftance from the city, feeing the flames, and imputing them to chance, immediately haftened thither to prevent the confequences, but when they beheld *Alexander* with a torch in his hand, they threw away the water they brought, and affifted him in compleating the deftruction of that fine palace, the glory of the eaft, and the feat of its kings This event according to *Diodorus*, *(e)* happen'd about the clofe of the fourth year of the 112th olympiad, in the year of the world 3621, according to *Helvicus*, the 4385th of the *Julian* period, and 327 years before the birth of our Lord *Jefus Chrift* It is faid that *Alexander* intended, by this action, to revenge the conduct of *Xerxes*, who had formerly deftroyed the temples of *Greece*, and particularly thofe of *Athens*, in the fame manner But *Arrian* cenfures the proceeding of *Alexander (f)*, and declares this to be an improper manner of avenging himfelf on the antient *Perfians* He adds, that *Parmenio* employed all his efforts to prevent the deftruction of that fine palace, and told *Alexander*, that he ought to preferve the rich acquifitions of his valour, and that he would infallibly draw upon himfelf the hatred of the *Afiatics*, who would imagine that his only intention was to deftroy *Afia*, inftead of deriving any real advantages from his conqueft of that country *(g)* He accordingly preferved it, but did not enjoy it for any long time, and this empire was rent, and divided after

(a. Chap. xi ver. 5, &c   (b) Ad Porpon Mel cap viii n m 5,9
(c) Vide Diod Sicul lib x ii p 620 Edit Steph lib p 544 Edit Wech Conf Curt lib v. cap 20
(d Conf Curt lib x cap 4 Arrian lib ii de exp Alex
(e. Lib & p c 100   (f) Lib iii p m 66
(g) Conf Curt lib v cap 22 feq

his

1704 his death among his captains And when these had weakened themselves by their continual divisions and wars, the *Parthians*, under the conduct of *Arsaces*, made themselves masters of *Persia* and several other of its dependant states But the *Persians* commanded by *Artaxerxes*, regained the possession of those territories, in the time of the emperor *Alexander Severus*, and the *Mohammedan Khaisahs* afterward made themselves masters of the same, and then the *Sophies*, from whom the present king is descended

Tho' *Arrian*, *Quintus Curtius*, *Justin*, and some others, call the palace of *Persepolis*, the palace of *Cyrus*, it would yet be difficult to point out the true founder, as has been already observed But if it was not built by *Cyrus* himself, it might possibly have been erected by *Cambyses*, *Darius*, or *Xerxes*, as far as can be judged by its architecture This conjecture is even strengthened by a passage in *Diodorus*, *(a)* who declares, speaking of the magnificence of *Thebes* and *Egypt*, that indeed the structures which were raised there, still subsisted in his time, but that all the ornaments of gold, silver, ivory, and stone, had been carried away by the *Persians*, when *Cambyses* caused the temples of *Egypt* to be burnt, and that out of the spoils of that kingdom which were transported into *Asia*, the palaces of *Persepolis* and *Susa* were built, and that workmen were sent from *Egypt* to raise those structures The same *Diodorus* indeed says in another place, that the palace of *Susa* had been built long before the foundation of the *Persian* empire, by *Memnon* the Son of *Tithonus*, whom *Teutamus* king of *Assyria*, is said to have sent to the succour of *Priam* during the siege of *Troy*, with 10000 *Ethiopians*, together with as many troops of *Susiana*, and 200 chariots, and

that the palace was called *Memnonia* from him *(b)* With respect to the city of *Susa*, it is said to have derived its name from the white lillies which grew in the adjacent parts, and it is agreed, that *Cyrus*, and the *Persians* caused a palace to be erected there, after they had subdued the *Medes*, in order to be nearer to *Babylonia*, and the other dominions that were subjected to their empire, at least, this is the opinion of *Strabo (c) Pliny* however declares, *(d)* that the palace of *Susa* was built by *Darius* the son of *Hystaspes*, which, with what has been cited from *Diodorus*, may have occasioned the opinion that this prince enlarged that city, and founded a palace there, especially as this is confirmed by *(e) Ælian*

It cannot, in my opinion, be doubted, that the palace of *Persepolis* was likewise built, or at least adorned and embellished with the spoils of *Egypt*, as *Diodorus* has observed There might, indeed, have been a city and castle of that name, in the time of *Cyrus*, but it certainly had not then attained to that degree of splendor and magnificence, in which it afterward appeared, at least it is not mentioned in that manner by any historian. And what is still more to our purpose, *Herodotus*, *Xenophon*, and the other historians of those times, do not rank even the palace of *Persepolis* among the royal mansions of *Cyrus Justin*, indeed, after *Trogus*, and some modern writers, slightly mention the city of *Persepolis*, but reckon only the palaces of *Babylon*, *Ecbatane*, and *Susa*, among those of *Cyrus* It is likewise certain, that the antient *Greek* historians, *Herodotus*, *Ctesias*, and some others, hardly take any notice of that of *Persepolis*, and positively declare, that most of the kings who reigned after *Cyrus*, resided at *Susa* Beside, *Cassiodorus (f)* ranks among the seven wonders

1704

The palace of Persepolis built, or adorned, with the spoils of Egypt

(a) Lib 1 p 50 Ed Steph seu p 43 Wech p 109 Wech Conf Herod. L v c 53 seq sub voce Σεσα   *(c)* L c p 727   *(e)* Lib 1 c 59 Conf Guil Hill in Comm Edit London   *(f)* Lib vii ep 15

(b) Vid L ii p 77 Edit Stephan. seu &L vii c 1 51 Strabo L xv p m 728 Steph   *(d)* Lib vi c 27 Hist Nat f10 ad Dionys Orbis descript Ver 1074 p 557

1704 of the world, the palace of *Cyrus*, founded at *Sufa* by *Memnon*, with the utmoft magnificence, and that the very Stones of it were riveted together with gold, and yet it cannot be denied that the feat of the *Perfian* empire and of all the caft was fixed at *Perfepolis*, in the Time of *Xerxes*, and *Alexander the Great* See *Quintus Curtus* to that effect (a) The palace of this capital may have even been called the palace of *Cyrus*, and this prince might formerly have made it the feat of his refidence, before that edifice had received the ornaments which were afterward added to it, but he can never be confidered as its founder For if it was really finifhed with fo much magnificence, and adorned with the fpoils of *Egypt*, as *Diodorus* declares, it muft have been after his death *Cambyfes* likewife could not be the founder of it, any more than his father, fince he died in his return from *Egypt*, and it is impoffible it fhould be *Smerdis the Magus*, who ufurped the crown after the death of that prince, fince he enjoyed it but fix months I therefore conclude, that it was erected by the fame *Darius* who adorned and embellifhed the city of *Sufa*, and that *Xerxes*, the richeft and moft potent of all the *Perfian* kings compleated the Work *Strabo* (b) confirms my opinion, when he declares,

that after the kings of *Perfia* had 1704 embellifhed the palace of *Sufa*, they did the fame by thofe of *Perfepolis* and *Pafagarda*, where their treafures and archives were depofited, becaufe they were fortified places, and had been the refidence of their anceftors Befide, the habits of the figures that are ftill to be feen among the ruins of this palace, have no correfpondence with thofe of the antient *Perfians*, but refemble thofe that were afterward introduced by *Cyrus* and his fucceffors We likewife find in *Quintus Curtius*, (c) that after *Alexander* had recovered from his intoxication, he repented of the action he had committed, and faid, that the *Perfians* would have been more mortified to have feen him feated in the palace, and on the throne of *Xerxes* at *Perfepolis*, than to behold the fame palace reduced to afhes But this hiftorian is miftaken, when he pretends, that not the leaft traces of this palace were to be feen after that conflagration, except the river *Araxis*, which marked out in fome meafure the place where it was fituated. For it is certain, that there are ftill to be found at *Chilminar*, moft of thofe particulars, which the antients afcribe to the palace of *Perfepolis*, though much impaired, as appears by the plates and figures inferted in thefe travels.

C H A P. LV.

The author's departure from Perfepolis. *His arrival at* Zue-raes, *or* Chiras. *The defcription of that city. His arrival at* Ifpahan.

1705 AFTER I had employed almoft three months in fearching after all the famous antiquities of *Perfepolis*, and had fully fatisfied my curiofity, I fet out from thence

the 27th of *January*, 1705, and re- 1705 turned through the plain, where I did not find fo much game as I had feen the firft time, the feafon being far advanced When I had

(a) Lib v c 23   (b) Cir 523   (c) Lib cit

proceeded

TROIS MONTAGNES AVEC RUINES DES FORTERESSES

LE PONT POL-ZJAE-SADE

proceeded half way in my journey, I drew the three mountains, on which had formerly been the fortresses already mentioned   The first and largest of these mountains is that which seems divided in the middle, the two others on the right, are near the bridge of *Jeminien*, and the remotest of them is generally covered with snow   The representation of them may be seen in plate 172 and with the bridge of *Pol-Chanie*, over the river of *Roetghoena* or *Bendemir*, in plate 173   There was so much water in the country adjacent to *Sergoen*, that the horses were up to their girts, which made me very uneasy with respect to my papers, the horse who carried them being frequently in danger of falling   After I had passed through this inundation, I left the town of *Sergoen* on my left, and advanced toward the mountains, which are very high and stony, and arrived there in the space of half an hour. I travelled over them to the southwest, and passed by several *Caravanserai's*, and some burying-places shaded with cypress, and came, that evening, to *Zji-raes*, which is nine leagues from *Persepolis*, and went to lodge at the convent of the *Carmelites*

This city begins to be seen a little beyond the mountains, which are then to be left 500 paces to the right, after which we discovered a great number of tall cypress-trees, with a wall cut out of the rock, from whence a stream of water falls like a torrent, after great rains   The road between the rocks is deep and narrow, and leads to the city. This is situated to the right, and has a wall of earth on the right and left, but much impaired on one side   It is about 300 paces in length, and adjoins to a gate which is five paces wide at the entrance, and enlarges into ten as you advance.   When we had passed through this gate, which is very large and lofty, we came to a narrow passage, called *Teng-alla-agber*, bordered with buildings, on the right and left, like the *Chiaer-*

baeg at *Ispahan*, but most of them are in ruins as well as the gardens, which are filled with cypress and fruit-trees   At the distance of 1500 paces from the gate, and in the middle of the public way, is a bason seventy two paces in length, and forty-six in breadth, lined with stone. On each side is a wall in form of a half moon, with arches and seats; and on the left a mosque, which extends one hundred paces in front. The bridge of *Pol-Zjae-Sade*, is *A fine bridge* ninety paces from thence, and as many in length   It is built of stone, with four arches, of which that in the middle is the loftiest   It crosses the river *Roetgone*, whose source is between two little mountains, twelve leagues to the north of *Zjie-raes*, and discharges itself into the sea of *Derjanemeck*, or the *Salt-Sea*   The pass of *Teng-alla-agber* begins at this bridge, and is thirty paces wide   At the end of this the way lies through another passage of the same extent, and which is carried on to one of the oldest gates of the city, called *Davase Hanie*, or the iron gate, which is greatly impaired, and serves at present for a *Bazar*.   It is vaulted, and extends to the length of eighty paces   Several *Turkish* characters are inscribed on this gate, and the ruins of a tower above it.   It affords a passage into a great street, on the left side of which is a burying-place, and a ruinous garden, with several edifices on the right   This street extends to the heart of the city, which is a small league in circumference   In the reign of *Abas the Great*, it was governed by a certain lord, named *Eman-Couli-Chan*, who was much esteemed by that prince, as well for the great services his father had performed for the state in the war against the *Turks*, as also for those which he himself had accomplished, by wresting the fortress of *Ormus* from the *Portugueze*, by the assistance of the *English*   This was a place of such importance, that it formerly constituted a kingdom of that name, with the territories and cities that were its dependencies, and

1705 it extended as far a _Laer_ The king, in order to recompence so signal a service, honoured this lord with the title of duke, or governor of all the country which lies between this city and _Gomron_ This prince likewise usually styled him his grand duke, and when the _Dutch India_ company first came to trafic in _Persia_, under the direction of _Hubert Ulfnich_, he gave this lord full power to treat with them, on what conditions he should judge most advantageous to the state, which was a very extraordinary concession in a country where the kings are so jealous of their authority and power, and it accordingly excited against him the jealousy of the ministers and lords of the court, who resolved to ruin him after the death of king _Abas_, who was succeeded by _Sophi_, his grandson, to whom they did not fail to render the governor suspected This prince being thus prejudiced against him, commanded him to appear immediately at court, under pretext of imparting to him an affair of the utmost consequence, but in reality to destroy him The governor resolved to obey this mandate, contrary to the sentiments of all his friends, who represented to him the danger to which he was preparing to expose himself, and that he could have nothing to apprehend, if he would continue where he was, since neither his enemies, nor the king himself, would attempt to offer the least violence to him there. But as this lord was conscious of his innocence, and, at the same time, was impelled by the fatality of his destiny, he set out for the court, where he was perfectly well received and caressed. He was likewise persuaded, that in case the king had been determined to destroy him, he needed only to have demanded his head, by vertue of the absolute power of the eastern monarchs, which as he had not done, his mind was free from all suspicion, and this occasioned his ruin: For the king caused him to be assassinated in a bath, by his greatest enemies, among whom was

A tragical account of a governor of Gomron

his own son-in-law, and not content with this victim, they sacrificed to their barbarous hatred his fifty natural sons, the eldest of whom they murdered, and caused the eyes of the rest to be plucked out Such was the catastrophe of this great man.

At the end of the street I lately mentioned, are several others, full of shops, and which cross each other to the right and left The _Indians_ have a _Caravanserai_ there, and some _American_ are likewise there, but the trafic which they transact, is not very considerable.

In the heart of the city is a large edifice, the facade of which resembles that of a mosque, with portals and two fine towers, the upper part of which is impaired This structure, which is called _Madre ze Imon Coult Chan_, is a public college, where all sorts of sciences are studied There are six great mosques in this city; the first of which is dedicated to one of the twelve _Imans_, and has the denomination of _Ghatoen Kjeomet_; the second is called _Zeyd alla dien Oseyn_, the third, _Sjegnoerbags_, the fourth, _Zadaed mier Mohammed_, the fifth, _Chja't Zieraeg_, and the last, _Mad-zyd nou_, or the new mosque. There is another great city on the side of this, and adjoining to the bridge already mentioned, and I was assured by some persons, that, beside the mosques which I have named, there are three hundred more, that are smaller, and serve for chapels, and 200 baths This city contains thirty-eight quarters, twenty one of which belong to the faction of _Heyderes_, and seventeen to that of _Mammet-ollaey_ There are likewise about 700 very poor _Jewish_ families in this place, they inhabit a particular quarter, and are vine-dressers for the generality Some of them, however, manufacture stuffs of gold and silks. They pretend to be descended from the antient _Jews_ who were carried from _Jerusalem_ to _Babylon_, and afterward settled in _Persia_ As for the _Indians_ there were about a thousand of them in this city, and they

The disposition of Chiras

acquired

1705

acquired their subsistence by changing gold and silver, and likewise by usury. But the number of the *Europeans* there is very inconsiderable The principal among them are two Carmelites, one of whom is of *Milan*, and his name is *Pedro d'Alcantere de Sante Terese* I may add too, that he is a gentleman with whom I have passed many agreeable hours The other is a *Pole*, seventy three years of age, thirty seven of which he has spent in *Persia*, where he has been three times The name of this gentleman is *Sladislaus* There is likewise an *Italian*, named *Francisco*, who supplies the *English* merchants with wines, and a *Portuguese*, who makes those which his countrymen yearly transport from *Gamron* to the *Indies*

Wretched buildings Most of the buildings of this city are in ruins, and the streets so narrow and dirty, that they are hardly passible in rainy seasons, and there are several places, where passengers are obliged to bend their bodies, in order to walk under the arches before the houses, and especially in the quarter inhabited by the *Jews* The streets are likewise rendered very offensive by a number of places of easement, which are all without, and render the air very unwholsome, in consequence of which the generality of the inhabitants are very lean and pale The *Europeans* themselves are subject to a certain indisposition, in the summer season, which frequently carries them off, and the burying-grounds lie open to the *Jackals*, or wild dogs, that are engendered by a dog and a fox These creatures often commit great disorders in the city, and in the night-time make dismal howlings which much resemble a human voice.

The cypress-trees are the principal ornament of this city, and indeed I never saw any so fine, nor in so great a number, in any other place. There are likewise several large gardens without the city, which are filled with these trees, as are also the avenues, where care is taken to plant them with great regularity.

Half a league from the city, to the north, are several tombs of saints, in the mountains · The name of the most considerable of whom is *Baba Koej*, or the saint of the mountain, where he lived a long time in the utmost solitude. The *Persians* have a singular devotion for that place, and daily resort to it These tombs have several apartments, and in the lowest of them is a court, with a fountain surrounded with cypress, and other trees, among which I took notice of some whose stocks were thirty palms in diameter We ascended from this tomb into another that is higher, by a stair-case of sixty two steps, each of which is about three inches high, and at the top of these, are five others covered with a small dome, under which the body of a solitary is deposited

Tombs for Saints

I chose this place as commodious for me to make a draught of the city, but the weather proved too unfavourable that day On a little rock, at the foot of the mountain, are the ruins of a beautiful structure, with a large bason without water, and likewise a spacious garden full of cypress, and other trees, with beautiful alleys, where the trees were planted in strait rows At the end of the middle alley are the ruins of another edifice, which corresponds with the former The garden was encompassed with a mound of earth, but it was all over-grown with weeds, and entirely neglected at that time. This amiable place is called *Ferrodous*, or *Paradise*, and two hundred years ago it was the residence of a king, named *Karagia* Half a league from the city are likewise to be seen the ruins of the antient fortress of *Kallaey-Fandus*. I climbed up with great difficulty, and found some remains of a wall on the rock, composed of small stones strongly cemented together with a composition as hard as the rock itself. This fortress was once half a league in circumference, as far as can be judged by the little that still remains There was likewise a second wall, higher than the first, and

A beautiful structure

1705

and as the top of the mountain is covered with heaps of stones, they are probably the ruins of a lesser fortress, that was at some distance from the other The rocky part of the mountain, forms likewise a kind of wall to the west, from whence one may see several stones, that have fallen from a higher wall, and the ruins of a tower, contiguous to the first wall There is a very steep way in this place, which extends to the summit of the mountain, and some remains of a wall, joined to the tower already mentioned. I drew the annexed design, on the south west, where I saw some fragments of a building on the rock, and the middle part, which is now separated from the rest, constituted

1704

RUINES DE LA FORTERESSE KALLAY FANDUS

The tomb of a fine Persian

ore of the towers of the wall I had likewise a view of another ruined edifice in the plain, together with the tomb of one of the greatest poets in *Persia*, known by the name of *Sieg-zady*, who lived about 400 years ago, and caused this tomb, which is large and well built, to be erected He was a Dervise, and a native of *Zjieraes*, and there are still extant twenty *Arabic* books, in his manner, and two in the *Persian* language On one side of this tomb, is a large octogon bason, the water of which is moderately warm, and plentifully replenished with fish The bason is surrounded with a low wall, and the water flows out of it toward the city, from under a building, and then forms several other fountains, which disperse their streams through the meadows, but no one is permitted to catch the fish that pass from one of these fountains to another. I, however, caught a few cray-fish All these structures are shaded with fine

cypress

VUE VERS LA VILLE ZJI-RAES

VUÊ PROCHE DE LA PORTE DE ZJI-RAES

FIGURES SUR LE ROCHER

... trees, and there is a beautiful meadow, which serves for whitening of linnen

As I observed the prospect of the city made a more pleasing appearance on the mountain I have mentioned, than it did on that where I first began to draw the intended design, I returned thither in a few days, to the east, and completed the drawing represented in the plate 174 where I have marked the particular objects with numerical figures 1 Ghatoen Kroment. 2 Siegh Zyed Oddien, a mosque demolished by the Turks 3 Zeyt alla dien Ossein 4. Saig noei bags 5 Zadaed mier Mohammed. 6 Cha't Zieraeg 7 Mad Zid Nou, or the new mosque Between the last of these is seen the college already mentioned 8 Bibie docten oen, a large structure, where are some tombs 9 Zeyt mier alie hamse, near the bridge of Pol Zja Zade, without the wall of the city 10 The Chraei-baeg 11 Zev adoen, a village, on the river of which is a bridge fifty six paces in length 12 the river of Roetgoen 13 Sem Verdoneck 14 Koev Sieg 15 Fenadous, or paradise There is likewise on the mountain, where I drew the design of the city, an exceeding deep well, hewn in the rock, the opening into which is fifteen feet long, and eight broad

We cast into it several stones, which made a surprising noise in their descent I had an inclination to found the depth, but the cords which I had procured, not being of a sufficient length, I caused them to be untwisted, and then fastened together, upon which I found the well to be 420 feet and eleven inches deep We afterward threw into it large balls of oiled cloth, set on fire, and fixed upon iron plates, in order to obtain a view of the bottom, and in what manner it was formed, but the depth was too great to afford us that discovery, notwithstanding those flaming balls shot forth a great blaze We then threw down others, which were not fastened like the former, and the light of them appeared, and then vanished from time

Vol II.

to time, which made us conclude that the cavity was not continued down in a strait line, and that there had been some other entrance It, however, was a real well, made for the preservation of water, and there was another, something less, in the same mountain

In my return to the city, I desired a man of letters to inform me, by whom these fortresses were built, and at what time? He assured me, they were erected by a Guebre king, named Fandus, and that the mountain of Kallav Fandus, on which they were situated, had received its denomination from him that it was surrounded with the sea at that time, and that 6000 years had elapsed, since they first began to build on that plain, on the side of Zjieraes, in the reign of Siemschid, who was then emperor of Persia, and has been already mentioned He added, that this prince was the founder of Persepolis, which was built after Zjie-raes, or Chiras This city is in the province of Fars, or Farsistan, to the south west of Persepolis, and on the river of Roetgoen, twelve easy days journey from Ispahan, and about twenty four from Gamron, which distances are very ill observed in the maps, that place this city at an equal distance from Ispahan, and Ormus

Without the gate of Dervasy Bagh Zjia, to the north west, is the lovely alley of Koet-Zjia-Baeg, which extends to the King's garden, which is ninety five paces wide, and 966 in length When we had passed through the lodge, at the end of this garden, we came into another beautiful alley, bordered with cypress-trees, this is 620 paces long, and twenty broad, and is covered over with flowers in the middle We there saw a delightful house, surrounded with a charming canal, there is likewise a fountain at each corner of the building, which is square, and they mingle their streams with the water of the canal. This house is spacious, and in the middle of it is a grand hall, covered with a dome,

O

1705

A fine alley

The king's garden

1705 a dome, which is filled with niches, both within and without Before we entered the house we had the view of a square bason to the left, whose angles are eighty five paces long This beautiful alley is bordered on each side with seventy two stately cypress trees, one of which was twenty two palms in circumference There is likewise another alley, behind the house, bordered with cypress and sena trees, and its extent is equal to that of the others This garden is called *Baeg Stae*, or the royal garden I was there the twenty second of *March*, when the festival of *Nouzroes* was celebrated, and the people then resort from all parts, for their recreation in this garden, so that the alleys resembled a fair among us

I walked round the city, without the wall, that I might have an exact knowledge of its circumference, and I set out from the house of the *Carmelites*, which is without the northern gates. I then turned to the right, and advanced to a little bridge with two arches, under which a canal flows from the north west, and serpentises around the city Its source is half a league from the old gate, already mentioned, and it flows through the plain, and gardens This canal is always full of water, and at the distance of half a league from it is another, which loses itself in its approach to the city There is likewise a third within the space of a quarter of a league form this, and to the south west of the city are two or three ponds, filled with reeds and wild herbage, among which a vast number of ducks from their nests Most of the houses, as well within as without the city, are in a very wretched condition, but the adjacent country presents a charming prospect to the view, and is covered with a luxuriant growth of corn, and all other grain at the proper seasons of the year, and as far as the mountains, which are distant about two leagues to the south-west The city itself is about two leagues in circumference, and before I returned to the fathers, who

The extent of the city

entertained me, I drew a design of this amiable view, which is represented in plate 175 where every remarkable object is distinguished by numerical figures As 1 the road to *Ispahan* 2 A little chapel consecrated to the sister of *Hali* 3 The chapel of *Elias* 4 The garden of *Chiar-baeg* 5. The tomb of *Zieg-Zady* 6. The governor's house 7 The ruins of the antient fortresses 8 The river, where the caravans stop

I likewise drew the prospect which the eye commands on the mountains toward the city, together with the garden to the right, on this side of the gate, and in which several *Europeans* are buried Particularly Mr. *Blockhoven*, a member of the *Dutch India* company, who died the tweny fourth of *May* 1666. One *Dupont*, a *Frenchman*, and some others, among whom are four ecclesiastics This draught is exhibited in plate 176, and another in plate 177, which was designed near the gate on that side

I have likewise represented the fine alley of *Teng-alla-agber*, and the mosque on one side of it.

Two *English* gentlemen arrived here from *Ispahan*, in the Month of *February* One of them was named *Gayer*, and the other *Maynard* We went together to take a view of a mountain, a league and a half from *Zjie-raes*, on the left side of the plain, and to see a mosque there, which is distinguished by the name of *Ma-Zjit-Madre-Sulemon*, or the mother of *Sulemon*. It was a square building, and extended about twenty paces, from one corner to the other. There are three portals still to be seen, like those at *Persepolis* The first is to the east, the second to the north west, and the last to the north east They are eleven feet in height, and on each of their pilasters is the figure of a woman as large as the life, and holding something in her hand, like those at *Persepolis* Below that, to the north west, and on each side of the rock, are nine small figures much impaired

The ruins of a mosque

1705 imp e t, a d half buried in the earth, and on the north eaft is a ftone which refembles a tub All the reft is enclofed with ftones, which were ranged there in fome later time Moft of the pilafters are out of their places, which muft have been occafioned by fome earthquake, but the cornice of that in the middle is very little damaged The reprefentation of it may be feen in plate 178 A quarter of a league from this place, are the ruins of a wall, which formerly enclofed this mofque, and at the diftance of another quarter of a league, are feveral trees, planted along a ftream of the moft agreeable running water in the world, which fprings from a little rock, and the neighbouring mountains, and then flows to the eaft, forming a finall river in its

ALLEE TENG-ALLA-ACHER

progrefs We found the depth of it to be fix feet in fome places It likewife abounds with fifh, which we did not fpare, and they afforded us an agreeable repaft, in a cool fhade of rocks and trees This place is called *Kadamga*, which fignifies *a welcome unexpected* We then proceeded half a league from thence, to fee fome figures carved on the rock, and diftributed into three compartments The firft contains three figures, one of which has its hand on the hilt of a large fword The fecond reprefents a man, with fome thing round on his head, and the third is a mitred figure, with its hand on the hilt of a fword, like the firft, but they are fo disfigured, that they are hardly diftinguifhable On the fide of the rock is a little pond fhaded with fena, and fome other trees, as may be feen in plate 179 When we had fatisfied our curiofity in this place we returned to the city at fun-fet

We there found three *French* merchants who came from *Gami on*, and

1705 and were going to Ispahan, and they set out soon afterward with the English gentlemen already mentioned. At .... I received a letter from Gamron the 20th of March, which informed me, that a vessel arrived there from Batavia, the 26th of February, but that it was not as yet known whether she was to return thither, and that Mr Kaabk our director, had received his dimission, which he to return to the Indies, but that he would not set out before the month of August. This account made me resolve to return to Ispahan, having no inclination to continue at Gamron, during the summer heat, which is the most unhealthy season of the year.

I departed from .... the twenty-sixth of March in expectation of travelling alone, but had the good fortune to find the English and French gentlemen who began their journey before me, still at Sirgen. The next day we crossed the plain, which was floated over in such a manner, that the beasts of burden were obliged to take another way. We arrived, about noon, at Mir-clas-kæn, but would not stop there, because we intended to be early at Persepolis, which these gentlemen had not seen. I accompanied them thither, and when they had satisfied their curiosity, we returned to the village, where we found our equipage, and then passed the night there. The next morning we proceeded on our journey, by Naxi Ruftan, the floods not permitting us to keep the usual road. After we had visited the tombs at that place, we continued our journey to the north, over the mountain, that rises to the east, and came to a place where we saw twenty three apertures hewn in the rock, the largest of which was about three feet in depth, and as many in breadth. The others were much smaller, and near to each other, but we could not judge for what use they were intended.

We there saw a fine country, 1705 well cultivated and full of villages, and flocks of sheep and goats, and observed that the young were separated from the others.

As some of us frequently alighted from our horses, to kill game on the plain, where a great number of mares and horses were feeding, three or four of ours began to run after them, and we found it very difficult to ride on those upon which we were mounted, and one of them threw his rider into a ditch. But after we had employed abundance of pains to catch them, and re-adjust our arms and equipage that were scattered over the plain, we could not forbear diverting ourselves at this adventure, after which we pursued our journey to the mountains, where we likewise found several cavities in the rocks, and a demolished fortress to the left. We then crossed a river, always advancing through the plain to the east, and arrived at Majien at the close of day, after a journey of nine leagues.

The rain, which fell that evening, and continued all night, obliged us to stay there the whole morning, after which we travelled by the side of the river, which was dry at my first arrival there, but was then full of water, and we came, about six, to the Caravanseray of Imanfada, four leagues from the place where we had passed the night. The next day we proceeded as far as the Caravanseray of Aad-lee, where we made an agreeable repast, with the provisions we had brought with us, and the addition of some good fish, which we found there, and arrived, at the turning in of the day, at the Caravanseray of Aes-pas, after we had travelled seven leagues. The wind blew from the north, full in our faces, and I never felt the cold more severe. We resumed our journey on the last day of the month, and came by noon to the ruinous Caravanseray of Dombaeyne, where we found plenty of water and wild fowl,

The Author's return to Persepolis

fowl, which afforded a fine collation, and we arrived, about four, at the *Caravanjerai* of *Koskiejar*, after a journey of fix leagues We faw a little hill in the village, on which the inhabitants pretend that there had formerly been a fortrefs, but no remains of it were then to be feen I think I never beheld any place which more refembled that mentioned by the evangelift *Mark*, in the fecond chapter of his gofpel, and where the paralytic perfon was brought into a houfe in *Capernaum*, where the Saviour of the world then was, while the four men who introduced him, uncovered the roof of the houfe, in order to let him down as he lay on his little bed.

We continued our journey, the firft of *April*, through the plain, with greater facility than before, and ftopped at the bridge of *Pol-Sia-koe* About one at noon, we paffed by the *Caravanferai* of *Kievielar*, and fpent the night at *Egerdoe*, after travelling feven leagues The next morning we proceeded to *Jef-degaes*, where no houfes of refrefhment are to be found, and we then beheld on a mountain, fome ruins of a wall which had formerly been part of a fortrefs This mountain is a real rock, around which feveral large inverted ftones are to be feen We renewed our journey on the third of this month, and took fome refrefhments in the town of *Ana-baet*, where excellent fugar candy is made This town has ftill a wall of earth, with the remains of a caftle built in the reign of *Abas the Great*. We then paffed by the town of *Abas-abaet*, where we

faw two towers, which now ferve for dove-houfes Thefe are the firft that are to be found in this part of the country, and the laft in the road from *Ifpahan* We paffed the night at *Mag-zoet-begi*, after a journey of fix leagues We there faw another dove-houfe, and fet out, the fourth of this month, by break of day. We croffed a plain full of villages, gardens, and dove-houfes Behind us were mountains covered with fnow, and we found it warm in that quarter

We travelled that day no more than five leagues, to the town of *Ko-minfia*, where we arrived about noon, and proceeded the next morning to *Majaer*, which is five leagues from thence I fet out, on the fixth, with Mr *de l'Etoile*, before day, and left my other companions behind, that I might arrive at *Ifpahan*, in two days We met on the road with Mr *Davoed*, interpreter to the *Englifh* factory, who was travelling to *Zjie-raes* with two *Armenians* We afterward proceeded to the *Caravanferai* of *Mierfa-elrafa*, where we fed our horfes, and found an *Armenian* prieft, who till then had accompanied the perfons we met We came about four, to the tombs of the chriftians, where the friends of Mr *de l'Etoile* waited for his arrival I likewife found our interpreter there, who expreffed the utmoft joy to fee me, and after we had refted there for the fpace of half an hour, we proceeded to *Ifpahan*, and went to our director, who was furprifed at my return, which I had concealed from every one but himfelf

Vol. II.   P   C H A P.

CHAP. LVI.

Fine gardens belonging to the king, and the queen-mother, at a little distance from Ispahan. *News from the* Indies. *A demolished fortress on the mountain of* Deif-selon. *The director of the* Dutch *company visits a* Persian *lord of great rank. The arrival of a new Director.*

I Returned to my old lodgings at the *Caravasera*, soon after my arrival, tho' the director importuned me to continue with him. I afterward went to visit my friends, and, amongst the rest, Mr *Billon*, a *French* gentleman, and minister of *Malta* at the court of *Persia*. He had acted in that character only from the month of *December*, and had already obtained his audience of leave, on the twenty-second of *March*, 1705. He likewise paid a visit to our director, with whom he supped, and he regaled us, in his turn, the twelfth and thirteenth in the *Easter* week. On the twentieth I went to visit, and pay the usual compliments of the season to, the gentlemen of the *English* factory, who entertained me at dinner and supper. The next day I went to see the *Armenian* ecclesiastics of that city, and likewise of *Julpa*, to wish them a happy festival, on the part of the director, whom they had already complimented on that occasion. On the twenty-fifth the mourning for *Hussein* was resumed, two days after which I accompanied the director to the new garden, which belongs to the king, and is near five leagues in circumference, and we there passed the time in a very agreeable manner.

In a short time after we received the news of the battle of *Hoch-p...*, wherein the *French* were defeated by the allies, which occasioned a universal joy among the *English* and *Dutch*.

On the first day of *May* the famous procession of *Hussein* was solemnized, almost in the same manner as it was the preceding year, but there is always some diversity to be observed.

I took a little journey on the eighth, about three leagues from *Ispahan*, to see one of the principal gardens belonging to the king, the name of it is *Konma*, and it is situated in a fine plain filled with villages, and a variety of other gardens, which afford a charming prospect to those who view them from the mountains. Several officers of the customs reside in that quarter, to ... duties on all mercantile commodities which pass that way. This garden is distributed into ... divisions, and surrounded with ... In the middle of the first is a large ... which those who visit the garden may recreate themselves in a boat. It is likewise covered with birds, that make an admirable effect, and on one side of it is a large edifice in ruins. It is supplied by another canal which flows into it, after it has traversed a long tract of land. As to any other particulars, this garden has nothing considerable to boast, except a lovely alley, and a few small canals. *The king's garden*

We proceeded from this garden to that which belongs to the queen-mother, whose name is *Marjambeek*. We arrived there at an early hour, and diverted ourselves with fishing, having prepared nets for that purpose. And we succeeded so well, that we renewed that recreation the next day, on the river *Roetgone*, over which is a fine bridge of stone. We were as fortunate there, as we had been the preceding evening, and we *The garden belonging to the queen mother*

sent

1705 lent part of our fish to Mr. *Kaste-lein* We likewife killed twenty pigeons before we returned to *Ispahan*

On the thirteenth of this month, the minifter of *France* paid a vifit to our director, who kept him at fupper The next day we returned the vifit, and continued with him two hours

A new general of the India company

On the twenty eighth, Mr *Kaste-lein* acquainted all thofe who were employed under him, in the fervice of the company, that Mr *William de Hoorn*, general of that company, had refigned his employment, in favour of Mr. *John de Hoorn*, and he then difcharged them from the oath of fidelity they had taken to the forme, and was to be renewed to his fucceffor The letters which brought this intelligance from *Batavia*, were read in public, and the cannon fired while each letter was reading, as is ufual in all places where a company has any factory, or other eftablifhment This ceremonial was performed in the garden belonging to the *India houfe*, and under the *Talael*, which is a kind of theatre, or open gallery, open before and on each fide, with a fountain in the middle The reft of the day was paffed in drinking healths, and it concluded with illuminations, and other rejoicings, and as it was then *Whitfontide*, the director entertained us in a very fplendid manner, according to his ufual cuftom

As there were feveral antiquities about *Ifpahan* which I had not feen, I determined to vifit them in order, and accordingly went firft to the

The giant's mountain

mountain of *Dief-felon*, to the north of the river of *Zenderoe*, where I faw feveral other mountains, feparated from each other in the plain The people of this quarter imagine they were antiently inhabited by giants The mountain of *Dief-felon* is feparated from another only by a cleft, through which a flow of water iffues On the fummit of the former, which refembles a fugar-loaf, moft of thefe antiquities are to be found, and on

the fouth weft is the wall of a fortrefs 1705 that formerly ftood there I however could fatisfy my curiofity only in part, becaufe the rock was too fteep to be afcended by me: Our lackey, notwithftanding this, climbed up to a confiderable height, but could not get over the wall fo that we could have no account of any thing on the other fide of it This mountain is extremely hard, and replenifhed with veins of iron Our huntfman attempted to afcend to the top of the other, which rifes much higher than this, and he was very expert at climbing We ordered him, that, in cafe he fhould find any thing worth obferving, to give us notice of his difcovery, that we might advance thither ourfelves, if poffible, but after we had waited above half an hour, in expectation of fome intelligence from him, we returned, with much difficulty, to the place place from whence we came, and when we had defcended to the foot of the mountain, we beheld our man greatly embarraffed on one of the fteep fides of the rock, where it was faid to be impoffible for any one to faften himfelf He however, accomplifhed his defign, tho' in a manner that made us tremble, for he fupported himfelf by his hands and feet, amidft the projections and fiffures of the rock, notwithftanding he was encumbered at the fame time with his gun, which hung at his back

Deep wells

He informed us, that he had found on the fummit of the mountain three wells, hewn in the rock, and that the opening was about twelve feet in diameter He alfo added, that he difcovered in one of them, an iron chain as thick as a man's arm, and faftened to the rock He likewife told us, that this well was funk the deepeft of any, in an oblique defcent, and that the aperture was larger than thofe of the reft He further declared, that he threw feveral ftones into the cavities of thefe wells, but they were fo exceedingly deep that he could only hear the found of one. He affured us befide, that he difcovered the ruins of a ftreet, built on both fides,

fides, with a ciftern in the middle, and two bridges that were partly demolifhed, and over which a paffage was ftill practicable, they being three feet wide, and ten in length That they had formerly afforded a communication, from one village, or neighbourhood, to another, and were carried over one of the cifterns He then continued to acquaint us, that the firft object which prefented itfelf to his view, was the way or ftreet already, mentioned, that he believed it might contain 155 paces in breadth, and that feveral divifions of the antient apartments, were ftill vifible among the ruins In a word, that the fummit of the mountain was a level furface I have drawn the reprefentation of the firft mountain, with the wall on the top It was inhabited fome years ago, by a fet of

robbers, who were afterwards chafed from thence, and all the paffages conducting to it were deftroyed, to prevent them from concealing themfelves there for the future.

We returned by the bank of the river, which we afterward croffed, on a very ruinous bridge, and then threw our nets into the water with very little fuccefs, but we had better fortune the next day, after which we returned to *Ifpahan*

Soon after this little expedition, I attended our director to the houfe of the firft minifter's fecretary, from whom he had received an Invitation to pafs an hour with him It was then but eight in the morning, and he entertained us with tobacco, accompanied with liquors and confections when this collation was over, they retired into another apartment, and rejoined us about half

an

1705 an hour afterward A variety of provisions and fruits were then served up according to the season, together with lemonade, forbet, rosewater sweetened with sugar, and several other forts of hot and cold liquors, of all colours, and perfectly agreeable

The author's observations

We continued there till one at noon, and I was afterward informed, that this invitation was made by the order of the first minister, who had his reasons for not receiving the visit at his own house I then began to be sensible, the court was desirous that the company should employ their good offices to obtain the liberty of some pilgrims, whom the *Mefket Arabs* had taken in the *Perfian* gulf, as they were returning from *Mecca*, and that they would likewise take upon them to accommodate the misunderstanding which then subsisted between the court of *Perfia* and the *Arabs*, without any intervention of that court

Unlucky days

The nineteenth, twentieth, and twenty first of *June*, are accounted unlucky days by the *Perfians*, who then discontinue all affairs, and the shops are shut up

A new director

On the twenty seventh in the morning, a courier belonging to the company, arrived with a letter to Mr *Kaftelein*, from Mr *Bakker*, who had lately succeeded him in his place, and gave him notice of his being at *Defdagaes*, which is twenty five leagues from *Ifpahan*, where he intended to arrive the next day Upon which Mr *Kaftelein* ordered his deputy, and the other officers of the company, to wait upon the new director, and congratulate him on his arrival. We set out, at seven in the evening, to the number of twenty three persons, all on horseback, with Mr *Kaftelein's* master of the horse, attended by eight couriers, at our head. We had likewise nine *Banians*, or *Indians*, on horseback, with four couriers, so that our troop was composed of forty four persons We made a short halt at the *Caravanferai* of *Margh*, and arrived about midnight at that of

Vol II.

Merfa-alie-reta We travelled another 1705 league, on the 27th, with two *Frenchmen*, and an *Armenian* merchant, who had joined us, but the heat was so stifling, that we were obliged to shelter ourselves in the shade of the mountain of *Ortfoertre*, where we supped in a very agreeable manner We there found a *Perfian* lord, who had retired into a grotto to enjoy the cool air, having, for that purpose, quitted his tents which were set up in a field, where he was causing some wells to be sunk, by the King's order The nobleman sent us refreshments of fruit, and ice, which he imagined we wanted extremely, though we were well supplied with all accommodations of that nature, notwithstanding which we accepted of his civility, and returned him our acknowledgments, with a present to his messenger, and likewise sent him some of our fruits, with thrice the quantity of ice we had received from him, and for which he thanked us, but gave nothing to the person who carried them to him

The arrival of the new director

About eight at night, we perceived, on the mountain of *Marfjal*, the flambeaux of our new director, agreeable to the custom observed by persons of rank, who travel by night in *Perfia* We then mounted our horses immediately, leaving some domestics to take care of our provisions, with an intention to return thither, provided the director would stop there, to wait the arrival of his lady, who had not advanced so far as himself, and this was accordingly consented to The lady herself came some time after, preceded in the same manner, by a flambeau, and we remounted our horses, in order to proceed to the last *Caravanferai*, which we had passed by as we came, and we arrived there at midnight

The order of his march

Our director and his train marched in this manner · His gentleman of the horse was at the head, followed by a led horse, two guides, and six couriers After these, Mr *Bakker* appeared, accompanied by a

Q *French*

F... gentlemen, then came he
I..., or the p...er who carries
the T... seated on a J...
wh ch has been a... described
This ser... was allowed by the
B......, or a man who carries
such furniture as m... happen to be
wanted on the road, and a water-
carrier, who has a leather bucket filled with ..., under the belly of his
hor.e, there were likewise two
grooms, and as many cooks, with
the proper implements, as also
another servant, who is charged
with the care of the bedding, a valet to sweep the chamber, beside
four *Morisco* slaves, seventeen horsemen, and six couriers

The director's lady was attended
by two *Dutch* women, who were in
the service of the company, she
had likewise two guides, and as
many couriers, with a footman who
led her mule by the bridle, and was
followed by another, who conducted four female slaves, there was
also another servant seated on the
jagtan, and likewise a torch-bearer.
The whole Troop was composed

of th... two persons, among whom
were the couriers

On the 2... h of this month, Mr
Ba... entertained us at dinner, and
we arrived, about the close of the
day, at *I...al...*, where he was received under a discharge of the
small arms of the company   His
lady, who was not inclined to enter the city till night, was received
in the same manner   She was of
Dutch extraction, but a native of
the *Indies*   Mr *Kastelein* treated her
with all imaginable politeness, and
entertained her at supper

On the first day of the month,
the king's music was heard all night,
on account of the festival of *B...
/ d/ a-adien*, which has been formerly mentioned   On the eighth
of *July*, that of *Mohammed* was solemnized, when his Majesty's music played anew, and most of the
shops were shut up.

On the 12th and 13th of *July* I
made all the necessary preparations
for my journey, and took leave of
my friends, in order to set out the
next day, with Mr. *Kastelein*

C H A P.

CHAP. LVII.

The author's second departure from Ispahan. The order in which he and his company began their journey. Very singular plants. Tombs. Vast swarms of Gnats. Their arrival at Ine-raes.

WE set out on the 15th of *July*, about ten in the evening, without acquainting any one with our departure, that we might avoid all ceremonials, and prevent the great number of Mr *Kastelein's* friends at *Ispahan*, as well *Christians* as *Persians*, from accompanying us out of the city, according to custom. They had, with that view, desired him to acquaint them with the day and hour of his departure, particularly the bishop of the *Armenians*, who had great obligations to him. But he acted with as much secrecy as possible, contenting himself with the unblemished reputation he had acquired, during his long residence in *Persia*, and with the esteem his friends entertained for him. He therefore was only attended by his deputy, and the company's interpreter, with whom some *Indian* couriers joined themselves. Our company, however, amounted at last to forty one persons, thirty of whom were on horseback. The daughter of Mr *Kastelein* placed herself, with her waiting woman, in a *Kasua*, which is a kind of litter. The women slaves had been sent away the preceding year.

The cooks, and four other servants, who carried tapestry, quilts, and all other necessaries for the journey, were ordered to set out before the rest of the company, that all things might be orderly disposed at the place where we were to lodge.

A Kasua or Persian litter. Two of Mr *Kastelein's* chief domestics marched on the sides of his daughter's litter, to oblige the *Moors* whom they might happen to meet to give them a free passage. She was likewise accompanied by two couriers, one of whom, an *Armenian*, led the mule of the litter, which was lined all round with red. These litters are very commodious for travelling, and there are some mules which carry two, in the nature of panniers. Camels are also employed in this service, but not with so much convenience.

The director of the carriages never advances to any distance from the litter, but to see that nothing is wanting. The *Kasua* generally sets out half an hour before the rest of the company, and as it is accompanied by a flambeau in the night, they never lose sight of it. Those who conduct the baggage are ordered likewise to march before, but they are frequently overtaken in the way.

We arrived, about two in the morning, at the *Caravanserai* of *Miersaresalesa*, where the interpreter *Sahid* entertained us very handsomly with some provisions he had ordered to be brought from *Ispahan*. The *Indian* couriers returned in the afternoon, and we came to *Majaer* at one in the morning, where our interpreter entertained us a second time. Mr *Oets* and he parted from us at that place, after having shed abundance of tears, and, indeed Mr *Kastelein* had acted like a father to the first, who had been his deputy, and the other was his intimate friend. This separation was made upon the way at some distance from the *Caravanserai*. We stopt twice near a small river, and arrived about midnight at the tombs of *Zia-reza*. Some domestics had been sent in good time to secure the lodgings, which were granted us by the inhabitants,

ones tents, who were sensible they should
be well paid. They also prepared
a ... ... against our arrival,
for the accommodation of the women
We passed the night very quietly,

and afterward diverted ourselves in
a beautiful place, where was a
bason full of fish. This place appeared to me so agreeable, that I
took a draught of it, and here

ZJA-RESA

present it to the reader. We continued there till the 19th, and after
having passed through the city of
Ceminsia, which lies all in ruins,
and drank coffee in the garden
of *Baba-ziel*, we ordered the flambeau to be lighted, and arrived a-
bout midnight at *Magsoet-begi*. We
saw the next day seven or eight
stags, and endeavoured to shoot
them, but they ran from us. We
passed the night at *Acp-nabaet*, and
came the next day to *Jes-dagaes*,
where we diverted ourselves in a
garden full of fruit. We afterward
cast nets into a small river, which
runs by the side of the garden, and
at the first cast drew out sixteen

large fishes, and a prodigious number of small fry, which we caused
to be dressed several ways, the fish
in that country being extraordinary
good. Five or six women, whose
habitation was in that garden, entertained us very agreeably, and
when we had returned them some
marks of our acknowledgment, we
repaired to the *Caravansei ai*, from
whence we proceeded four leagues
on the 24th, and stopt at the village
of *Gombes-Lala*, where there are but
few houses. We saw abundance
of deer in the mountains, without
being able to approach them; but
in recompence for that disappoint-
ment, we met with several peasants

in

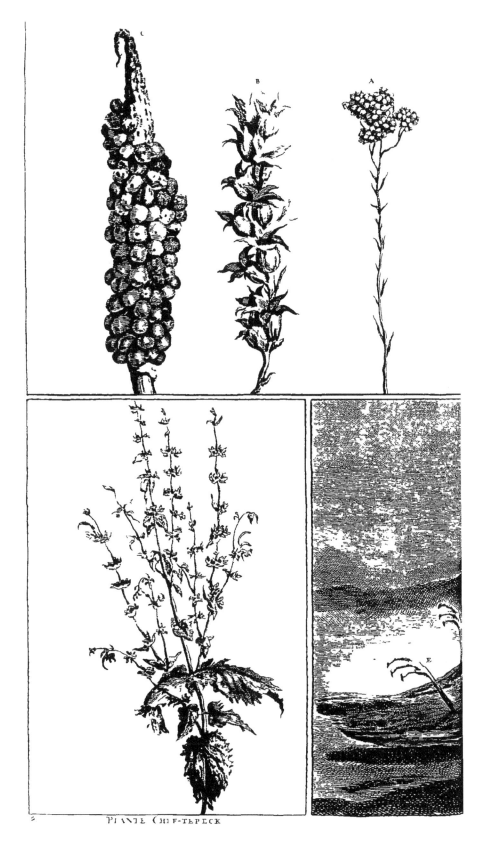

PIANTE CHIF-TEPECK

OISEAU SJOERAKAN ET BECCASSINE

18.

1705 in tents, who supplied us with good fresh butter, milk, eggs, and chickens, which afforded us an agreeable repast, and we came about ten in the evening to *Degerdoe*, where we were obliged to pass the night in a very bad *Caravanserai*, but this was not the only inconvenience, for the inhabitants of the place are very uncivil, being privileged, because they are in the king's service, whose horses are fed in this quarter Those of *Koskiesar*, seven leagues from thence, are not much better

On the 26th we passed the greatest part of the day, and also the night, at *Poelsakoe*, where we caught abundance of fish, in a small river, and among the rest three fine carps. As there is no *Caravanserai* in that place, we were obliged to divide ourselves into several companies. The next morning, as we were going out of the village, we met two of the company's couriers, who came from *Gamron*, and were carrying to *Ispahan* the news of the death of Mr *Wichelman*, director of the company's affairs in that city, where he died the sixth of this month of a violent fever, which carried him off in two days. This was very unwelcome news to Mr *Kastelein*, who feared this unfortunate circumstance would retard his journey to *Batavia* He ordered these couriers to return with him to *Koskiesar*, three leagues from thence, that he might have time to examine the letters which they had in charge. This news created him so much uneasiness, that he was unable to close his eyes for the whole night, and it deprived us of all the pleasure we had promised ourselves in the remainder of our journey, as we had reason to be apprehensive that the death of this gentleman would oblige the director to stay at *Gamron*, to look after the affairs of the company He wrote the next day to *Ispahan*, and *Gamron*, but delayed sending the letter designed for the last place, because he imagined he might probably meet another courier, which afterward happened accordingly

The death of the director at Gamron

We, however, continued our journey through a plain well inhabited, and plentifully stocked with game, and other animals, especially sheep and goats, and after having repassed the high mountains, we came to *Assa-pas*, where we found a good *Caravanserai*

I rose early in the morning, and found in that village a dry plant, which they call *Madroen* It rises about two feet from the ground, with a growth of several small branches, which are very short, and closely compacted together, and full of yellowish buds at top, as I have represented them at the letter A in plate 180 The inhabitants distil from this plant a liquor as strong as ginger, which the plant, as dry as it is, resembles in the smell. I found also another plant, with little bells hanging down at top, with five points like the flower of the pomegranate, having some small leaves on the stalk, which is something taller than that of the other plant The bells of it are full of large blackish seeds, which are contained in a shell like an acorn. The inhabitants are unacquainted with the name of it, and know only that the seed causes a kind of giddiness in the head This plant is exhibited at the letter B I found likewise a plant of wild *Spanish* wheat, something taller, and it glows with a beautiful red when ripe, till which time it is tinged with green. The reader will find it represented at the letter C, without leaves, which differ in nothing from those of the *Spanish* wheat. As to its qualities, it is so hot, and costive, that one cannot bear it in one's mouth The fruit of these three plants are drawn as they appear in their natural growth. At a little distance from thence we saw a few turpentine trees, the gum of which the peasants carefully collect, in order to sell it at *Ispahan*. The fruit of them, which consists of small green berries, is pickled, and

The Madroen plant

Wild Spanish wheat

Turpentine trees

1705 and ufed inftead of capers There is a bough of it in plate 181 and on one fide of it a white flower call'd *Geel-najra'it*, the ftem of which is pretty high, and bears a profufion of branches, fpotted in the infide with yellow and red We had a prodigious ftorm that day, which however did not incommode us more then the duft, as we had the wind on our backs, and were then in a large plain full of canals, marfhes, and *Wild-boars* bull-rufhes This part of the country is infefted by a vaft number of wild boars, that march in troops, and deftroy all the feed and fruits of the earth, and purfue their ravages as far as the entrance into the villages The inhabitants, in order to remedy this mifchief, fet fire to the rufhes which afford them a retreat, and deftroy'd above fifty in that manner, but thofe that efcaped the flames fpread themfelves all round, in fuch a manner, that the people themfelves were obliged to have recourfe to flight, and have never difturbed them fince, for fear of drawing upon themfelves fome greater calamity They affured me, that fome of thefe creatures were as large as cows The fame day, in the afternoon, we met upon the road the domefticks of the duke or governor of *Laer*, with fifteen Kafuas full of women, and we arrived about nine at *Oed-joen* We had difpatch'd fome fervants before to fecure us lodgings in a garden, which the king had in *A royal tomb* that quarter, where we found the tomb of *Sultan Hoffen Man eth*, a king's fon, whom they pretend has been buried there 280 years This monument is in a fmall apartment, cover'd with a little dome, and the coffin is of ftone, cas'd with wood, and is cover'd with a pall, which reaches to the ground, and has a turban upon it As there were feveral other apartments, we were very well lodg'd And as foon as the fun appear'd above the horizon we went a fifhing, and had excellent fport, in a fmall river, which runs by the fide of the village We returned thither the next day, and were as

fuccefsful as before After which we 1705 fet out out about five in the evening, and when we had croffed the mountains of *In ai faae*, we came about nine to the town of that name, after having been expofed to exceffive heats all that day

The firft day of *Auguft* we went *The tomb* to fee the tomb of *Imon Sadde Ifmael, of a faint* who, if the Inhabitants may be believed, has refted there 700 years, and the veneration for the tomb of this *Santon* is fo great, that even the grandees of the court and the great officers of the army, are prohibited from approaching it, or even the town, when they are travelling, (in order to fecure the people of the place from the infults which others fuffer) This tomb, which is built of ftone, is tolerably large, it is likewife cover'd with a dome, and furrounded with a wall, to which there is a door

We fet out at four o'clock, and arriv'd by eight at *Maj-ten*, where Mr *Kaftelein* and his Daughter took lodgings in a pleafant garden, and we went to a *Caravanfer ai*, which was not far off I found in that gar- *A fine dry* den a plant call'd *Chef-terick*, which *plant* is about four or five feet high, and bears a great many branches, and large leaves It likewife produces little berries, which contain four grains of feed, of a clear chefnut brown, and has a very ftrong fmell, proceeding from the flower, which is fmall, and variegated with colours of white, blew, and violet, ftreak'd with red This plant is in great efteem for its agreeable odour, which is the only known virtue it enjoys. The reader will find it reprefented in plate 182 I took alfo a bird, called *Singular* *Sicei akan*, very like a duck, and as *birds* big It has a yellow head, with a red beak and feet, and is reprefented in plate 183 I caught alfo another bird, which paffes there for a fnipe, the plumage of which is black, grey, and white, and the feet red, the reader will find it at the letter E.

The next day we proceeded on our journey, and had a diftant view of the mountain, mentioned before, upon

1705 upon which there was formerly a fortrels

As we continued to advance, we found the plain full of cattle, and the country people employed in cutting the corn with a crooked knife, like a fickle, grafping as much of it as they were able in their left hand Inftead of threfhing it they ufe a fmall carriage, with four wheels, which they roll feveral times over the corn, after they have laid it it little heaps, in order to bruife the ftraw, and force out the grain, after which they tofs it up and down in the wind, and nothing is left but the grain and the ears When this is done, they feparate the ears, and beat them again, in order to force out the reft of the grain As all the people were then come out of the villages, the country was entirely covered with tents

In the evening, after we had croffed the river of Bendemir, upon a bridge, near the two mountains already mentioned, on which a fortrefs formerly ftood, we paffed the night at the Caravanferai of Abgerm, at half a league diftance from that bridge, and from thence proceeded with our flambeaux to a mountain, at the foot of which a fine fpring of water gufhes out as clear as chryftal This ftream abounds with fifh, that eafily flide under the rock into feveral fubterranean hollows It is about three feet in depth, and the water is fo extremely clear, that all the fifh may be eafily feen This gave us an inclination to employ our net, and we brought out at the firft draught twenty fifh, three or four of which were a foot long

The in on-venience occafioned by Gnats But it was impoffible for us to clofe our eyes any part of the night, the Caravanferai being full of gnats, which continually difturbed us, and obliged us to quit that incommodious lodging One of our domeftics, who refolved to continue in bed, was fo ill treated, that we hardly knew him the next day Our young lady had likewife her fhare, although fhe had taken all poffible

precautions not to be difturbed, and was continually moving about, without once lying down. Even the very horfes were extremely incommoded by thefe noxious vermin. 1705.

We fet out from fo difagreeable a place by break of day, and paffed over a ftone bridge, half a league in length, and built over a marfh, but as moft of the arches are very fmall, the waters, when they happen to fwell, flow over the top The plain is cut into a variety of channels, and likewife abounds with rice

About ten in the evening we came to the Caravanferai of Porlegoor, where we met with a courier from Gamion to Mr Kaftelein, who informed us, that the widow of the deceafed director, Mr Wichelman, died the 12th of the fame month of June That place was alfo full of gnats, which rendered it impoffible for us to read the letters which the courier brought, fo that he was obliged to go back with us to the Caravanferai of Baeits-gardie, two leagues from Zyie-raes

The author's arrival at Zyie-raes On the fourth we fent back the courier to Ifpahan, where he had alfo letters to deliver, and then we proceeded to Zyie-raes, where we we alighted at a houfe of Mr. Kaftelein Father Alkantera came immediately after, and I went to vifit his companion about noon.

The next day the merchants, who traded with the company, came to wait on Mr Kaftelein, and the moft confiderable perfon among them, whofe name was Hazje Nebbie, made him a prefent of feveral bottles of oil of Santal, together with fome diftilled waters, fweetmeats, and fruits, for which the bearer was handfomely gratified The next day we were vifited by feveral Perfian merchants, who had great dealings with the company.

That day we went in great ceremony to pay a vifit to Hazje Nebbie, who entertained us after the manner of the country, with hot liquors, fweetmeats, and tobacco, by the fide of a beautiful fountain.

His

His house was the finest in all that town, and he pressed Mr *Kastelein* to defer his journey for some days, in order to take the diversion of the country, but he excused himself from accepting the civility. On the eighth in the morning two couriers from *Ispahan* passed by with letters for *Gamron*,

---

C H A P   LVIII.

The author's departure from Zjie-raes. Fertile fruit-gardens. The retreat of the Pagans *The author's arrival at* Jaron, *with an account of its situation. Abundance of dates, &c Wild pistacho and turpentine-trees The ruins of some antient fortresses. Hot winds The author's arrival at* Laer

The author's departure Zjie-raes

WHEN we left *Zjie-raes*, we entered upon a plain, and the bridge of *Pol-saffa*, which is partly in ruins, and the great drought had drained all the water from under it. At a little distance from thence, upon the middle of the plain, is a high mountain separate from the rest, and we struck to the right of it, in order to proceed to the *Caravanserai* of *Babba-had-jie*, five leagues from *Zjie-raes*, and where we arrived at midnight

The 9th in the morning Mr *Kastelein* had a fit of a fever, which obliged us to stop in a garden, after a journey of four leagues. In our way thither we passed by several pleasure-houses, and fine gardens, and then began to ascend the mountains, from whence we had a view of *Zjie-raes*, at the end of the plain We continued our course to the village of *Paroe*, half a leaguee from the high road, where the garden was in which we were to stop, and by the side of it ran a small river, in which we found crayfish We renewed our journey the next day in the afternoon, and arrived about 9 at the *Caravanserai* of *Mosse-farie* Immediately after which we went a fishing with flambeaux, and caught some carp and cray-fish. This part of the country is full of villages,

the inhabitants of which were out in the field under their tents, along the river side, with their cattle

We pursued our journey at six in the morning, and passed by a village of extraordinary length, all the houses of which were built with rushes We then crossed very stony mountains, and stopt at the *Caravanserai* of *Paeyra*, which is surrounded with villages, and lies about four leagues from the place where we had passed the night. The country is watered by a small river, and the mountains are full of willows, and wild fig-trees, and they likewise produce plenty of sage, the figs of these trees are not unpleasant, but they are very little coloured

We continued our journey on the 12th, and found several great heaps of stone in the way, which the people would persuade us were the ruins of some antient city, but I could not discover any part of its foundations A great number of villages and gardens appear on the right, towards the mountains.

It was eleven at night when we arrived at the *Caravanserai* of *As-mongeer*, after having passed over several hills, and stony mountains, and some valleys On the 13th the people of the place brought us for

A ... ld
cit

figs, raifons, and citrons from the mountains I here faw a fmall citamountain coloured like thofe of the ifle of *Cyprus*, with long legs, and ftrait ears, that are likewife of a confiderable length, and a tail like that of a rat, but I obferved when fhe licked herfelf, that her tongue was not fo pointed as thofe of common cats We fet out the next day at fix in the morning, and came to feveral handfome houfes with gardens, in the fhade of which we refted ourfelves, after we had travelled three leagues, the fun being very hot, and moft of our company tired Thefe gardens are fituated in the town of *Tadawoen*, which fubfifts by their produce, and they are filled with pomegranate orange, peach, and fig trees, befide large growths of palm, and moft of them are loaden with fruit at the fame time We likewife found abundance of melons there, and all thefe fruits are produced in great plenty by the copious ftreams of water that enrich the foil They are carried from thence to *Ifpahan*, and as this place is encompaffed with mountains, it appears like a wood at a diftance.

Antient grottoes

About half a league from thence, and among fome fteep rocks, are feveral grottoes, which I went to fee on the 14th after the heat of the day was over I perceived before thefe grottoes fome remains of a ftone wall well cemented, and a fmall tract in the moft fteep part of the rock, which flopes from the mountains on the right and left. Thro the valley, between thefe mountains flows a river, round which a fevere cold always reigns The inhabitants of the country pretend that the *Guebres* retired formerly into thefe grottoes. But I fhall hereafter be more particular in my defcription of them, having paffed that way on purpofe, in my return from the *Indies*.

We were prevented from proceeding on our journey that day, becaufe Madamoifelle *Kaftelein* had the misfortune to be indifpofed with

Vol II

a fever, which encreafed to fuch a degree in the night, that fhe became delirious, which fenfibly afflicted her father, who loved her tenderly, and alarmed us on his account, becaufe he would not ftir from her, though he himfelf had but a weak conftitution, and was fubject to feveral diforders That lady's waiting maid was likewife taken ill, which added to our embarraffment, and made us refolve to fit up with her miftrefs, one after another, to relieve her father, who had great need of reft The violence of her fever continued till the feventeenth, when it came to a crifis, and fhe flept toward morning It was then thought proper to have her carried in her litter, by four men, to *Jaron*, and we chofe out eight of the ftrongeft peafants in the village to relieve one another

An extraordinary fifh

A fifh was brought to us that day, as big as a *Kabeliaeu*, or *Melwel*, to which it had fome refemblance, and a great deal of the relifh, but I had never feen one fo large in that country. We had it dreffed after the *Dutch* manner, and as we had fome carps, we made a tolerable good repaft, and continued our journey as far as the mountains As the litter, which was carried by men, proceeded but flowly, we did not arrive till midnight at the *Caravanferat* of *Michgeck Sogte*, after we had travelled about three leagues.

We purfued our journey on the 18th, and paffed over fome craggy mountains, after which we entered into a champion country, cut out into canals, over which were fmall bridges, and arrived at midnight at *Fagra-baet*, where we took up our lodging in a pleafant garden full of palm-trees, with a row of fena in the middle, and a variety of pomegranate, orange, quince, and pear trees, with many others, the fruits of which were admirable This garden had not any confiderable extent, but was the fineft I ever faw There was a houfe in it raifed very high, the walls of which were extremely thick. It was likewife

S adorned

adorned with two fine fountains, and a handsome bason in the middle, with a fountain spouting before the front of the house. The water of this bason was conveyed by a subterranean channel, to the two fountains, and served also to water the whole garden. This place belonged to the duke or governor of *Gamron,* called *Mameth-Momien Chan,* whose ancestors had likewise been governors of that place.

The author's arrival at Jaron

On the 19th we set out in the evening for *Jaron,* which is but a league from the garden, and arrived there about nine o'clock, at a *Caravanserai* near the city, where we found a good well, covered with a kind of stone dome.

The situation of the city

At break of day I went into the city, which is very mean, and looks more like a village, the houses being all built of earth, and separate from one another I saw two or three poor little mosques, in which they were performing service. As this city is full of palm-trees, it looks at

a distance like a wood This, of all the trees in that country, is what is esteemed most, both for its beauty, and the goodness of the fruit, which is the best in all *Persia* They reckon the annual product of each of these trees at seven florins, and they bear, one with another, 300 pound weight of fruit, every pound being worth two farthings They furnish the principal revenues of this city, the inhabitants having no other trade by which they can subsist The government belongs to *Ibrahim Chan,* duke of *Zjie-raes,* but as that lord is always at court, he keeps one of the king's lieutenants here, as well as at *Zjie-raes.* I have exhibited a view of that city, which extends from east to west as far as the mountains. We staid till the 21st, and hired eight fresh men (those whom we employed before not being willing to go any farther) to carry the sick lady, who continued very weak, to *Laer* Mr. *Kastelein* wrote from thence to *Gamren* to order another litter to meet him.

We

JARON

RESTES D'UNE FORTRESSE

We set out about one in the afternoon, and proceeded fouth-weft over the mountain of *Jaron*, which rifes very high, and we were always mounting aloft, or defcending between rocks, where we found the way very difficult to our horfes. We had advanced to the middle of the mountain by break of day, and came to a place where the fteepeft part of the rock is furrounded with a wall, and the way very ftony. We faw upon this mountain feveral large cifterns, cover'd over, and without any water at that time, but there is generally too much in winter. There are alfo abundance of piftacho and turpentine trees, which produce great quantities of gum. I found a piece fo hardned by the heat of the fun, that I could keep it without melting. It was nine by that time we had paffed the mountain, and we arrived an hour after at the *Caravanferai* of *Ziatalle*, a beautiful ftone building, and very commodious for travellers, fituated likewife in a plain bordered with mountains, at five leagues diftance from the place where we had before paffed the night.

We fet forward at midnight, and paffed over feveral plains and mountains, which latter were not fo high as thofe we had croffed before, and yet the ways were very bad. We arrived by day-break at a fpring, which is fupplied from the mountains, and from thence defcended into a valley, through very ftony ways.

We arrived, about eight, at the *Caravanferai* of *Mou-feer*, where we found a *Carmelite*, who came from *Gamron*, and whofe companion died on the road, by a fall which broke his leg. He had alfo been fick himfelf for fome time, and was going to *Ifpahan*. We ftopped at this *Caravanferai*, which, tho' fmall, is tolerably commodious, a garden full of orange and other trees, furnifhed us with fruits for our refrefhment. I found under thefe trees a plant, the lower leaves of which were a fpan in length, and half as much in breadth. Thofe which grew higher up the tree were

Perfian Plants

fmaller, and had a kind of down upon the ftalk. The inhabitants of the place call it *Goes-foutoor*, or camel's ear, but are unacquainted with the virtue of it. I found another plant, call'd *Zia-raek*, whofe leaves fteeped in butter have an admirable effect in curing thofe people who have worms in their arms or legs, a difeafe very common about *Gamron*, where this plant is carefully cultivated. It produces only one cucumber, which is crooked and very pointed, the flowers, which rife on the top of the ftalk, are red and white, and the plant itfelf is reprefented in plate 184.

We fet out from thence at midnight, and arrived in the morning at *Dom-banje*, where we difperfed ourfelves into feveral houfes, the *Caravanferai* of the village lying in ruins. I went to fee, about half a league from thence, weftward, a mountain, feparate from the reft, upon which there was formerly a fortrefs. I found upon the top a well dug into the rock, the mouth of which was ten feet in diameter, but the depth was not very confiderable, as appeared by the fall of fome ftones, which I threw in. There was a vault on one fide of it nineteen paces in length, and twelve in width, with a dome above it, containing feventeen feet in diameter. It was round and open atop and on the fides, but it then appeared in a very ruinous condition. This mountain, which is very fteep on the north fide, has toward the fouth-fouth-weft, a path of fixteen paces in length, and a width of fourteen in the middle, it is partly cut out of the rock, and begins at the dome, from whence it extends to one fide of the mountain, but grows much narrower at each extremity than it is in the middle, as may be feen by my reprefentation of it in plate 185.

The fun being upon the decline, we returned over the plain, which was filled with feed, and I faw a field near the village with a growth of cotton, of an extraordinary height, which however was not yet in flower

1705 er We found in the night a well of extraordinary good water, with which we filled our leathern facks, that were empty before. The heat was then exceſſive, the wind being more fultry and infupportable than I had ever experienc'd it in any other country, and travellers are extremely incommoded by it. This quarter is full of villages.

Mr. Kaftel m and I reſolved to go before that night without the flambeaux, being fatigued with that troubleſome pace. We proceeded to our right, and obſerving ſome perſons ſtretched under tents, we engaged them to ſhew us the way. After we had travelled five leagues, we arrived about one in the morning at the village of *Aes Zjeraf*, but as it was unprovided with a *Caravanferai*, we took up our lodging at a tolerable good houſe, where we found the water a little brackiſh. Several travellers had written their names on the walls of this houſe, and among others, I read theſe words *Mr Director* Keits *died here in the year* 1640, *the* 29*th of* May. This happen'd during the travels of Mr. *Van Leenen*, counſellor extraordinary of the *Indies*, whom the company ſent at that time to *Iſpahan* in quality of ambaſſador, and to whom the director was to ſerve as a deputy. He was interr'd in that place without any ceremony, and even without a ſtone over his grave. This village is large, and contains a great number of gardens, full of palm and other trees. We here received letters from *Iſpahan* and *Gamron*, and after we had diſpatch'd the couriers who

Director Keits tomb

brought them, we purſued our journey the twenty-fixth, an hour after ſun-ſet, over ſome craggy mountains, and through bad roads, and arrived about one in the morning at the *Caravanſerai* of *Burtes*, which is ſeated in a plain, and we had then travelled about five leagues. This *Caravanſerai* is a large and beautiful ſtone edifice, well built, as is alſo the reſt of the village, which is full of palm and other fruit trees. About a league from thence are the ruins of an antient fortreſs, together with a wall round the mountain, and ſome ruinous fragments upon the top. This place is call'd *Koetel-Bieries*. There is alſo a well cut into the rock. The whole is exhibited in plate 186, together with ſome palm-trees and houſes.

We ſet out the next morning before day, and arrived about ten o'clock at *De-Faloe*, a large handſome village, accommodated with a good *Caravanſerai* of ſtone, and a large growth of palm and other trees. The conductor of the beaſts of burthen entertain'd us here, and we ſet forward a little before night. We paſſed over the mountains, and then perceived a water-mill on our left hand, with a large ciſtern above it, made for the reception of part of the water which flows from the mountains through a ſtone channel. The reſt runs into the plain by other canals. The road from thence to *Laer* is full of country-houſes and gardens. We paſſed through this city, and took up our lodging on the other ſide, after we had travelled about four leagues.

1705

C H A P.

CHAP LIX.

A defcription of Laer. *A great number of wells The reception of Mr* Kaftelein. *A fine* Caravanferai. *The author proceeds to* Gamion *The arrival of the fleet from* Batavia. *A new governor of* Gamion. *The author's indifpofition.*

The city of Laer THE city of *Laer* is the metropolis of an antient kingdom, which the *Perfians* with much difficulty have reduced under their government, and it is at this day a place of great commerce It has alfo a filk manufactory, and the beft cannons in all *Perfia* are caft here

Its fitua-tion I found all the avenues to that city in good repair, and the houfes for the moft part very high, among which there were many with openings for the admiffion of air The ftone *Bazar,* which is in the middle of the city, is the moft beautiful of all the buildings It is arched over, and full of fhops, with two ranges in the middle,

and the length of it is 216 paces At the end of this *Bazar* is a fine fquare, and, below the gate, the *Ragoine,* or the place where the mufick of the city may be heard. Oppofite to the *Bazar* is a large building, with a delightful entrance, and it ferves for a manfion-houfe for the duke or governor, *Ywas Chan* The caftle, which is entirely built of ftone, is fituated on an high rock, whofe fummit it almoft furrounds The avenues to this city refemble a wood, the land being covered with palm, orange, and citron trees, which almoft fhroud the city from the eye I now fhall prefent the reader with a draught of this, and likewife of the

LAER

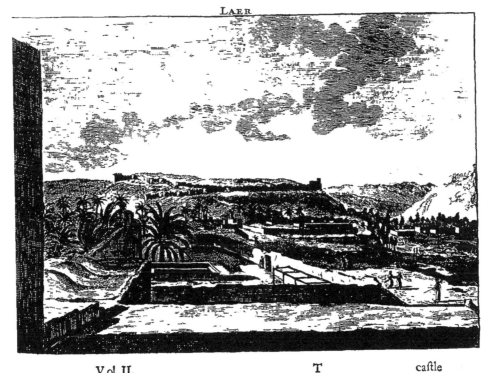

caftle

1705 castle, which I took from the top of the *Cidaraira*. It extends itself much farther on the left-hand than on the right, but the trees prevent it from being seen. It lies open like a village, and is extended very far on each side between the mountains. It has a great number of mosques, but none that are beautiful. The chief of them, which has a large dome, is called *Pir-Pansa*, from one of their saints. The city is filled with cisterns, vaulted above, to preserve the water.

Aug. 26 The governor sent this day, a congratulation to Monsieur *Kastelein*, upon his arrival, with a request, that he would continue there some days, to afford him sufficient time for acquitting himself of that duty in person; adding, that he should not have failed in sending before, if he had known of his arrival. Monsieur *Kastelein* returned him his acknowledgments for the civilities he had rendered him, and assured him, that his being obliged to depart immediately, gave him a sensible regret. A few moments after he received a handsome present of fruit from one of the principal merchants of the city, who came to pay him a visit, and was entertained agreeably to the manner of the country.

We continued our journey till evening, through a charming plain, bordered with trees, and houses on one side, which are said to form great part of the city, and after having passed through several villages, we came about midnight to the *Caravanserai* of *Basha-tary nae*, at the distance of four leagues from the city. We quitted that place on the 30th, and passed three times over a little river, which, at that time, was very shallow, but forms a considerable stream in the winter, and we arrived about two hours after at *Basta*, where we waited for the litter. We then pursued our journey, and came in eleven hours to a little *Caravanserai* half demolished, where we found an aged woman with some provisions. This part abounds with covered cisterns, the water of which is exceeding

good, and many people are employed to dig others, and likewise wells, without which neither they nor the cattle could subsist. They are also extremely diligent in searching for springs, as in the first ages of the world, of which we find an example in the first book of *Moses*, where it is said, that *Isaac* repaired the wells, which his father had dug, and the *Philistines* had filled up after his death.

As this was the season for hot winds, and sultry heats, which left no room to expect any favourable change of weather, we travelled by night as much as possible. The last day of the month we passed over a stoney plain, at which time fell a thick fog, accompanied with a kind of drizling rain, which occasion a disagreeable smell, which is a common circumstance in this country, in the night, and at that time of the year. We then passed over some mountains and rocks, and arrived about one in the morning at the *Caravanserai* of *Gormoet*, after a journey of five leagues.

The 1st of *September*, we again took the road, and found all the country filled with palm-trees, to the distance of a league from the town. Care had been taken to cover the parcels of dates with wicker baskets, as well to keep them from the sight of passengers, as to prevent the birds from devouring them. We then proceeded, not without much difficulty, over rocky mountains, and some rivers, which were very scanty of water, to make amends for the frequent inundations, in other parts of the year. Sometime after we met the *Kafua*, or new litter, which had been sent for from *Gamron*, attended by twelve bearers, who were to carry it by turns. They placed in it the sick lady, who then found herself more easy than she had been in the other; and we arrived about two in the morning, at the *Caravanserai* of *Tangboedalou*, where we met Monsieur *Bakker*, inspector of the magazines, (of whom I have already taken notice,) together with the

1705 the company's fecretary and houfe-keeper at *Gamron*, and who were come to meet Monfieur *Kaftelein* A fmall canal paffes through the *Caravanferai*, which is not very large, but extremely agreeable, and well-built It is all of ftone, and the water of the canal, which runs thro' it, flows from a little rivulet at a fmall diftance from it It has like-wife the advantage of being fhel-tered from the hot winds. The earth alfo in all the adjacent parts, is filled with little fubterranean ca-nals, which convey the water into the cifterns round about All forts of provifions are daily brought from the villages, to a water-mill, which is at the foot of the mountains, and near the *Caravanferai*

The next day we advanced eaft-ward, and at midnight arrived at the *Caravanferai* of *Goei-Bafer-goen*, after a journey of four leagues The company's houfe-keeper at *Zypeftein* then found himfelf fo much indif-pofed, that we were obliged to place him in the *Kafua* We arrived a-bout eleven that night at the great town of *Korefton*, which is feated in a plain, and took up our lodgings at the houfe of the bailiff, without ftopping at the *Caravanferai* As it was extremely hot, I laid myfelf down under the trees, where the wind was not quite fo ftifling, but the heat returned towards morning We continued there till fun-fet, and then paffed over a large plain full of wild trees, and croffed the river of *Korefton*, which was then very low, but it frequently overflows in the winter There is a bridge a quarter of a league in length, but entirely ufelefs, by reafon of its being ruinous in the middle I found this to be feven paces wide, it had likewife feveral arches, and a parapet on each fide We arrived about one in the morning at the *Caravanferai* of *Gefje*, after a journey of five leagues, and found fome women there, who fold frefh butter, with eggs, and good fowls, but the water is very indifferent.

We renewed our journey on the 1705 5th at fun-fet, and arrived about midnight at the *Caravanferai* of *Band-alie*, after having travelled five leagues That building is open on all fides, for the commodious ad-miffion of the breezes, which blow from the fea, and are very refreft-ing, that place being not above 3000 paces diftant from the gulf of *Perfia*, which much refembles the main fea

The interpreter *Varyn* vifited us that evening, with fome of the *In-dian* courtiers, to congratulate Mon-fieur *Kaftelein* upon his arrival, and prefent him with fome refrefhmen's The next day they brought us a re-gale of fmelts, and fmall pike, to-gether with plaice, and a few little oyfters, which were none of the beft, and thefe were accompanied with a prefent of *Englifh* beer In the morning I took a walk by the fea-fide, but found nothing worth my obfervation It was exceeding hot, but a wind which blew from the fea toward the fouth, was very refrefhing The *Caravanferai* where we were, lies north of the *Perfian* gulf, which extends itfelf from eaft-north-eaft, to weft fouth-weft to-ward *Konge*, which ftands upon its fhore From hence one may per-ceive the ifle of *Kifmis* in the gulf, at fouth-fouth-eaft, and at eaft-fouth-eaft, that of *Lareek*, between which the fhips ufually pafs The way from thence to *Gamron* lies eaftward, and partly along the fhore We travelled on in the evening, and a-bout a league from that place met Monfieur *Clerk*, the deputy director, with the treafurer, and we arrived at the town about ten in the evening, where Monfieur *Kaftelein* alighted at *The au-* the company's houfe, and I at the *thor's ar-* houfe of one of the company's fer- *rival at* vants. Five *Englifh*, and two *Dutch* *Gamron* veffels, were then in the harbour, with many others that were built in the country On the 8th Monfieur *Lid*, director of the *Englifh* factory, came to vifit Monfieur *Kaftelein*, and I went next day to his houfe, where I was very well received

On

On the 18th a yacht arrived from *Batavia*, and we were informed by those on board, that she was followed by five other vessels. She brought letters from the company, who had constituted Monsieur *Kastlin* director at *Gamron*, in the place of Monsieur *Backelaar*, who had desired to be dismissed from that service before his death. As soon as this account was made publick, the new director received the usual congratulations, the cannon belonging to the company were fired off, and answered by those of the fleet, and the evening passed in all manner of rejoicings. Our vessels also discharged some vollies. The next day the director of the *English* factory came to congratulate ours on his new dignity, and on the 26th one of the *English* vessels set sail.

On the 12th of *October* one of our vessels sailed for *Bassora*, and the five ships which were expected from *Batavia* arrived the next day, and their sloops came to anchor about noon. They were commanded by admiral *Baar*, who hoisted his flag on the top-mast. The *Eleonora* was to accompany those ships which were to sail for *Surat*, and had on board Monsieur *Six*, the company's deputy, to adjust the differences that were arisen between them and the people of that country, and to remain there in the quality of director. The baron *de Larey* embarked in one of those vessels for *Ispahan*, where he was also to continue as deputy to Monsieur *Backer* the director.

The king having about that time conferred the government of *Gamron* upon *Mamtb Alie Chan*, great rejoicings were made for the space of 3 days successively, and the cannon of the castles in the city were fired off, as likewise were those of *Ormus*, *Larek*, and *Kismis*. This lord had already enjoyed that government about eight or ten years before, but he afterwards obtained that of *Kirman*, from whence they have all their wool, and where is also a mine of silver. The last governor of *Gam-*

son had been deposed, in consequence of several complaints which were made against him at Court, and it was thought adviseable to leave his son there by way of precaution. *Mirja-Mocella*, who was to command in the absence of the governor, arrived on the eleventh, when most of the inhabitants went out to meet him, and he was received with a salute from the artillery of the castles. The people likewise received orders not to work that day, and were not permitted even to load or unload the ships.

On the 12th I was seized with a violent fever, which continued all that night, and increased the next day. As soon as I was sensible of its attack, I drank a large glass of wormwood, which had been very serviceable to me two or three times before, and I then walked by the seaside, in hopes that exercise would relieve me, but was obliged to take to my bed at my return. In the mean time the director went to pay a visit to the king's new lieutenant, who received him with a salvo of the cannon that were planted before his house, and the same was done at Monsieur *Kastelin's*, when the governor came to visit him.

My fever still continued, and made me delirious in the night. All the nourishment I then took was broth, and I drank nothing but tamarin water sweetened with sugar. I afterward became very laxative, which weakened me extremely. The fever left me in ten days, but it was a considerable time before I could recover my strength.

The *Banians*, or *Indians*, were at that time celebrating their new year. It is customary for the courtiers of that nation to make presents on that occasion, to the director, and all the officers employed under him, each in his order, even to the meanest, to whom they give little pieces of stuff flowered with gold and silver, and they likewise make illuminations. The director returned the visit to the two principals, who

1705 who are very rich, and they entertained him with artificial fire-works.
Their house is very large, but without any manner of ornaments

The 21st was attended with prodigious claps of thunder, and a very
boisterous wind, followed by some 1705
rain, which proved very serviceable
to the fruits, and for which they
returned thanks, by singing after the
manner of the country

CHAP. LX.

A description of Gamron. *The air unhealthy, and
very hot   The author resolves to depart from
thence.*

Description of Gam-ron.

THIS city was formerly called by the name of *Cam-
rang*, by the *Portuguese*, on account
of the small cray-fish, which are
called *Gamberi*, and abound there in
great plenty   The *Persian* appellation of this place is *Bander-Abassie*,
or the port of *Abas*, who made himself master of the town, and likewise of *Ormu*   It is computed to
be 200 leagues from *Ispahan*, but
it is certain that *Zyre-raes* is but seventy two or seventy three leagues
from that metropolis, and the distance from *Zyre-raes* to *Gamron*,
does not exceed 131 leagues, which
added to the other, make in all but
186, as I found a second time in my
return. This city is a small league
in circumference   It is likewise open,
and extends itself along the sea-shore
from east to west, or from north-
east to west-south-west   It has no
considerable buildings, and most of the
houses have a very mean appearance
on the outside   The best are those
which belong to the *English* and
Dutch factories, that of the governor
being but indifferent   It is very incommodious for strangers to reside
there the common sort have only a
set of wretched huts, and even the
Bazar itself is but a mean place
There are, indeed, four structures
which have the name of castles,
but they are low, small, and ruinous
That of the four which is farthest in
the city, has some pieces of cannon

to salute the ships. The poor people dwell there in cottages made of
boughs, and covered with the leaves
of the palm-tree, of which there
is great plenty in that city   The
principal houses are furnished with
machines to draw and receive the
wind   They are made like square
towers of a considerable height, and
are accessible to the wind on all parts,
except the middle, which is closed
up   Those two sides, which are
most exposed, have two or three
openings, which are long and narrow, and those of the other two
sides are less   There is likewise between each opening a small advanced
wall, which receives the wind, and
turns it back into those apertures,
by which means the houses are always rendered airy, when there is
the least gale of wind   The inhabitants generally take a short nap a-
bout noon, and pass the night upon
the terrasses during the hot seasons,
which would otherwise be very incommodious   But when these are
over, they lie in chambers, as in other
places. These towers, for the reception of wind, are very ornamental
to the city

A flag is always streaming upon
the houses of the *English* and *Dutch
India* companies, and serves for a
signal to their ships   The house
which belongs to our company, is *house belonging to
the* Dutch
factory
the most beautiful structure in the
city, and is built on the edge of it
toward

... toward the east The first foun-
d on was laid there in 1698 by
Mr H... n r, the company's minister It is very large, and furnished
with ... magazines, the chambers
t ... and of a confi-
derable length There is likewise a
very magnificent and beautiful hall
in the middle of the apartments a-
bove, whose windows, as well as
those of the directors, and his de-
puties lodgings, have a prospect to
the sea, from whence these apartments are refreshed with the most
agreeable air in the world But this
house is not finished as yet

I drew the city from one of our
barks, the large vessels lying at too
great a distance The reader will
see the representation of it in plate
187, and the whole is distinguished
by numerical figures 1 The governor's house 2 One of the castles
3 The house belonging to the *French*
company 4 The *English* company's house 5 That of the *Dutch*
company 6 Another of the castles
7 The *Dutch* Company's new house
The *Europeans* are buried in a tract
of ground to the north of the city,
and it is filled with lofty tombs covered with domes One need not
be surprised at the great number of
them, since the air is very unhealthy, and the excessive heats carry off
a vast multitude of people But
nothing is more pernicious than the
burning fevers, which are there more
common than in any other place and
frequently prove fatal in the space of
twenty four hours The months of
October and *November* are not less
dangerous, for the air is then either
very damp, or exceeding dry The
latter is the least dangerous, and the
water is fresher, and better to drink
than in a rainy season, the humidity giving it an ill flavour and
rendering it very unwholsome Camels are sent for water to L... n
upon the mountains, about four
leagues from the sea, and this is the
wholsomest water in all the country The inhabitants likewise send
for it to Na... ban, which is a league
from the city, near the sea, but this

latter is not so good We had to- 1705
lerable weather during my continuance there but the heat lasted longer than usual, and was extremely
incommodious It is sometimes in-
supportable, and I have been assured, that it has even melted sealing-
wax In this extremity they throw
off all their upper garments, and
cause themselves to be sprinkled
over with water Our interpreter
had a well, in which he passed a
great part of the day These im-
moderate heats always occasion
severe distempers, as I have already
observed, and happy are those who
escape them But even these are not
exempted from great inconveniences, of which one of the most remarkable is the worms, which eat
into the arms and legs of persons,
and which are not drawn out without their being exposed to apparent
danger, by breaking them in the
flesh In a word, one could not
find a more rigorous punishment for
malefactors than confining them in
a place like this One, however, seldom fails of finding some people of
merit and distinction here, whom
interest, and the hopes of raising a
great fortune, have drawn thither,
and whom death often snatches a-
way before they have attained to
the height of their desires

The vessels anchor about half a *Ships in the*
league from the city, from whence *harbour*
small barks are sent to load and unload them, by the assistance of persons appointed for that purpose

The principal isles of the *Persian* *Isle of*
gulf are, 1st that of *Ormus*, three *O mus*
leagues distant from *Gamron* The
capital of that isle, and of the kingdom of that name, was formerly
very famous among the cities of *A-
sia*, for the greatness of its commerce,
it lies at the mouth of the gulf, near
the south-side of *Persia*, and was
formerly governed by a king of its
own, under the protection of the
Portuguese, who demolished the citadel The *Persians*, assisted by the
English, made themselves masters of
it in 1622, nor has the city ever
flourished since They even yet va-
lue

GA

LES ISLES D' ORMU

ON

REKE, ET KISMIS

1705

lue their caftle, into which ftrangers are feldom admitted Nor are even their fhips allowed to appro ch it, for fear of giving umbrage There was forme ly a bed of fand near this ifle, on which were found pearls, which have fince been poifoned, as is reported The ifle of *Lareke* is five leagues fouth-fouth-eaft from *Gamron*, and that of *Kifmis* is four leagues and a half at fouth-fouth-weft This is the largeft of the three, and about fix or feven leagues in length, it fupplies them with moft of the wood uled by the carpenters of *Gamron*, and likewife with timber for refitting foreign veffels which put in there, it extends almoft to *Conge*, and fhips may pafs between them

Each of thefe iflands has a citadel, but none of them are confiderable,

except that of *Ormus* They are reprefented in plate 188, that of *Ormus* is marked with A, its citadel, which is at the extremity of it toward the north-weft with B, *Lareke* with C, and *Kifmis* with D

The *Meydrecht*, one of the company's fhips, being ready to fail for *Batavia*, I ordered all my goods to be carried on board, and two days after embarked myfelf, although I was not then fully recovered, but found myfelf fo very weak, that I was fcarce able to fupport myfelf I, however, preferred the fea to travelling by land, which appeared to me more dangerous, flattering myfelf that the air of the fea would be more healthful for me, in which I was not deceived

Marginal notes: *Lareke* · *Kifmis*

1705

CHAP. LXI.

The author fets fail from Gamron for Batavia The coaft of Malabar The ifle of Kover. The rocks of St. Mary. An Englifh fhip at anchor before Mangeloor. Dolphins, flying fifh, and other kinds A fea monfter. The author's arrival at Cochin. The civility of the governor.

WHEN I had taken leave of the director, and all my friends, I went on board the 25th of October We hoifted fail in the night-time, and fteered our coaft fouth-eaft by fouth, between the ifles of *Ormus* and, *Lareke* in the *Perfian* gulf, and between the kingdom of *Perfia*, *Arabia deferta*, and *Felix* On the next day about noon, we difcovered the cape of *Monfandon*, at north-weft by weft, and the cape of St *James* at eaft by fouth, and at the diftance of about five or fix leagues

On the 29th, the wind being at fouth-eaft, with a brifk gale, we faw again the cape of St *James* at

eaft by fouth, and, toward the fouth, the ifland itfelf, and north of the bay of wood, upon the coaft of *Arabia* at north-weft by weft, and the bay at fouth-weft by weft, and when we had advanced within three or four leagues of the fhore, we found ourfelves in 25 degrees 38 minutes north latitude, at fixty fathom water

The wind changing in the evening to fouth-weft, we fteered our coaft eaft by fouth, the night being very clear The wind increafed the following days, and the weather continuing fine, we purfued our voyage fouth-fouth-eaft, in order to reach the coaft of *Arabia*.

The

Marginal notes: The author's departure from Gamron · Capes of Monfandon and St James

1705 The first of ...., and the following days, the wind proved various, and the sea calm. On the 7th we came to the height of 21 degrees 1- minutes north latitude, steering our course east-south-east. The next day we advanced to 19 degrees 4- minutes, and on the 12th to 1- degrees 5- minutes. About noon a brisk gale rose at north by east. We sounded, but found no bottom at 100 fathom that day, nor for some days after.

On the 1-th at break-of-day, we discovered the coast of ...., from south-east by east to south-east, at seven or eight leagues distance from us. We then steered south-east, the wind being north-north-east, and very strong. We sounded again, but without finding any bottom. After sun-set, we lost sight of land, the air being thick and cloudy. The wind was tolerably calm in the night, and we steered our course eastward, and entered into the *Indian* sea, which is between the eastern coasts of *Africa*, and those of *Arabia*, *Persia*, and the *East-Indies*, the isles of *Sumatra*, and *Java*, and other small eastern isles, and the southern continent.

On the 16th, the air being cloudy, we found ourselves in the northern latitude of 15 degrees 12 minutes, and the 17th at 14 degrees 19 minutes. On the 18th we were becalmed, and had a cloudy season, with some lightening in the night. In the morning the weather proved fine, but the wind was variable. On the 20th there was so great a calm, that we went backward rather than forward, the tide, which is very strong at west by north, being against us. On the 22d the weather continued the same, and we had still the tide against us north-west by west, while we steered to the north-west. The weather did not change the next day, and having sounded in the night, we found from seventy to seventy five fathom water, upon a greyish bottom, mixed with sand and ooze. The next day at dawn we had another view of the coast of

Melobar, sailing under the wind in nifty to fifty five fathom water, the bottom being still the same. At noon we were obliged to cast anchor in fifty eight fathom, by reason of a calm, and the strength of tide. We were now in the latitude of 15 degrees 35 minutes, and within sight of land, but were unable to distinguish what particular land it was, because the weather was foul and very cloudy.

The 24th some of us imagined we saw the cape of *Comar* at south-east, and I am persuaded we were not mistaken, though others doubted it, because the water was changed, and they found no bottom. We stood out to sea again that day, and as the wind was easterly, and we were sailing to the south, the tide carried us off again from the coast, and we found that the ship had advanced fourteen or fifteen leagues to west-north-west, and that we had been driven back from the shore above sixty leagues.

The 25th, the weather being cloudy, we were surprised by a great calm, and came about sun-set within three or four leagues of the point of *Anchediva* at east by south, and toward morning, within five or six leagues of *Onor*, likewise at east by south, in the latitude of 14 degrees 17 minutes, we continued our course south-east by south in the night, the wind being north-west.

The 27th, at break of day we discovered the isle of *Kovers*, to the south east, and at the distance of three or four leagues, and we came within two leagues of it about noon, at east by north, in the latitude of 13 degrees 50 minutes. At sun-set we discovered the most southern continent at south-east by east, and the isle of *Kot n*, at east-north-east, about five leagues from us. We continued our course in the night, south-east by south, from east-north-east, with little wind, having from twenty-six to thirty fathom water, upon an oozy bottom. The next day, being about four leagues from land, we had some rain and a calm,

which

1705

The cape of Comar

The isle of Anchediva

Onor

The isle of Kovers

1705 which obliged us to anchor in nineteen fathom water, that we might not go back any more, because the tide was very strong. The 29th, at break of day, we sounded, because of the shoals of St *Mary*, which were about a league and a half from us, at east by north. In the mean time the calm and the tide continuing favourable to us, we remained at anchor till noon, when we stood out to sea again, with very little wind, steering south-east by south.

The 30th, at break of day, we discovered a vessel at anchor before *Mangeloor*. We were then about two leagues from land in sixteen fathom water, and passed before noon by that place, which belongs to the *Dutch India* company, and has a small citadel. There are several high mountains in the inland part of the country, and one upon the shore. About noon a bark came up to us with ten *Malabars*, who informed us, that the vessel we had seen upon the coast, was an *English* ship, and that the captain had given them a letter for ours, and desired him to let that bark accompany us to *Kananor*, from whence the master was to carry by land to *Calicut*, a letter for the director of the *English* company, who resided there. To this our captain consented, and ordered his men to furnish those in the bark with all the accommodations they wanted.

That place is in the northern latitude of 12 degrees 29 minutes. At sun-set we came within about two leagues and a half of the *White Beacons* at north-east, and to the point of *Monstadely*, which lay south-south-east, at the distance of three or four leagues. The next day the *Malabars* left us, in order to proceed to *Kananor*.

We had frequently the pleasure of seeing and taking many sorts of fish. *Dolphins* We first caught a dolphin with harping irons and hooks. It is customary to fix a little bundle of feathers on them, and then cast them into the sea at the end of a rope fastened to a pole. The dolphins,

Vol II

who take these tufts for flying fish, 1705 upon which they continually feed, follow the bait till they are taken. This is the less extraordinary, as those little fish, who are apprehensive of the dolphins, fly as long as they are able above the surface of the sea, but as they are obliged frequently to plunge themselves into the water, the dolphins, who pursue them, seize upon them, as I have often observed. I have preserved in spirits of wine three of these fish, that fell as they were flying upon the deck of our ship, a circumstance which often happens. We took one of these dolphins which was four foot long, and the head was ten inches thick. They have a yellow belly, speckled with blue, up to their eyes, and the rest of the body is tinged with a light blue, blended with spots of a deeper complexion, especially upon the top of the head. The fins are purple, green, and white, with a small intermixture of yellow near the edge. Their colour changes when they die, and resembles that of the purple-fish. They have one fin upon their back, from the head to the tail, and another from the middle of the belly to their tail, two others under the body near the neck, and one on each side of the head. Their tail is forked, and their eye-balls are encircled with a ring of white. Their mouth and teeth are small, the head of the male is much larger than that of the female, and they have but few intestines. The sailors eat them dressed in the same manner as the *Cabillau*, or *Melwell*, and they afford a tolerable good relish.

The first we took was the largest and finest, but as my eyes were then out of order, I could not make a draught of it. My fever likewise returned, which I attributed to too great a repletion, having had an extraordinary appetite at sea, and using no exercise. I even believe that this contributed not a little to impair my sight. When I had continued three weeks in that condition, I recollected that I had brought from

X *Holland*

H found a microscope, and some o-
ther glasses, which employed and
diverted me very agreeably, and by
the help of these I drew one of the
dolphins, which the reader will find
represented in plate 189 They
likewise helped me to read in the
night, when I was prevented from
sleeping by an itching, and a heat
which had continued upon me ever
since my sickness at Gamron We
took a variety of other fish, some
of which were a foot long These
were sea-perch, usually called
P , and they have some resemblance to river perches Their bodies are speckled with brown and
blue spots, an inch in breadth, and
which grow narrower near the tail
These fish are continually playing
about the rudder of a ship, and are
commonly accompanied by another
fish called Ha They are likewise
dressed for eating like river perches
I preserved a small one in spirit, and
the reader will find it exhibited in
plate 190

We also frequently saw on the side
of our ship, a fish which the sailors
call the Devil, or sea-monster It
is a large flat fish very like a turbot,
and has a great deal of the taste,
as they told me, but is not quite so
large, nor so long His wings, or
fins, are always expanded, and from
his tail issues out a long narrow
streamer, which in the sea appears
white, and in its motion resembles the
undulation of a serpent The rest of his
body is brown, intermixed with white
spots, and is about twelve feet in
length, and more in breadth, when
his fins are extended We endeavoured to hook him with a
harping-iron, but could not succeed,
though he appeared two or three
times at the head of our ship Our
captain assured us, that he had
struck several times at one, but that
he always made the harping-irons
fly back with great violence, and
without receiving any wound Some
of these fish are reported to be large,
and strong enough to over-set a
sloop

We came within a small distance
of Cochin the 3d of December, and
anchored in the evening in six fathom and a half water, at the distance
of a league from the city The gates
were then shut, but were soon opened
to us, and we went to wait upon the
governor, to whom our captain delivered the letters he had received
for him He favoured us with a
very civil reception, and obliged us
to sup with him, he likewise pressed
me to accept of a bed at his house,
but I excused myself, chusing rather to lodge with my fellow-tra-
vellers

The author arrives at Cochin

CHAP.

1705   1705

C H A P. LXII.

A description of Cochin The author's departure from that city. The cape of Komerin The island of Ceilon Point Adam The author's arrival at Gale The taking of a crocodile A description of it. An account of some extraordinary animals, plants, and sea-herbs

I Returned the next day to the governor's house, and defired him to lend me a bark to cross the river, that I might take a draught of the city from the other side, and he immediately granted me that favour I there beheld an infinite number of trees of a surprizing beauty, and different from any I had ever seen before From this situation I drew the north prospect of of the city, as it appears in plate 191 No 1 represents the company's fishery 2 The station appointed for the guards of the citadel, and its entrance 3 The bastion of *Gueldres* 4 The port of the bay. 5. The governor's house 6 The church 7 The captain's house 8 The deputy's house 9 The flag hoisted upon an old ruinous tower 10 The company's magazine 11 The purveyor's house 12 The place where the sailors lodge 13. The extremity of the well.

The situation of the city This city is about half a league in circumference, and has two gates, one of which, that fronts the shore, is called the gate of the bay, and the other the river gate. They have dug a canal on this side, where the company's barks ride, and by the side of it is the timber-yard From thence one passes over a great wooden bridge, in order to arrive at this last gate, near which is a river, that flows into the ditches of the city, and bears large vessels The bastions of this city have the several names of the provinces of *Gueldres, Holland, Utrecht, Frieseland,* and *Groninghen*, and the little bastion, which is near the fishery, is called *Overyssel* The captain's

house is at *Stroomenbourg* The governor's hall, which has a prospect to the sea, forms also a kind of point or bastion, and there are likewise two half-moons among the other works The place is very agreeable both without and within, the streets are spacious, and the houses handsomely built with brick There is also another wood-yard for refitting ships, and for the use of those who come in or go out The governor's house is a large structure, composed of fine apartments The Sieur *Moormans* is the present governor, and he is a gentleman of a very obliging disposition He presented our captain with several plants that grow in that part of the country, and are esteemed as great curiosities, and we sent him a present of corn in return They have great plenty of fish, and all sorts of flesh, so that a cow is sold for three or four crowns, a hog for a crown and an half, a hen for two pence, and a duck for six pence They are likewise as well supplied with rice, but the soil produces neither corn nor wine, nor have they any of either, but what is brought thither *Stroomenbourg* is also under the jurisdiction of the commander of the city, whose deputy is named *Bitter* We took up our quarters in one of the handsomest houses in the city, with Monsieur *de Graef*, an ensign in the service of the company Their money is of two kinds, *viz Fanums*, which are equal to a quarter of a *Dutch* shilling, and *Besaroeles*, thirty two of which are equivalent to a penny

This

This city, which lies in ten degrees of north latitude, is the capital of an antient kingdom of that name, and had formerly a bishop. It is situated in the eastern part of *Asia*, near the coast of *Malabar*, which extends itself partly from south to north. It has a high mountain in the eastern part of it, and the soil is very fertile and pleasant. A continual spring flourishes there, and the ground is always enamelled with every kind of flowers, as has been observed by the famous *Antsord*.

Malabar was formerly subject to an Emperor, whose dominions extended from cape *de Komeryn*, as far as *Mangeloor*, on the frontiers of the kingdom of *Chanara*. But I found in the memoirs left by the governor of *R de* to his successor, that this powerful empire, which formerly contained four millions seven hundred thousand men fit to bear arms, was, after the death of the last emperor, divided into thirteen or more kingdoms, governed by the principal men of the empire. The chief of these princes is the sovereign of *Cochin*, descended in a direct line from *Ceeram-Perumal*, and from the great *Samorin*.

As I made but a short stay in that country, I could not inform myself of any other particulars, except only that the flat part of the country is watered by many navigable rivers, some of which are very large.

The governor entertained us this day at dinner, and we embarked in the evening with much difficulty, by reason of the violence of the waves, which beat continually against the rocks. We set sail in the night, and there fell a heavy rain, accompanied with thunder and lightening; after which we discovered some high mountains about two leagues distant from us, while we steered south-east. Toward the next evening we were again threatened with a storm, and were obliged to furl the sails. We advanced an hour before night, near the cape *de Komeryn*, when the weather grew fine again, but the wind changed, and continued against us all the next day. It rained part of the night, and we doubled the cape on the 8th in the morning, the wind being at north-east, and we lost sight of it in the afternoon, steering to east-south-east, and to south-east by east. In the night we were surprized by a calm. However, we continued our course every day with a changeable wind, and *Isle of Cei-* discovered the isle of *Ceylon* the 10th *lon* in the morning, with a high mountain in form of a sugar-loaf, which *Adam's* is called the *Peak of Adam*. This *Peak* peak is visible only at some particular times, because it is involved in clouds, which descend even to the bottom of it. The reader may see a representation of it in the following plate.

We cast anchor at eight in the evening, in thirty nine fathom water, and hoisted sail again the 11th at break of day, so that we advanced in a short time within sight of the city of *Gale*, but were not able to arrive at it till the evening, by reason of a calm, which obliged us to cast anchor a league and a half on this side of it in seventeen fathom water. The next morning, our captain sailed in the sloop to the city, in order to deliver the letters he had in charge. We weighed anchor about ten, but the wind being against us, and very strong, we could not get into the harbour.

When any ship approaches the *Rocks* bay of *Gale*, a cannon is fired every half hour, to give notice to the pilots to come on board, because there is no passing farther without being exposed to apparent danger, from the rocks which are hidden under water; some seventeen feet from the surface, others fifteen and twelve, and many less. I went in the evening to the city with the pilot, and lodged at an inn. The next day I visited the governor, whose name was *Welters*, and he received me in a very obliging manner, and offered me all the service in his power. He was but newly arrived from *Kiin*, where he had been director. As I intended to continue some time in that city, to refresh myself, and recover my health,

I left

1705

PIC D'ADAM

I left the inn, and went to lodge with one of the company's fergeants It rained inceffantly till the 17th, tho' it had continued above two months, and the preceding year had been exceeding dry. But the weather grew fine again in a fhort time

I found five of the company's fhips in the port, three of which returned to *Holland*, and two other veffels after arrived here from *Bengale*. On the 18th the governor gave an entertainment to thofe who were preparing for their return to *Holland*, and above fixty perfons were prefent, but my ill ftate of health prevented me from being one of the number

A terrible accident About midnight there happened a fad accident One of the men who had drank too freely, fet fire accidentally to one of the fhips that were to return, but they had the good fortune to quench it before the flame, which had already feized the rigging, could reach the powder, otherwife the fhip, with all her tackling and cargo, had been inevitably deftroy'd, and the others expofed to very great danger

Two of thofe fhips failed out of the harbour on the 20th, and anchor'd in the road, the third follow'd them the next day, and I took this opportunity to write to my friends in *Holland*. In the mean time the drum was ordered to beat in the city, to fummon the failors on board, upon pain of being put in irons, and after the cargo had been reviewed, they fet fail on the 24th The fame day arrived a veffel from *Amfterdam*, and two *Englifh* fhips paffed by the port, fteering weftward My fever returned then with a Diarrhæa, which weakened me extremely.

On *Chriftmas-day* a crocodile was *A crocodile taken alive* taken alive, fixteen feet and a half in length, and five and a half in breadth We were affured that he had devoured thirty two perfons upon that coaft, befide feveral others whom he had doubtlefs deftroy'd in different places They had often given him chace, but to no purpofe till then After they had

1705 killed him, they dragged the body to the governor's house, from whence he was sent to the surgeons of the hospital to be diffected. My curiofity drew me thither to fee the infide of that monfter, and examine whether he had not in his body fome remains of any human creature. And we accordingly found the trunk, arms, and legs of a man, together with the skull, feet, and hands, and a prodigious quantity of fat, which is ufed as a medicine, and is faid to be excellent for the palfy, and all relaxations of the nerves, and likewife for rheumatifms.

§ of crocodiles that are not hurtful It is pretended that there are fome places where thefe animals are not injurious to any. When they lay their eggs, they place them in a hole in the ground, where they are hatched by the heat alone. As foon as they are opened, the parent crocodile appears, and fwallows down all the young ones that chance to run into her mouth; the reft jump into the water. There are fome as big again as that I am defcribing. They have no tongue, fo that when they open their mouth, one perceives a frightful cafm. When they are upon land, on a fandy foil, they run with fuch a prodigious fpeed that a man cannot efcape them by flight; but upon a hard and ftony ground they are not fo fwift, becaufe the bottom of their feet is exceeding tender. They devour cattle without any difficulty, and even a wild ox, and their teeth are fo long, that they grind their horns to powder. But their eggs are fcarce bigger than a pullets, and are altogether as white. Their yard is but fmall in proportion to their bulk, and is flit at top with a kind of fmall tongue beneath. They dry'd that of this crocodile, as a prefent for me, and gave me one of the tefticles, which had a fmell fomething like amber. I likewife received from them a bottle of the greafe of that monfter.

The manner of taking them They take thefe crocodiles with a large hook faftened to a chain of forty or fifty ftrong threads, which infinuate themfelves between the monfter's teeth in fuch a manner as renders him unable to difengage himfelf, or break his hook, which penetrates as far as the ftomach, and faftens there; but if the hook were to be fixed to a thick cord o chain, the crocodile would eafily bite them in funder. Thefe threads ferve alfo to conceal the hook.

These monfters are alfo found in the ponds in the ifle of *Ceilon,* and other parts of the *Indies.* There is another manner of deftroying them, and even of preferving them for a fhew to the people, which is this. *Another manner of deftroying them in feveral* They take a very dry tube, three or four feet in length, which they fill with quick lime, and faften to a dead pullet; the crocodile, as foon as he perceives it in the water, never fails to fwallow it. But when it has remained in his body for the fpace of twenty four hours, the wood burfts, upon which the fire flies about, and then burns, and confumes him, fo that when he is thus filled with fire, which continually preys upon him, he leaps out of the water, and expires in an inftant.

One may judge of the ftrength of thefe crocodiles by the efforts they make after they are caught with a hook, and have been opened, in order to take out their entrails, fince, even in that condition, they rife again, and frequently run twenty or thirty paces. *Their ftrength* I was told, upon this occafion, that about fourteen years ago, the crew of a fhip, called *The King of Bantam,* took a * *Haai,* that had forty five little ones in its belly, which, when it was opened, came out, and began to fwim in a veffel of water prepared for that purpofe, and that the leaft of thefe fifh was larger than a *Merlan.* ** A large fea fifh, ＆c. a kind of devour, men*

I ought to take notice here, that they prefented me with two large bottles filled with various forts of animals preferved in fpirits, among which were little crocodiles, young fea-lizards, cameleons, fcorpions, millipedes, a blind ferpent, and feveral other creatures. *Strange creatures*

They

1705 They gave me likewise some other productions of the sea, which were not very considerable I went my self, but with no great success, to search along the shore for others, and appointed some persons to do the same, but what they brought me was in a manner useless, and among other things were a great number of stones I chose what I liked most out of them, and threw away the rest, which they had picked up without much curiosity, I not being able to accompany those to whom I gave that employment, by reason of my weakness This island likewise produces plants, and medicinal herbs, which are extraordinary good, as the inhabitants pretend, but strangers ought to be well acquainted with them.

Physick herbs

I sent into the woods to seek for some of these productions, particularly for an herb called *Hacke-melle*, of which they report wonders; and among other particulars, that if one wraps up a flint stone in one of its leaves, the moment any one takes it into his mouth the flint breaks into a thousand pieces, and that the juice of these leaves is a specifick remedy for the gravel: They much resemble those of celery, only the leaves are tinged with a deeper green I intended to extract some of the spirits, but not having sufficient time for that operation, I was obliged to content my self with bringing away some dried leaves, and the exterior buds, which are used like tea, and are extremely good to bring down the stone, and dissipate the gravel

1705.

CHAP. LXIII.

The revenue which the India *company receives from the isle of* Ceilon *A description of the city of* Gale. *The people converted to the Christian religion The habit of the* Singales *Abundance of elephants. Cinnamon trees.*

THOUGH I was offered in this place all manner of information necessary for a circumstantial description of the isle of *Ceilon*, and the satisfaction of the readers curiosity in these particulars, I did not make any use of them, because my ill state of health, and the little time I had to continue there, would not permit me to go far up into the country to make any discoveries myself, and to see those pieces of antiquity which are said to be there I was likewise unwilling to trespass upon the resolution I had taken, not to relate any thing which I had not seen with my own eyes, for which reason I shall content myself with mentioning the principal revenues which the company receives from that famous island.

The most considerable is that produced by cinnamon, which is better there than in any other part of the world As soon as the governor has ordered the number of cinnamon bales, required by the company, the *Chalins*, whose business it has always been to peel off that valuable bark for the sovereign of the isle, fail not to furnish him with it at a very inconsiderable expence.

The company's revenues from the island Cinnamon

The second revenue is, that which proceeds from the *Areek*, the trading in which, without the company's permission, is prohibited to all the world. The servants of the company are obliged to carry the rice into their magazines at a very reasonable price, and they carry on a very advantagious trafic with the merchants of *Coromandel*, who come

Areek

this

1705 thither for it   Beside which the company likewise frequently sends that fruit to *Bengale* and *Surat* in their own ships

Gen

The third is that which arises from the sale of the coarse cloth of *Madura* and *Coromandel*, which are sold as they come from the manufacturer, without being whitened, and this commodity produces a considerable profit.

Elephants

The fourth arises from the sale of elephants, which are brought from *Columbo* and *Maturan*, as well as from the kingdom of *Jaffnatnam*, where they are sold very advantagiously to the natives of *Golconda*, and the other *Moors*

The manner of transporting those animals

The elephants, which are taken in the countries of *Columbo* and *Maturan* were formerly transported, with much difficulty, in the company's ships, to *Jaffnapatnam* But they have found out, some years since, the secret of cutting a passage, for near fifty leagues, through a very thick and wild wood, from *Negomb* through the country of *Kande*, as far as *Jaffnapatnam* This difficult undertaking was accomplished by the assistance of the natives, who have at length performed it at a small expence

The capture of these elephants is also performed by the inhabitants of the country, under the direction of the company's officers If I had ever had an opportunity of being present at one of these exploits, I should not have failed to have given a particular account of it   But as I have never been an eye-witness to it, I shall content my self with saying, that several persons worthy of credit have assured me, that in one single chace they have often taken, in the country of *Columbo*, near 160 elephants, and sometimes more

Pearl fishery

I might here likewise mention the advantage which accrues to the company from the pearl fishery which is carried on in that island, and in the dependant countries, as well at *Tutucorin*, upon the coast of *Madura*, as in the gulf of *Arippo*,

under the government of *Manna* But as that revenue is altogether unsettled, and produces sometimes more, sometimes less, I cannot give an exact account of it   However, as they are continually fishing in one or other of these places, it is not to be doubted, that the company find their account in it. I have before me some pieces which might authorise me to speak more exactly, for I have made it a maxim with myself, not to mention any particular of which I have not a certain knowledge. I shall therefore only say, that the principal revenue which the company receives from this fishery, results from a tax laid upon the *Tax upon stones* stones which are used for that purpose, every diver who works there, being obliged to have one, to make him sink to the bottom of the water   Each bark contains more or less, the largest of them are from sixteen to twenty pound in weight, and the smaller weigh about six or eight pound   So that when that fishery shall be brought to perfection, and they can employ 450 vessels, the profit will be very considerable

The *Parruwas*, who are those *The Parruwas* that profess the *Roman* religion, pay seven rix-dollars for each stone, the inhabitants of the country nine and a half, and the *Moors* and *Mohammedans* twelve, a custom introduced by the *Portuguese*, and continued by the company.

I shall now proceed to a description of the city of *Gale*, which is *A description of Gale* rendered very strong by its situation, being surrounded on the side next the sea, with shelves of sand and rocks which render it inaccessible, without the assistance of pilots from the port, which forms a half-moon in the eastern part of the city, and is well provided with cannon   It has also strong walls, and good entrenchments cut into the rock, and bulwarks in many of the angles, the principal of which bear the names of the sun, moon, and stars   Between these bastions are the city gates, and there are some other fortifications,

1705

FEMME MEXTIETSF

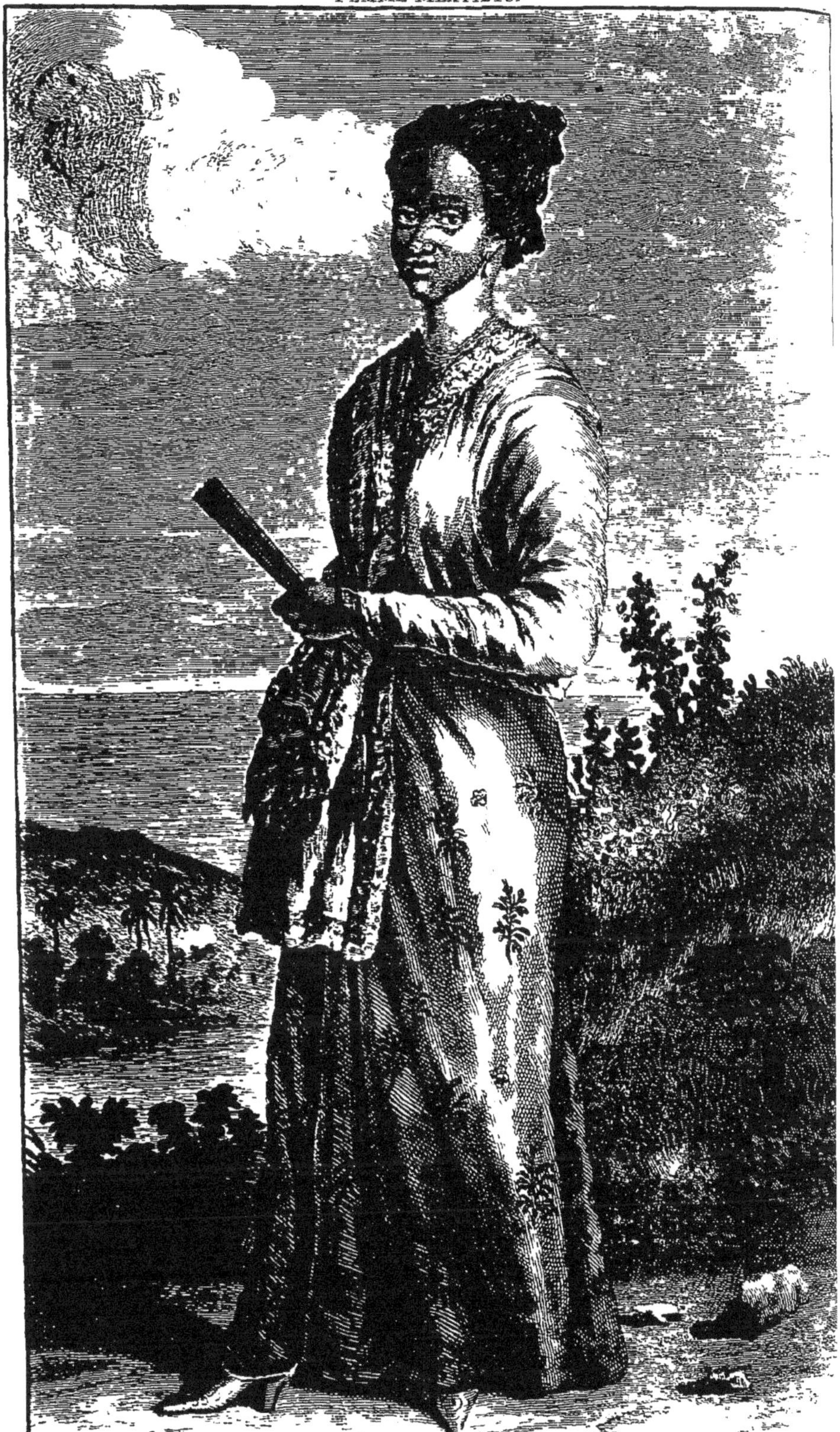

fications, namely, that of the *Sailors*, of *Utrecht*, of *Venus*, of *Mars*, of *Æolus*, and the *Standard Rock*. There is but one gate to the eaft, which is that on the fhore. The city is about half a league in its inward circumference, for there is no walking round it without. It has some tolerable ftreets, which are not paved, but covered with turf, and feveral of the houfes make a handfome appearance, particularly that of the governor, which is fpacious, and full of beautiful apartments. It is built upon an eminence, over-againft the company's magazine, which is very large, but the walls which are next the water are very damp, and the upper part of the ftructure, which is of wood, is rotted and eaten by white ants, of which there are vaft numbers in that country. The entrance into this magazine is at the city gate, and one end of it has been formed into a church, where the *Hollanders* perform their devotion in the morning, and the *Singalis* in the afternoon. The country adjacent to this city is full of gardens, fhaded with fine trees, and formed into beautiful alleys. The mountains, which rife in the eaftern part of the country, are cover'd with woods, and from thence one may eafily pafs along the fhore to the port. Thefe woods are full of wild-goats, hares, and birds, but the market is feldom furnifhed with any of this food, but with refpect to other provifions, it is almoft as well fupplied as that at *Cochin*, butter excepted, which is very dear, and far from being good. When any fhip is difcovered out at fea, a flag is hoifted upon an old building fituated on a rock, where a guard is always ftationed.

The money of that ifland is all of copper. The largeft fpecies of it amount to near two of our *fols*, and the fmalleft to about a *denier*. But the *Dutch* money is likewife current there.

They have feveral fchools for the *Singales*, who are converts to Chriftianity, and good mafters, who are inftructed by the minifters to inform them of the articles neceffary to their falvation, and to give them a good education. Thefe minifters vifit the fchools every fix months, which produces a very good effect.

Thefe *Singales*, who are half *Moors*, have, for their whole clothing, but one piece of linnen wound about them from the waift to the knees, all the reft of their body being naked. The women wear this habit fomething longer, it refembles a petticoat, and is tinged with feveral colours. They have likewife a little waift-coat of cloth, hanging loofe below. The better fort of them have two of thefe waiftcoats, with an ornament of fringe on the uppermoft, when they appear abroad, and go to church, they put on white ftockings, with embroidered flippers, but in the houfe their legs are without any covering, and they have wooden fandals on their feet. Their heads are alfo uncovered, and their hair is tucked up behind. Their necks are ornamented with a fmall chain of gold, to which is faftened a jewel, which falls upon their bofom. They likewife wear another larger chain, which hangs down to their petticoat. They have alfo over their left fhoulder a white flowered fcarf, or of fome other colour, which defcends as far as their knees before, and is fhort behind. The fleeves of their waiftcoat flow to their wrifts, around which they wear bracelets of gold, or any other metal, as reprefented in plate 192. There are among the moft confiderable of them fome *Mextietjes*, who fpeak good *Dutch*. Thefe are the offspring of *European* and *Moorifh* parents.

This ifland abounds with elephants, as I have already obferved, and two hundred of them are fometimes taken in one chace, with fnares made of ofier, and which are extended to the diftance of three leagues. Thefe captures are made every third year, after which the elephants are fent by the company to *Coromandel*, and

Side notes:
Fortifications
Provifions
Their money
The fchools
Habits of the Singales
Elephants

1705

Surat, as well as to other places The largest of thele animals are fold for 2000 rix-dollars, and the others at a price proportionable to their age.

The tree which bears cinnamon, is the moft confiderable of all those that grow in the island The oil of it is produced by the flower, and has the confiftency of foop It is likewise as white as tallow, and has not any fmell It is faid to be an excellent remedy for chilblains Monfieur *M.d* the treafurer, was fo obliging as to prefent me with a quantity of this production

This island of *Ceilon*, or *Ceylan*, which the inhabitants call *Lankavon*, and *Tinariffim*, is fuppoled by fome to be the *Taprobane* of the antients It ftretches into a large extent, is almoft round, and its fertility is very

great It lies fouth-weft of the *Eaft-Indies*, north of the *Indian* fea, and fouth-eaft of the coaft of *Coroman-del*, in the gulf of *Bengale* It likewife comprehends feven different kingdoms, the chief of which is that of *Kandee* Its moft confiderable cities are, *Kandee*, *Columbo*, *Punte-Gale*, *Zegombo*, *Jaffnapatnam*, and *Baticalo*

The firft day of the year 1706, I went to pay the cuftomary civilities to the governor, who received me in a very obliging manner On the third, letters arrived from the governor of *Columbo*, with orders to fend away our fhip without any other company, though we had agreed with two others to return together to *Batavia* We fet fail on the 5th, after having taken leave of the governor

1705

C H A P. LXIV.

The author's departure from Gale. *The ifle of* Engano *The coaft of* Zillabar *The ftreights of* Sunda *The author's arrival at* Batavia *The civility of the general of the* Indies

I WENT on board the 6th of *January*, about fix in the morning, at which time the treafurer came to take a view of our loading, and when he had fatisfied himfelf in that particular, we weighed anchor, the wind being north north-weft, we fteered, at firft, fouthward, and then to fouth by eaft, with a favourable wind, which changed in the night, and then ceafed on a fudden. The next day we loft fight of the ifle of *Ceilon*, proceeding fouth-eaft by eaft, with variable weather, accompanied with rain, and ftormy-winds, which obliged us to lower our top-maft On the 13th at night we had a view of the north ftar before us, which was a very extraordinary circumftance, becaufe it is very feldom

feen by thofe who advance toward the line; and efpecially in bad weather The 18th the wind fhifted to north weft, and we fteered our courfe fouth-eaft by eaft, and paffed the equinoctial line to 31 minutes of fouth latitude, and the longitude of 124 degrees, and 32 minutes. The 19th the wind being at weft-fouth-weft, we continued our courfe to fouth-eaft by fouth, in 38 minutes, and the 20th we came into 1 degree 45 minutes, and about morning, the wind being weft-north-weft, and blowing a frefh gale, into two degrees 8 minutes, fteering our coaft fouth-eaft by eaft, favoured by fine weather, which lafted all the next day, but then changed, and continued bad to the end of *January*

At

Les Isles du Passage et

Pointe du Bantam, Côte di

L'Isle Longue, la Montagne Bleue i

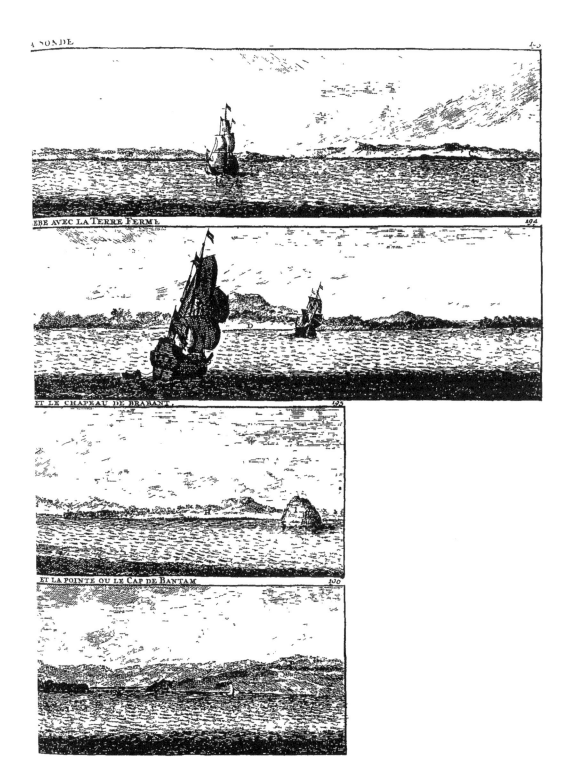

ÈBE AVEC LA TERRE FERME   *194*

ET LE CHAPEAU DE BRABANT.   *195*

ET LA POINTE OU LE CAP DE BANTAM   *196*

1706 At the beginning of *February* it grew fine again, and we had hot weather, with fome calms But on the 4th the wind varied, and the sky grew cloudy, which made us hope for a change, for we greatly feared the calms, which might have retarded our voyage for a long time The wind rifing at fouth-weft, we continued our courfe fouth-caft by eaft The 5th, the wind continuing favourable to us, we came into 4 degrees 32 minutes fouth latitude, and the weather changed a little after, otherwife we might have difcovered land, fteering continually fouth-eaft We afterward had thick, heavy weather, and much rain in the night, both which are very ufual on the weftern coaft of the *Indies* in winter We, however, continued our courfe eaft-fouth-eaft, making little fail, becaufe we were near land We at laft came into 4 degrees 38 minutes of fouth latitude, and into the longitude of 127 degrees 25 minutes, where we were driven up and down by ftorms till the 11th of the month, when the wind fhifted to fouth-weft, from whence it blew with great violence About noon we found ourfelves in 5 degrees 3 minutes, always fteering eaft-fouth-eaft, the weather being wet and cloudy, we likewife founded, but found no bottom We had feen in the evening fome white gulls, which, the feamen fay, is a fign that one is not far from land, becaufe they never fly far from the fhore The next day we faw another, and proceeded in the night to weft-fouth-weft, making but little fail, till at length, having been tofled about for fome time by changeable wind, we difcovered the ifle of *Engano* to fouth-weft, at the diftance of feven or eight leagues, and on one fide of us, the mountains of the high land of *Zillabar* at north-eaft

We continued our courfe between them with great fatisfaction, for having difcovered land, after we had fo long wifhed for that fight, we then failed firft to eaft-fouth-eaft, the weather continually changing, and being gener-

ally rainy, we then fteered to fouth- 1706. eaft by eaft, and at length to eaft, and to eaft by north When we were about feven leagues from the eaftern coaft, the men founded, but found no bottom at eighty fathom. The 16th we difcovered high land at north-eaft, being about five leagues from the coaft, and found ourfelves toward *The Impe-* noon in the latitude of 6 degrees 15 *rial ifland* minutes We afterward faw the *Imperial* ifland, to eaft-north-eaft, at fix or feven leagues from the cape. We then directed our courfe eaftward, being favoured with very fine weather, and the wind blew fo briskly toward evening, that we approached the ftreights of *Sunda*, where we found feveral pieces of floating wood, with birds upon them We then fteered eaft by fouth, with cloudy weather, and unexpectedly *The* found ourfelves on the 17th, with- *Prince's* in a quarter of a league of the *Prince's ifland* ifland The mafter of the fhip was the firft who perceived it, which greatly furprized him, and not without reafon, becaufe we fhould infallibly have run afhore, if the weather had not fuddenly cleared up. Two or three men, who had been ordered to look out carefully, were punifhed for their negligence on this occafion We then tacked about immediately to north-weft, and north-weft by weft, and found by founding, that we were three leagues from the point, having been carried back by a ftrong tide fince the laft founding, eight leagues and a half to fouth-weft, though we had been favoured by a good wind from the weft during the night A refolution was then taken to proceed without delay to fouth-weft, while we had it in our power, and this was immediately put in execution. We then advanced to fouth-foutheaft, in order to double the weftern point, and then kept to eaft-northeaft, till by fteering in this manner, we came about two in the afternoon to the fartheft point of the ifland of *Java*, where we found forty-two fathom water upon a bottom of thick fand, covered with fhells and small

1706 small hints The wind, by good fortune, favoured us, and had it not been for this advantage, we might possibly have been obliged to put into some neighbouring port for two or three months, in order to wait for a favourable gale

The Streight of Sunda.

This streight of *Sunda* is about a league and a half in breadth, within thirty seven or thirty eight leagues of *Batavia*, forming a passage from the *Indian* sea to the south, between the coast of the island of *Sumatra* to south-east, and the western side of the island of *Java*, on which the city of *Bantam* is situated When we had made some advance into this streight, I drew the prospect which was then presented to me The *Prince's* island lying north of *Java*, and this latter bearing to the south, beyond which is seen another island at a great distance, but not quite so high, and the name of it is the *New Island* I have represented this view in plate 193 where the *Prince's* island is distinguished by the letter A, that of *Java* by B, and the *New Island* by C The depth of water is from thirty to forty fathom in this streight, but sailors cannot find any bottom at the entrance on the other side, to the north of the *Prince's* island, where the streight opens to a great breadth At sun-set we continued our course east-north-east, about three quarters of a league from land, the wind being north-west, but blowing very moderately, and the tide was also against us The wind changed in the night, after which we were becalm'd, and had showers of rain. The weather likewise continued thick for some days, but this did not prevent us from proceeding to the fourth point, which lies north-east about two leagues from *Krackatouw* Some fishermen of that coast advanced toward us, and we sent out our sloop in order to be supplied with some refreshments from them Some of them came on board, and brought us several *Pampes*, a species of small flat fish, together with some *Masbankers*, another little flat-fish, which is none of the best They furnished us likewise with several sorts of fruits, and, among the rest, *Kaffers*, which are round, and red, and very like sea-chesnuts, only they are smaller than those, and covered with prickles This fruit grows in large clusters, like grapes, with small stalks, they have also a large kernel, which resembles a plumb-stone, and the flavour has a sweetness tempered with acidity, which is not disagreeable to the taste They brought us also another sort of fruit called *Lanp*, which is very round, and its colour an intermixture of yellow and red, not unlike an *Abricot*, and it grows in the manner of grapes beside these, our fishermen supplied us with young *Arecks*, and *Betelsbladeren*, or leaves of the betel, of which I shall treat more largely in my description of *Batavia*. The 19th we had unsettled weather, and steered our course north by east, and to north-north-east, and the wind and tide being against us, obliged us to anchor about noon in twenty fathom water We, however, soon set sail again with a favourable wind, bearing to north-north-east, and to north-east by north, but did not continue long in this course We cast anchor again on this side the point of *Bantam*, which lay north-east by north, at the distance of a league and a half The wind changed frequently in the night, and abundance of rain fell We sailed again in the morning, and continued our course to north and north by east, in nineteen, twenty two, and twenty three fathom water, but were obliged to come to anchor again about noon, in sight of several high islands. In the afternoon, the wind shifting to south-west, we came about evening into the latitude of the point of *Bantam*, at north-east by north, being then about two leagues from land We then cast anchor again, not daring to advance amidst the darkness of the night, lest we should run upon one of the islands, we had likewise much thunder and lightening The 21st, the wind

1706

blew

1706 blew against us at north-east, and the tides were so strong, that we found it impossible to advance In the morning we were supplied by a bark from Jccr, with fruits, and a parcel of lean crackers We had the point of *Bantam* to the north-east, and the isle called *Toppers-hoedt-je*, at north-east by north, about a league and a half from us. In the afternoon, the wind shifting to the south-west, we set sail again with a favourable tide, and steer'd our course north-east by north We came in the evening to the point of *Karac-katouw*, which was about a league and a half from us to the north-north-east, and about two leagues from the isle of *Toppers-hoedt-je* As soon as it grew dark, we perceived some fires upon land, and had several flashes of lightening About ten o'the clock we were becalmed, and obliged to cast anchor in twenty seven fathom water, but that calm was immediately followed by a violent storm

On the 22d I drew two beautiful prospects, the first of which is exhibited in plate 194 where D marks out the isle of *Passage* E that of *Selebes*, and F the northern side of the continent of the inner western coast The point of *Bantam* is represented at the letter G, in plate 195 together with the coast of *Java* at H, and the *Chapeau de Bra-bant* at I There is likewise a view of all the mountains, and islands filled with trees, which form a very agreeable prospect. We had then the point of *Bantam* to the north-east, and the *Chapeau de Brabant* to the north north-east, about a league and a half from us, and toward noon we perceived a *Batavian* vessel under sail, with a bark belonging to the company The vessel was a *Dutch* pink, on her return to *Europe* As soon as we saw their flag, we hoisted ours, and sent our sloop out to enquire after news, she on her part sent two pilots on board us, who did not stay long, and in the mean time the company's bark arrived, according to custom, to exa-

mine and take an account of the 1706 ships which arrive in that sea. The master of the bark ordered the captain of our ship, on the part of the magistrate of *Batavia*, to send his clerk on shore with the company's letters, upon which he immediately obeyed, and we then set sail again with a westerly wind We had the point of *Bantam* at east by south and the *Chapeau de Brabant* at west-south-west Advancing in thirty two fathom water, about eleven at night, we anchor'd in sixteen fathom, beyond the point of *Bantam*, 18 leagues from *Batavia*. The 23d at break of day we hoisted sail again, the wind being at west-north-west, and blowing with a brisk gale. We then discovered the Gulf of Bantam gulf of *Bantam*, which extends itself to a great length

On one side of this gulf we had a view of *Long-Island*, which we left The blue mountain on the right. We had also a prospect of the blue mountain, which is very high. This is represented in A description of that quarter plate 196 in which *Long-Island*, otherwise called *Pen-Panjang*, is exhibited at K, the blue-mountain at L, the gulf of *Bantam* at M, and the point of *Bantam* at N. We passed by that city, in which we could partly distinguish the highest buildings We had *Baby* to the north- Baby north-west, at the distance of about a league and a half, and we steered with a wind from north-west, and from south-west, to east-north-east, and east by south, in ten, twelve, and fifteen fathom water This part of the sea has several islands, where we were often obliged to anchor by reason of the calms At last we approached *Batavia* the 24th. The commander *Broueg* came to meet us in his bark, and brought me the agreeable news that I was expected by the governor-general, Monsieur de *Hoorn*, who had received notice of my coming by letters from Monsieur *Witsen*, burgo-master of *Amsterdam*

The commander offer'd me a The author's arrival at Batavia passage in his bark to the city, where we arrived about ten, and were in-

formed

formed that the governor was gone to pass the day at a country seat M *de Garlegh* was so good as to lend me his chariot to carry me thither The way to it was exceedingly agreeable, being bordered with trees, and pleasure-houses on each side The house to which I went was not above half a league from the city I met with good company there, and the governor in particular received me with open

arms, and invited me to dine with him In the evening we all returned to the city, and I lodged in the castle with him He gave me a packet of letters, in which there was one from the burgo-master *Witsen*, dated the first of *May* 1705 After supper I was conducted to my apartment, where I immediately went to bed, being much fatigued, and indisposed

---

CHAP. LXV.

The author's indisposition. The inhabitants of the South A rigorous punishment Extraordinary fruits Chinese comedies The director general's pleasure-house.

MY indisposition increased to such a degree, as obliged me to keep my chamber M *Brouer*, the company's first physician, attended me, by order of the governor-general, and gave me hopes of recovering my health in a few days, nor was he deceived, for he had such good success, that I was in a condition to walk out the beginning of *March* I had not the least relish either for wine or beer since my sickness at *Gamron*, and had drank nothing but water, and sometimes a little brandy But the refreshments with which I was now supplied, recovered my appetite, and I began to print several *Indian* fruits, which afforded me an agreeable amusement As soon as my health was a little improved, I went to visit M *Outhoorn*, who formerly had been governor-general of the *Indies*, and he received me in a very obliging manner He was about seventy years old, and very healthy and vigorous for his age. He had likewise executed that important charge for the space of thirteen years, and then quitted it with no other view

than to pass the rest of his life in peace and tranquility I had a long conversation with him, which proved very satisfactory to us both, and he made me promise to visit him frequently, and show him all the curiosities I had then in my possession. I afterward visited M *de Riebeek*, director-general of the company, and the general *de Wilde*, together with some members of the council of the *Indies*, as also M *Garsin*, first secretary to the company, who all received me with great civility, and especially my old friend M *Hooghamer*, who had formerly been ambassador to the court of *Persia*, and was then vice-president of the council of justice, and I took this opportunity to renew my acquaintance with that gentleman

Some days after I went to pay a visit to M *de Roy*, major of the citadel, where I found four men, whom a ship, called the *Pincon*, had taken from the southern coast, with two or three women, who were permitted to enjoy their liberty These savages, who were six in all, had been brought to *Batavia*, from

HOMME SAUVAGE DU SUD

1706 from whence two of them escaped, and the other four remained in the service of the company, who sent them aboard their ships in order to learn our language, and that some account might be obtained from them of their own country, to which they were intended to be sent back after they had made those discoveries which were then wanted. They were treated in this manner, that they might have an opportunity of representing the humanity of the company to their fellow native, and to induce them to engage in a commerce with our nation, for till then they had never permitted strangers to enter their country, and the ship of which I have been speaking, was the first that ever arrived on that coast.

These savages had something so peculiar in their air, that I had an inclination to paint one with his bow and arrow in his hand, agreeably to their manner, and as may be seen in plate 197. They have no other covering than a slight cincture of cloth round their waist, and which hangs down a little before. They have also a small ivory bracelet round their left arm. I took one of their bows, and several arrows which I have kept by me. Their letter are made of cane, some larger than others, and have a great many points which render the wound they make very dangerous, but their extreme slenderness prevents them from going very far.

A scene of punishment   Several of those were executed about that time, and two of those unhappy wretches had their flesh torn off with red hot pincers, after which they were broken upon the wheel.

The former governor sent me his chariot to convey me to a pleasure-house which he had without the city. I passed some hours there very agreeably, and shewed him part of the designs I had taken in *Persia*, with which he seemed very well satisfied. In the evening I returned to *Batavia*, and on the 30th of *March* a galley called the *Noghtte*,

set sail from thence with the company's letters. I took this opportunity to write to my friends.

I had already painted several species of fruits, which the reader will find exhibited in plate 198, where A is a certain fruit called *Frot Kas*, the flavour of which is sweet, and the colour a beautiful red, it has likewise a great resemblance to the sea-chesnut, and the tree has very large leaves. B a fruit called *Mangustans*, which has an agreeable sweetness, and is likewise very salutary. The size of it is equal to that of a *China* orange. It is also white within, and cover'd on the outside with a chesnut brown. C represents two *Goyaves* ripe and open, the fruit is red within, and it resembles a water melon. On one side are exhibited others of the species, which are small and green, together with their leaves. This fruit is certainly very pleasant and is about two inches in diameter when ripe. D represents another fruit called *Klapper Royal*, the juice of which is very pleasant, and there are several sorts, this is properly the cocoa-nut, which is about the size of a melon, and has a white pulp within, which adheres to the shell, and is good to eat. E is placed at a fruit called *Frota Rottan*, which is very grateful to the taste, and much esteemed, it has likewise a bright violet colour, spotted with brown. F exhibits an orange called *Piepienje*, or rather a large cucumber, with its blossom and leaves. G a red and white *Jamboes*, with its foliage, this fruit much resembles a peach in its flavour, and on the side of it are drawn two of a smaller kind. A in plate 169, marks out a fruit called *Ta natu*, the cort of which resembles a shell. This fruit is beautifully tinged with red on the outside, and full of kernels like a cucumber, its flavour is likewise agreeable, especially in sauces. B an *Annona*, whose outside is grey and rough while the fruit continues unripe, but it afterwards assumes a violet colour, and is something bigger than an orange. the flavour of this

1706 this fruit is agreeable enough The leaves are about the length of one's finger C represents a large citron full of a delicious juice, inclosed in a very thin rind D exhibits two *Pompelmoses*, one large and entire, the other opened This fruit is red within, but there are some of a white hue, and which have fewer kernels Its flavour and scent resemble those of a *Chine* orange, it is shaped like a melon E represents a sweet and pleasant fruit, called *Fiesang*, which the inhabitants peel like a fig It has a green texture before it is ripe, but this deepens into a yellow when the fruit has attained its due maturity It is about five inches in length, and at the top rises a flower blended with violet and red, and which falls when the fruit is ripe The stalk produces another flower a foot and an inch in length, and five inches in diameter This flower is tinged with a violet colour, intermixed with red and blue The leaves of the tree which bears this fruit are about two fathom in length, and one in breadth, they likewise glow with a deep red on one side, and between them and the flowers from whence the fruit springs, one sees a profusion of other long flowers, some yellow, others blue and red, and they form a most agreeable view The trunk of the tree is not above three fathom high, but the thickness of it is very confiderable The rind is full of sap, and they stew the inside like cabbage

Chinese comedies I went about this time to see a theatrical performance in the *Chinese* manner The stages are erected in the street, and front the houses of those who give these entertainments, or contribute to the expence on that occasion. I observed in the vestible of one of these houses, a large high table covered with all sorts of provisions, finely disposed, as well wild-fowl as fish, and among the rest a hog's head split There were likewise confections, and other delicacies, on one side of which were a great number of round flat loaves

heap'd up one upon another A little higher (for this table had the form of an altar) were all sorts of fruits, embellished with flowers, and before the table a man stood in the habit of an ecclesiastic, with an open book in his hand, adorned with very extraordinary figures, the place was likewise finely illuminated: The person I last mentioned frequently threw pieces of copper on the ground, and then resumed his reading He was likewise joined by a second actor, who made several motions, which seemed to express some of their sacred ceremonials, and gave me reason to believe, that the piece they were then performing had an intermixture of religious worship. However, as they all continued silent, I went to another theatre, where the performance was already begun This structure resembled the other, but was not altogether so magnificent Eight or ten actors appeared upon the stage in comic habits, and among the rest two women, who alternately sung and spoke Every one of these persons uttered soliloquies at particular intervals, with extraordinary gestures and contortions of body The performance closed with a circular dance, and the actors retired in good order, moving to the musick of their own instruments Among other things were several basons, which they struck one against another, agreeably to the manner practised at *Ispahan*, these were accompanied with a clang of lesser basons, intermixed with the modulation of soft flutes, and the theatre was illuminated with *Chinese* lamps and candles. When I went from thence, I returned to the place from whence I came, and where the performance was also begun The actors were more numerous, and the theatre was likewise larger than the other These representations are exhibited in most parts of the city, and continue all night, some beginning sooner in the evening, others later, and they continue from the beginning of *March* to the end of *April* They represent

1706

fent

sent the adventures and history of the antients, as well in tragedy as comedy, as is the practice among us, and I was informed, that all the actors in these pieces were maidens in disguise I have frequently seen performances of this nature in the *Indies*, but am apt to think they are executed to more advantage in *China*

The next day the director-general *Riebeek* invited me to accompany him into the country, and we accordingly went out of the city in a chariot, but afterward mounted on horseback, because we found the roads very bad We passed over part of his lands before we arrived at his country-seat, which was about a league and a half from *Batavia* I found the soil which lies nearest to the city of different colours, and rising in several little hillocks, which form a very agreeable prospect All the lands which belonged to the director were covered with rice, which, instead of being mowed, is cut down at the proper season, with a small sickle As this production is sown at different times, it is ripe in some places before it is quite green in others He had also planted a great number of fruit, and other trees, which were not yet come to per-

The direc t r gene ral s coun try house

fection. His house was all finished, except the stables and kitchen, upon which they were at work every day He told me that he employed above an hundred oxen in the cultivation of his land, and other rural works We returned in the evening to the city, along the river side, where a great number of delightful seats are built, as in our country I found myself very much fatigued at my return, being still very weak, and I began to be much incommoded by the heat, as well as by several small pimples which came out all over my body. But this is a common disorder in that country, it is even counted very wholsome, and I really found my self better. The worst circumstance which attends this distemper is, that it indisposes one from sleeping, and, indeed, it is impossible for those who are seized with it to rest above two or three hours in a day There is an easy method of curing it, but the remedy is worse than the disease, because it exposes one to great danger, by driving the pimples in My sight did not grow any better, so that I was always obliged to use spectacles, but age, perhaps, might contribute very much to this defect

---

CHAP. LXVI.

Pleasure-houses in the parts adjacent to Batavia. *The manners of the* Baliers *Pepper-plants Vast numbers of apes. The rejoicings occasioned by the taking of* Batavia

A little journey of the author s to the estate of Mr Kastelein

I HAD again some fits of my fever toward the end of *April*, but they did not prevent me from accompanying a few friends to Mr. *Kastelein's* estate He waited for us with a coach and two horses at a small distance from the city, and at a place called *Wellevret*, a little

beyond the fortress of *Noortwick*. The domesticks were gone before to the *Corps de garde* of Mr *Corneille*, about three quarters of a league from thence. This is a square wooden building, surrounded with a quickset-hedge, and has some resemblance to a fort, having a high centry-box

Vol II

box on each point toward the plain Here is commonly stationed a guard of thirty or forty soldiers, commanded by a lieutenant or ensign We were seven in number, with three domesticks, guarded by five or six *Indians* on horseback, and eighteen *Bahers* on foot armed with long pikes, among which were two streaked with black, and finely adorned with gold at the extremity, the rest were red embellished with silver Most of them wore a large dagger at their girdle, like the *Ganjaers* of the *Turks* These *Bahers* are natives of an island, which lies to the east of *Java*, and they have the reputation of being the most warlike people of that quarter, chusing rather to suffer death than shrink a step from their enemies, forty or fifty of them will often put to flight two hundred of the *Indians* of the isle of *Java* This quality is accompanied with an assiduity, and inflexible fidelity to those masters who use them well, for they are not to be treated with severity When we had proceeded about half a league on our journey, we came to the suggar-mills of a *Chinese* named *Tansianko,* upon the great river *Tjulican*, or the river of women, which in some places is eight or ten fathoms wide, and in others not above two We dined there in a very agreeable house, with a handsome garden belonging to it, and continued there till three o'clock I here found some butterflies of a surprising beauty, and have preserved a dozen of them We had sent away our domesticks and horses before us, that they might pass the river before our arrival there, in order to gain time, and we followed with three chariots, each of which was drawn by a buffalo, which we were obliged to change three times in an hour, the ways were so very bad and rugged When we came to the river I have already mentioned, we were obliged to pass over it in little boats, made of the bark of a tree, and, an hour after, we arrived at Mr *Kastelein*'s country seat at *Se-*

ring-sing It is situated upon the declivity of a point which projects from a hill, and from whence one enjoys a full view of the great river. This point much resembles an amphitheatre, the seat upon it is entirely built of wood, very neatly compacted together, and raised upon a good foundation of stone, which advances three feet above the ground This situation was chosen in order to preserve the building, and secure it from rotting, and being infested with white ants The house is two stories high, the first of which is inhabited by the domesticks, and is used as a conservatory for all the provisions The second story is reserved for the master of the house, and it contains a fine hall, with a small apartment on each side, together with a large one fronting the entrance into the court. Under this is a room furnished with seats, for the use of the servants, and over it is a place open at the top, and glazed on the sides, for the use of those who play on *Bahers*, which instruments I shall hereafter describe This edifice is square, and surrounded with wood painted green On each of its sides is another building, one of which serves for a kitchen, and has likewise two small chambers for the slaves The other is the magazine, where the rice is deposited, and it has likewise two small chambers for the servants Behind the magazine is a large hen-house, and a stall for cattle There is likewise a spacious yard for poultry, surrounded with a quick-set hedge, and a fine gate is intended to be built at the entrance into this place On the right of this yard, is a piece of ground covered over, for the accommodation of passengers with a shelter, and the chariots and other carriages are likewise set up here The garden is on the east-side of the house, and has a descent of thirty-six feet toward the river, together with thirty six steps divided into three flights The first consists of fourteen steps, and is furnished with seats for the conveniency of those

who

PLANTE D UN POIVRIER

1706 who have an inclination to reft themfelves   The fecond has twelve fteps, the feats like thofe of the former, and the third has ten, at the bottom of which is a paffage over a little bridge, to a place of eafement on the river.   Thefe fteps are railed on each fide in a very elegant manner   There is likewife another defcent, like that already defcribed, toward the river, and on the north-fide of the houfe, together with fteps of the fame ftructure with the others   On the edge of the water is a fummer-houfe, and at the end of the garden a fine hall, where the mafter of the houfe ufually dines, and which commands an inchanting profpect   There is likewife another hall raifed on pillars, upon the bank of the river, and from whence there is a communication with the preceding by a fmall bridge, handfomely railed, and a defcent to the river is alfo formed by a flight of fteps   This feat is reprefented in plate 200.   There is a place over the gate, where the muficians feat themfelves when they perform upon their inftruments, as they frequently do ten, or twelve, or fourteen fometimes in a band, to entertain company   Their mufick confifts in ftriking feveral bafons one againft another, in conjunction with the beat of drums, and the found of pipes   They have alfo a kind of a harp, and a large tabor, which ferves for a bafe, and is ftruck only with one ftick   They, however, form a harmony not difagreeable to the ear.

After we had been fufficiently diverted in this place, we mounted our horfes, in order to accompany our hoft to his eftate at *Manpang*, and *Depok*, which lie fouthward of the feat I have been defcribing   In our way thither, we paffed over feveral fields full of fugar, and *Sering-fing*, a fmall plant like a reed, from whence the country received its name, and which fhoots out even on the trees   We then entered a wood newly planted, and covered with fhort grafs, that makes the moft

agreeable appearance in the world; 1706. it is likewife difpofed into beautiful alleys   When we had travelled a league, we came to the fource of a fmall river fhaded with thick trees, where travellers often ftop to enjoy the frefh air, and repofe themfelves. Half a league from thence we entered upon the lands of *Depok*, in a valley through which the great river flows   I there faw two pepper *Pepper* plants, which grow round poles, or *plants* green props, like beans in our country, at the diftance of fix feet from one another, and the poles are about eighteen feet high.

As the rays of the fun cannot penetrate their foliage, one may walk in their fhade during the greateft heats.   The pepper fprings out in clufters that refemble a growth of goosberries, and the grains are green at firft,   but afterward affume an orange colour, which proceeds from a fhell that enfolds them, and which peals off when rubbed in the hands, the pepper which then remains being of a white hue.   I gathered a fmall branch from this plant,   and the reader may fee it reprefented in plate 201

After dinner we went down the river in a fmall canoe, and found the current run with great violence over a rocky, flinty bottom, notwithftanding the winding flow of the river. We arrived in two hours at *Sering-fing*, having paffed by feveral cottages inhabited by *Negroes*.   The banks of the river are very fteep, and bordered with trees   We there *Aøes* faw abundance of apes, on the branches, as well as on the earth, which was covered with them. Moft of thefe animals are grey, but we faw a few that were black   Several of the fame fpecies are likewife to be found in the woods.

I drew two *Balters*, who were *Balters* flaves to Mr. *Kaftelein*, with the drefs they wore in this as well as in their own country   They fold part of their habit, which is ufually made of a ftriped ftuff, round their waift, to which they faften it by one end, and fuffer the reft to flow
down

1706 down to their feet. The upper part of their attire, which is of a different colour, covers their breast, and then descends to their knees. They generally have a handkerchief in their hand, and their hair is plaited into a point on the upper part of the head. Their arms and feet are naked, as may be seen in plate 202. The 203d plate represents them in the habit they wear on horseback, a black mantle being cast over their body, and their head covered with flowered linnen, and a red hat. They have likewise a handkerchief in their hand, on this as well as on other occasions.

When we had passed some time in that place, I took my leave of Mr *Kastelein*, who was so obliging as to lend me two slaves, who were to be my guides, one on foot, and the other on horseback. I again crossed the river, in order to proceed to *Batavia*, through the woods, which is the best way, *Sering-sing* being but five leagues distant from that city. At my return a blast of thunder fell upon a house, which received great damage from that casualty.

The author returns to Batavia

I determined at that time not to engage myself any farther in the *Indies*, contrary to my first intention, which was to visit all the coast of *Coromandel*, in order to discover the antiquities, customs, and religion of those parts. But I found my self too weak for an expedition of that nature, and was likewise apprehensive of a relapse into my former illness, having had some fits of my fever at *Sering-sing*. I was therefore in no condition to bear the fa-

The author's resolution

tigue and inconvenience of so long 1706 a voyage, and had need of rest for the recovery of my health, and to qualify me for my return by land. I had also some other reasons, which shall be mentioned by and by.

The 30th of *May*, being the anniversary of the taking of *Batavia* in 1619, under the conduct of general *Koen*, was celebrated by a festival, according to custom. The governor general gave a magnificent entertainment to the members of the council of the *Indies*, and the magistrates of the city, who were elected that day. Two counsellors of justice were also invited, together with two of the principal merchants; four ministers, and several private persons, among whom I was one. The rejoicings began on *Sunday* about five in the evening.

Rejoicings on the anniversary the taking of Batavia

In the general's court was placed a long table, with chairs for that officer, and the members of the council of the *Indies*. The rest of the company disposed themselves according to their respective ranks, but in a standing posture, tho' there were several seats in the court. They drank prosperity to the city, and its magistrates, the cannon firing at the same time from the citadel, ramparts, forts, the neighbouring isles, and from the ships which lay in the road. Part of the citizens also appear'd under arms, fifteen in each company, with colours flying, and there were six of these companies in the whole. There was also a body of horse, headed by the proper officers. The company at last broke up, after they had partaken of a very splendid entertainment.

CHAP.

CHAP. LXVII.

The situation of the isle of Edam *Remarkable fishes A* Chinese *feast. The manner of preparing sugar, indigo, &c*

Isle of E-dam

THE weather was hot and rainy at the beginning of *June*, and then I went to the isle of *Edam*, about five leagues from *Batavia* General *Kamphuisen*, to whom it had belonged, consigned it at his death to the present general of the *Indies* In our passage thither we met a vessel coming from *Amboyna* with the late governor of that colony, whose name was *Coyet* Our pilot was intrusted with the direction of affairs in the isle of *Edam*, where ships are sometimes obliged to

Onrus

stop, or else at that of * *Sans-repos*, till the arrival of new orders He enjoin d the master of that vessel to go into the road of *Batavia*, and he immediately obeyed

This isle is half a league in circumference, the shore is covered with stones and coral, and the inland part of the country with fruit and other trees There is also a good promontory which shoots out into the sea, to a considerable length, and beyond it is another, upon which the deceased general built a handsome house with two facades, and a flight of stairs on each side. This was the usual place of his residence, and he took great pleasure in collecting plants, and productions of the sea. The same curiosity drew

Remark able fish

me thither, and I had the good fortune to take some remarkable fish, which I failed not to delineate, having provided myself with cloth, and colours for that purpose, and likewise with spirit of wine for the preserving these creatures I took,

Sea cray-fish

among others, a sea cray-fish of a surprising bigness, a beautiful colour, and finely spotted, together with a

A crab

crab near the same size, coloured with a bluish brown, intermixed with white spots The two claws

Vol II

were tinged with a bright purple variegated with white, and covered with little prickles The feet, which were almost blue, were shagged with small prickles, which were red within, and others of a white complexion, rose on the body The reader will find five of these fish represented in plate 204, from the life That which is distinguished by the letter A, is called

The box-fish

Ikam-peti, which signifies the Box-*fish* It is almost square, flat on each side, and hard as wood, and the colour is yellow, spotted with black On each side of the head is a small fin, and another on the body near the tail That which is marked with B, is blue, and has a circle of golden yellow round its eyes, and a streak of the same colour upon one part of its body: The mouth is full of teeth, the eyes are large, and black, and the tail is coloured with a violet dye, blended with yellow and white This little fish is called *Ikam-batoe*, or the *Stone-fish*, because it generally shrouds itself among stones and rocks The letter C exhibits a very small fish, of a beautiful red, with three blue streaks, bordered with black on the body. The largest that I ever saw of this kind was not above two inches long It has one small red fin, which, together with the tail, that is coloured in the same manner, makes a very beautiful effect My fisherman brought me three of this species, which usually swim together in that number, and are easily seen in that water, which is altogether as clear as chrystal, and the bottom itself may be discovered without any difficulty This fish is not called by any particular name D shews another small flat fish, whose length exceeds his breadth, the body has a bluish cast on

C c the

the upper part, and toward the belly, but all the rest of it is brown Round the head is a black circle, out of which the eyes project, the throat is black both within and without, and all the space between the mouth and eyes is of a beautiful yellow, as is also the tail It is without a name, as well as the former That which is exhibited at the letter E, is called *Ikam-ka se*, or the *Wood-fish*, because it delights in streams shaded with trees It is of a bright blue, but has the back tinged with yellow, the body is likewise mark'd with four large brown streaks, which are not extended to the belly It has also one pointed fin upon its back, another between that and its tail, and two at the belly. A, in plate 205, marks out a small round fish, called *Ikam-bato*, or the *Rock-fish*, and it resembles one of the former It is of a reddish blue, and has seven or eight little blue streaks on the body, the nether part of which is black Its short and white tail is formed like a pair of scissars, with a little red streak toward the end, on each side of its head is a fin dyed with yellow and blue The body of this fish, which has some resemblance to a plaice, is a dusky blue, the flavour of the flesh is very agreeable, and the skin is extremely thick B marks a *Ikam-tamar*, or kind of carp, the colour of whose body is an intermixture of red and white, and part of the head glows with a fine red Out of the mouth issue two points, which are two inches in length, it has two red fins under its belly, and a third extends from thence to the tail There are likewise two upon the back with sharp points, and one on each side of its head, red and white like the tail, which parts into several sharp extremities This fish is about a foot and four inches long, from which one may judge of the others, that are represented in miniature in the same plate C points to an *Ikam-Kapak*, which signifies a *Stonebream* This fish has the top and each side of its head of a fine red

The rock-fish (margin)
Carp (margin)
Stonebream (margin)

and the under part mixed with blue and white, the body is blue, with large streaks of a violet hue, and red fins D marks an *Ikam-garga-sie*, or *Saw-fish*, the body of which is of a clear blue, streaked with brown and black, the belly is white, and the mouth yellow, as are also the fins, especially that which is upon the back, the whole is sprinkled over with black spots, and the points of its fins are as sharp as a saw It has likewise a yellow tail, spotted with black E is an *Ikam-boeian*, or *Bird-fish*, which is white, and formed like a plaice, with two large black streaks on the body, from between which there comes out a white kind of a streamer, pointed at the end, and a foot in length, the lower part of the body and the tail are yellow, as are also the fins, which grow out from the black streaks, the head is small and pointed There are but few fish of this species

F marks an *Ikam-maes*, or *Gold-fish*, it is of a bright blue, with red streaks along its body, and spotted with yellow, which looks like gold, the fins and tail are red, yellow, and white, and the top of the head all red

G represents an *Ikam-kakatoua*, so called from a bird of the same name and colour It is of a transparent bluish green, and has several reddish spots, which resemble network, and a yellow spot on each side the head, which is red and green The fin upon the back is of a fine green, intermixed with blue and yellow, those on the sides are green and blue like varnish, and that which is under the body has a yellow cast I omitted taking notice that the cray-fish I mentioned before was all green, except the tip of the head, which was red, as were also the two large horns which come out of it, and are four inches long, and three quarters of an inch in breadth, at the extremity of these are two other horns, which are a foot and seven inches long, and likewise another pair, which are but half

1706 (margin)
Saw-fish (margin)
Bird-fish (margin)
Gold-fish (margin)
Ikam kakatoua (margin)

half as long as the former, and are contorted at the end, one being white, and the other almost entirely black. This cray-fish had all the upper part of his body full of black and white spots and streaks, as well as the tail, and two large yellow and white streaks upon the sides. The feet were long and pliant, and finely streak'd with green, black, yellow, and white It was a foot and five inches in length, but there are some of a smaller size, and they afford an admirable relish I painted all these fishes from the life, and have preserved some of them in spirits This cray-fish is represented at the letter H, and the crab at I I found also some flying insects in this island, and among the rest several butterflies. But they have nothing singular in them

As I commonly accompanied the fishers, when the weather was fine, and as the water is so clear and transparent, that one may see the bottom, I found several short branches of coral I even undress'd myself sometimes, that I might advance farther into the sea, and gather some of these productions I was then convinced that coral is formed of a certain thick slime produced by the sea, and which fastens to the rocks, and then hardens, and grows into the form in which we now see it. It appeared very beautiful under the water while it was liquid, and was tinged with a fine yellow, mixed with white and brown, I pulled off several pieces from the rocks in that condition, in hopes they would preserve their beauty and colour by drying in the sun, but the event proved otherwise, and they changed to a deep dirty brown, nor could I attain to the art of drying them in any perfection

The isles of Alcmaer, Frikhuisen, and Leiden After I had dispatched all my affairs in this island, I embarked, in order to return to *Batavia*, and passed by the island of *Alcmaer*, which lies nearest to that of *Edam*. That of *Enkhuisen* lies a little more to the south, that of *Leiden* in the midway, *Of Hoorn and Smith* and that of *Hoorn* over-against

this last This is inhabited by fishermen, and the isle of *Smith* lies on one side of it toward the south As the wind was fair for us, I arrived in a short time at *Batavia*. 1706.

At my return I took a walk with our governor-general through the city, to see some new buildings, which he had lately caused to be erected; and in the way thither I observed green boughs upon the houses of the *Chinese*, which were shut that day, by reason of the feast of *Phelonaphie*, which they celebrated at that time

I had before observed in the port, *The feast of Phelonaphie among the Chinese* several neat barks full of *Chinese*, who were all in motion on account of the feast, the origin of which is as follows

The *Chinese* have a particular regard for those who have signalized themselves in the service of their country, or made any discoveries advantageous to the publick, and celebrate their memory after their death A certain man, called *Phelo*, *The discovery of salt by one Phelo* having first made a discovery of salt, and not receiving any acknowledgment, took umbrage and retir'd, nor could they ever learn what became of him. His countrymen, who did not at first perceive the advantage of salt, having at length discovered it, were so angry with themselves for their ignorance and ingratitude, that they sent several persons in quest of *Phelo*, but could never gain any intelligence of him. They then resolved to celebrate in his honour this feast of *Phelonaphie*, which they do with very particular solemnity and devotion, by launching about the sea in several barks, as if they were in expectation of finding that great man.

Soon after Mr. *Kastelein* invited *A plantation of Mr Kastelein* me to one of his plantations, where I saw them make all the preparations of sugar. He had erected for that purpose a mill, which was *A sugarmill* worked by two buffalos A man was stationed to take care of that part of the mill where the sugar canes were deposited, and which in the first working are only bruised, and

1706 and then drawn through an aperture on the other side The juice flows into a well, and passes from thence thro' a subterranean gutter to the place where the sugar-pots are, and the boilers At the second operation a larger quantity of sugar is drawn out of these canes, and the rest at the third It is then boiled and poured into earthen pots peirc'd thro', in order to discharge the grosser particles, and the mouth of the pots are strongly closed up with fresh clay This is the first and best part of the sugar They afterward draw out a second juice, and then a third I found the sugar-canes were like those I had seen in *Egypt*, being about seven or eight feet in length, and three or four inches thick

Indigo This place likewise furnished me with the sight of indigo, which grows on small shrubs, that have several little branches twined together. They commonly shoot up to the height of a foot and a half from the ground, and the leaves, which are pressed in order to extract the indigo, are small The seed grows in long and slender clusters, agreeably to the representation in plate 206

Coffee The letter B exhibits a branch of the *Kauwa*, or the pods which contain the berries of coffee, which are green before they have attained their maturity, yellow when half ripe, and of a reddish violet colour when their growth is completed The flower very much resembles that of *Jessamine*, having six long pointed leaves, which are yellow in the middle These pods were brought from *Arabia* some years since, but the best plants were destroyed in 1697, by an earthquake, which shook the whole city of *Batavia*, and overturned all the gardens around it, in so destructive a manner, that nothing was left in the general's garden But some curious people having afterward discovered a few shoots of this plant, were industrious to cultivate it anew, and succeeded so effectually, that there is reason to believe these plants will be

rendered very numerous in a few years 1706 Those persons therefore are very much deceived, who imagine that this fruit grows in no country but *Arabia*, and that the trees which produce it cannot be cultivated in any other climates

At the letter C the reader will *Leaves of a wild tree which grows in the woods* find a representation of the leaves of a wild plant which grows in the woods Some of these leaves are red, others white, but the plant bears only one red flower The three branches which are there exhibited, are almost as large as they appear in their natural size Here is likewise a growth of cocoa, of which *Cocoa* chocolate is made This fruit has a charming appearance on the tree · It is red and yellow, and one often sees five or six of them one above another, and about six inches in length The leaves are large, and long, some of them are tinged with yellow, others with red The tree itself is represented in plate 207

I likewise observed a growth of *Citrons of China* *China* citrons, shaped in a peculiar manner, and shooting out several points They have some resemblance to those which I have described in that part of the first volume of these travels which treats of *Rama*, but they are not so large. This fruit has not any kernels, and is of a beautiful yellow It flourishes to great perfection in this soil, and is exhibited in plate 208

I saw likewise another fruit, which the *Portuguese* call *Jaka*, *Jaka* the *Indians Nanka*, and the *Dutch Soorsaeke* It is very large, and something like a bagpipe, the colour is of a reddish green before it is ripe, but it changes to a dusky, as it advances to its maturity This fruit inclofes several other large fruits of a yellow complexion, and which contain white kernels As the flavour of it is sweet, it pleases most people, and is reckoned very wholesome. Two of them are represented on a tree, in plate 209

There is also another fruit called *Nomnam* by the *Portuguese*, *Nomnam,* and *Poekis anjang* by the *Indians* The
t fte

288 CITRON DE CHINA

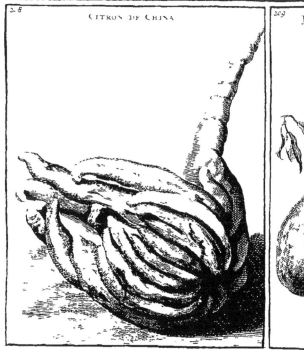

209 JAKA OU SOURSAK

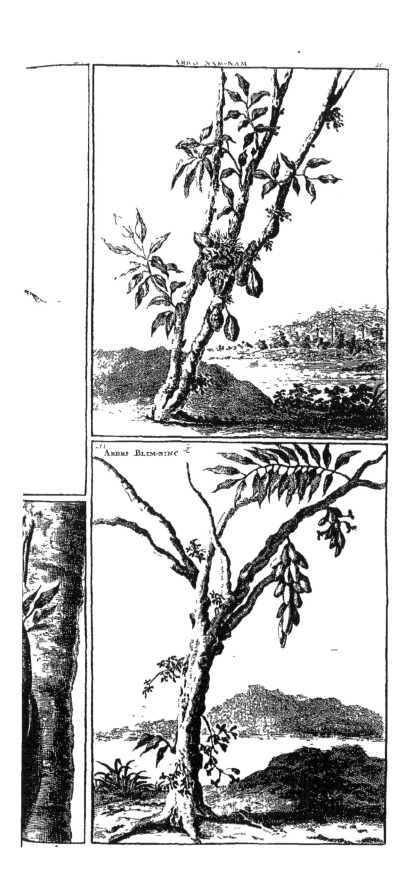

ARBRE NAM-NAM

ARBRE BLIM-BING

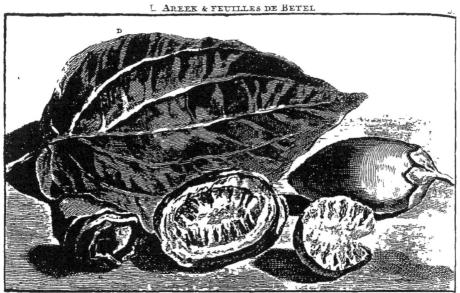

FILANDER

1706. tafte of it is agreeable; it is likewife coloured with a greyifh yellow, and greatly refembles a pear The flower is red, yellow, and white, and grows in clufters, the leaf and form of it are reprefented in plate 210 The *Blimbing* is alfo a plant, the fruit of which is large, and long Its flavour refembles that of a goosberry, and the flower of it is red Where any perfon has corroded his mouth, with vinegar, or any other acid, he cannot have a better remedy than this fruit, which is reprefented on a tree in plate 211.

Areek The *Areek* is a fruit which grows in thick bunches, on a large high tree, the bark of which is very thin, and the leaves long It is of univerfal ufe, not only with the natives of the country, but alfo among ftrangers It is fhaped like a plumb, and grows yellow in ripening I have reprefented one of them mark'd with A in plate 212 Another, which is ripe, with B, and half a one without the outward rind They divide this half into feven or eight parts, which they wrap up in the leaves of *Betel*, rubb'd with a red of *Siam*, or elfe with white lime This is chewed till the faliva becomes as red as blood, and this they pretend s an excellent remedy to preferve the teeth and gums. But I could never be prevailed upon to ufe it, finding fomething very difagreeable in the flavour, befide which it often happens, that thofe who are not accuftomed to it, find themfelves indifpofed, and faint away, though thefe circumftances never happen but when they take a bad fort This leaf of *Betel* grows like thofe of *French* beans, and the reader will find fome of them reprefented at the letter D It is commonly of a dark grey, but there are fome of a green tincture, and thefe are the beft The manner of wrapping th s fruit in the leaf may be feen at the letter E

Filanders When I was at our general's country feat, I faw a certain animal called *Filander*, which has fomething very extraordinary in it. There were five al that ran loofe with rab-

Vol II

bits, and had their holes under a 1705 fmall hill, encompaffed with a rail This animal which I have reprefented in plate 213, has its hind leggs much longer than the fore, and has the fame skin as a large hare. It has a head like a fox, and a pointed tail; but what is moft extraordinary in it is, that it has a bag under its belly, into which the young ones retreat even when they are very large One may frequently fee their heads and necks extended out of the bag, but when the dam runs, the young are not vifible, but keep at the bottom of the bag, becaufe fhe leaps very much in her fpeed Some days after I went to fee a review of a company of *Bougis*, in prefence of the go- *Bougis* vernor and the general *de Wilde* The officers firft faluted them, and then fixed their pikes in the ground, and drew their daggers, with which they performed feveral exercifes, crying out at the fame time with loud voices, that they would kill all enemies that would prefume to confront them They afterward, to fhew their vigour and addrefs, made feveral motions with their bodies, which were more like contorfions of wreftlers, than an exercife of military men. They likewife found themfelves animated with frefh ardour by being well fhod, inftead of which they were formerly accuftomed to go barefooted The airs they gave themfelves in their march, were fufficient to create a hearty laughter, and the general *de Wilde* could not help faying to me, *They give money among us to fee comedies and farces, but can there poffibly be a more diverting fight than this?*

The foldiers were all habited in *Their ha-* different manners Some had large *bits* bonnets, fmall waiftcoats, and fhort breeches, others had hats with broad brims made of the bark of certain plants twifted together There were fome, who had bonnets in the form of fugar-loaves, others who had only a cloth twifted round their heads. Some had machines on each fide their heads, like gilded horns, which

D d

1706
Tber
eroʃs

which formed a very ridiculous fpectacle Some were even covered with armour, they were likewife armed with firelocks, daggers, and pikes, longer than thofe of the officers, who had all piftols at their girdles

While thefe were employ'd in performing their exercifes, there paffed by fome other companies of foldiers, who were to take their arms, in order to embark in fome veffels defigned for the kingdom of *Samaran*, upon the eaftern coaft of the ifle of *Java*, about fixty leagues from *Batavia*, under the government of king *Pangeran Poega*, who

had been depofed by his nephew, 1706 and afterwards re-eftablifhed by the company's forces And as *Ade-Patti*, the nephew of that prince, had efcaped, and endeavoured to create his uncle frefh troubles, thefe troops were fent in purfuit of him.

The governor having informed me foon after, that a veffel would fhortly fet fail for *Bantam*, which I was defirous to vifit, I embraced that opportunity, and he was fo good as to give me letters of recommendation to the governor of that place ; and likewife to the adminiftrator of the company.

C H A P. LXVIII.

The author's voyage to Bantam *A defcription of that kingdom. The author is admitted to an audience of the king*

The author's voyage to Bantam

THE 11th of *July*, after I had taken my leave of the general, I went on board the *Munfter*, a veffel of twenty fix guns, and fixty feven failors, all *Europeans*, with a referve of ten *Indians*, and we advanced about noon, into the latitude of the ifle of *Hoorn* As the wind ftood fair, we prefently after paffed by thofe of *Amfterdam*, and *Middlebourg*, which lay fouth between two rocks, that are about fix or feven feet under water, and are always vifible, by reafon of the clearnefs of the water

The ifands of Hoorn, Amfterdam, and Middlebourg.

Of Combuis.

We advanced weftward toward the ifles of *Combuis*, which we faw on the right, and found ourfelves about five o'clock near the ifle of * *Anthropophagi*, four leagues from *Bantam* The night, which was very dark, obliged us to caft anchor, but we continued our courfe at break of day, in cloudy damp weather We doubled the point of *Pontang* at eight o'clock, and coafted along the great *Poelemadi*, which

* *Men-eaters.*

Ifle of Poelemadi.

we had on the right, and a little after by a fmall ifland of the fame name, where we found but four fathom water, and after having touched at the ifles of *Poeledoa*, we came about ten into the road of *Bantam*, and about noon to the city I went directly to the houfe of the commander, Monfieur *de Rheede*, who received me with a great deal of civility, as alfo did Monfieur de *Wys*, adminiftrator of the company

Poeledoa

I took a walk the next day with an intention to take a view of the city both within and without, in order to which I went out by the water-gate, where there is always an advanced guard It is a fmall gate of the old wall, near the point or baftion of *Speelwick* toward the north, and from thence I proceeded along the fea-fhore, by a way which is often floated over with water when the tide is high, and it was then fo wet that I was obliged to ftrike into another road bordered with trees between feveral gardens

A defcription of Bantam

I faw

1706. I saw a range of wretched houses, covered with leaves, and inhabited by fishermen, who go to *Batavia* to sell their fish. The first place one meets with in this quarter, is the bastion of *Caranganto*, rebuilt with stone in a square form, with a battery of ten pieces of cannon. There are six other bastions on the side next the sea, another toward the east, and three small ones toward the west. From thence there is a passage over a draw-bridge, and another of stone, under which runs a river that derives its source from the mountains, and discharges itself into the sea. It flows at the extremety of the city, on the side next the sea, and near the *Bazar*, which is full of *Chinese* shops, where fruits, and other provisions are sold. On one side of the *Bazar* is a large *Chinese* building, where the captain or chief of that nation lives, and on the sea-shore are erected a great number of fishermen's huts, and some salt-houses. The *Dutch* landed near this place on the 7th of *April* 1682. In the way as one returns back, a road is struck out between the two bastions of *Caranganto* and *Speelwick*, to the Palace, where a stone bridge is built over the river already mentioned. The king commonly diverts himself the last day of the week with running at the ring in this place, and over the bridge, with the lords of his court. The great mosque called *Mit-zid*, is at the end of this bridge on the right hand.

I was informed at my return, that they had already weighed and counted out the pepper money, which the vessel in which I came was to carry to *Persia*, and that the prime minister of state was to go at four o'clock to the commander's

The author demands audience of the king

house to receive it. I took this opportunity to desire that minister to introduce me to the king, and as our commander had already told him (in pursuance of the order he had received from the general) that I was greatly desirous of the honour of paying my duty to that prince.

He assured me, that he would not fail 1706 to represent my request to his majesty that very day, and return me his answer as soon as possible. That lord, who was named *Pangeran*, prince of *Pour-ba-nagara*, was accompanied by ten inspectors of pepper, and he seated himself in a chair between the commander and chief inspector of the barriers. The others were placed on the contrary side, after the manner of the orientals. He came by water to *Speelwick*, attended by sixteen domestics. The commander entertained them with confections, and fruits, accompanied with bread, cheese, tea, and tobacco. They afterward counted the money, and sealed it up in bags of 1000 *Spanish* rials. The commander then took the prime minister by the hand, and conducted him as far as the river. The next day about nine o'clock the chief inspector of the barriers came to acquaint me, that I should be admitted to an audience of the king at two in the afternoon, and that his majesty was gone for that purpose to a pleasure-house, which he had about a quarter of a league from the city. He asked me, if I would accept a horse, or choose to go on foot, upon which I thanked him, and gave him to understand, that I preferred walking. He came to me at the appointed hour, and we were attended by M *Kaef*, who had been the company's resident at *Bantam*, before they had possessed themselves of that place, and had returned thither about three months, in order to transact some negotiations, by virtue of which he was admitted to the audience with me. We were likewise attended by a secretary, who was to be our interpreter. We found at the gate of the city four led horses, which the king had sent us, but we did not use them. The prime minister waited for us at the entrance into the palace, in order to introduce us to his majesty, and we proceeded by a stone conduit raised about two or three feet above the surface of the ground,

ground, in which is a leaden pipe, which extends from the pleasure-house, where the king then was, as far as his palace. This conduit had been made about two years, and is supplied with water from the mountains, which rise at the distance of about two leagues from thence, and this water discharges itself into a river, which flows through the country. It was three o'clock when we arrived there, and after we had waited some time, a lady of the court came to acquaint us we might enter. We saw, as we were passing along, one of the king's lodges, in which stood three coaches, the drivers of which were *Hollanders*, who were habited in scarlet after the *Dutch* manner.

When we had passed over a wooden bridge, railed on each side, we entered by a small door into a vestible, where the king was seated on a couch, on the side of which were five or six ordinary chairs. He tendered his hand to us, and received us in a very favourable manner, after which he ordered us to sit down, which I accordingly did, after having paid him my compliments. The prince was seated at the upper end of a table, and we placed ourselves on each side of him, and were immediately served with confections, fruits, and other refreshments, after which tea, tobacco, and pipes were brought to us upon silver salvers, with two lighted candles. Some time after we were entertained with hot provisions, such as *Pilau*, ragouts, chickens, roast-meat, and fruits, together with hard eggs, and radishes cut into slices. Every one had his napkin, and a plate filled with meat. What appeared to me most extraordinary was a large dish full of a particular food, which resembled starch, and slices of pears, the taste of which I found to be admirable, but as for liquor, we had nothing but water, which was poured out of a beaker, as well for drinking as washing of hands.

Nothing surprised me more than our being served by none but women.

The prime minister was seated on the ground, at the lower end of the table, with his legs crossed after the manner of the eastern people. His wife served at table, like the others, and even I had the honour to be waited upon by that lady. Monsieur *Karf* was seated on the right hand of the king, and served by three or four women of the first rank. There were others behind him, seated on the ground, and among the rest one who held a firelock in her hand, her companion grasped a small pike, and a third held the king's cane, varnished with black, with a silver apple. They rose from time to time, as I shall afterward relate more at large.

Behind these were five or six of the king's youngest sons, from three to six years of age, all very beautiful, and of a tolerable good complexion. This prince had no children by his first consort, but had eight by his second, who was his cousin german, and the widow of his brother, who had no children by her. The eldest is about thirteen years old, and the king has several other children by his third wife. This numerous off-spring did not prevent him from espousing a fourth, who has not the title of queen. This prince has likewise forty concubines, and 850 women who wait upon him in his palace.

Fifteen or sixteen ladies were behind these young princes, and three or four other companies of women appeared in the vestible, so that above 200 of them were then in motion. All of them had their necks uncovered, their arms and legs were likewise naked, a kind of petticoat was fastened to their waist, and a small piece of linnen above their bosom, their hair was also plaited back on the top of their heads.

The king wore that day a small bonnet about five inches deep, the white borders of which were about an inch in breadth, the rest was of a violet colour. His vest was shaped after the *Turkish* fashion, it was

was likewise of a brown colour, and the buttons of it were silver It was girded about him with a small sash of a violet colour, the ends of which hung down before He likewise wore a dagger studded with gold, his legs were naked, but he had red slippers after the *Dutch* fashion

When the dishes were removed from table, the king offered us tobacco, and asked me, if I had an inclination to take any I answered in the affirmative, but added, that I could do very well without it I also took the liberty to ask, whether the king smoked, and they answered yes, but that it was very moderately. He then enquired of me, if I would smoke provided he did? To which I reply'd, that this would be too much honour for me He asked me likewise, if I had any tobacco? because he thought mine might be better than his own As I happened to be provided with some, I filled a pipe, and had the honour to present it to that prince, who smoked half of it, and then gave the rest to his secretary, who had none

His affability

This prince, who is very affable and curious, asked me several questions concerning the countries thro' which I had passed, and the most remarkable things I had seen In particular, he enquired, who were the most powerful kings on earth, what was the extent of their dominions, what the manners of the inhabitants, and which were the largest and most famous rivers in the world? I then related to him all the particulars of the *Nile* and *Volga*, which I had measured both at their sources and outlets, and afterward gave him a description of several other rivers

In speaking of the world in general, he asked me how long the *Christians* thought it had subsisted, and how much longer they believed it would continue? To which I returned him the best answers I was able to make The king took such

Vol II.

pleasure in my replies, and the other particulars with which I had the honour to acquaint him, that he desired me to transmit them to him in writing from *Batavia*, and I accordingly promised to obey him

The king informed me, in his turn, that all the inhabitants of that country were formerly pagans, and that it was about three hundred years since they embraced the doctrines of *Mohammed*, at the solicitation of one of his ancestors, whose name was *Soefoehoenan Aboel Machajin*, who was reckoned a saint by the people, and to whose empire they submitted themselves He then conversed with me about *Turky*, the *Holy-Land*, and *Jerusalem* He also caused a *Turkish* merchant of *Bethlehem*, to be introduced, whom chance had brought into that part of the world, after he had lost all his cargo at sea

We had a long conversation together, with which the king was so well satisfied, that he often shook me by the hand. He desired me likewise to visit him again the next day at nine in the morning in his palace, and to bring with me the journal of my first voyage, for I am informed, says he, that your book is in the hands of Mr *de Wys* He then turned to Mr *Kaef*, and told him, that he had no need to give himself the trouble to come again, for the letters which he was to carry to *Batavia* should be delivered to him the next day, and that he might depart immediately after

The king conducted me into every part of his pleasure-house, which consisted of three stories, each containing a variety of apartments He likewise informed me of his sentiments, with relation to the grandees of states, and the counsellors of princes, and in what manner they ought to be rewarded, or punished He highly extolled virtue and fidelity, and added, that a prince could never sufficiently repay the services of his subjects, and whenever they committed any faults, to which

E e human

human nature is obnoxious it was incumbent on princes to pardon them, in consideration of their past services, and that instead of using violent remedies, every circumstance should be softened as much as possible He added, that kings ought not to suffer themselves to be swayed by their passions, nor to act with precipitancy and inconsideration To which he subjoined, that he was not ignorant of the mischief which jealousy occasions in courts I afterward took the liberty to tell him my sentiments, which I strengthened by several examples drawn from history and the antients

Crude n c ne h re is a (are-...

The situation of the house where we then were, is charming as well on the land side, as on that next the sea, and it is likewise surrounded with a beautiful canal, the bottom of which is paved While the king conducted me from place to place, and discoursed with me in the manner I have related, he was attended by the ladies armed as I have already described. As the night drew on, I took my leave of his majesty

We found three coaches at the gate, in one of which the king desired me to place myself He then mounted his horse, with three or four of the young princes, and the ladies of the court placed themselves in the other coaches I was informed that queen *Ratoe-anoem* was among them, and that she diverted herself with fishing with the women of her train, while we were with the king. The other women returned on foot, every one loaded with baggage There were likewise two hundred guards armed with pikes, who followed the king Those who are nearest his person are called *Kejorans*, and the others *Souranagaras* All the subjects of this prince are *Javanites*, and the strangers who reside in his dominions are *Malayans*, *Makaßares*, and *Baliers* When they are not in his service, they are obliged to retire out of the way while he passes with his women, after the manner of the orientals We arrived by night at the castle, where we took leave of his majesty, and were conducted to our habitations with two large lanthorns

The author takes leave of his majesty

CHAP. LXIX.

The author is admitted into the King's presence a second time Comic dancers He takes leave of the King The language of the Javanites *Their worship The Origin of the Kings of* Bantam

A friend auther t

I Failed not to go the next day at the appointed hour, with secretary *Gobius*, to the prime minister's house, in order to wait there for the lady who was to conduct me to the palace I was very much surprised at the plainness and simplicity which appeared in the house of that great lord The lady, for whose arrival we waited, came soon after and conducted us to the king,

whom we found upon the castle wall over the great gate, employed in viewing a chariot which the magistrates of *Batavia* had presented to his majesty, and it arrived there the preceding evening in a bomb-vessel

As soon as we were seen by that prince, he made a sign to us to come up where he was He was surrounded by women, who supported six parasols behind him From thence

1706 thence we were conducted into the hall of audience, which is separate from the rest of the building This hall was also full of women, among whom were three dancers, the principal of whom was perfectly beautiful, and dressed in a very elegant and singular manner There was here also, as on the foregoing day, a large table covered, at the upper end of which the king placed himself, and ordered me to seat my self on his right hand, and the secretary to sit next me

They presented us at first with tea, and presently after the queen appeared, and placed herself on the left side of the king. As soon as we saw her come in, the secretary and myself rose, and made a profound reverence, but the king obliged us to sit down again We were afterward served with several sorts of provisions, and among the rest, a plate of *Dutch* cheese, which the queen placed by me, thinking to please me, for which I testify'd my acknowledgment, by eating a piece of it, and likewise tasting of every dish upon the table The king, who saw this with pleasure, asked me if the sauces were to my liking, and what I thought of their manner of dressing their meat, to which I answered, that I thought every thing exceeding good, and that I could not give a better proof of that opinion, than by eating as I did. The king smil'd, and seemed contented Then the dancers began to exercise themselves The queen *Ratoe-Anoen,* who is the second of his majesty's wives, and the most considerable of them all, and whom I have *A description of the queen* already mentioned, was in the flower of her age, her person was very amiable and genteel, her complexion was admirable, her air majestic, and her behaviour perfectly agreeable and engaging She was habited after the manner of the country, like the rest of the ladies of the court This princess returned in an hour's time, and after the tables were cleared, the king read over part of the relation of my voyage,

which I had brought by his order, 1706 and explained it to him as well as time would permit In the mean *One of the king's con-* time the king ordered one of his *cubines* concubines to come in, and placed her over against me This lady was fat, and very fair, with fine light hair, but her cheeks were bloated, and her eyes half shut She asked me of what country I took her to be, I reply'd that I did not know, but if she allowed me to guess, I thought she might be a *Ruffian,* since I had seen some ladies of that country like her at *Constantinople.* However, I was mistaken, for she was a mountaineer of the isles situated southeast of *Ternate,* the inhabitants of which are called *Kackerlackes* These people have a much longer night than day, and cannot bear the light of the sun, which makes them always keep their eyes half shut, and they seldom appear in the day, this lady was so fat that one could hardly see her eyes The king then *The king's* ordered six of his children to be *children* brought in, and they were placed upon the table, two by two in a chair, because they were yet very little, and they were his majesty's children by that queen whom I last mentioned. They were beautiful, and finely shaped, and their complexions were as white as snow There were two princes and four princesses, the eldest of whom was nine years of age At length the king asked, if I was satisfied with the reception he had given me, and I replied, that his majesty had been pleased to honour me infinitely more than I deserved Upon which this prince added, *You are the first* European *whom I ever admitted to my hall of audience, and it is an honour which I have never granted to the counsellors of the* India *company, nor even to the commander, nor should I have accorded it to you, if you had not been a stranger in whom I discover something agreeable and entertaining This I tell you with my own mouth, that you may have no reason to doubt of the truth of what you have now heard* I then rose, and made a proa profound reverence to his majesty, and humbly thank'd him for all his favours, upon which he again did me the honour to present me his hand The secretary had already told me, when the queen appeared, that it was a favour, which the king had never granted to any person, and that when the commander and his lady came to pay their duties to her majesty, she thought it sufficient to receive them in an upper apartment, that princess never appearing before strangers in publick In the mean time we amused ourselves with smoking, and the principal dancer began to dance She wore a crown of gold, with a chaplet of flowers, which hung down as far as her waist, her head was likewise graced with a variety of other ornaments She was clothed with a beautiful vest, and a rich petticoat, her arms were all naked up to her shoulders, except those parts of them which were ornamented with large golden bracelets But what appeared to me most extraordinary, was, that she had green spots on her cheeks, and eye-brows of the same colour Her dance consisted in certain movements of the body which bended forward to her waist, without any air, or agreeableness, and she advanced very slowly, and almost without moving her arms She afterward took two drawn daggers, one of which she placed with the point toward her throat, continually dancing with surprising gravity The other dancers had black spots like flies, upon their faces, and all their habits consisted only of a vest, with drawers over their shifs They performed a comic scene, and acquitted themselves with great perfection One represented a *Dutchman*, and the other, who had some smattering of our language, complained that he gave to others what was justly her due She gave herself a variety of airs, and made a thousand grimaces, and motions that were not very decent, with a surprising agility, which raised the laughter of the whole company

Two of the king's dwarfs then appeared, and endeavoured to imitate, and turn into ridicule, that dance The king had married the least and most diverting of them, to one of the ladies of the court, whom he shewed me The principal dancer appeared a second time with a silver porringer full of *Pinang*, a fruit which they usually chew, and has been already mentioned She presented it to me and the secretary, upon which we took some of the fruit, and put money in the place of it, as is customary While the farce was representing, they brought in hot slices of meat, wrapped up in green leaves, and the king gave one to the dancer who expressed the most humour in the part she performed. She pulled it to pieces in a very odd manner, and then filled her mouth with several morsels of it, but without discontinuing her discourse, though she uttered her words in a very imperfect manner While she threw one piece into her mouth in this manner, she drew out another, and then approaching us, as if she intended to speak to us, she distorted her face into horrible grimaces

This kind of entertainment continued till two in the afternoon, when the whole being over, the dancer brought us again the money which I had just put into the porringer, but instead of receiving it, I desired her to keep it, telling her it was not the custom among us to take back any thing we had already given The king then conducted me into all the apartments of his palace, from the top to the bottom, after he had pulled off his shoes in order to go up, and we followed his example, that place being esteemed sacred He even conducted me into the queen's apartment, the chambers of which were very small. Having at length had the honour to entertain his majesty with various subjects of conversation, and for a considerable time, he took his leave of me, and desired me to pay his compliments to the general. I returned my

1706 my acknowledgments to his majesty, for the honour which he had vouch-fifed to afford me, and wished him the enjoyment of a perfect health, together with a happy and fortunate reign, and that those princes who were to fucceed him, might equal in glory their illuftrious predeceffors. The king, on his part, had the goodnefs to wifh me all imaginable profperity, and a happy return to my native country, and then conducted me through a wooden gallery into another edifice, having been accompanied thither by the two eldeft damfel, who advanced no further When we were come down the king put on his flippers, and we our fhoes I then took leave of that good prince, who again did me the honour to tender me his hand, after which I returned to my lodging

The author takes leave of the king

The complexion of this prince is very brown and finguine, and there is fomething noble in his mein His eyes are brown, his eye-brows almoft black, and the muftachos he wears are fmall I have already fufficiently defcribed his habit. He was then about thirty three years of age, and had as many children.

The perfon of this prince defcribed

The reader will find in plate 214 all that appeared moft remarkable in the hall of audience, where the king received and entertained me. I drew a sketch of the whole fcene upon the fpot, without being ob-ferved, becaufe I was thought to be writing down particulars of the audience, that I might not forget any of the honours I had received For I had acquainted the king, that I fhould not fail to publifh the inftances of his goodnefs to me, in order to preferve the memory of them, and the ladies of the court were exceedingly pleafed with this declaration.

1706

I fhall now defcribe the ornaments and enfigns of honour with which the king is accompanied when he appears in publick Thefe are generally near his perfon, and are fupported by ten ladies of quality, 1. a *Tsjelor*, or fword of ftate, 2 a *Sawo-eniggaling*, or golden cup, 3 an *Ardawilika*, or wooden bird gilt, upon which are borne the veftments of the king, 4 a *Servpienangdoor*, which is found in the *Maldive* iflands, 5 a *Lante*, or little meafure, 6 a *Souaffe-kuifpidoor*, or fmall cane made of the root of a tree, 7 and 8 two carabines, 9 a *Sjaratan*, or fmall drinking can, 10 a bowl of *Souaffe* Thefe are the ornaments, or ordinary enfigns with which the king is ufually accompanied, and which he changes, increafes, or diminifhes at his own pleafure.

The enfigns of the king

As I am unacquainted with the language of the *Javanites*, I fhall content myfelf with exhibiting their alphabet, which confifts of twenty characters.

The Javanefe alphabet

A	B.	C.	D.	E.	F.	G.
Ha.	na	tzja	ra.	ka.	da	ta.

H	I.	K.	L.	M	N	O.
fa	wa.	la.	pa.	da.	dja.	ija.

P	Q.	R.	S	T.	V
nija	ma.	ga.	ba.	ta.	nga.

With respect to their religion, that of *Mahomed* prevails more than any other, in the island of *Java*, where it has been established for the space of 300 years, as I have already intimated, but the inhabitants of the eastern side are nothing near so zealous as those of the western. The king who governs these last has assumed, with the *Cirebeans*, the *Arabian* title of *Sultan*, which the king who rules the people that inhabit the eastern side of the island has ever refused to this day. It is even said, that there is still a third part of the island which has not submitted to the *Mohammedan* doctrines, but still retain the worship of idols, after the manner of the antient *Javanese*, whose descendants still inhabit the isle of *Bali*.

King *Machdeem*, or *Seyso euang-Geneng-Diat*, who has been already mentioned, was, according to the chronology of the *Bantamites*, grandson of king *Ben Ifrael*, who reigned in *Arabia*. This prince, who had an inclination to see the world, passed through *China*, in order to arrive at the island of *Java*, where he landed at a place called *Damack*. After he had continued there for some time, he proceeded to *Sirrebon*, where his interest was espoused by many of the inhabitants. He dyed, and was buried there, and it is reported that his tomb, which is held in great veneration, is yet to be seen. This prince was the first, who introduced *Mohammedism* into this country, and his tomb, which is surrounded by several buildings and walls, is esteemed so sacred, that it is yearly visited by a great number of *Mohammedan* lords, and ecclesiastics, who bring presents from their respective princes, and especially from the king of *Bantam*.

This king *Machdeem* or *Seyso koeteng Geen eng-Diat*, espoused, at *Sirrebon*, the daughter of *Kiay Gaudling Bahaar*, by whom he had no children. He afterward married the daughter of *Ratoe Ayoe*, by whom he had one son named *Paneumbahan Srien*, and sometime after he

espoused another daughter of the same *Ratoe Ayoe*, and the younger sister of the former, by whom he had a son called *Hasanodin, Pang, or Dipoti Socrasouan*, whom he declared his successor, and who, after the death of that prince was known by the title of *Seyso euang*, or *Pangeran Seda Kingkingh*. This *Hasanodin* quitted *Sirrebon*, and caused himself to be declared king of *Bantam*, by the name of *Pangeran*. His father had married him to a daughter of the king of *Demack*, called *Pangeran Ratoe*, by whom he had several children. He afterward espoused a daughter of *Radja Indrapora*, who had for her dowry the country of the *Sillabars*, a people of *Banca Houlon*, on the western coast of *Pellombang*, and he had two children by this princess. I omit those he had by other wives, and by his concubines. He died at the age of 120 years, and left his crown to his son *Joseph*, who took the name of *Pangeran Passaruan*. This prince had several wives, who brought him a numerous off-spring, and he was succeeded by his son *Maclomed Pangeran Seedangrona*, who had likewise several wives and children, and left his crown to *Aboema Vacher Abdul Kader*, the son of one of his concubines, who was the first that assumed the title of *Sultan*. He married *Ratoe Adjoe*, daughter of *Pangeran Aria Ranga Singa Sari*, by whom he had several children, and among the rest *Absel Moah*, who was his successor. This prince had several wives, and a numerous issue, and by his first wife *Ratoe Koelon*, daughter of *Pangeran Djaya-karta*, he had a son called *Abdoulphatach*, *Abdoel-plata*, to whom he left his crown. This latter prince, who had several children, was succeeded by his son *Abdsel Kahar Aboenasar*, who had five wives, and several children, and among the rest, *Moechamad Jachun*, who reigned after him, and *Aboe Machasin Moechamad disjenoel abidin*, who now fills the throne.

CHAP

CHAP LXX.

The situation of Bantam A lady of an extraordinary age The author's departure from Bantam, and return to Batavia

The sit of Bantam AFTER I had satisfied my curiosity at court, I resolved to take the like prospect of the city of *Bantam*, and the governor lent me a bark for the more commodious execution of my design, in the road which lies on the north side of the city Number 1 marks out the governor's house, which is white, and covered with red tiles 2 the guard at the bastion of *Speelwyc* 3 the house at the corner of that point, this is an agreable mansion, where the king generally diverts himself

BANTAM

when he visits the governor On the top of this house, (which is built of stone) is a platform with a balustrade of lattice-work, and this situation commands a delightful prospect 4 the gate where the advanced guard is stationed. 5 the wall 6 the gate, through which is a passage to the governor's house. 7 the pepper mountain 8 the hills of *Saringa* 9 the mountain of *Pienang* 10 the port into which the small vessels come It advances into the sea to a great extent, and is very shallow, it likewise passes through the whole city as far as the back front of the castle The few small houses in the adjacent parts, make but an inconsiderable appearance, and the trees with which the city is surrounded, obstruct the view of the rest, together with that of the castle While I was drawing this prospect, I saw a crocodile, who appeared at different times, and frequently raised himself above the surface of the water *The castle* The castle is a large oblong square, surrounded with a high wall, and likewise fortified with four bastions, and two half-moons rocks between them It is near a quarter of a league in circumference ... furnished with ar... together with a D... gate ... of ... men

The ... built upon the ... two good league in circuit Most of the houses are ... buildings, being made of the branches of trees, and covered with leaves There are also suburbs, ... the court of the ... on the ... side It is very po... and the number of children there is very extraordinary

I here found very good ... and in great numbers with which I filled several pots, or presents to my friends at B...

... the commerce of that quarter consist only in pepper The great haven comprehends near three leagues in circumference, and is as wide at its ... at the entrance, so that ships ... there with all possible security, ... is likewise the largest I ever saw. This kingdom, which is in the southern part of the East-I..., lies in the north-west tract of the island of Java... near the streights of Sunda, and at the distance of about twenty-five leagues from Batavia, which is westward from it I took the diversion of the water in a canoe, which is a small vessel of that country, pointed at both ends, and made of the hollowed trunk of a tree called Bar-..., which is generally of a surprising thickness These boats go very well with oars I was accompanied by a Prussian, who had been settled some time in that country and was well acquainted with the language and all the customs of it We went to a place called Carams, which is filled with tombs It lies about a league from Bantam, upon the bank of the great river, which flows from the mountains These tombs were erected for the families of the kings of Bantam The chief structure is entirely ruinous, all the rest are inconsiderable, and disposed in covered places Several bodies are to be seen, ranged by each other, without any tombs,

and only covered with earth raised to a small height above the surface of the ground, with little stones joined together in the form of tombs This place is surrounded by a single wall We went to bathe ourselves at our return, in the river near the garden where the king sometimes resorts to refresh himself in the same manner

We landed at a little distance from the city, in order to visit a lady who was 130 years old She had been mentioned to me by the king, who likewise ordered me to go and see her She lived with the king's great aunt, who had the direction of all the dancers. As we came from that place, we were introduced into the apartment of the women, who were desired to dance, as thinking we came for that purpose But I returned them my acknowledgments, and declared, I had already enjoy'd that pleasure; upon which they conducted us to the king's aunt, to whom I testified my gratitude for the honour she intended me, and told her, that I only desired to see the antient lady upon which some of her women, who were curious to see me, took upon them to be my conductors I found her in a very mean apartment, seated upon a kind of table, covered with grey cloth, after the manner of the country, and her head bare She was yet very fresh, and had a tolerable strong voice, but her legs were so weak that she could not stand, and she was reduced to meer skin and bones. As the day began to close, I desired a candle might be lighted, and when I had taken it in one hand, I held the other before it, and asked the old lady, if she could distinguish the light *How should I*, reply'd she, *since you hold your hand before it?* She, however, was incapable of distinguishing the features of a face. I then asked her, in order to try her memory, from what country she came? *I am a native of* Jackatra, said she, (this was the antient name of Batavia, before it was taken by the company ninety seven years ago,)

and

1706 and I came, when I was young, to dwell at Bantam, where I have known *seven kings*, whom she particularly named, she always ate with a good appetite, but grew childish at some particular times, when she no longer asked for food, upon which occasion care was always taken for her supply. Her eyes were funk deep in her head, her hair was entirely grey, and very thin, and her great age had bent all her fingers inward After we had satisfied our curiosity, we took leave of the king's aunt, and thanked her for the civility with which she had treated us

I employed the next day in making preparations for my departure, the ensuing evening, in one of the barks of the country, having no inclination to return in the vessel that brought me hither, and which set sail the preceding day, because contrary winds frequently retard the course of these vessels, for a considerable time, in that season of the year I desired Mr *de Wys* to hire me one, but he was so good as to lend me his own, which was larger and more commodious than the common ones, and I embarked about seven in the evening with Mr *Kaef*, who returned with me. The governor and Mr de *Wys*, gave me their answer to the general, and I returned them my acknowledgments for all their civilities The governor would even accompany me out of the city gate, where I found Mr *de Wys*, and the secretary, who waited to take their leave of me

The haven on that side is neither 1706 broad nor deep, the sailors therefore were obliged to use a pole to push *The author's departure from Bantam* the bark forward, which is very tiresome, because they make but a slow advance As soon as we were got out, we were obliged to cast anchor, in order to wait for a land-wind, which rose soon after We made such way in the night, being favoured by a fine moon-light, that at break of day, we gained sight of the vessel which set sail in the evening, and had the wind against it Thus by continually coasting, and passing between the islands, we arrived about three in the afternoon at *Batavia*, *His arrival at Batavia* where I surprized the general, who did not expect me so soon I acquitted myself to him of the compliments, with which I was entrusted on the part of the king, and gave him the letters I had for him. I likewise entertained him with an account of whatever had happened to me, and with which he appeared very well satisfied I then went to pay my duty to the old general, who was overjoyed at the good success of my voyage

I carried with me from *Bantam* *Strange birds* some little birds, which I put into spirits of wine to preserve them. The most beautiful of them had a violet spot upon the top of his head, his breast and tail were tinged with a fine red, and all the rest of the body was green. There were also several other small birds with red breasts and tails, and others that had those parts of a grey complexion

Vol. II.   G g   CHAP.

C H A P. LXXI.

The manner of receiving the letter of the king of Bantam *Wild fruits A present, and letters from the emperor of* Java. *The arrival of captain* Dampier.

THE letter of the king of *Bantam*, which Mr *Kaef* had in charge, being arrived in the road of *Batavia* the 19th of *July*, Monfieur *Sabandhaer*, mafter of the ceremonies, was immediately fent, with feven or eight principal officers of the company, and fome of the chief merchants, to receive it This letter was placed in a large filver difh, covered with yellow damask, richly flowered, and borne by a halberdier, accompanied by a flave in livery, who fupported the damask covering When they were come to the caftle, they paffed between two ranks of foldiers of the garifon under arms, and who were pofted from the great gate, as far as the governor's apartment, with enfigns difplay'd, and drums beating A treble volley of fmall arms, and the cannon of the caftle, were then difcharged, and a magnificent entertainment was prepared in the hall of the council of the *Indies*, where the governor, and the general of the company were feated, the fecretary appear'd ftanding, and the halbadiers were difpofed round the table

The company received on the 23d a prefent of thirty three horfes from *Soeffenang Pakuboana*, emperor of *Java*, thefe were fucceeded on the 26th by letters from that prince, which were received with the fame ceremony as thofe of the king of *Bantam* This prefent was accompaned by fifteen or fixteen young female flaves This is the fame emperor, whom the company replaced on the throne the preceding year, after having driven out his nephew *Adipati*, who had poffeffed himfelf of the kingdom of *Metaram* This empire, which is called *Samataram*, is on the eaftern coaft

of *Java*, about fixty leagues from *Batavia* The war lafted three years, but the depofed prince could never prevail upon himfelf to give up his pretenfions Time, however, decided them at laft

I received, much about that time, a prefent of wild fruits, which are found in the woods, and I took a draught of fix different fpecies of them on paper The *Atap*, or *Piek*, of which they eat the infide, grows in cluftres, about a foot and a half in diameter, the leaves are long and narrow, as may be feen in plate 215 The *Froet Mieri*, is a fruit with white kernels, fo very malignant in its nature, that no one can tafte it without immediate death The reader will find one, open, with fome of the leaves at the letter A, in plate 216 The *Froete Tiackou*, is alfo a fruit, of which they eat the infide, it is green, and incircled with eight leaves, and is as large as it appears at the letter B The *Kandeke* is a long fruit, the flower of which bears no feed, but they fet the branches of it The leaves are very beautiful, and agree with the reprefentation at the letter C in plate 217 D marks a fruit, the name of which I could not learn, it is of a beautiful red when ripe, the leaves are long, and narrow, and clofe to one another The 6th is the *Baple Kammie*, a fruit of which they eat the kernels, of the middle part, which are very large They are likewife planted, becaufe they contain the feed of the fruit, which is very foft The leaves refemble thofe of ivy, and the fruit is reprefented in plate 218, as it grows naturally I have alfo added in plate 219 a fine red flower, which fomething refembles a rofe, though it is

formed

PROFIL MERI ET TASSOI

c

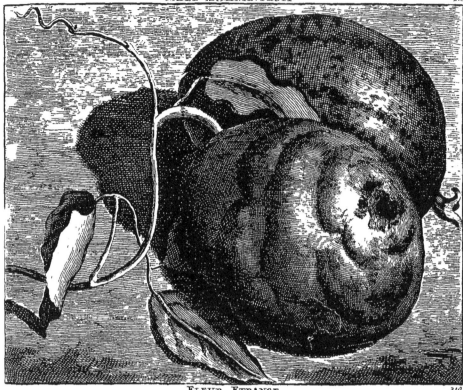

1706

Mineral productions

An extraordinary plant

An admirable remedy

Sagoe

First book of Kings ch ix ver 28

formed of feveral fmall floweis joined together

I likewife received, among feveral other curiofities, a parcel of gold, filver, antimony, chryftal, and gold duft, taken from the mines of *Cilhbaer*, on the weftern coaft of *Sumatra*, together with a fea-plant, which is found at *Amboina*, and called by the *Indians Akkar-bahaer*, a name compounded of *Akkar*, which fignifies a root, and *Bahaer*, which fignifies the fea, as if one fhould fay a fea-root The *Arabs* call this plant *Kalbahaer*, the firft fyllable of which fignifies the heart, and the fecond the fea, that is to fay the *Sea-heart* They pietend that it is an admirable remedy againft the ftrangury, and in order to prepare it for that purpofe, thefe branches, or roots, muft be reduced to powder, and infufed in watei, a fmall tea cup of which is then to be taken The fame preparation is alfo faid to be excellent for relieving the pains of a woman, newly brought to bed, but it muft be mixed up with two thirds of *Den-ty de bada*, *Adas*, and *Poole Sary*, and a large tea cup of it fhould be taken thrice.

In *Amboina*, and *Ternate*, are found whole forefts of a tree called *Gabbe-gabbe*, which the inhabitants ufe inftead of rice They cut off the ftem and branches, and take out a kind of pith that refembles a fponge, and which they drefs like rice When this tree is feven or eight years old, they fell it, and then cut it into pieces, which are fteeped in water, after they have been well cleanfed Thefe are afterward made into *Sagoe*, which the *People of Amboina*, and moft of the orientals, ufe inftead of bread, they alfo make them into bifcuits, which will keep feveral years

The ifland of *Sumatra*, which is oppofite to *Malacca*, is thought to be the place from whence ophir was formerly brought, and where both the *Syrians* and fervants of *Solomon* gained fuch large treafures, as I have obferved in my firft voyage There is ftill to be feen a fmall ifland before *Malacca*, and which the inha-

bitants call *Ophu*, but failors and geographers diftinguifh it by the name of the *Red Ifland* There is alfo found, both on the eaft and weft fide of the ifland of *Sumatra*, abundance of gold, of which I faw feveral pieces almoft round, and very neai as big as a pigeon's egg, and others longer, without any mixture of ftone

North-weft of the ifland of *Sumatra*, lies the city of *Atchem*, or *Achim*, where the queen keeps her court, that territory, as I was informed, being governed only by women, who derive their principal revenue from the mines The *Dutch* company had foimerly a facto y there, but it has been removed for fome time

A *Dutch* veffel, called the *Waveren*, being accidentally fet on fire in 1691, feventy perfons, among whom was a young *Dutch* lady, faved themfelves in the floops, and after having been upon the fea for the fpace of nineteen days, and as many nights, were caft upon the coaft of *Sumatra* They arrived ten days after at the city of *Achim*, in a deplorable condition, after having fuftained the utmoft feverity of hunger at fea The queen being informed of their arrival and adventures, oidered them to be brought before her, and treated them with abundance of humanity, fhe caufed two pieces of cloth to be given to each of the officers, and one to every failor, to cover them, and endeavoured to comfort them under their calamity, by affuring them that fhe would take care of them She likewife gave orders for fupplying them with provifions, and all neceffary accommodations, and even continued to provide for them with all the goodnefs and generofity imaginable, till they could find means to tranfport themfelves to *Malacca*, from whence they went to *Batavia* in the company's veffel

The laft day of the month, the famous captain *Dampier* arrived at *Batavia* from *Ternate*, with twenty eight of his crew on board one

of

1706

The city of Achim

A melancholy accident

The generofity of the queen of Achim

The arrival of captain Dampier

1706 of the company's veſſels He ſet ſail from *England* in *September* 1703 with two ſhips, and after he had coaſted along *Braſil* to ſixty degrees ſouth latitude, he doubled the cape of *Horn* The tenth of *February* he advanced as far as *Iſla de Fernando*, where he met a *French* veſſel, with which he had a ſharp engagement, but was obliged to quit it, becauſe he ſaw two others making up, and he then made all the ſail he could toward the coaſt of *Chili* and *Peru* At length being come into eight degrees north latitude, he landed with a few men at the river of *Saint Mary*, but was repulſed from thence, after which the ſhip which accompany'd him, and was called the *Cinque Ports*, left him near *Panama*, and from that time he never heard any thing of her Toward the middle of *May* one of his pilots fled from his ſervice, together with twenty of his ſailors, in a *Spaniſh* veſſel which he had taken in the bay of *Nicaya*, and while he was abandoned in this manner, he met a large veſſel of *Manilkas*, with which he fought a whole day without being able to make himſelf maſter of her Theſe diſaſters created a miſunderſtanding between him and his factor, and likewiſe his ſecond pilot, and the reſt of the crew, and it roſe to ſuch a height, that the factor and the pilot, accompany'd by thirty two ſailors, forſook him, and went to the *Indies*, in a *Spaniſh* prize in 1705 In this condition he arrived at *Amboyna* the twenty-eighth of *May*, from whence, after he had ſold his veſſel called the *St John*, which was no longer capable of being ſerviceable to him, he embarked in one of the company's ſhips, in order to proceed to *Batavia*, and from thence into *Europe* He had taken at different times and before his ſecond ſhip left him, thirteen or fourteen veſſels, and ſome *Spaniſh* barks in the *South-Sea*, without acquiring any conſiderable booty Finding his company, therefore, reduced to twenty-eight men, after he had been forſaken by part of his crew a ſecond time, he continued ſtill to cruiſe for ſome time, and took four prizes, till at length, his ſhip, the *St George*, being no longer in a condition to keep the ſea, he left her, and went into one of the barks he had taken, and to which he gave the ſame name He alſo reſolved to ſail through the *Indian* ſea, and at laſt arrived in a very bad condition at the iſland of *Batlan*, where he ſold his veſſel, and proceeded from thence to *Ternate*, and then to *Batavia*, where he embarked for *England*, with ſome of his men, in a ſhip of that country, and the reſt, who greatly diſagreed with him, went after in the company's ſhips which were returning to *Holland*

1706

CHAP.

CHAP. LXXII.

A description of Batavia The castle or citadel A-
greeable pleasure-houses Strange nations A great
number of Chinese Wild animals. Abundance of
fish, plants, and pulse.

A description of Batavia

THE city of *Batavia*, former-ly called *Jacatra*, was redu-ced under the government of the u-nited provinces of the *Low Coun-tries*, in the year 1619, as has alrea-dy been intimated The governor-general *Koen*, who made himself master of it, rebuilt it by the ad-vice of his council, and added a ci-tadel to it, with an intention to make it the feat of government of all the countries and places which were in subjection to the united pro-vinces in those parts, and the com-pany from that time gave it the name of *Batavia*

Its situa-tion.

This city is in *Asia*, southward of the *East-Indies*, and in the we-stern part of the island of *Java*. It is situated in 6 degrees and 16 mi-nutes of southern latitude, and in the longitude of 127 degrees 15 minutes, it has likewise a fine port, and a good road

Its arms

Its arms are a sword of azure in an orange field, the point of the sword is raised, and passes through a crown of green laurel The bor-ders, and jurisdiction of this city, are extended eastward, as far as the kingdom of *Siriebon*, westward to that of *Bantam*, southward to the *South-fea*, and northward over all the neighbouring isles in this part of the sea

Religion

The reformed religion is establish-ed in all the places which have any dependance upon the company, in the fame manner as it is in the u-nited provinces, and all other doc-trines are prohibited from being taught, under very severe penalties The *Sunday*, and all the festivals, are observed there in the fame manner as they are in *Holland*.

Vol II

The city has a delightful situa-tion, and I was assured that it has been very much embellished within by several beautiful structures, and the country round about it by a variety of fine pleasure-houses, within the space of six years All the avenues are bordered with fine trees, and small canals, and yet the natural beauty of the country, which is covered with a continual verdure, surpasses all the ornaments of art The city of *Batavia* is a league and a half in circumference, and the ditch from twelve to fifteen fathom in breadth The walls, which are of brick, are twenty one feet in height, and the rampart a fathom and a half in thickness, there are likewise five gates, namely, that which fronts the water, to the north, that of *U-trecht*, to the west, that of *Diest*, and the new gate, to the south, and that of *Rotterdam* to the east.

The beauty of the city

The citadel has two gates, one toward the land, on the south-side, and the other next the water, on the north It is a quarter of a league in circumference, and is fortified with four bastions, called the *Ruby*, the *Diamond*, the *Pearl*, and the *Saphir*. These are all well provided with brass cannons, and have hand-some stone walls of a confiderable height, together with large maga-zines, stored with ammunition, pro-visions, and mercantile commodities. The entrance by the land-gate opens into a large square, surrounded with handsome houses, of which that which belongs to the governor-gene-neral takes up the greatest part of one side of the square That of the director-general is over-against it, and the chappel of the citadel between

The citadel or castle

H h them

them There is a communication, by a gate, between this and the house of the governor, who has a feat next the pulpit There is likewife another for the director-general, the general of the troops, and the members of the council of the *Indies* The reft are feated according to their rank and dignity There are alfo chairs oppofite the pulpit, for the women who belong to the citadel, and whofe number is inconfiderable General *d. Wild*, and two or three other members of the council of the *Indies*, are placed next the director-general The paffage into the large fquare lies between feveral magazines over which are fome apartments The watergate opens into a fquare which had fome refemblance to the former, and where is alfo a range of houfes inhabited by the two principal merchants of the caftle, and other of the company's officers On the fide of this gate, are feveral magazines like the former, together with the chancery, into which there is a paffage by a back door of the governor-general's houfe This is what is moft remarkable in the citadel At the entrance by the land-gate is a flight of ftairs, which afcend to the apartment of the major of the place, as likewife to the arfenal, and the quarters of the foldiers of the garifon, and from the top of this place a delightful profpect opens every way to the view

The governor's palace The governor's palace has a handfome ftair-cafe, baluftraded on each fide with ftone, its front is likewife very beautiful, and built after the Italian manner At the entrance into it is a fine veftible, where the halberdiers are ftationed, and fome apartments on the right hand, which front the fquare, and on the left hand a handfome gallery, with large beautiful windows on the right, which look into a court, on the other fide of which are feveral apartments At the upper-end of the gallery is a hall, where the governor gives audience, and over the gallery is another hall of much the fame ftructure, together with a range of

apartments The top of the building is ornamented with a fine tower, which commands a delicious profpect The principal officers of the palace are lodged on the other fide of the court, which I juft now mentioned, where is alfo the kitchen Beyond the veftible is a fmall garden, which affords a paffage to the council-chamber, which is a large apartment, adorned with the pictures of all the governors in full length, except the prefent one, and his predeceffor, which I was refolved to paint, notwithftanding the diforder in my eyes, but I could not finifh that of the laft, by reafon of his indifpofition, and fome difappointments which happened at that time

I fhall now fet down a lift of the governors general, who have been employed in the fervice of the company, and have exercifed that important charge

The firft was *Peter Both*, elected *A cata- logue of the governors* by the chamber of feventeen in the year 1609 he poffeffed this place till the year 1615, and died the fecond of *January* in the fame year, in his return to *Holland* His fucceffor was *Gerard Reinft*, who died of a bloody flux at *Jacatra*, the 7th of *December* in the fame year

The 19th of *June* 1616, the council of *Ternate* nominated in his place *Laurent Reael*, who was recalled the 25th of *October* in the following year He was fucceeded by *John Peter Koen*, who fet out from *Holland* in 1618, made himfelf mafter of *Jacatra* the 30th of *May* 1619, and gave it the name of *Batavia*, the 21ft of *Auguft* 1621 He returned to *Holland* the 2d of *February* 1622, and left in his place *Peter Charpentier*, who returned to his own country the 12th of *November*, 1627

The 25th of *September* in the fame year, Mr *Koen* returned to the *Indies* a fecond time, in quality of governor-general, and died there the 20th of *September* 1629 His fucceffor was *Jacob Spelx*, who returned to *Holland* the 4th of *December* 1632

Henry

1706 *Henry Brower* succeeded him, and returned to *Europe* the 31st of *December*, 1635 His office was conferred on *Anthony Van Diemen*, who died the 9th of *April* 1645

He was succeeded by *Cornelius Vander Lyn*, who returned to his own country the 11th of *June* 1650, and was succeeded by *Charles Reyners*, who died the 18th of *May* 1653 *John Marsuyker* was nominated to this important charge, and confirmed in it the 16th of *June* He died the 4th of *January*, 1578 *Ryklof Van Goens* succeeded him, but having voluntarily resigned his generalship, was succeeded by *Cornelius Speelman*, who died the 11th of *January* 1684

The same day was employed in the provisional election of *John Kamphuisen*, who was confirmed the 7th of *August* 1685 He laid down his post the 27th of *November*, 1691, and died the 18th of *July* 1695

His successor was *William d'Outshoorn*, who resigned it the 15th of *August* 1704, and it was given the same day to *John Van Hoorn*, who quitted it the 29th of *October* 1709, and had for his successor *Abraham de Riebeck*.

As the hall where the pictures of these governors were hung was antient, it was thought advisable to pull it down, and workmen are now employed in rebuilding it The council in the mean time assembles in the hall which fronts the fish-pond This apartment is very spacious, and rises on an eminence above the pond, it has likewise a cabinet which affords a fine prospect On each side of the hall are small gardens full of fruit-trees, with a low wall on the side next the pond

In the passage from the citadel through the land-gate to the city, is a large stone bridge, built over the ditch, and the *Esplanade*, beyond it, leads to a pleasant road bordered with trees At the end of it is a *Corps de Garde* upon the bank of a river, which has a bridge over it, and a gate in the middle, where a centinel is stationed

The governors stables, and grooms 1706 lodges are on the other side of this river, opposite to the *Corps de Garde*, and not far from thence is a scaffold, on which are executed those who are condemned by the courts of justice or the citadel, but those who are condemned by the magistrates of the city, are executed in a spacious square before the town-house This was a large building of a considerable height, and adorned with a beautiful front, but the whole structure was so very antient, that they are at present employed in pulling it down, in order to rebuild it. Leaving this edifice on the left hand, the passage lies through the new street, and from thence into the suburbs, which are to the south About the distance of one hundred fathom from thence is a reservoir, the water of which falls from the mountains, and is conveyed to this place by stone gutters, and as this water is very good to drink, it is transported to the city in small barks The passage is continued, with this reservoir to the left, and five powder mills, together with several beautiful gardens, and on the right a large number of brick and lime kilns, to the left of which runs a small river, which turns the mills, and the river *Carrot* flows to the right

The advanced guard of *Ryswick* is a league from thence, and half a league from a fine estate or farm of the director-general of *Riebeek*, it is distinguished by the name of *Tanna-aban*, or red-land, the red-lands already mentioned, beginning at this place, four leagues from *Sering-sing*, and twenty from the blew mountain.

After passing through the same gate, and leaving the great river on the right, one comes into a charming road bordered with trees, and fine gardens This leads to the fort of *Jacatra*, near which are the tombs of the *Chinese*, and at a little distance from these is the governor-general's garden *Nordwick* house, which belongs to Mr *Kastelein*, is not far from this place, and beyond it is another guard near a place called *Struiswick* A

1706   A league from the gate of *Rotterdam* is a small gulf, and the fort of *Anjol*, where a garison of thirty *European* soldiers is stationed There is likewise an oyster-fishery in this place, and the gulf must be crossed in order to go to *Tanjonpree*, where there is a noble house, with beautiful gardens and fish-ponds, from whence a fine prospect opens to the sea This estate belongs to the heirs of captain *Egberti*

A passage along the sea-shore leads to the two *Marotdes*, which were formerly the residence of the rebel *Jonker*. This place, which is three leagues from *Batavia*, supplies all the wood which is burnt in that city, and there is no proceeding farther, by reason of the thickets which fill this part of the country

In passing through the gate of *Dijl*, one advances half a quarter of a league to the east, where the road then turns to the west, and leads to two little forts, one of which is half, and the other three quarters of a league from the city At a little distance from hence is the canal of *Mocker*, which flows from *Tangeran*, and was made by the bailiff of *Mook*, who has been re-imbursed his expences, which amounted to a very considerable sum The money, however, may be considered as lost, since no use can be made of the canal If, indeed, it could be rendered navigable, it would prove of vast advantage to the city, that quarter producing a plentiful growth of wood *Tangeran*, to which this canal extends, is five leagues from *Batavia*, and separates the territories of that city from those of *Bantam*

From the gate of *Utrecht* one may proceed in the same road, to the north, as far as a place called the *Flute*, where a guard of fifteen soldiers is stationed, with a sergeant and two corporals This guard is on the western point of the sea-shore, by which means it renders any farther passage impracticable

All the out parts of the city are filled with beautiful gardens and fruit-trees, and are very populous as well as the suburbs, some of which extend to a great length, and on the side of them are several agreeable canals

1706

Every quarter of the city is full of *Chinese*, who are an indefatigable people, and very ingenious, especially in imitating whatever they see performed These people cultivate most of the landed estates in the country, and have the direction of all the sugar-mills, and those other places where arrack and brandy are made They likewise keep all sorts of shops, dress provisions, and sell liquors Their houses therefore are always filled with sailors. Malt-spirits being a very profitable commodity, a vast quantity is accordingly consumed

When I came to this city, I found thirty vessels in the road, and there were almost as many when I left it, exclusive of the barks which belong to that country

No appearance can be more agreeable than that of the canals, which are bordered with trees, and adorned with the finest houses imaginable The canals of most note are the *Tygersgraft*, the *Jonkersgragt*, the *Kacimangragt*, and the *Rhinocerosgragt*, and that which is formed by the great river, the rest are not so considerable The largest streets are those which are distinguished by the names of the *Prince*, the *Lords*, and *Newport* There are three churches, namely, the *Dutch*, the *Portuguese*, and the *Malayan*, where service is performed in those languages There are also several other ministers, who are sent to those places where the *Dutch* have any settlements

This city is inhabited by a great number of strangers, some of whom are habited in a very particular manner, while others are almost naked. The *Chinese*, who are most numerous, wear a kind of shirt, and under it a strait pair of drawers, which hang down to their feet Some of them have wide sleeves to their shirts, others those which are very narrow,

and

(margin notes: Chinese. Canals Streets Churches Strangers that are Chinese habit is)

1706 and buttoned on their wrifts Their legs are naked, and they wear flippers Their hair is plaited round a bodkin, on the top of their heads, like that of women, and they always go bare-headed, and carry a fan in their hand Their wives are habited after the manner of the country There are also abundance of *Metifs*, who are a people defcended from *Moors* and *Europeans* The *Kaflietfes* have a nearer refemblance to the *Europeans*, or *Whites*, and there are a third fort of them, called *Poeflietfis*, whofe complexion differs very little from ours They fpeak broken *Portuguefe*, and pretend it is their natural language Moft of them underftand *Dutch*, and are likewife acquainted with the language of the country Their habit refembles that which I have defcribed before in my account of the ifland of *Ceilon* The other ftrangers whom one finds at *Batavia*, are *Makaffares*, *Bougis*, *Baliers*, *Malayans*, and *Moors* of *Amboina*, or *Turnate*

Provifions With refpect to their provifions, their meat is not extraordinary, efpecially their beef, which is very lean, and they have no mutton but what is brought from other places The fmall quantity of milk which their cows yield is very furprifing, but thefe defects have fome compenfation in the abundance of fmall game in the woods But the confumption is not confiderable, tho' they are brought to market Their chief food is pullets, which are brought from the coaft of *Java*, together with ducks and geefe, and fometimes deer, and elkes The circumjacent woods are full of wild boars, and they likewife harbour Tigers, and Rhinoceroffes, with great numbers of apes, and other animals.

This city is plentifully fupplied *Fifh* with fifh, the largeft of which are moft efteemed, namely, the *Kakap*, the *Jacob Evertfen*, the *Bream*, the *Cabillau*, the *Royal Fifh*, and the carp There are alfo fmelts, foles, and a kind of plaice, &c together with cray-fifh, crabs, oyfters, and eels, and a large kind of cray-fifh, whofe flavour is admirable

Herbs are equally plentiful, and *Herbs* there is no want of good *French* beans, green peas, carrots, parfnips, large and fmall raddifhes, and potatoes, of which fome people make bread

I have prefented the reader with *The profil* a profil of the city in plate 220, *of Batavia.* which I took in one of the company's barks, and the whole is marked with numerical figures, 1 fhews the ftructure where the great bell is hung, 2 the advanced guard, 3. the magazines of oil, 4 the ftores of wood, 5 the place where rice is depofited; 6 the caftle, or citadel, 7. the gate which fronts the water, 8 a gate of lattice in the caftle wall, 9. a fmith's fhop, 10 the wood-yard, 11. the magazine for cloves, 12 the free port, 13 the eaft cape or point, 14 the weftern cape, 15 the river, 16. the fea-mark, called the duke of *Alva*, erected upon a bank of fand at the mouth of the river As this city is very low, one can fee nothing on the fide next the river, but the land which lies above it, together with one fide of the citadel, and the mountains which are covered with trees.

Vol. II.   I i   CHAP.

CHAP. LXXIII.

The retinue of the governor-general of the Indies. *The dignity which attends that employment. The difficulties inseparable from it, as well as from those of the other directors. The author resolves to return by land. A recital of the honours he received*

I Shall now give some account of the honours which are rendered to the governor-general of the *Indies*, who, in the name of the company, governs all the territories they possess in this country

The governor's state He usually devotes *Wednesday* and *Saturday* to his recreation, at one of his country seats, on which occasion he is preceded by a quartermaster, and sixteen horsemen, together with a trumpet, and two halberdiers on horse-back He is seated in a light coach, made after the *Spanish* fashion, and drawn by two horses His master of the horse rides by the side of it, followed by six other halberdiers, who ride two in a breast. These are succeeded by two other coaches, in which are those who accompany the governor, and the procession is closed by forty eight horsemen, with their captain, two quarter-masters, and a trumpet at their head He is attended almost in the same manner when he passes through the city, only his guard is then composed of foot, but his master of the horse, and the halberdiers, are always on horseback, unless he be going either to a wedding or a funeral, for then the halberdiers march on foot with their partisans in their hands But the master of the horse rides always beside the chariot

The manner in which he troops are exercised On *Sunday*, after divine service, he causes his guards to parade in the court of the citadel before his palace First appears a led horse richly caparisoned, and led by the bridle by an *European*, next a company of cavalry, armed with cuirasses, and attended by a trumpet, then a company of granadiers, followed by a battalion of fusiliers, pikemen, and musquetiers, armed with head-pieces, and preceded by six hautbois. They march twice round the place in good order, and are well acquainted with every branch of their exercise.

These marks of grandeur contribute in some measure to soften the *The arduous state of a governor* fatigues of so weighty and arduous a charge, for this great officer has never any rest or vacation, as among us He is harrassed with letters and pacquets, from the moment day begins to break, and is continually employed in the affairs of the company, by reason of the vast extent of the country which is under his jurisdiction Beside all which, he has a variety of business to transact with the ships that yearly come from *Holland* The sun is no sooner risen than the two principal merchants, the commander of the citadel, the major, the architect, the chief engineer, and several others, come to give him an account of what passes, and to receive his orders About eleven o'clock the *Sabandhaer* waits upon him, to give him a particular account of the barks, merchandises, and persons that are arrived, and the place to which they are bound, after which he dispatches the necessary pass-ports, and must likewise give audience to those who have any affairs to transact at the palace

These attentions engage him till dinner-time, when he has not above half an hour's rest, and he even employs part of that time in talking of business, after which he returns to the duties of his province till supper So that to form a true judg-

1706 judgment of things, without being influenced by outward appearances, one muſt needs pronounce him a meer ſlave, who has not a moment to himſelf, and dares not paſs one night out of the citadel He is likewiſe obliged to give the company an account of all that paſſes on the coaſt of *Java*, and its dependent territories Every member of the council is obliged to do the ſame by a courier, with reſpect to thoſe affairs which are under his direction

The aſſembling of the council
The council aſſembles conſtantly twice a week, and ſometimes oftner, as any extraordinary occaſion may require Foreign miniſters who arrive at *Batavia*, are not permitted to depart from thence before they have been conducted to an audience of the governor

Theſe conſtant employments, which were always preſented to my view, cauſed me to recollect the manner in which I had paſſed my time at *Moſcow*, where, when I asked my friends, how long their feſtivals and rejoicings were deſigned to be continued, they immediately replied, that their diverſions began with *January*, and ended with *December*. How different is this manner of living, from that of perſons of diſtinction in this country ! I was therefore ſo far from envying their grandeur and proſperity, that, on the contrary, I thought myſelf very happy in being able with a moderate fortune to enjoy a pleaſing tranquility of mind, in conjunction with a ſtate of liberty, without which all other advantages are of no ſignification

The director general
The moſt important charge next to the governor's, is that of directorgeneral, which is altogether as fatiguing, ſince he is obliged by his ſtation to buy up, and diſpoſe of all the merchandiſe of the company, of what nature ſoever it be, and to what place ſoever they ſend them , beſide the other employments incident to this office In a word, he has the management of every particular that relates to commerce,

and all the merchants and officers of 1706 the company render an account to him of what paſſes, and receive from him the keys of the magazines, the charge of which is conſigned to his care This director alſo iſſues his orders with reſpect to the particular cargo each ſhip is to take on board

The general of the company's troops
During my continuance at *Batavia*, no one was more eſteemed than Mr *de Wilde*, general of the company's troops, and the third officer in their ſervice He is alſo a member of the council of the *Indies*, and a perſon of extraordinary merit I ſhall not give any particular account of the members of the council, nor of thoſe who poſſeſs inferior ſtations, ſince what relates to them is ſufficiently known in our country For which reaſon I ſhall only add, that I do not believe there is any place in the world where they write ſo much as in the offices belonging to the company, where a number of extraordinary penmen are employed.

As I had no longer any affairs to detain me at *Batavia*, I thought of returning home by *Perſia*, and found myſelf the more inclinable to undertake that journey, becauſe I was informed about that time, that four *French* men of war were cruiſing on the *Indian* coaſts, and had taken the *Phœnix* on the coaſt of *Coromandel*, in her return from *Bengale*, and two *Engliſh* ſhips in the beginning of the year , beſide which *A miſunderſtanding between the Mogul and the company*
there was ſome miſunderſtanding between the great *Mogul* and the company, in conſequence of which that monarch would no longer permit them to trade on the coaſt of *Coromandel* As it therefore was impracticable for me to go thither without hazard, I reſolved to return by land as ſoon as poſſible, though I was adviſed to the contrary, and was alſo preſſed to take the opportunity of embarking in one of the ſhips that were returning, to which I had no manner of inclination The governor-general, perceiving my reſolution was fixed, informed me, that in eight

1706 eight or ten days, he should difpatch two fhips for *Perfia*, and that I might have a paffage in one of them I then defired a pafs port from the director-general, which he granted me immediately, telling me at the fame time, with all imaginable civility, that he was forry to lofe me fo foon, and before I had feen one of his eftates, which he intended to have fhewn me

A pleafant houfe belonging to the governor general

I, however, went to divert myfelf once more at *Struifwick*, with the governor, and general *de Wilde*, together with other perfons of diftinction This place, which belongs to the governor, is beautified with the fineft avenues and moft delightful walks in the world It is likewife full of fruit-trees, and watered by the great river, which runs on one fide of it The houfe is built of wood, and contains a fpacious hall, with a variety of other apartments We breakfafted here, and went afterward to another houfe belonging to this lord, where we arrived before noon, and found fome members of the council of the *Indies*, with other friends, and were entertained in a very elegant manner The governor told me in the evening, that the director-general was to go the 11th of *Auguft* to the

* Onruft

ifle * *without reft*, and that I might take this opportunity to fee it. The director likewife was fo obliging as to defire me, two days before his departure, to accompany him thither, and fent me the following order the fame day

Thofe who have the command of the fhip called the Prince Eugene, *are hereby authorifed to receive on board the perfon and baggage of* Cornelius Le Bruyn, *in order to conduct him into* Perfia, *and they have orders to lodge, and entertain him in the captain's cabbin*

Given at the caftle of *Batavia*, the 6th of *Auguft*, 1706

A. DE RIEBEEK

I failed not to go at the appointed 1706 time to the director's houfe, where I found above twenty perfons, who were to accompany us to the ifle *without reft*, which is about three leagues from *Batavia* We fet out on this little progrefs with the found of feveral trumpets, and hautboys, and all the fhips in the road hoifted their flags and ftreamers, which afforded a very agreeable profpect We arrived there about eight o clock, and took a view of the ifland, and the fort, which is well provided with cannon, and has a good garifon They make in this ifland all things neceffary for refiting fhips, and there is fuch a continual noife of hammers and anvils, that it is juftly called the ifland *without reft* It is furrounded with banks of fand, which prevent the approach of larger veffels, and none but fmall barks pafs between that and the ifle of *Kuiper*, which is over-againft it, at a fmall diftance I went over to it, and took from thence a draught of the former While I was thus employed, the director vifited fome of the members of the council, and about noon they gave me notice by a floop, that it was dinner-time I had then juft finifhed my work, which the reader will find in plate 221 The galley in which we came appears at the point of the ifland, and upon the bank are three cranes with feveral fmall veffels

Several fifhes of extraordinary beauty were fhewn me at my return, and as dinner was not then ferved up, I haftened to the fhore, in order to take a draught of the ifland of *Kuiper*, which is exhibited in plate 222, for I was very fenfible that the company would not part with me after dinner, becaufe it was the director's lady's birth-day, for which reafon they intended to devote that time to pleafure We were entertained in a fplendid manner both with flefh and fifh, under a tent, and there was no want of wine upon that occafion. General *de Wilde*, and

1706 and five members of the council of the *Indies* were there alfo About the middle of the entertainment fome *Dutchmen* made their appearance , two of them were habited like women, and they diverted us with feveral agreeable fancies We returned in the evening to the fame place, where we continued our diverfions, and drank the governor's health, which was accompanied with a difcharge of the fhips cannon, and the found of the trumpets, and hautbois About feven we arrived at *Batavia*, and went to congratu-

late madam *de Riebeek* on her birth-day 1706.

As the time of my departure drew nigh, I went the next day to take my leave of the members of the council of the *Indies*, and to return them my acknowledgments for all their civilities. General *de Wilde*, preffed me with his ufual complaifance to dine with him, and I fhall always retain a grateful remembrance of the obliging manner in which he treated me . I muft add too, in juftice to his character, that I never faw a more polite gentleman than himfelf

CHAP. LXXIV.

Tombs of the Chinefe *Their funerals. An entertainment given by the governor-general. His civility to the author.*

Chinefe tombs

TWO days before my departure, I went with the governor's mafter of the horfe, to take a view of fome *Chinefe* tombs , and I made a draught of them, which the reader will find in plate 223 Thefe tombs are all built in the fame form, only fome are larger, and more ornamented than others

Their fentiments with relation to their tombs

The reafon they affign for this uniformity in the ftructure of their tombs, is, that all Men are alike fhut up in the womb of their mothers, and therefore there ought to be no diftinction between them after their death They firft dig a grave in proportion to the coffin, which is longer, but not deeper than ours, and is likewife very thick, and varnifhed over They cover it at the fame time with paper, and bind cords about it After which they caft money into the grave, more or lefs, according to the rank and eftate of the deceafed perfon, and place the coffin upon it They then make the cement which is to be employed in building the tomb, and is compofed of the whites of eggs,

and other ingredients, which render it fo hard, and binding, that it is impoffible either to break or remove it from its place The top of the tomb is raifed fome feet above the earth, in a round form, and encompaffed with ornaments that refemble fteps. They place likewife on the forepart feveral branches, and fome fquare bafes, upon which they fix the heads of beafts, fuch as lions, tygers, &c painted in green, with a fmall intermixture of red, by way of ornament They likewife raife, on the middle of the fteps which lead up to the tomb, a fmall work in form of an altar, with a red border in the middle of the front, and fome *Chinefe* characters in gold. The pavement which is laid before the tomb, is of the fame mafonry with the reft of the work, it is likewife white, and divided into three compartments feparate from each other, with a little elevation on the backpart There is another altar on the right, in the front, with a kind of a niche in the middle.

Vol II.

K k

Thefe

These tombs coft fometimes two, three, or four hundred crowns, but there are fome which have no ornaments beftowed upon them The mafonry and form of the work is the fame in all, becaufe it is thought that the dead, by thefe means, will repofe in perfect fafety

When I arrived at this place, I faw fome people employed in making one of thefe tombs for a perfon whom they were going to inter The proceffion advanced foon after, and I beheld feveral tents furnifhed with every thing neceffary for a kitchen, and for preparing a repaft I carefully obferved all the ceremonials practifed by the funeral train, which refembled a proceffion, with refpect to the number of perfons that compofed it, and the ornaments which were carried on that occafion, fuch as ftreamers, parafols, and canopies, under one of which was carried one of their faints, known by the name of *Jeffe* , and I likewife heard the found of feveral bells When they came to the place where the corpfe was to be laid in the earth, every thing was difpatched with great expedition, and in very good order Over-againft one of thefe tombs was a pavilion, and feveral parafols, under one of which I obferved a large table covered with all forts of provifions brought from the city, and among the reft a raw hog, and a he-goat, which were to be offered to the faint I have already mentioned In the mean time thofe who attended the funeral threw money into the grave, and then the corps was let down A prieft, who ftood at one end of the grave, held a book in his hand, in which he read, and by the fide of him ftood another, who held a filver plate full of feeds, of which he threw now and then a handful toward the attendants, as likewife upon the coffin, and the deceafed woman's child, who ftood on the other fide of the tomb, covered with a robe of unwrought flax, which flowed over his head after the manner of the antients, who covered themfelves in

this manner with fack-cloth in times of mourning and affliction, and caft themfelves upon the earth This child, who was but ten years old, did fo feveral times, and then rofe up again by the direction of the attendants, among whom was his father clothed in white The prieft then ordered the child to approach him, and made him fprinkle fome handfuls of feed upon his mother's coffin, which concluded the ceremony Nothing appeared to me more extraordinary then the fcattering of the feed, which was certainly emblematical, and fignified to the attendants, that the perfons who performed the ceremonial wifhed their pofterity might be multiplied in the fame manner

While fome were employ'd in making the cement already mentioned, the reft feated themfelves at table, to the number of five hundred perfons, among whom were feveral women clothed in white, with a kind of pointed cap of the fame colour upon their heads, and which hung down to the middle of their body The company continued there till the evening, under the trees Thefe tombs are but a fmall league from *Batavia*, and there are feveral which are not fo far The reader will find them reprefented in plate 224 The circumftances of this funeral repaft correfpond with the cuftom I have elfewhere mentioned, of bringing provifions to the tombs of the dead in other places There are even fome who come thither to fmoke, or drink coffee, &c others to pay their devotions, as I have feen practifed at *Chiras*, or *Zjterunes* in *Perfia* They frequently make thefe repafts, foon after the interment of the body, upon carpets fpread on the earth. This ceremonial is practifed among the oriental Chriftians, namely, in *Georgia, Armenia,* and among the *Greeks,* who pour out their lamentations around the tombs of their anceftors, as has been obferv'd in the account of *Ifpahan* The more forrow they teftify on
　　　　　　　　　　　thefe

The funeral repaft

FUNERAILLES DES CHINOIS.

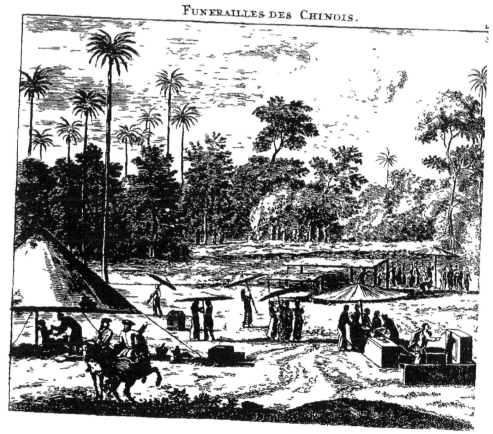

TOMBEAUX DES CHINOIS.   223

1706. thefe occafions, the greater is the honour which they render to the relations of the deceafed They alfo hire mourners of both fexes, who perform the ceremony of weeping for the dead, in the greateft perfection. This cuftom has prevailed in all ages, and the prophet *Jeremiah* mentions it in his *Lamentations*.

I returned about noon to the citadel, where the governor had caufed a fplendid entertainment to be prepared for fome ftrangers, who were lately arrived from *Holland*, as well as for thofe, who were returning thither, or going to other places. I had the honour to be one of the guefts, whofe number amounted to fifty five perfons, among whom were general *de Wilde*, feven members of the council of the *Indies*, and moft of thofe who conftitute the council of juftice The feaft was ferved up in the great council-chamber, with inexpreffible magnificence The company withdrew about five, and the governor then asked me if I had compleated the preparations for my departure? To which I replied, that I had, and that nothing remained but to return him my humble acknowledgments for all his civilities He was again fo obliging, as to defire me to tell him, if there were any other particulars wherein he could be ferviceable to me? Upon which I endeavoured to exprefs my fenfe of his goodnefs in the beft manner I was able.

I went the fame Day to take my leave of his Predeceffor, Mr *Outfhorn*, who treated me with the utmoft civility, and made me a prefent of feveral curiofities. The next day I went to take my leave of the director-general *de Riebeek*, and Mr *Kaftelein*, to whom I had very particular obligations, and who did me the honour of a vifit in his turn In fhort, I muft again declare, in juftice to all thefe gentlemen, that no perfon could be entertained in a more obliging manner than I was by them, and I fhould think myfelf the moft ungrateful of mankind, if I did not conftantly retain a grateful remembrance of their favours I went alfo to take my leave of my old friend Mr *Hoogkamer*, vice-prefident of the council of juftice, whofe memory I fhall always honour, I then embarked my goods on board the fhip, which was to convey me to *Perfia*.

I fupped that evening, for the laft time, with the general of the *Indies*, and gave my baggage into the hands of Mr *Pauli*, a gentleman of merit, and fteward to that lord; and he had the goodnefs to charge himfelf with the care of its conveyance to *Holland*. I then went on board the *Prince Eugene*, a fhip of forty guns, and one hundred and thirty men, and it was one hundred and forty five feet in length.

CHAP.

CHAP. LXXV.

The author's departure from Batavia. *Observations on the water near the Line. The southern coast of* Arabia Felix *His arrival at* Gamron.

The author sets sail from Batavia.

WE set sail the 15th of *August*, in company with another vessel called the *Monster*, from which we had orders not to separate ourselves, by reason of the war of which I have already spoken, and we met the *Beverwick*, and several other ships coming from *Holland*. A calm obliged us to anchor in the evening near the isles of *Combuis*, in eleven fathom water We continued our course at break of day, but were obliged to stop again in the evening, and anchor in seventeen fathom water. The next day we did nothing but shift up and down, the wind being against us to the west, and a small bark came up with us in order to sell us fruits, and other provisions. We cast anchor again, toward evening, in twenty three fathom water, and continued our course at day-break, steering west-south-west, with the wind south-south-east That day the captain of the *Monster* came on board us, to agree with our captain, on the signals to be used in the voyage About evening we cast anchor again near the second point of *Java*, and sailed again at day-break. We were obliged to anchor again between the second point and the *New Isle*, in twenty four fathom water We found here a small *English* vessel that set out from *Batavia* before us, and we sent her to fetch water from the corner of the *terra firma* of *Java*, where it is *The New Isle, and that called Prince's* very excellent. I made a draught of the *New Isle*, which the reader will find in plate 225, as also of the *Prince's Island*, opposite to it, and which is exhibited in plate 226.

The next day we continued our course, and left the *English* vessel at anchor, which by all circumstances, was to take in pepper, instead of water, in that place. As the wind was south-south-east, we passed on in the evening, at the distance of two leagues from the western point of *Java*, which lay south-east of us. We steer'd west-south-west and by south, and soon lost sight of land, the wind blowing a fresh gale. That night, and the two following days, the wind continued south-east, and we had exceeding good weather The third day we steered westward, the wind being east-south-east The first of *September* the captain of our ship went on board the *Monster*, and as it appeared in the evening, that we were advanced into the longitude of 104 degrees, and 45 minutes, it was resolved that we should steer westward, as far as 89 degrees, and forty or fifty minutes longitude, and 9 degrees south latitude, and then proceed northward, passing the line to the tenth degree of northern latitude, and from thence, north-north-west, as far as the cape of *Rasalgato*, or toward the coast of *Arabia*. On the fourth, the *Monster* hoisted her flag upon the main-mast, and we took down ours toward evening, and discharged a cannon, as had been before agreed The fifteen days, in which we were to have the lead, being expired, we lay by, to let her advance before us, and as she was a very bad sailor, we were obliged to do so very often, without being able to take the opportunity of the wind, which at that time stood fair for us This circumstance created us much uneasiness, since we were apprehensive it would prove a great impediment to our voyage

The

1706 The 5th we loſt ſight of the Monſter's lanthorn, during the night, but continued our courſe directly weſt, with few ſails up The 6th in the morning, we perceived her ſouth-weſt of us, at a vaſt diſtance, upon which we ſteered that courſe, and ſhe came up within two leagues of us On the 8th ſhe made a ſignal for changing the courſe, and advancing weſt-north-weſt, and on the 9th the weather was changeable On the 10th ſhe made another ſignal for ſome of us to come on board her, and we advanced northward in the evening The next day we had a view of her to the north-weſt, at the diſtance of two leagues from us, and in the ſouthern latitude of 6 degrees 42 minutes, and 88 degrees 30 minutes longitude On the 12th, about noon, having advanced about 25 degrees northward, we came into 5 degrees 2 minutes of ſouth latitude, ſteering north, and north-weſt, in order to come up with the other ſhip, which, in the evening, was within a league of us to the weſt

The water very ſalt near the line

The 15th we drew near the line, and found the water much ſalter there than in other parts of the ſea, not only to the taſte, but even to the ſight, the waves which beat againſt the prow of our ſhip leaving a thick foam of a whitiſh complexion, and full of ſalt Some people have formerly been deceived with this appearance, in their approaches to the line, and imagined that it was occaſioned by the ſhallowneſs of the water, but they were ſoon convinced of their error by ſounding, without finding any bottom The 16th we advanced twenty three leagues north-north-weſt, as far as fourteen minutes north latitude, and 88 degrees 21 minutes longitude on the other ſide the line. The diſtance from *Batavia* to this place is computed to be 686 leagues, and from the line to *Gamron* 480. The wind blew weſt by north, and weſt-north-weſt, and weſt by ſouth in the night On the 18th we came into 2 degrees 31 minutes of north-

Vol II

ern latitude, and 88 degrees of longitude The *Monſter* took down her flag in the evening, and we hoiſted ours the next day, with a diſcharge of cannon, and found ourſelves about noon, in 3 degrees 44 minutes of northern latitude, and in the longitude of 87 degrees 21 minutes The other ſhip was three leagues from us, and we were obliged to lie by and wait for her. The following days we ſaw ſeveral ſmall red cray-fiſh playing round our ſhip On the 23d we ſteered our courſe north-north-weſt, with little wind, which blew from ſouth-ſouth-eaſt. The 24th we changed our compaſſes, from the fifteenth to the tenth degree north-weſt, and advanced on the 26th to the north by weſt, after having given the ſignal. We here ſaw a flight of land birds, together with ſome grey ſwallows, and afterward a white butterfly. We took one of the ſwallows, but reſtored it to its liberty again.

On the 27th, I obſerved an extraordinary greenneſs in the ſea, together with a ſhoal of ſmall fiſh, and a parcel of floating eggs At the ſame inſtant appeared a large fiſh, very different from any I had ever ſeen before His head was ſix feet or more in length, and he immediately diſappeared

The captain of the *Monſter* came on board us that day, and we were then, by agreement, to ſteer north by weſt, till we ſhould come within ſight of the *Arabian* coaſt. They ſounded twice in the evening without finding any bottom A little after the *Monſter* made a ſignal to notify that land was ſeen As it was very high, we ſoon perceived it likewiſe, from weſt-ſouth-weſt, to north-weſt by north, having ſailed ſeventeen leagues ſince noon to north by weſt. We then ſteered north-eaſt by eaſt, till morning, when we perceived the weſtern coaſt riſing very high, and ſteep toward the weſt, and alſo another tract of land of the ſame form, to the north-weſt, and to the north a round hill like an iſland, about three

L l   leagues

1706

1706 leagues from us, the greateft appearance of land was toward the weft, and weft by north This was the coaft of *Arab a Felix*, near the cape of *Curia Maria*, according to the maps I drew the plan of it in the morning, and perceived to the north-weft, a kind of gulf between lofty mountains, and in the middle of it an ifland, as it appears in plate 227 The mountains which appear on the other fide of it are reprefented in plate 228 Before thefe mountains is feen an ifland which rifes to a confiderable height, but is not taken notice of in the maps, any more than the gulf itfelf One can fee there only two or three points, without any appearance of the ifland As the weather was a little cloudy, we could not have a diftinct view of the land We afterward advanced, between the *Red Sea* and the *Perfian Gulf*, fteering firft fouth-eaft, and then fouth-eaft by eaft, the wind being fouth-weft by weft, and weft-fouth-weft About ten in the morning we faw the laft appearance of that land, to the north-north-weft, and at the diftance of about four or five leagues from us Our bowfprit then happened to break, and we were obliged to repair it as well as we could About noon we came into 17 degrees 12 minutes of north latitude, fteering directly eaft, without feeing any land We afterward directed our courfe eaft-north-eaft during the whole night, the wind being weft-fouth-weft On the 30th the wind fhifted to the fouthward, and we fteered north by eaft at break of day About noon we found ourfelves in 18 degrees 8 minutes of northern latitude, and 81 degrees 15 minutes longitude, having failed but twenty five leagues north-eaft by eaft, in twenty four hours, and as we did not difcover any land, we fteered to eaft-north-eaft In the evening the *Monfter* fired a gun, and kindled a blaze upon her fkuttle, being weftward of us, fhe likewife fired a fecond time, and we faw again the fire upon her fkuttle This was the fignal to found, upon draw-

ing near to land, but we found no 1706 bottom at 150 fathom depth We lay by till the fecond watch of the night, with two lanthorns lighted, that the other fhips crew might fee us, but as we heard nothing of them, nor faw any light, we continued our courfe, eaft-north-eaft, as before, the wind being fouth-weft, and weft-fouth-weft, and the fky very clear In the mean while we founded feveral times without finding any bottom The firft of *October* we entirely loft fight of the *Monfter*, and imagining that fhe had changed her courfe, we refolved to continue our voyage without waiting for her, and advanced to the north-eaft by north, the wind being fouth-weft, and came about noon into 20 degrees 8 minutes of north latitude

The 3d in the afternoon we difcovered land, and a range of high mountains, to the north-weft, advancing continually north-north-weft In the evening we faw the weftern coaft, to the weft by fouth, about eight leagues from us We likewife found a change in the water in the night, and advanced eaftward upon that account On the 4th there was a fog, which prevented us from having any diftinct view of the land, and about noon we perceived a fhip to the weft-north-weft, about three leagues from us We immediately fired our cannon, and ftruck the fkuttle fail twice, a fignal which had been agreed upon between us and the *Monfter*, and fhe did not anfwer, fo that we concluded it was not her

We were foon after furprized by a calm, and at fun-fet we founded, about eight or nine leagues from the high cape of *Rafalagata* As we had fcarce any wind, we came near the fhip I mentioned, and found it to be the *Monfter* About noon we came into 23 degrees 30 minutes northern latitude, under the tropic, and found at fun-fet that land was not above fix leagues from us During the night we fteered weft-north-weft, the wind being eaft-fouth-eaft The next day

The cape Rafalaga ta

227 COTE MERIDIONALE DE L'ARABIE HEUREUSE

229 BAYE DE MUSKETTA

231 ISLE DE LAREKE

COTE MERIDIONALE DE L ARABIE HEUREUSE 228

RIVAGE OU COTE D ARABIE PROCHE DU CAP DE MONSANDON. 230

ISLE DE KISMUS. 232

1706 day we founded within fight of a small ifland, or rock, about two leagues and a half from us, without finding any bottom We found that the diftance between the cape of *Rafalagata*, and the bay of *Musketta* is not fo confiderable as is reprefented in the maps This little ifle, or rock, is directly oppofite to that bay, and is called by fome the *Grey-Rock*, the reader will find a reprefentation of it in plate 229

The grey-rock.

On the 7th, we came into 24 degrees 26 minutes north latitude, and at the diftance of feven or eight leagues from land, and founded, but found no bottom The next day we failed but feven leagues, and difcovered the coaft of *Arabia*, from the fouth to the north-weft by weft

The next day we found ourfelves in 24 degrees 35 minutes, but ftill without finding any bottom On the 11th, we founded in the latitude of cape *St James*, to the north-eaft and by north, and about noon came into 25 degrees 25 minutes, where, founding by the rock on this fide the cape, to the eaft-fouth-eaft, we found fixty fathom water. We then advanced northward, and in the evening weftward We approached in the night fome iflands that are fituated before the cape of *Monfandon*, where we found a depth of water from fixty to forty fathom, and fteered to the north, with the wind at fouth-fouth-weft

Cape St James

The cape of Monfandon

The next day I made a draught of the *Arabian* coaft, near the cape, with the adjacent rocks, in the manner as the whole is exhibited in plate

The coaft of Arabia

250 We continued our courfe to north-north-weft, with the fame wind, and founded at fome diftance from a rock called *Leeft*, which lay north of us, and the ifle of *Ormus* north-north-weft, toward which we advanced in a direct courfe, and found there from forty to thirty fathom water About noon we founded again, at the point of *Ormus*, to the north-eaft and by north, and at the inner point of *Kifmus* to the fouth weft, and by weft I took a draught of *Laieke* to the eaftward, as it is reprefented in plate 231, and likewife of the ifland of *Kifmus*, which appears in plate 232. We found here a depth of water from twenty-four to twenty-two fathom, and being come, about evening, into four fathom two feet, we thought it advifeable to caft anchor, after which I landed, and went to the new lodge, where the director, and other of the company's officers then refided They were furprifed at my return, becaufe, when I fet out from thence, in the preceding year, I was in a very bad ftate of health I was informed that the fteward of *Sypeftein* was dead, and likewife two merchants, one of whom died at *Zjieraes*, as he was travelling to *Ifpahan*, and that Mr *Prefcot*, the *Englifh* minifter at the court of *Perfia*, had followed them I have given a reprefentation of the ifle of *Ormus*, as it appears from the lodge at *Gamron*, when the air is clear and ferene, with the caftle on the extreme point to the left

1706

Ifle of Ormus.

Ifles of Lareke and Kifmus

CHAP.

I ISLE ORMUS

CHAP. LXXVI.

Remarkable things at Gamron *The situation of* Effin. *Cotton-trees. Extraordinary plants The arrival of the governor of* Gamron. *The author's departure from thence. His arrival at* Laer, *and* Jaron

THOUGH I had determined to go immediately to *Ispahan,* I was obliged to continue some days at *Gamron,* to wait for the carriages from *Zjie-raes* or *Chiras,* I therefore accompanied the director to his country-house at *Naeibacn,* which is situated not above a mile from the city, at the foot of a mountain, from whence there is a very beautiful prospect both to the sea, and toward the city Near this place is the tree greatly commended by Mr *Tavernier,* but which is far from corresponding with his account of it All that can be said is, that the branches bend down to the ground,

A mistake of Mr Tavernier

and some have taken root, and shoot out like young trees, as to any other particulars, the tree is not very lofty, nor does it afford a large shade. I have seen several of the same species in the *Indies,* near *Malakka,* and upon the coast which goes by the name of *Pasyaei* There is in this place a small house, which serves for a retreat to the *Banians* in the night In our return we met with some courtiers of that nation, who were diverting themselves in the open field with two of the dancers of the country, and other buffoons, who performed several ridiculous feats, by torch-light, for the

sun

1706 fun was down We went to them, and they entertained us with hot liquors, confections, and other delicacies

On the 23d, I hired two men, and as many affes, according to the cuftom of thofe parts, together with a guide, to conduct me to *Effin*, where he himfelf dwelt, and from thence to any other places which I fhould be inclinable to vifit This place is three leagues from *Gamron*, and feated on a plain, half a league from the mountains. It chiefly confifts of gardens, and little huts, inhabited by poor people There is a houfe here belonging to the company, which fupplies *Gamron* with the beft water that is to be found there

An extraordinary tree

The moft remarkable thing I obferved here, was a tree, the trunk of which was fifty two fpans in circumference · It was ftrait in the middle, and full of branches of a proportionable bignefs, with fmall leaves

This tree is called *Dragtoe*, and it bears a kind of a wild apple. The reader will find a reprefentation of it in plate 233, and one of its branches, with the leaves upon it, drawn from the natural one, in plate 234. There were feveral names carved on the bark, and upon the trunk is a fmall piece of white mafonry, for which the *Bantans* have a great veneration, becaufe this tree is facred to one of their faints, the garden, in which it grows, formerly belonged to them, but they fold it out of a foolifh fuperftition, having taken it into their imagination, that all who inhabit it will die young It belonged at that time to the *Englifh* interpreter They believe, however, that thofe who are afflicted with a fever, or any other difeafe, may obtain a cure, by making a pilgrimage thither.

Cotton plants

I faw here fome cotton-trees, as large as a common apple-tree, moft other trees of that fpecies refemble fmall plants more than trees, but the leaves are exactly the fame

Ju-a

I likewife found here a white flower, or rather the leaves of a plant, or tree, known by the name of *Ju-*
Vol II.

ca, and which the *Perfans* call *Go-lie-kielie* This plant, which comes from *Surat*, has a ftrong, but very agreeable odour, and the inhabitants pretend that it attracts ferpents The flower of it is nine inches in length, and grows in bunches inclofed in the leaves of the plant, which are ten inches long · This flower produces feveral others in its middle part I have kept one, which was prefented to me, and it ftill preferves its fragrancy, notwithftanding it is now dry It is five or fix inches in circumference, with the leaves that enfold it

I returned the next day to *Gamron*, through a rocky road, the tracks of which are fo narrow and bad, that there is no paffing but upon affes, which are fmall, but very fwift. They are fomething like thofe in *Egypt* in the country adjacent to *Grand Cairo*

The arrival of the governor of Gamron

Alie Chan, duke or governor of *Gamron*, arrived there the next day, and was faluted with a difcharge of cannon from the citadel, and likewife from the fhips which lay in the road I went to pay him a vifit, an hour after his arrival, with the director, and other of the company's officers, and he entertained us after the *Perfian* manner, with hot liquors, and tobacco

Two days after the governor came to vifit the director, with a train of forty perfons, on horfeback, and thirty five couriers, among whom were thirty that fupported fmall banners He was likewife entertained agreeably to the cuftom of the country, but did not ftay long

As the governor had brought feveral mules from *Zjie-raes*, whither they were to return, I took this opportunity, and hired them to carry my baggage, having before provided myfelf of a horfe, and other neceffaries, and I fixed my departure for the 30th I then took leave of my friends, and of captain *Helma*, in whofe fhip I came, and to whom I had many obligations

The next day I gave the director the letters which I had written to the governor-
M m

governor-general of the I..., and others of my friends at Batav... after which I took my leave of him, and all the other officers belonging to the company

To assist at the funeral of Mr Cross

We went in the evening to the *English* lodge to assist at the funeral of Mr *Cross*, director of the *British* company, and I set forward at the same time, in order to arrive that evening at *Bandih*, three leagues from *Gamron*, in the road to *Ispahan*, being accompanied only by a muleteer, and one footman, because I had sent my equipage before. I renewed my journey at three in the morning, and proceeded as far as the *Caravanserai* of *Gitpie*, after having travelled five leagues. We passed the day there under a tree, and set out again in the evening, when we passed over a large plain, and advanced as far as the old *Caravanserai* of *Koreftan*, which is six leagues from the former.

We arrived, about ten in the morning, at the *Caravanserai* of *Goer-bafar-goen*, after a journey of four leagues, and the next day, at the same hour, at that of *Bilon*, which is five leagues from the former, and where we found no company, which had likewise been our fate at that of *Goer-bafar-goen*, but the peasants brought us pullets, and other provisions. This quarter, which confists of ftony plains fituated between mountains, is very unfertile. We found there, under a tree, our fmall caravan which came from *Gamron* before us, and set out again on the fourth of *November*. We followed it about three or four hours after, and arrived about nine at the *Caravanserai* of *Germoet*, after we had travelled five leagues. I there drew part of the village, and a well covered with a stone dome, as may be seen in plate 235.

We continued our journey next day with the *Caravan*, and found the water of that quarter to be very bad and falt. But travellers commonly provide themselves of a fufficient quantity at places where it is good : After we had travelled six

leagues farther, and paffed over feveral plains, we arrived about evening at the *Caravanserai* of *Sempon gien*, where we paffed the night. It was very hot during the day, and cold in the night.

The next day we passed over a beautiful plain full of villages and gardens, as far as *Laer*, where we refted after we had travelled six leagues. We found here feveral travellers, and a caravan from *Zjie-raes*, loaded with wine, for the members of our company at *Gamron*. We continued here till the 8th, and then purfued our journey over a plain, at the end of which, and oppofite to the mountains, we found a refervoir of water, with a building, near which we had paffed the night, when we travelled that way before, the water is conveyed hither by a canal walled in, and which runs crofs the mountains ; the reader will find a reprefentation of it in plate 236. From thence we paffed over fome high and fteep mountains, and then defcended into a beautiful plain, where we faw a handfome ftone *Caravanserai*, and a few houfes inhabited by husbandmen. After we had paffed over this plain, which is two leagues and a half in length, we entered among the mountains, and paffed the night at the *Caravanserai* of *Dikoe*, a confiderable village, full of trees and gardens, and fituated upon a plain of a roundifh form, and partly cultivated into arable land.

The next day we proceeded three leagues farther to *Bieries*, a large well-built town, which furpaffes feveral of their cities. We there found a handfome *Caravanserai* of ftone, from whence there is a profpect of a ruined caftle, which has been already mentioned, and is fituated on a neighbouring mountain.

My courier was taken fo ill there, that I was upon the point of leaving him behind, but finding himfelf better the next day, he followed us upon an afs. After we had paffed over the mountain, we came into a beautiful plain, where we faw feveral flocks of fheep, and a ruinous

Ca-

1706 Caravanſerai, where there were some caravans, with camels, horſes, and mules We advanced as far as the village of Ais-Zjtiraſu, where we ſtopped after we had travelled five leagues As there was no Caravanſerai here, we took up our lodgings in a very agreeable houſe, which has likewiſe been already mentioned

The next day we paſſed over a plain, which was ſandy in ſome places, and cultivated in others In the midſt of it is a rock, and a large ciſtern finely ſhaded by a ſingle tree which grows near it We arrived about evening at the Caravanſerai of Dedomba having travelled four leagues

We purſued our journey on the 12th, over the ſame plain, as far as the Caravanſerai of Mouſel, where I found father Pedro d'Alcantara, with whom I had lodged at Zjieraes, he was accompanied by three other Italian monks, and was going to embark at Gamron, in order to take a voyage to Sicopolis in the Mo- 1706 gals country, in quality of biſhop, and apoſtolical vicar

The next day we continued our journey in the afternoon, but as I was obliged to leave my courier behind me, I furniſhed him with what was proper for his ſubſiſtence, and ordered him to follow me to Iſpahan as ſoon as his health would permit him After we had travelled five leagues, we ſtopt at the Caravanſerai of Zatal, where the perſon who had the care of it being indiſpoſed, deſired me to give him a little wine, which I very readily did, and he in return made me a preſent of ſome citrons and oranges

We ſet out again in the afternoon, and after we had paſſed over the mountains, or rocks of Jaron, which are very dangerous, the bad roads frequently obliging travellers to alight from their horſes, we arrived late at the city of Jaron, having travelled five leagues that afternoon

✹✹✹✹✹✹✹✹✹✹✹✹✹✹✹✹✹✹✹✹✹✹✹✹✹✹✹✹✹

C H A P. LXXVII.

The authors departure from Jaron *An account of ſome antiquities His arrival at* Zjie-raes. *A robbery committed on ſome merchants.*

The authors departure from Jaron

WE ſet out from Jaron on the 15th, and when we had paſſed through the city, we came into a beautiful plain, full of cattle, we paſſed the night in a pleaſant garden, which was walled in The roads are very good in this quarter, and the plain is cut into ſeveral canals, over which we paſſed on ſmall bridges of ſtone

We met on the road ſeveral troops of aſſes laden with rice for Laer I ſaw alſo a tower of a conſiderable height, but unaccompanied with any other building, there were likewiſe ſeveral tombs entirely ruinous, and a few ſmall houſes in-habited by poor people The name of this place is Demonaer

After we had travelled ſome leagues, we paſſed over a bridge of ſeven arches, under which a current of water flows when it is high, but at that time there was none Toward evening we forded a river, and after we had travelled about ſix leagues, arrived at the Caravanſerai of Moogack

The next day we met two of the company's couriers, who were carrying letters from Iſpahan to Gamron. We left the common road at this place, in order to go to Tadurwan, along the river ſide, and

Demonaer

we

1706 we kept this road near an hour, before we arrived at that village, which is very difficult of access on this side, and the ways are so bad that some of our beasts of carriage fell down, one of which we were obliged to unload

This village very much resembles a wood, by reason of the trees, and inclosed gardens all around it It is situated on the river-side, upon a small hill, and surrounded by gardens walled in, which latter was a very uncommon circumstance

At the end of this village is a passage over the river, which flows by the side of the mountains, and upon their decline to the north I had formerly been here with Mr. *Kastelein*, but we came in on the other side, where the entrance is much easier However, I had an inclination to visit it a second time, having found at *Batavia* in the memoirs of Mr *Curcus*, ambassador to *Ispahan* in 1652, that he had found several curious pieces of antiquity near this village, together with several subterranean passages that extended as far as *Zyé-ra*, or *Chiras*, which is twenty five leagues from that place, and a well of an extraordinary depth

I set out early the next morning, with a servant belonging to the caravan, and one of the inhabitants of the town, in order to take a view of those curiosities I went much farther than I had done before, and found a grotto in the rock, with an aperture at the top, into which I made the countryman enter As the bottom was visible through two or three openings near to each other, I could easily see him, and perceived that he was at the end of the grotto after he had gone about thirty paces We met again in the common road by the river side, where I enquired of him which was the way that led to *Zyé-raes*, and found that those persons from whom I had the description, had only taken their account upon trust, without examining the truth of the fact It was the same with regard to the well

upon the mountain, which I took the trouble to ascend on the north side. I found that there had formerly been a fortress in that place, of which a few ruins are still to be seen, together with some remains of the walls, and upon the summit, a small square building covered with a dome, agreeably to the representation in plate 237 As for the prodigious fissure which is mentioned in the same memoirs, it is nothing but an uncommon gap on the east side of the mountain, where the height is very considerable, and the declivity as steep The river flows on one side of it The buildings which have been raised on the side of this mountain by the *Pagans* or *Guebres*, *Buildings of a peculiar structure* are of so strange a structure that one knows not what to make of them, and I believe nothing like them was ever seen They are built on the steepest part of the rock, on each side, and there is still to be seen a small aperture I have exhibited a representation of them in plates 238 and 239, as they appear on the east side, where a prospect opens on the river between the mountains, on the highest part of which is a canal full of reeds It is pretended that these people stretcht iron chains from one side of the mountain to the other, that they might secure a communication one with the other in time of war, it is also said, that on the other side of the mountain to the west, is another aperture like that which I have already mentioned As to other particulars I was unable to obtain any certain information from the inhabitants of the village, who call this place *Goenegabion*, or the habitation of the pagans They likewise declare, that this place was founded by giants, who lived 1300 years ago, under the government of one *Rustan*, but they have no foundation for this pretence, as has been already observed in my account of *Persepolis* This place is about half a league from the village, and the subterranean passage, which has already been mentioned, a full league

A little

1706

BÂTIMENS ANCIENNES 232.

BÂTIMENS ANCIENNES 232

A little on this side, toward the east, is a water-fall, which extends itself westward among the lands, on the side of the village. There is great plenty of fruit in this quarter, and some admirable melons, the weather was so excessive cold that we were obliged to have a fire.

We set out the next day at another part of the village, where we found the river much easier to be passed, and about a league from thence, we came into the high road, where we found a *corps de garde*. We then entered upon a beautiful plain, and arrived late in the evening at the *Caravanserai* of *Af-mongui*. The greatest part of the land which lies adjacent to it, was cultivated, and the country people were employed in making canals for the distribution of the water. This place is about four leagues from the other that was last mentioned.

We continued our journey the next day, over the plain, where we saw many tents covered with black, and also met several families, the women and children of which were mounted on camels and asses, some caravans also, with several *Persians*, accompanied by women in litters, passed by us. We arrived in the evening at the *Caravanserai* of *Povia*, after a progress of five leagues, and continued our journey, the next day, notwithstanding the cold was excessive, and the wind very boisterous, but had scarce travelled 300 paces, when we were informed by two couriers, that the road was infested by a great number of robbers, who were well furnished with arms. This information made us think it advisable to return from whence we came, and wait till evening for some caravans which we had left at the *Caravanserai*. We set out together at one in the morning, and met a caravan at break of day, but heard nothing of the robbers, whom we had escaped, and we arrived about eight at the *Caravanserai* of *Moejafaru*, where we found so much company, that there was not room to lodge above half of them, tho'

Vol. II

the *Caravanserai* is very large and commodious. We continued there till midnight, and then proceeded on our journey, the moon shining exceeding bright. We met on the road some *Persians*, and a troop of asses, laden with rice, and after we had passed over a beautiful valley, we arrived at the *Caravanserai* of *Babasite*, which is seven leagues from the former.

We found there a caravan, and a *Persian* lord, attended by seven or eight domestics, and going to *Gamron*, we continued our journey at seven in the morning, and arrived about three at *Zjie-raes*, after we had travelled five leagues.

I took up my lodging, as usual, in the convent of *Carmelites*, where I found the old father, and the *Fleming*, whom I met the preceeding year, in my journey to *Gamron*, and they were extremely glad to see me. My old friends Mr *Latoul*, and Mr *Batar*, a *French* clock-maker, came to congratulate me upon my return. The people were still employed in their vintage. I acquainted the conductor of the caravan with my inclination to set out the next day, but he happened not to be quite ready. In the mean time a courier brought me a letter from the baron *de Larix*, dated the 28th of *November*, at *Mahyn*, which is three days journey from *Zjie-raes*. As he was desirous to see me, he had sent another by the way of *Persepolis*, having been informed by a letter from the director of *Gamron*, that I might possibly take that road. I wrote him an answer immediately, and took horse two hours after, with a *Carmelite* of the *Low-Countries*, in order to meet the baron, whom we found in a garden near the mountains, from whence we returned together to the city, where Mr *De Larix*, who had a large train of servants, took up his lodgings with the man who prepares the companies wines. On the second of *December* we paid a visit to Mr *Hasjie Nibbie*, a famous merchant, whom I formerly mentioned. We went thither on horseback, attended

N n   by

1706 by a numerous train of servants, mounted on fine horses, of which those that belonged to the baron and myself, had their bridles and housings all embroidered We were entertained in a very polite manner, and continued there till noon That *Persian* had already visited Mr *de Laria*, and had sent him presents This gentleman did me the honour to sup with me in the convent, where we passed the greatest part of the night in a very agreeable manner The next day he continued his journey, and I accompanied him some leagues from *Zjre-raes*, and Mr *Latoul* as far as *Gamron*. We pursued a deer, which the hunters who belonged to Mr. *de Larix* afterward took

The mosque of Solomon's mother I changed the design I had formed of going by the way of *Persepolis*, and resolved when I came five or six leagues from *Zjie-raes*, to travel through a place called *Mazit Madre-Sulemoen*, or the mosque of *Solomon's* mother, tho' I am not able to comprehend by what means the knowledge of that prince extended as far as *Persia*, for I could never learn from the *Persians* themselves, how they came to erect a temple in honour of his mother, since neither the scripture, nor any historian, has once intimated that he was ever in *Persia*, or that he ever travelled out of the *Holy-Land*. It is therefore very probable that this structure was only dedicated to the mother of one of their kings, whose name was *Solomon* I had indeed often heard the ruins of this place mentioned by Mr. *Hoogkamer*, and likewise by Mr *Bakker*, who had been his secretary, and had taken a draught of part of this building, which is of stone, and higher than all the rest There is still to be seen a large apartment, which has no tomb in it, and there are some other buildings raised about it At the distance of two musket shots from thence toward the north, upon the plain, there are also some ruins, and a large portal without any figure, and two leagues and a half from thence a

wall, built with large stones round a mountain, on whose top there appears to have been some structure in antient times, but it is impossible to form any judgment of it, by the little which is now left These ruins are about a league from the village of *Sefahoenia*

A robbery committed on some merchants I was informed, at my arrival at *Zjie-raes*, that it was not long since twenty robbers, in the middle of the night, and near the village of *Mazten*, attacked a caravan that was coming from *Iman-sade*, in which were three christian merchants, from whom they took 13300 ducats, and even their rings from their fingers. The merchants defended themselves with great bravery for some time, being provided with fire-arms, and each of them having a servant, who was likewise armed They killed one of the robbers, who having no fire-arms of their own, attacked with their sabres the merchant who had shot their companion, and killed him on the spot, after which they retired with their booty

Messieurs *Latoul* and *Batar*, whom I lately mentioned, were of the number of this caravan · The former was director of the *French* company, though he was an *Armenian* by birth, and for that reason those unhappy merchants had placed themselves under his protection But the director and his companion had recourse to flight, the moment the robbers appeared, and about an hour after rejoined the caravan, where they found matters in the condition I have related If they had stood firm to each other, this calamity might, in all probability, have been prevented, since they were furnished with fire-arms, whereas the robbers were only armed, some with sabres, and others with clubs One of these merchants was a native of *Aleppo*, the other two of *Diarbekir*, the capital of *Mesopotamia*, and they were trading to the *Indies*

In reality they had acted very imprudently, having counted, and changed their money, in a publick manner, in the *Caravanserai* at *Ispahan*,

pahan, where some of this gang of robbers happened to be present, and observed upon which beast the money was laid. This accident, and some others of the same nature, obliged me to keep the high road, and not trust my self to any person. The youngest of these merchants retired hither, and the other went to *Ispa-* *han*, to try if he could obtain any intelligence of his money, and of those who had taken it. For my part, I agreed with one of the masters of the caravan, who furnished me with two horses to carry me to *Ispahan*, with a courier, whom the baron *de Larix* had given me.

CHAP. LXXVIII.

The author's departure from Zjie raes. Remarkable fortresses. His arrival at Ispahan. The departure of the king and court from thence.

The author's departure from Zjie-raes.

ON the 4th in the evening, I pursued my journey, and was accompanied by some friends as far as the garden, where we went to meet Mr. *de Larix*, and I arrived, about two in the morning, at the *Caravanserai* at *Baet-siega*, three leagues from *Zjie-raes*, from whence I set out at break of day, to take the advantage of the morning light, since the nights were very cold, for this reason I had no inclination to accompany the caravan, which commonly travels in the night. When I had passed over some mountains, and a valley, no water was to be found, I entered upon the plain of *Sergoen*, leaving on my right hand, the village of that name, and the bridge of *Pol-chame*. I was much surprised at not finding a drop of water in the plain, which is commonly floated over. I afterward forded a river, because it was the shortest way, and arrived about evening at the *Caravanserai* of *Abgergm*, after I had travelled 8 leagues. I proceeded on my journey the next day, and at the distance of a league from thence, passed over a large stone bridge, near which are two mountains, on whose top was formerly a fortress. I was accompanied that day by a caravan, which durst not travel in the night, by reason of some robbers who infested that quarter. We passed over two or three marshes, in order to shorten the way, leaving on our left hand another mountain, upon which a fortress had formerly been erected, and I then, for the first time, had a distant view of snow upon the mountains. We afterward passed a river, which was dry, and arrived about noon at the town of *May-ien*, after a journey of five leagues.

I there found a *Persian* lord, with a numerous train of servants, provided with fire-arms, which he was pleased to shew me, but they were not then charged, and had very bad flints, notwithstanding he was provided with those that were very good. He afterward shewed me a fine musquet, of *European* make, and to which I fitted a good flint. I then gave him a sight of my arms, which consisted of a good fusee, and two pair of pistols, one for the pomel of my saddle, and the other for my girdle. That lord set out soon after for *Zjie-raes*, and as the caravan, which had accompanied me the preceding evening, did not move fast enough for me, I went before, and passed over a rock, where the way was so bad, that I was obliged to alight, and lead my horse by the bridle. One of the horses that carried my baggage, fell down two or three times. I here met three travellers, who were likewise going to *Ispahan*, and

1706 and when we had passed over the rock, we descended into the plain, and arrived about three at the *Caravanserai* of *Oedsja*, after a journey of seven leagues. We set out from thence at break of day, and found the water frozen over in a fine plain that was well cultivated, and full of villages; we stopped at the town of *Assepas*, about five leagues from the place where we had passed the night, and found a caravan loaded with wine for our director at *Gamron*. The next day we continued our journey, and saw a vast number of small birds in a field sowed with rice, and a little farther, in a marshy ground, several snipes, ducks, lapwings, and storks. We arrived in good time at the *Caravanserai* of *Koes-kiesar*, after a journey of seven leagues.

The next day we passed through a fine plain, that was cultivated, and full of villages, and little hills. We here met some *Persian* lords, with a train of twenty-five servants, who were all well armed, and afterward several caravans. We arrived about three at the *Caravanserai* of *Dedergoe*, seven leagues from that where we had passed the night. The next day we passed by a ruinous castle, which was situated in a place full of little hills, and then continued our journey over mountains, that were very difficult of access, and where we were frequently obliged to alight. We descended, with inexpressible difficulty, into the plain of *Jesdagaes*, where we rested ourselves at the *Caravanjarai* of that name, being much fatigued, though we had not travelled above seven eagues. The next day about noon, we arrived at *Magsabegi*, where I found Mr *St John*, who came from *Ispahan*, and was going to *Gamron*, in quality of director of the *English* company. He was accompanied by Signior *Francisco*, who had the management of that company's wines at *Zjie-raes*. He continued his journey in the night with the caravan, and I mine at break of day, over a beautiful plain, full of inclosed gar-

dens, and dove-houses, as far as *Commsja*, which is a large town, and furnished with several very commodious *Caravanserais*, and by the side of it runs a river. The next day I passed over another plain, which was likewise full of gardens, and houses, and is watered by a canal, that extends to *Majaer*, where we arrived about two in the afternoon, after a journey of six leagues. I there drew the inside of the beautiful *Caravanserai* of *Majaer*, from my chamber window, which opened toward the great gate. I have already given given a description of the outside of this structure, and of the country around it, and have represented it in a plate. I departed from this place at break of day, and passed by *Micrja-Elrasa*, which is two leagues beyond it, and three from *Ispahan*, where I arrived about three in the afternoon. I alighted at the convent of the *Capuchins*, where I was very well received by the father guardian. I chose this retreat, that I might be a little at ease, beside which, I did not intend to tarry long in that city. I was informed at my arrival, that the king went from thence the 28th of *August*, and stopped at his garden of *Sadets-abaet*, till the 16th of *September*, and afterward at that of *Koes-gonna*, and the 24th at *Douwht-abaet*, three leagues from this metropolis. He was accompanied by all the grandees of his court, and likewise by his concubines: the principal design of his journey was to visit the frontiers of his kingdom, agreeably to the custom of the antient kings his predecessors. He consigned the regency, in his absence, to the eunuch *Sefi-Coeln-Aga*, whom he invested with an absolute authority.

The next day after my arrival, Mr *Bakker*, the director, did me the honour to send his steward to congratulate me upon my return, and to invite me to dine with him, from which I excused myself, with a promise to visit him in the evening. He received me with great civility

vility and friendſhip, and offered me an apartment in his houſe, for which I returned him my thanks, and went back to the convent

The next I paid a viſit to Mr *Locke*, the *Engliſh* agent, who was alſo ſo good as to offer me his houſe My friends came to welcome me, and among the reſt Mr *Joſeph*, an *Italian* ſurgeon and phyſician, who arrived at *Iſpahan* ſince my departure for the *Indies*.

I afterward wrote to my friends at *Batavia*, particularly to Mr *Kaſtelein*, and the baron *de Larix*, by a courier who was ſetting out for *Gamron* with ſome diſpatches I

then went for my diverſion into the country with the director, to the garden of *Koes-gonna*, where the king had ſtopped for ſome time, after his departure from *Iſpahan*

There is a noble building in the middle of this garden, with a large hall, very finely painted. From the top of this ſtructure, the eye commands a proſpect of all the country around, and there is a ſeparate ſeraglio, diſtributed into ſmall apartments I paſſed the night at the company's houſe, where ſeveral other perſons, as well as myſelf, were entertained the next day with the utmoſt civility

Vol. II.   O o   C H A P.

CHAP. LXXIX.

Congratulations on the new year, &c An entertainment given by an Armenian *merchant. The extraordinary conduct and death of a minister of* France. *The* Guebres *Their calculation of the world's duration Their opinions and manners*

First of January congratulations

ON the first day of the year 1707, I went to congratulate the director, and to wish him a happy year, in conformity to the custom of the country He pressed me to dine with him that day in company with father *Antonio*, burgo-master of *Julfa*, together with most of the principal *Armenian* merchants, and the greatest part of the *European* monks Abundance of rain fell this day

I went likewise, on the 6th, to pay my compliments to the *English* agent, who provided an entertainment for the same company as dined the first day at the director's The time we passed there was rendered very agreeable by the sound of several instruments, and the discharge of five small pieces of cannon

On the 7th, the *Persians* solemnized the last day of their grand fast, which had continued a whole month A few days after the director honoured me with a visit, and we went the next day to dine at *Julfa*, with Mr *Gregory Sumael* As we were passing over a plain on horseback, the director's horse fell with him into a ditch full of snow, from whence we drew him out with great difficulty When we came to the *Armenian*'s house, we found the patriarch there, together with father *Antonio Destiro*, the second director of the *English* company, some *French* ecclesiastics, and a great number of *Armenian* merchants, in all above fifty persons We were entertained at first with sweetmeats, hot liquors, cordial wa-water, and tobacco, and afterward with all sorts of provisions When

the patriarch had blessed the table, he took a loaf, and broke it, and then presented the pieces to several of the guests, which was a ceremony I had never seen before The hall, which was very spacious, was covered with a carpet of cotton, around which we placed ourselves, agreeably to the custom of the country, and the servants were very diligent in supplying each of the guests with provisions and wine We drank to the health of all the guests, and of several persons who were absent, and the company parted about the close of day On the 17th, was solemnized the baptism of the cross, the particulars of which have been formerly related

The death of a French ambassador

Much about this time we were informed that Mr *Fabre*, who came to the *Persian* court, in the quality of a *French* ambassador, died at *Erivan* the 20th of *August*, and that he had left no more than four ducats behind him, though he had contracted debts to the amount of above a hundred thousand livres at *Constantinople*, where was likewise his wife, who was a *Grecian* It was also said, that he had brought another wife from *Paris*, and that she repaired to *Ispahan*, where she had the boldness to assume the character of the deceased, and made her entry on horseback, habited like an *Amazon*, and bare-headed, which was a conduct directly opposite to the manners and customs of the country. The event of this affair was impatiently expected, when intelligence came that Mr *Michel*, secretary to the *French* embassy, at the Port, was to set out for *Persia* It

was

was likewise known, by the way of *Aleppo*, that his most christian majesty had sent orders to apprehend Mr *Fabre*, and send him prisoner to *France*, but this misfortune was prevented by his death

We afterward understood by letters from *Erivan*, in the month of *February* 1707, that a quarrel arising between the servants of that ambassador's retinue, and the inhabitants of the city, on some difference which was said to be entirely owing to the ambassadress, the contending parties came to blows, and several *Persians* being killed in the fray, the inhabitants were so provoked, that they immediately slaughtered a considerable number of the *Frenchmen*, and dragged the rest of them to prison, among whom were found some *Armenians*, who were all beheaded It was afterward reported, but without any certainty, that the court of *Persia* had given orders for sending back the ambassadress, but I shall give a more particular account of this affair in the sequel.

The author's conterfit on with a priest of the Guebres

I was very desirous at that time, to converse with some priests of the *Guebres*, and was favoured with an opportunity of that nature by means of the *English* agent, a man of merit and learning, and in whose friendship I had the honour to enjoy a considerable share He procured me a visit from one of these priests, who was attended by an interpreter, that served him in the quality of secretary, and we enter'd into discourse together I first ask'd him, his opinion of the creation of the world, and of God's omnipotence To which he reply'd, that he considered God as the Being of Beings, and a spirit of light, above the comprehension of human faculties, that he is immense, and present in all places, almighty, and from all eternity, and will exist to eternity, that nothing can be concealed from him, or done in opposition to his will They have likewise a tradition amongst them, that some of the angels rebelled against God, and

had the insolence to wage war with him, and that one of those *Angels*, named *Ablies* before his fall, and after it *Zeyloen*, or *Devil*, was thrown headlong into the *Doesag*, or *Hell*, which they suppose to be in the center of the earth They say, that God created the earth in six periods of time, which they call *Mey-deserem, Mey-doesjem, Peti-esjaeyhem, Eoos-aen, Meydie-jeriben*, and *Ammaespas-miediehem* He could not inform me whether these were years, months, weeks, or days, but was inclinable to suppose they might be days. He added, that after God had created the world, he likewise created man, and called him *Babba-Adam*, from whom all his descendants have received the name of *Adam*, but in a more particular manner amongst the *Persians* and *Turks* That this *Adam* was formed out of the four elements, fire, air, water, and earth · That God afterward created his spirit, which they imagine to be a wind, and then extracted from the left side of *Adam* some part of his body, and a portion of his soul, with which he formed woman, in the image and resemblance of *Adam* · That likewise in process of time, some one, with whose name they are unacquainted, presented to *Adam* a certain species of corn, larger than a melon, whereof he ate, and for that offence was expelled by the deity from the seat which he had granted him for his habitation. He likewise told me, that when man was first created, his eyes were placed on the uppermost part of the head, and that they did not descend below his forehead, till after he had eaten the fruit This notion makes it evident, that they believe his view was directed toward heaven before the fall, and after it to the earth. He added, that *Adam* afterward presenting himself before God, the lord demanded of him, what he had seen at his first creation? To which he replied, that he had beheld his creator, and God having further enquired what he then saw, he answered,

1707 fwered, that he then faw himfelf in a deplorable ftate The prieft likewife declared, that he knew not in what manner *Adam* and his wife afterward conducted themfelves, but was certain that they had multiplied their kind, and peopled the earth That there appeared, a long time after this, a prophet, whom they call *Zaer-fios*, and that the *Perfians* to this very day take him for *Abraham* That this prophet recommended to mankind the practice of virtue, and the deteftation of vice That mankind murmured at him, faying, *Why do you enjoin us the performance of this, and why forbid us the other?* To which he anfwered, *I come by the command of God* They then returned, *If your affertion be true, draw yourfelf through the gold and filver we are preparing to melt, if you do that, without receiving any injury, we will readily believe you, and yield obedience to your injunctions* This experiment he confented to fubmit to, and performed it with fafety · from this circumftance they gave him the name of *Zaer-fios*, or *Zaer-fioeft*, which fignifies a perfon wafhed with melted gold or filver He then gave them the books of their law, that they might be inftructed in the performance of his precepts, with refpect to God and their neighbour Thefe laws obliged them to reverence whatever was above them, namely, the fun, the fire, the water, and the earth, without paying adoration to them The prieft added, that many perfons thought they worfhipped the four elements, though in reality they entertained a veneration for fire, only on account of the many advantages they derived from it, for water, becaufe it afforded them drink, and purified them, for air, becaufe it furnifhed them with light, namely, the luftre of the fun and moon, which they honoured for their beneficial brightnefs, and paid the fame regard to the earth, becaufe they proceeded from it Their veneration for fire is deduced from the antient *Perfians*, in the days of *Cyrus*,

Darius, and *Alexander*, who efteemed fire as facred and eternal, and carried it on filver altars before their armies They alfo bore the image of the fun in a chryftal veffel, and placed it over their tents, that it might be feen by all The prophet *Ezekiel* had this practice in view when he faid, *Your images of the fun fhall be thrown down* 　1707

They are not permitted to eat crows, ferpents, nor camels, and even the blood of thofe creatures is prohibited them, as is alfo the hog, unlefs they have kept them two or three months in their own houfes, and prevented them from eating any impure food

They are forbidden to eat

As to births, the third day after the infant's nativity, they fend for a prieft, who pours holy water into the child's and the mother's mouth At the fame time he gives the infant the name of one of his predeceffors, after which he invokes the affiftance of God, who created the heaven and the earth, and entreats him to grant a long life to the child, together with all things neceffary for its accommodation. They have no circumcifion

Their cuftoms, with regard to the birth of infants

When a virgin becomes marriageable, and has been folicited to enter upon the nuptial ftate, fhe makes choice of fome perfon of her own fex, whom fhe authorizes to appear in her name, and with witneffes, before the judges of the place, when this commiffion has been difcharged, the judges enquire of the witneffes, whether the pretenfions of the man are well fupported? After which the intended bridegroom appears, and is thrice afked by the judge, whether he be inclinable to efpoufe that woman? To which the man having replied in the affirmative, he is ordered to pay forty *tomans* in filver, and five in gold, which amount to 1575 livres, in cafe the woman fhould require it, and this fum is ufually paid in jewels, but if his circumftances fhould not permit him to advance it, his wife may difpenfe with the payment

Their marriages

When

1707

When thefe preliminaries are fettled, the fuitor goes with five or fix of his oldeft relations, to the houfe of his intended fpoufe, who is accompanied by feveral women The perfon whom fhe had authorized to act for her on this occafion, then takes her by the hand, and prefents her to her husband, upon which all the relations take each of them a candle, and conduct her to the habitation of her fpoufe, and into the chamber where the marriage is to be confummated, but perfons of quality have no interview with each other before the celebration of their nuptials When a woman happens to prove barren, the husband may efpoufe another wife with the confent of the former.

Their burials

When a perfon is at the point of death, it is ufual for a prieft to attend on that occafion, and he then reads what is fuitable to the condition of the fick perfon, and when death has done its work, the body is conveyed to a place appointed for that purpofe, and called *Lefcona* There they leave it for the fpace of 4 or 5 hours, while they affemble the relations of the deceafed After the body has been dreffed in white linnen, and wrapped up in a fheet, it is placed on an iron bier, in order to be carried to a certain mountain, that contains an apartment, formed into feveral divifions, in one of which the corps is depofited while fome paffages are read out of a certain book When this ceremonial is compleated, the body is left in that fepulchre for the fpace of a year, at the end of which the bones are collected together, and buried in the earth. Thefe people are of opinion, that the moment the foul quits the body, it paffes into another world, where it continues excluded from the fight of God till the day of judgment At which time it makes its appearance before him, in order to be configned either to heaven or to hell, as it fhall appear to have been innocent or guilty

Their days of prayer

They never obferve any day of reft, but have four days of prayer in

each month, and affemble themfelves in their temples, for the celebration of their ceremonies They have their ftated prayers three times a day, namely, at fun rife, noon, and evening, and they curfe *Mohammed*, whom they account a falfe prophet

Thefe *Guebres* have been driven from their own country by the fatalities of war, and are now reduced to an inconfiderable number. They are likewife difperfed in feveral cities of *Perfia*, in which places they enjoy more liberty than is allowed them at *Ifpahan*, where they who have fettled themfelves at *Julfa*, are now obliged to embrace the *Mohammedan* doctrines In the reign of king *Abbas* they enjoyed the fame liberty as was granted to the *Armenians* and *Chriftians*, and they were treated with this indulgment in order to prevent them from fettling on the frontiers of *Turkey* They had likewife lands given them to cultivate, as well there as in other places With refpect to other particulars, thefe *Guebres*, or *Gaures*, are all reduced to a low degree of poverty. Their women are clothed after the *Arabian* manner, and always go with their faces uncovered, in conformity to the antient cuftom of that nation · They have a language peculiar to themfelves, and the characters of it entirely differ from thofe of the *Perfian*

Their calculation of the years of the world

They compute the years of the world's duration from *Adam*, whom they call by that name, as we do, but they give other denominations to his defcendants They fay, that when he had attained to the 30th year of his age, *Oufhyn* was born, and they confider him as the chief of a family, the next perfon in their genealogy of this race of mankind, they call *Siem-fiet*, and pretend that he was their firft king They add, that he lived 700 years, and was fucceeded by *Soohaet*, who lived a thoufand years, and left his crown to *Freydoem*, who refigned it to *Pfoom*, at the age of 500 years. As to this laft, they neither know in what manner he lived, nor how he

Kings of the Guebres

con-

Vol II

P p

conducted the reins of government After him they place *Mamoet-Se-Ler*, who reigned 120 years, and then *Noufar*, who reigned twelve, and was depofed by *Aef-raeffia*, a *Tartar*, who feized the *Perfian* crown, and reigned fifty years His fucceffors, according to their computation, were *Khekobaet*, who reigned 120 years, *Khekodoes*, 150, *Loraes* and *Goftaes*, 120 together, *Baman* ninety-nine, and *Homa*, the daughter of *Baman*, thirty This princefs was fucceeded by *Darop*, the fon of *Darius*, who reigned fourteen years and three months, and had for his fucceffor the fon of *Baman*, who reigned but twelve *Sebandaz-roemie*, or *Alexander the Great*, enjoyed the kingdom after him, and reigned fourteen years, as thefe people think, for they reprefent them all as kings, after the two firft fathers   The fucceffors which they affign to that conqueror, are *Afht*, the fon of *Afht poes*, *Niercef-Jein-Coffcro*, fon of *Ardewoen*, and *Babokoen*, who reigned 265 years, *Ardisjier Babokoen* forty one years, *Armoos*, the fon of *Siapoer*, five, *Baroen Senogormoes* three years and three months, *Pieroes-ger* ten years, *Baroem*, the fon of *Baroem-m cen*, four years and five months, *Narfie*, the fon of *Baroem*, nine years, *Ormoes*, the fon of *Narfie*, likewife nine years, *Sapoer*, the fon of *Sapoer*, five years and four days, *Zaardezjer afzia*, ten years, *Zia-poer*, the fon of *Zia-ardezier*, eleven years, *Jefdegerd* thirty years, *Baroem-mi-*

gier fixty fix years, *Jesdigerd*, the fon of *Baroem*, eighteen years and four months, *Flinoes*, the fon of *Jesdegerd*, fourteen years, *Narfia*, the fon of *Fhieros*, feven years, *Bellaes*, the fon of *Fhieros*, five years, *Cobaet-Sinnefer oes* forty years, *Noufer-woen*, the fon of *Cobaet*, a very juft and equitable prince, forty feven, *Ormoes*, the fon of *Nosjeva*, twelve, *Cofroes*, the fon of *Ormoes*, thirty eight, *Cobaet*, fon of *Cofroes*, feven months, *Ardi-sjiei Sinnecobaet*, eighteen months, *Afermien*, the daughter of *Cofroes*, fix months, *Kofwar-bonec*, another daughter of *Cofroes*, one year, *Jesdegerd* twenty years.

These were fucceeded by a race of *Mohammedan* princes. This computation of years fince *Adam*, excepting thofe of the princes who have been mentioned, and whofe age is not known, amounts to 3632 years, one month, and five days, to which 1135 years, from the coming of *Mohammed* to the prefent time, being added, the total amounts to 4767 years, one month, and five days

This is all the information I could obtain, with refpect to the *Guebres,* and the princes of that race, who have governed *Perfia*, as thefe people pretend   I will now fubjoin an exact lift of the *Perfian* kings, who have reigned fince the time of *Alexander the Great*, and fhall offer a few concife remarks, that are neceffary for the illuftration of this fubject.

C H A P.

CHAP. LXXX.

A lift of the Perfian *kings, who have reigned in fuc-ceffion, from the death of* Alexander the Great, *to the prefent time; extracted from the antient* Greeks, *and modern* Perfians

AFTER the death of *Alexan-der the Great*, who poffeffed the empire of *Afia* for the fpace of 7 years, great diffentions arofe between the captains of that conqueror, with refpect to the fovereign power, to which they all formed pretenfions In order, therefore, to prevent the eff cts of fuch a competition, they unanimoufly ag eed to give the crown to *Aridæus*, the brother of *Alexan-der*, and the fon of *Philip* by *Phi-lene* But as this prince was not mafter of thofe qualifications that were requifite for fuftaining fo great a weight, the regency of the ftate was configned to *Perdiccas*, and the government of feveral kingdoms and provinces, was conferred upon the other princes and lords, who acted at firft in the name of the new king, but foon afpired to the fovereign power As thefe facts are known by all the world, and have been large-ly treated of by feveral hiftorians, I fhall think it fufficient to prefent the reader with an exact lift of all the *Perfian* kings from that time

It may be neceffary to obferve, that the *Greeks* did not long con-tinue mafters of the *Perfian* empire Their difunion, and continual wars, contributed not a little to the de-clenfion of their power We find, however, in antient authors, a fuc-ceffion of *Macedonian* princes, who governed this kingdom *Alexander* conferred the government of it on *Peuceftes*, during his life, and he retained it after the death of that prince, till he was dethroned by *An-tioclus*, a natural fon of *Philip*, and brother of *Alexander*, after the de-feat of *Eumenes*

1 *Antiochus* therefore was the firft *Macedonian*, who, after the death of

Alexander, affumed the title of king of *Perfia* He had been invefted before with the government of *Afia Minor*, and after the defeat of *Eumenes*, he made himfelf mafter of *Afia*, together with *Syria*, *Baby-lon*, *Perfia*, and all the provinces that depended upon them But this prince was vanquifhed in his turn, by *Seleucus Nicanor*, who conquered *Perfia*

2 *Seleucus Nicanor*, or *Nicator*, which name fignifies a conqueror, governed this fine kingdom for the fpace of thirty years

3 *Antiochus Soter*, or the prefer-ver, who fucceeded him, reigned twenty one years.

4 *Antiochus Theos* fifteen years

5 *Seleucus Callinicus*, eighteen years

Hiftorians differ, with reference to the time when the *Parthians* re-volted Some place this event in the reign of *Antiochus Theos*, and others in that of *Callinicus*. I fhall not mul-tiply remarks on this difference, which has but little affinity with our prefent fubject, and fhall therefore content myfelf with obferving, af-ter *Scaliger*, and fome others, that this revolt was carried on under the conduct of *Arfaces* (who, ac-cording to *Strabo*, was a *Scythian* by birth, though others will have him to be a pyrate) in the 12th year of the reign of *Antiochus Theos*, and the 3d of the 132d Olympaid, or, according to *Helvicus*, the 3700th year of the world, and 248 years be-fore the nativity of *Jefus Chrift*

We, however, are not to infer from hence, that *Arfaces* afcended the throne of *Perfia*, immediately after this revolt, fince there are rea-fons to believe it was at that time when

Seleucus Callinicus was engaged in a war againſt his brother *Antiochus Hierax,* or the *Rapacious,* and about the 17th year of his reign But it is generally agreed, that the *Parthians* made themſelves maſters of *Perſia,* in conſequence of that revolt, and poſſeſſed it for the ſpace of 479, or 476 years

I ſhall now preſent the reader with a liſt of the *Arſacides,* or kings who aſſumed the name of *Arſaces,* in honour to the memory of that prince. I have likewiſe added the number of years they reigned

Years of their reign

Kings of Perſia
1 *Arſaces* I
2 *Arſaces* II   reigned 20
3 *Pampatius, Phraates,* or   12
   Arſaces III
4 *Pharnaces,* or *Arſaces* IV   8
5 *Mithridates,* or *Arſaces* V   47
6 *Phraates,* or *Arſaces* VI   28
7 *Artabanus* I or *Arſaces* VII.   2
8. *Pacorus* I or *Arſaces* VIII
9 *Phraates* II or *Arſaces* IX
10 *Mithridates* II or *Arſaces* X.
11 *Orodes,* or *Arſaces* XI
12 *Phraates* III or *Arſaces* XII
13. *Tiridates,* or *Arſaces* XIII
14 *Phraataces,* or *Arſaces* XIV
15 *Orodes* II or *Arſaces* XV
16 *Boaones, Vonones,* or *Arſaces* XVI

His ſon *Meberdates* did not reign after him, another family having aſcended the throne

17 *Artabanus* 2 or *Arſaces* XVII
18 *Bardanes, Vardanes,* or *Arſaces* XVIII
19 *Gotarzes,* or *Arſaces* XIX
20 *Vologeſes* I or *Arſaces* XX
21 *Artabanus* III. or *Arſaces* XXI
22 *Pacorus* II. or *Arſaces* XXII
23 *Coſores,* or *Arſaces* XXIII
24 *Vologeſes* II or *Arſaces* XXIV
25 *Vologeſes* III or *Arſaces* XXV
26 *Artabanus* IV or *Arſaces* XXVI

This *Artabanus* was the laſt of the kings of *Parthia,* who ruled over all the ſtates of the *Perſian* monarchy, and maintained long wars with

the *Romans* This prince was aſſaſſinated by a *Perſian,* named *Artaxerxes,* who ſeized the crown in the 5th year of *Alexander Severus* the emperor, according to *Agathias,* or, as others ſay, in the 10th That is, according to *Scaliger* and *Helvicus,* 228, or 232 years after the birth of *Jeſus Chriſt,* and in the year of the world 4176, or 4179 It is pretended that this *Artaxerxes* was the ſon of *Pavecus* a tanner, or, that this *Pavecus,* who had no child, and was ſkilled in aſtrology, having found by his conſultation of the ſtars, that the offspring of *Sannus* a certain ſoldier, who lodged in his houſe, ſhould become illuſtrious and fortunate, he perſuaded his wife to receive him to her bed, in conſequence of which ſhe became the mother of this *Artaxerxes* It is at leaſt certain that this prince underſtood magick, and that all the kings of *Perſia* who have reigned ſince his time, are deſcended from him The princes in the following ſeries are ranged as I find them in *Agathias,* and other authors, who have tranſcribed the *Perſian* records

		Ye.	Mo.
1	*Artaxerxes* I who reign'd	14	10
2	*Sapor* I	31	
3	*Hormiſdas* I.	1	
4	*Varanes* I	3	
5	*Varanes* II	16	
6	*Varanes* III. furnamed *Seganeſna*		4
7	*Narſes*	7	9
8	*Miſdates*	7	9
9	*Sapor* II	70	

The deſcendants of Artaxerxes

He was declared king while he was in the womb of his mother, on whoſe body the crown was placed

		Ye.	Mo.
10	*Artaxerxes* II the brother of *Sapor,* reign'd		4
11	*Sapor* III ſon of *Artaxerxes*		5
12	*Varanes* IV furnamed *Kermenſat*		11

13. Iſ-

Ʒe Mo

13 *Ifdigerdes* I to whom the emperor *Arcadius* configned the guardianfhip of his fon *Thodofius*, according to *Procopius* — 21

14 *Varanes* V — 20

15. *Varanes* VI or *Ifdigerdes* II. — 17 — 4

16 *Perozes* — 20

17 *Valens*, brother of *Perozes*, or, according to others, *Obalas* — 4

18. *Cabales*, fon of *Perozes*.

This prince being defirous to introduce a law, which fhould authorize every man to enjoy as many women as he pleafed, whether virgins, or married women, was depofed, in the eleventh year of his reign, and imprifoned in a caftle. His brother *Zambafes*, or *Zamafper*, fucceeded him, and reigned but four years, others fay two *Cabades* having been preferved by the affiftance of the queen his wife, who for his fake expofed herfelf to the fury of his guards, retired among the *Euthalites*, and efpoufed the daughter of their king, with whom he returned into *Perfia*, and refumed the crown, which he had enjoyed thirty years before, fo that *Zembafes* and he reigned in all forty one years.

19 *Cofroes the Great*, and the fon of *Cabades*, fuftained furious wars againft the emperors *Juftinian* and *Juftin*, and reign'd 48 years.

Ʒe Mo

20 *Hormifdas* II — 8

21 *Cofroes* II — 39

22 *Sirocs* — 1

23 *Ardifher* — 7

24 *Baras*, or *Sarbaras* — 6

25 *Baram*, or *Barnarim* — 1 — 7

26 *Hormifdas* III — 2

27 *Jezdegird* II or *Jazdgerd* — 1 — 8

The *Arabs*, and modern authors among the *Perfians*, affign other names to thefe princes, that correfpond with the genius of their re-

Vol II

fpective languages, but I fhall not multiply remarks upon them, fince I am defirous of avoiding all prolixity, and efpecially as an account of them may be feen in the abridgment of the *Perfian* kings, p. 702, &c written by *D T V Ʒ* one of the gentlemen of the bed-chamber to the moft chriftian king. This work is entitled, *An Account of all the ftates, empires, kingdoms, and principalities, in the world*.

Perfia had fuffered greatly under the adminiftration of the laft fix kings, and was at laft fubjected to a foreign yoke. *Mohammed* the impoftor was born in the 802d year of the *Alexandrian Æra*, the 22d day of the month *Nifan*, which correfponds with the 22d of *April*, in the 572d year of the *Chriftian Æra*. He publifhed his falfe prophecies, in the year 611, in the 40th year of his age, and was driven out of *Mecca*, in 622, upon which he retreated to *Medina*. In time, he won, by force of arms, *Chaibar*, *Mecca*, and the better part of *Arabia*, and died of the falling ficknefs, accompanied with a fever in the year 634, and the 11th of the *Hegira*, or his efcape from *Medina*. After his death, *Abubecr*, or *Abudaker*, the fon of *Amer* and *Salma*, and father of *Aifcha*, *Mohammed*'s third wife, was proclaimed *Khalifah*, or chief of the *Mohammedans*, in fpiritual and temporal affairs, and was fucceeded by *Omar*, or *Homar*, the fon of *Elkateph*, who drove out *Jefdegird* in the year 640, and made himfelf mafter of the city of *Madajina*, where *Cofroes* had held his court, and he afterward conquered the greateft part of *Perfia*. This prince kept his court at *Bagdad*, and was affaffinated in the 4th year of his reign, by *Abululua*, a *Perfian* of mean extraction. The *Khalifah* who fucceeded him was *Othman*, or *Ofman*, the fon of *Affan* and *Bifa*, who challenged and flew *Jefdegird*, who had partly reinftated himfelf in his dominions. This event happened in the 31ft year of the *Hegira*, and the 651ft of *Jefus Chrift*, after

ter

1707 ter which this prince continued in the peaceable poſſeſſion of all the ſtates of the *Perſian* monarchy, which the deſcendants of *Iſraells* had enjoy'd for the ſpace of 461 years, or, as others ſay, 457. I ſhall now inſert a liſt of the *Khalifals*, or *Mohammedan* kings of *Perſia*, and they are here collected from the *Perſian* authors, namely, *Mirtond, Abul Pharajus,* &c.

Kings of Perſia, as mentioned from the Arabians, called Ommiades

		Ye	Mo
1	*Othman* or *Oſman* III Khalifah, reckoning from *Aboubecr*, and the firſt king of *Perſia*, reign'd	11	4
2	*Ali* IV Khalifah	4	9
3	*An Haſſen*, or *Acem*		6
4	*Muavi*, or *Mauvia* I	19	6
5	*Jezid*, or *Yhezid* I	3	8
6	*Muavi*, or *Mauvia* II		4
7	*Abdalla,*		
8	*Marvan* I } together,	1	
9	*Abdomalic*	21	1
10	*Walid*, or *Oelid* I	9	8
11	*Solyman Ben Abdolmalec*	2	6
12	*Omar*, or *Homar*	2	5
13	*Jezid*, or *Ylezid* II	4	8
14	*Ochon*, or according to others, *Hiſiam, Haſchan, Heſchan,* or *Evelid*	19	8
15	*Walid*, or *Oelid* II	1	2
16	*Jezid*, or *Yhezid* III		6
17	*Ibrahim*, or *Ebrahem*		3
18	*Marvan* II	5	

The 6th of theſe *Khalifahs*, who was the 4th king of *Perſia*, named *Muavi*, or *Muaviab Ben Abu Soſian*, deſcended from an *Arab* of quality, named *Ommiab*, and for that reaſon this prince and his ſucceſſors were ſtiled *Ommiades* by the authors of that time, down to the reign of *Marvan* II. But the deſcendants of *Ali* called them, in deriſion, *Faraena Beni Ommiab*, the ſignification of which is *Foraoos*, or tyrants, of the race of *Ommiab. Marvan* II, and the laſt king of the *Ommiades* was defeated in *Syria* by the *Abbaſſid*, after which he was taken and put to death in *Egypt*, in the 130th, or the 132d year of

the *Hegira*, which accords with the 747th, or 749th year of the Chriſtian account. This *Khalifah* was ſucceeded by *Abul-Abbas-Saffah*, an *Abboſſide*, deſcended in the fourth degree from *Abas*, the ſon of *Abdalmotoleh*, grandfather of *Mohammed*. His ſucceſſors reign'd 500 years.

1707

Khalifahs named A-baſides

		Ye	Mo
1	*Abul-Abas-Saffah*, the ſon of *Mohammed*, grandſon of *Ali*, the ſon of *Abdallah*, and great-grandſon of *Abbas*, uncle to *Mohammed* the impoſtor, reign'd	4	9
2	*Abugiafar*, the ſon of *Almanzor*, brother of *Saffah*	22	
3	*Mahadi Billa*, the ſon of *Abugiafar*	3	1
4	*Hadi*, or *Eladi Billa*, the ſon of *Mahadi*	1	3
5	*Harum Raſchid Billa*, the brother of *Hadi*	23	2 ½
6	*Abu Abdalla Amin*, the ſon of *Harum*	9	9
7	*Al Mamum*, the brother of *Amin*	20	8
8	*Abu Ezach Motaſſem*, or *Matacon*, the ſon of *Harum*	8	8
9	*Harum Watec*, the ſon of *Motaſſem*	5	9
10	*Al-Moto Wakkel*, the ſon of *Motaſſem*	14	9
11	*Montaſſer*, the ſon of *Moto-Wakkel*		6
12	*Ahmed Abul-Abas Muſtain*, the ſon of *Motaſſem*	3	9
13	*Motas*, or *Almatez Billa*, the ſon of *Moto-Wakkel*	3	
14	*Mothadi Billa*, the ſon of *Wathec*		11
15	*Ahmed Abul Abas Motamed Billa*, the ſon of *Moto-Wakkel*	23	
16	*Motadbed*, or *Motazed Billa Ahmed*, the ſon of *Muaffic*, and grandſon of *Moto-Wakkel*	9	9
17	*Motaſi Billa*, the ſon of *Motadbed*	6	7 ½
18	*Gia-*		

		Ye.	Mo.
18	Giafar Abul Fadlus Moctader Billa, the son of Motadhed	24	11
19.	Mohammed Al Man-fur Al Kaher Billa, the son of Moted-hed	1	5
20	Ahmed Al Radhi, or Razi Billa, the son of Moctader	6	10
21	Ibrahim Abu Ifhacus al Moctafi Billa, the son of Moctader	6	$11\frac{1}{2}$
22	Abdalla Abulcafin Moctacfi, the son of Moctafi I	1	4
23	Fazih Abulcefin Mothi Billa, the son of Moctader	29	6
24	Abdel Kerim Abubicr Al Thai, or Thayaha, the son of Mothi	17	$10\frac{1}{2}$
25	Ahmed Abulabbas Al Kader Billa, the son of Ifhac, and grandson of Moctader	41	4
26	Abdalla Abugiafar Al Kayem, Beamaryla, the son of Kader	44	6
27	Al Moctadi Billa, the son of Mohammed, and grandson of Kayem	19	5
28	Ahmed Al Moftadher or Moftazer Billa, the son of Moctadi	25	6
29	Al Moftarfhed Billa Abu Manfur, the son of Moftadher	17	7
30	Abu Jaafar Al Manfur, furnamed Al Rafhed Billa, the son of Moftarfhed		2
31	Mohammed Al Moctafi Beamrilla, the son of Moftadher	24	11
32	Iffuf Al Moftanyed Billa, the son of Moctafi		11
33	Abu Mohammed Al Haffan Al Moftadhi Beamrilla, the son of Moftanyed	9	8
34	Aleman, Al Nafer Ledinilla, the son of Moftadhi	40	11

		Ye.	Mo
35.	Al Dhaer Billa Odatoddin Abu Nazr Mohammed, the son of Al Nafer		$9\frac{1}{2}$
36	Abugaafar Almanzur Al Moftanfer Billa, the son of Al Dhaer	18	11
37	Al Moftazem Billa, the son of Moftanfer	11	7

This prince was defeated and put to death, together with his sons, by Hulacu Chan, emperor of Mogul or Tartary, in the 654th or 656th year of the Hegira, or 1256th or 1258th of the Christian Æra, and was the last of the Kalifahs of Bagdad or Bagded, who reigned in Perfia to the number of fifty seven, without including Movammed the false prophet. It is necessary to obferve, that the Khalifahs had already loft one part of their dominions in the reign of Ahmed Al Rhadi, whose successors scarce retained the title of sovereigns, though Tarik Al Abas, Akhbar Beni Al Abas, and Abdalla Ben Huffan, in his book, intitled Affas Fifadhl beni Abas, always gives them the ftyle of kings of Perfia. In the mean time the Tartars of Mogul, who had made great devaftations in Perfia, Armenia, and the Leffer Afia, in the reign of the Khalifah Al Nafer, were driven out of Perfia, under that of the Khalifah Al Monftanfer Billa, in the 623d year of the Hegira, and in the 1226th of our Saviour. But Hulacu Chan made himfelf mafter of all this monarchy in 1258. The following is a lift of the Tartarian kings, who reigned in Perfia since the beginning of their conqueft, according to Abul Pharajus, Marafche, or Marakfchi, Mirkond, Edward Pocock, and some others.

1. The firft was Gingiz, or Jingiz Chan, whose conquefts were interrupted in the year 1226, by the valour of the Khalifah Abujafar Al Manfur, Al Moftanfer Billa, who divefted him of the greateft part of Per-

Kings of Perfia of the Tartarian or Mogul race

1707 *Perfia* This prince reigned, as well over his proper ftates as in *Perfia*, for the fpace of twenty five years

		Ye	Mo
2	*Oktay*, or *Jegtai Chan*, his fon	13	
3	*Gajuk Chan*, the fon of *Oktay*	1	
4	*Manibuk Chan*, the fon of *Tuli*, and grandfon of *Jingiz Chan*.	9	
	But, a o hers fay	13	
5	*Hulacu*, or *Holagu Chan*,	6	
	Or, according to others	9	
6	*Abaca*, or *Haib Ka Chan*, the fon of *Hula-cu Chan*	17	
7	*Ahmed*, or *Hamed Chan*	2	2
8	*Argun Chan*	7	
9	*Caichtu Chan* (to whom *Texeira* and fome others give the name of *Gamatu*) the fon of *Abaca*, reigned about	4	7
10	*Baidu Chan*, the fon of *Targibi*, or *Targai*, and grandfon of *Hulacu Chan*	1	
11	*Kazan Chan*, or *Gazun* the fon of *Argun Chan*	8	10
12.	*Giyatho'ddin Chodabende Mohammed Chan*, whom other call fimply *Mohammed*, or *Abaptu Chan*, the fon of *Argun*	12	9
13	*Abu Said Bahadur Chan*, the fon of *Mohammed Chodabende*	19	
	Others fay that he reigned no more than	9	

This prince was the laft of the race of *Gingiz Chan*, though *Marafchi*, in his hiftory of *Mogul*, adds another, whom he calls *Arba Chan*, the fon of *Sengli Chan*, and grandfon of *Malec Timur*, who was the fon of *A tak Bega*, grandfon of *Tuli*, and great grandfon of *Gingiz-Chan*, and to whom this author affigns a reign of about five months Thus this race of the kings of *Perfia* was extinct about the 736th year of the *Hegira*, that

is to fay, 1335 years after the nativity of *Jefus Chrift* For after the death of *Bahadur*, or *Arba Chan*, the governors of the provinces arrogated the fovereignty to themfelves. This lafted till the time of *Timur*, furnamed *Lenc*, or *the Lame*, and who is known by the name of *Tamerlan* among the *Europeans* This prince afcended the throne of *Tartary* in the year 771 of the *Hegira*, which correfponds with the year 1369 of the *Chriftian Æra*, and feventeen or eighteen years afterward, he made himfelf mafter of *Perfia*, and was fucceeded by the following princes

		Ye.	Mo	
1	*Timur Lenc Sultan*, reigned over *Tartary* and *Perfia*	30		Kings of of Perfia of the race of Tamerlan
2	*Shah Ruch Bahadur Sultan*, the fon of *Timur Lenc*	43		
3	*Al Malec, al Said, Mohammed Ulug Beg*, the fon of *Shah Ruch*	2	9	
4	*Abdo'llatif Mirza*, the fon of *Ulug Beg*		6	
5	*Mirza Abdollah*, the fon of *Ibrahim*, and grandfon of *Shah Ruch*	1		
6	*Mirza Sultan Abufayd*, the fon of *Mohammed*, grandfon of *Miran Shah Gurga*, and great-grandfon of *Timur*	18		
7	*Mirza Sultan Mohammed*, the fon of *Abu-fayd*, or, as others fay, of *Baifankor*, the fon of *Shah Ruch*	28		
8	*Mirza Babor Sultan*, the fon of *Omar Schetkh*, and grandfon of *Abu Said*			
9	*Mirza Al Malec*, or, as he is called by others, *Mohammed Sultan*, the fon of *Abu Said*, and great-grandfon of *Timur Lenc*	20		

1707

10 *Sultan Hosain Mirza*, the son of *Manzur*, and grandson of *Baikia*, the son of *Omar Scheickh*, son of *Timur*, reigned about ⎫
⎬ 28
⎪

11 *Mirza Badio'zzaman* or *Badi Abzaman*, the son of *Hosain*, reign'd with his brother, *Mirza Modhaffer* ⎫
⎬
⎪

12 *Abu'l Mahan Mirza*, and *Gil Mirza* ⎫
⎬

Ye. Mo

These two princes are the last of the race of *Tamerlan*, who reigned in *Persia*. This race did not possess all the *Persian* monarchy, but enjoyed only a part of it, like those who succeeded them, for it appears, there were in the fifteenth century two other races, descendants of the *Turcomans*, who have likewise reign'd over one part of *Persia*, and for that reason are ranked in the number of its kings. The first race was called *Kara Koyunli*, or the *Black Sheep*, whence all the following kings are deduced.

Kings of Persia of the first race of the Turcomans

1. *Kara Iffuf*, or *Joseph* the black
2. *Amir Scandar*, the son of *Iffuf*
3. *Joon-xa*, or *Jean Shak*, the son of *Scandar*
4. *Acen Ali*, the son of *Joon-xa*.

These two last princes, the father and son, were destroyed by *Hasan Al Tawil*, of the race of the *Turcomans*, whom the authors of that time call *Ak Koyunli*, or the *White Sheep*. The kings of that race are,

Kings of Persia, of the second race of the Turcomans

1. *Tur Ali Beg*.
2. *Phacio'adin Kofli Beg*, the son of *Tur Ali*
3. *Karah Ilug Othman* · He was killed in the war he undertook against *Amir Scandar*, at the age of ninety years, and about the 809th year of the *Hegira*.
4. *Hamzah Beg*, son of *Ilug Othman*, reigned about thirty nine years.

Vol II.

5 *Jean Gir*, the son of *Ali Beg*, 1707. and grandson of *Othman*, reigned twenty four years.

6 *Hasan' Al Tawil*, or the *Long*, whom *Texeira* calls *Ozun Azenbek*, and *Leunclavius*, in his *Turkish* History, *Ufun Chazan* (*Ufun* signifies *Long* in the *Turkish* language) was also the son of *Ali Beg*, and brother of *Jean Gir* It is said that he espoused *Despina*, the daughter of the *Greek* emperor, *Calo-Jean*, who reigned at *Trebisond*, and in *Pontus* This *Hasan* dy'd the 883d year of the *Hegira*, and the 1478th year of the *Christian Æra*, after he had reigned about eleven years

7. *Chalil Beg*, whom *Texeira* calls *Sultan Kalil*, the son of *Hasan*, reigned but six months and a half.

8. *Yacub Beg*, the son of *Hasan*, and brother of *Chalil*, was a learned prince, and a fine poet, he reigned twelve years and two months

9 *Mafih Beg* IV. the son of *Hasan*, did not long enjoy the crown, because of the divisions which prevailed among the nobility, one party of whom placed *Ali Beg*, the son of *Chalil* upon the throne, and the other, *Bai Sankar Mirza*, the son of *Yacub Beg*, and who was but twelve years of age, and was killed in a battle, after a reign of one year and eight months.

10. *Ruftan Mirza*, or *Roftmbek*, the son of *Makfud*, and grandson of *Hasan*, reigned five years and six months

11. *Sultan Ahmed*, or *Hagmed Beg*, the son of *Ogurlu Mohammed*, and grandson of *Hasan*, reigned about a year.

12 *Alwan Mirza*, whom *Texeira* calls *Alwen Bek*, the son of *Yufeph*, or *Iffuf Bek*, and grandson of *Hasan*, reigned likewise a year.

13. *Mozad*, the son of *Yacub Beg*, reigned about seven years

This *Mozad* was the last king of that race, and was divested of his dominions by *Shah Ifmael*, in the 194th year of the *Hegira*, and the 1507th of the *Christian Æra*, since which event *Persia* was governed

R r

1705 verned by another race of princes, for the space of 200 years since, as appears by the following list

Scheich Haidar, the son of *Jonaid*, who is said to have descended from *Ali*, the son-in-law of *Mahamm d*, was the first of this race His father *Jonai d*, or *Gionaid*, is ranked among the saints, as is his great-great-grandfather. *Scheck Sofi*, or *Sayodin*, the son of *Gibriel*, and a descendant from *Hossin*, the son of *Ali* This *Jonaid* had acquired so extraordinary a reputation, and was followed by such a number of sectaries to *Ardevil*, in the province of *Adherbijan*, that the king *Joan-xa*, of the race of *Kara Koiunli*, or the *Black Sheep*, grew jealous of him, and opposed the adherents to *Jonaid*, who was so exasperated by this proceeding, that he retired, with his followers, to *Diarbekir*, in the country adjacent to *Bagdad* and *Mosul*, where he obtained a favourable reception from the king of the country, whose name was *Hasan Al Tavil*, *Azenbek*, or *Usun Chasan*, who gave him either his daughter or sister in marriage, for authors vary in this particular The name of that princess was *Kadija Katum*, she had one son by this marriage, named *Scheich Haidar*, who is considered as the chief of that race This *Jonaid*, and his followers, passed afterward into *Gurgistan*, where he obliged all those who were unable to oppose him, to join with his party, under a pretence of zeal and sanctity They likewise made themselves masters of *Trebisond*, whose king they slew, and then placed *Haider*, the son of *Jonaid*, on the throne His father or brother-in-law, *Hasan* or *Azenbek*, made himself at the same time, master of the greatest part of *Persia*, after having defeated and slain *Joan-xa* the king, and his son *Acen Ali*, and *Jonaid*, animated by the success he had obtained in *Gurgistan*, advanced with his followers, into he province of *Schirvan*, situated on the *Caspian-Sea*, where he was destroyed by the inhabitants, who hated him It is

said, that his son *Haidar*, after having espoused another daughter of *Hazan*, named *Alemcha*, ravaged all *Gurgistan*, with an army he received from his father-in-law, or which he himself levied in haste, and that having afterward attacked *Feroxhzad*, king of *Schirwan*, in order to revenge the death of his father, he himself perished in the battle with all his sons, except *Ismael* and *Yar Ali*, whom others call *Ali Paicla*, and who were imprisoned by their uncle *Yacub Beg*, after the death of their father They, however, recovered their liberty in the reign of *Rustan Mirza*, the successor of that prince, on this condition, that they should continue at their father's tomb, habited like poor people. This condition they complied with till the death of *Rustan*, of which they no sooner were informed, than they fled from that retreat, being apprehensive of *Ahmed Sultan* his successor At length *Ismael* having found means to raise an army of the followers of *Ali*, in the reign of *Alwan Mirza*, defeated this prince and his son *Morad*, together with the kings of *Schirwan*, *Diarbek*, *Bagdad*, and some others, and made himself master of all *Persia*, which his posterity possess to this day · He assumed the name of *Sophi*, an *Arabic* word, which signifies a person dressed in wool, and a zealous *Mussulman*, perhaps likewise to denote the state to which he had been reduced He was but fourteen years of age when he ascended the throne, and he reigned as many The kings descended from this prince are,

1 *Shah Ismael Sophi*, who reigned twenty four years

2 *Shah Tahmasp*, or *Xa Tahmas*, who was poisoned by the queen his wife, by whom he had a son named *Haidar* This happened in the year of our lord 1576, in the sixty eighth year of that prince's age, and after a reign of fifty four years.

3 *Shah Ismael* II the son o *Tahmasp*, reigned but one year and ten months, and died in 1578.

4 *Shah*

4 *Shah Mohammed Chodabende*, the son of *Tahmasp*, and brother of *Ismael*, died in 1585, after he had reigned seven years, or, as others say, six

5 *Shah Abas*, the son of *Chodabende*, a prince of great abilities, died in 1629, at the age of sixty three years, and after a reign of forty five

6 *Sam Myrza*, the son of *Sefi Myrza*, (who was put to death by his father *Abas*, because he was the darling of the people) ascended the throne, and assumed the name of *Shah Sefi*, as the king his grandfather had desired He died in the year 1642, having reigned twelve years

7. *Shah Abas* II the son of *Sefi*, died in 1666, after a reign of twenty four years

8 *Shah Selim*, the son of *Abas* II. died in 1694, and reigned twenty eight years

9 *Shah Selim* II. or *Soliman Huffain*, his son, succeeded him on the throne, and is the prince who now reigns

I shall now return to the continuation of my travels, till my return to *Holland*

C H A P. LXXXI.

The author's departure from Ispahan. *His arrival at* Cachan, Com, *and* Sauwa *Meets the* French *ambaffador. A defcription of* Casbin *and* Sultania. *His arrival at* Zim-gan, *and* Ardevil

ABOUT this time the river of *Zenderoe*, near the bridge of *Alla Wardie Chan*, was begun to be dug by five or six hundred men The intention, however, was to employ 70000 men in that work, of which number the *Armenians* of *Julfa* were to furnish 6000 at their own expence The work was undertaken in order to facilitate the course of that river, which frequently overflows, and lays all the plain under water The banks were accordingly raised, to prevent that inconvenience for the future, but as nothing more than earth and slime were employed on this occasion, all the labour that had been bestowed, was soon rendered ineffectual by the violence of the waters, and the country was again floated over as usual, as soon as the rain and melted snow had swelled the river

On the 25th of *February* we received intelligence from *Tauris*, that Mr. *Michel*, the *French* ambassador, whom I have formerly mentioned, was arrived thither from *Constantinople*, together with the mistress of Mr *Fabre* This minister had received orders from the court to seize this woman at *Erivan*, from whence she was to be conveyed to *Aleppo*, and from thence to be transported into *France* But as soon as she heard he was coming to that city, she retired to *Tauris*, and placed herself under the protection of the governor, who allowed her thirty *Mamoedies*, or two ducats, *per* day, to enable her to pursue her journey. It was likewise reported, that she was accompanied by a *French-man*, and had a train of thirty of the governor's domesticks This affair made a great noise, and the event was expected with impatience. I intend to relate it at large in the sequel of this work

In the mean time, as the day of my departure drew near, I went to take leave of all my friends in the city, and at *Julfa*, after having first wrote to *Batavia* and *Gamron*. I went then and waited on our director, who engaged me to sup
with

The author's departure

with him   The next day, his deputy accompanied me, with seven couriers, as far as the *Caravanserai* of *Koesgonna*, oppofite the king's garden   We fupped there by the light of torches, and after my friends were returned to the city, I likewife went to repofe myfelf a little, being exceedingly difordered with a cold   I was joined the next day by two *Armenians*, one of whom, who fpoke *Dutch*, intended to accompany me in my travels

We fet out the 2d of *March*, at nine in the morning, and found the plain all under water · We, however, advanced forward by the aid of feveral fmall bridges, and arrived in about three hours, at the *Caravanferai* of *Riek*, after a journey of five leagues   The wind blew very cold, and the mountains were, for the moft part, cover'd with fncw   Our caravan confifted of nine perfons on horfeback, and eight beafts of burthen, befide fervants   I had three horfes, and the others belonged to two *Armenians*, who had three couriers to accompany the baggage.   We had likewife two *Armenians*, who had a confiderable charge of merchandife , the reft of our company confifted of fome *Georgians*, and the conductor of the caravan   As we had agreed to travel by day, and repofe ourfelves during the night, by reafon of the cold, and to avoid many other inconveniences, we proceeded in our journey at feven in the morning, and found two *Caravanferais* at the end of the plain   From thence we entered the mountains, and arrived about night at *Sardaban*, after having travelled eight leagues.   We there paid eight pence for every beaft of burthen, as is cuftomary in that place   The next day we came to a garden belonging to the king, and called *Garftasjabaet*, whence there is a profpect of many other gardens and villages, and a great plain bordered with mountains, which we left on the right hand   We found the water frozen over in moft places, and arrived about two at the

Caravanferai of *Gaef*, five leagues from that, where we had paffed the night.   We renewed our journey at four in the morning over a large and beautiful plain, and advanced as far as the *Caravanferai* of *Baefabaet*, which is five leagues from the laft.   As yet we had not feen many pleafure-houfes, but the ways were exceedingly fine   The next day we met two *Georgian Mohammedans*, accompany'd with a retinue of thirteen or fourteen perfons, well provided with fire-arms, lances, bucklers, bows, and arrows.   They were travelling in order to join the king, and diverted themfelves with drawing the bow, and running races on horfeback   We made a fhort halt to obferve them, and likewife to wait for our beafts of burthen, and we arrived about two at *Cachan*, after a journey of fix leagues   I walked into the *Bazars*, where I purchafed feveral pieces of filk, which are exquifitely fine, as has been remarked before, and especially with refpect to the colours.

The great faft of the *Armenians* began on the 7th of this month, and continues forty nine days, during which they are not permitted to eat either flefh, fifh, butter, eggs, or milk, not even on a journey   As this is exprefly the injunction of their patriarch, they never violate it, but limit their diet to bread, rice, oil, herbs and fruits, which are very unfuitable food for a traveller ; but they have a full allowance to drink wine.

We continued our journey the next day, over the fame plain, where we faw feveral country-houfes, and met a fecond time the *Georgians*   I mentioned before, over againft the town of *Siefin*, where we breakfafted, having the mountains in our rear, and we arrived about four at the *Caravanferai* of *Abbi-fifterien*, after having travelled fix leagues   The next day we met feveral caravans, and advanced to *Gaffum-aba*, five leagues from the place where we lodged the preceding night   The day following we found the field full
of

1707 husbandmen, whose ploughs were drawn by two oxen, and we arrived at *Com* about noon. We continued there no longer than the break of day, and then renewed our journey over the plain, which is intersected by several streams, into one of which two of our saddle horses fell, thro' the carelessness of the guides, but we had the good fortune to disengage them from the danger, and did the same good office by an *Armenian* servant who fell from his horse. We returned thanks to God, for preserving us in that manner, but were frequently exposed to the same hazard, our horses being very restive, and I was frequently obliged to lead the horse that carry'd my baggage, to prevent it from being wet, though I had taken care to cover my chests 1707. with waxed cloth at *Ispahan*. At length, after having crossed many other canals, we arrived at a place where we found several black tents, and in about three hours we came to the town of *Sauwa*, which is very large, and resembles a city, being encompassed with a wall of earth. We there saw a number of fine towers, and a large mosque cover'd with a blue dome, and a spacious church-yard without the gates. At a distance this place resembles a forest, on account of the trees with which it abounds, and whose effect on the eye is extremely agreeable in the summer. The representation of it is exhibited in the following plate.

SAUWA

It was formerly a fine city, but is entirely ruinous at present, like many other cities in *Persia*: Yet we found several *Caravanserats* that were commodious enough, and we there payed twelve pence for every beast of burthen.

We were informed by an officer of the custom-house, who came from court, that the mistress of Mr. *Fabre* was arrived there, and had em-

embraced the *Mohammdan* religion

It was likewise reported, that the *French* king had made the king of *Persia* a present of this woman

We were also informed in that place, that the roads swarmed with robbers, and we had in our *Caravansera* a *Georgian Christian*, who had been robbed of all he had We supplied him with what was sufficient to carry him back again to *Cachan* , and the governor of the place gave us two horsemen for a guard, there being no soldiers there He likewise favoured us with a letter to the magistrate of the first village we were to pass through, with an order for him to furnish five or six armed persons for our safe conduct We remained here till the fourteenth, to rest our horses, and then renewed our journey, crossing over a range of mountains, after which we arrived at *Gangh*, where there is nothing but gardens and *Caravanserais* · We were furnished here with five men armed with fusees and sabres, with which convoy we continued our journey to *Goskaroe*, having travelled eight leagues The next day we entered the mountains, that were full of water, and at noon passed by the place which the robbers usually make their retreat, after which we dismissed our convoy, and proceeded by the *Caravanserai* of *Hoskaroet*, where robbers frequently skulk I entered it alone, and found it empty, and observed several apartments that were altogether in ruins We travelled on from thence in order to pass our night at *Alla-Sang*, a village full of gardens The next day we proceeded over a plain bordered with villages and gardens, and crossed several small rivers, having mountains covered with snow frequently in our view to *Abbesabath* When we passed on from this place we found the country full of ice, and a valley abounding with villages and gardens, whose prospect must certainly be delightful in summer, though the mountains are always covered with

snow About eleven we crossed a river, together with several bridges, and proceeded through a large paved way We afterward met a caravan of camels, and passed another river, where one of our servants fell into the water, but was immediately drawn out We found another spacious road paved like the former, with two canals on the right and left hand, but all the way was over-flow'd as far as *Casbin*, where the ground rises higher We arrived there very late, having travelled eight leagues

The day following, the interpreter of Mr *Miclel*, the *French* ambassador, whom I have so often mentioned, came to me by the order of his master, who understood that an *European* was arrived in that city, where he had been detained for the space of several weeks I went to wait on him after dinner, and he received me in the most obliging manner. He was still in the youthful part of his life, but had been employed in several courts, and had likewise served in *Poland* I continued with him a considerable time, and he informed me of the uneasiness he had sustained in *Persia*, where he was received in a very disagreeable manner, under a pretext that he was not invested with the character of the king his master. He, however, assured me, that he was the first minister who had been sent thither by the court of *France* , and the truth of what he declared was rendered evident not only by his credentials, but also by the rich presents he had in charge, and of which he favoured me with a sight He likewise shewed me a letter written from *Paris*, by Mr. *Fabre*'s mistress, wherein she intreats his permission to accompany him in his journey, though it were only to wash his linnen, and take care of his other apparel He added, that she was received at the court of *Persia*, though she had conducted herself in a very exceptionable manner in her journey thither, and that the court had refused to deliver

1707 liver her up to him, in order to her being fent into *France*, agreeably to the command he had received from the king his mafter, and that he himfelf was not permitted to make his appearance at court This minifter, however, fet out from hence with an intention to proceed thither, notwithftanding all the obftacles that were created in his disfavour, and departed by night without the leaft noife, leaving two or three fervants in the tavern where he lodged A report was current, that twenty perfons on horfeback were difpatched after him, but this was what he had no occafion to be alarmed at, becaufe he was attended with eighty domeftics well armed. We were obliged to continue three days at *Casbin*, our horfes not being in a condition to go any farther. We fold one fet of them, and bought others in their ftead

The fituation of Casbin — This city is fituated in a plain, in the northern part of the province of *Yerak*, to the north-weft of *Ifpahan*, and one league northward of the mountains The extent of it is very confiderable, and it abounds with plantations of fena and other trees

Its principal mofque, which is that of *Jumma Mat-zijt*, or the fabbath, has a fine cupola of a blue colour, well glazed, with two walks around it, and a beautiful portal, like thofe at *Ifpahan* There are likewife two or three others, which are very agreeable, and feveral that are more common. The royal palace is a very large ftructure, but the *Chiaer-baeg* is fmall, and bordered with fena-trees. The *Meydoen*, or great fquare, has nothing in it confiderable : the fhops of it are perfectly mean, and moft of the houfes are in a ruinous condition, as well as the *Caravanferais* The perfon at whofe houfe we lodged had four large fena-trees in his court-yard, with a canal of running water The *Armenians* refide in this city, and have a little chapel of a moderate height, and which, at a diftance, refembles a dove-houfe. There are likewife a number of poor *Jews* in this place, and a 1707. houfe where the king's mufick is heard at particular times

We purfued our journey on the 22d, through a plain filled with villages Toward noon we entered among the mountains, and travelled but five leagues that day We found, the day following, abundance of water in the plains, and advanced as far as *Corondara*, which is fix leagues from the *Caravanferai* where we had paffed the night We afterward proceeded through arable lands, and met feveral caravans : About four, we had travelled a league beyond *Sultania*, and we paffed the night at the *Caravanferai* of *Kara-boelag*, after a journey of eight leagues A greyhound of mine caught in that plain, a fmall animal called *Zits-jan*, which he brought me alive, and likewife another in a fhort time after, and I caufed the entrails to be taken out of them, in order to preferve them. This creature is a kind of field-rat, about the fize of a fquirril Its tail is fhort, and it has the hair and colour of a young rabbet, whom it likewife refembles in fhape, only it has a larger head, and the two under teeth are half as long again as thofe in the upper jaw. The two fore-feet of this little animal are fhorter than the hinder, they likewife end in four large claws, and one that is fmaller. The hinder feet have five, which much refemble thofe of an ape This animal is exhibited to view in the following plate

We arrived next day at *Zingan*, The aurival at Zingan — where we found the *Caravanferai* in fuch a naufeous condition, that we were obliged to take up with a ftable, at the other end of the city, and were compelled by the badnefs of the weather to continue there all the next day. *Zingan* is a mean place, where nothing remarkable is to be found. Upon our fetting out from hence, we croffed a plain full of water, having the mountains at fome diftance on our right and left. We likewife paffed a kind of torrent twice, into which one of our
horfes

ANIMAL ZITS-IAN.

horſes fell, and as he was loaded with coffee, we were obliged to dry it We arrived, about noon, at *Mubuʹ*, where the bad weather obliged us to halt, and the cold was ſo exceſſive in the night, that I found it very difficult to preſerve my ſelf from it. I was covered all over with furs, and had likewiſe two good blankets, and a large fire in a cloſe place

The next day about ten, we arrived at the mountains, and were unable to proceed farther than *Serg-Abeth*, which is four leagues from the place where we lodged the preceding night We here ſuffered as ſeverely by the cold as we did the day before, our courſe being directed to the north, and the wind being equally violent, but we were lodged more commodiouſly at a private houſe. The next day proved rainy, and we travelled but four leagues, as far as *Agkaut*, having paſſed over high mountains, and thro' valleys filled with water I was indiſpoſed with an ague a little before night, and immediately went

to bed, after having drank a little burnt wine ſweetened with ſugar, in which ſome particular herbs were infuſed In ſhort, we were obliged to continue in that place till the end of the month, in order to reſt our horſes When we ſet out from this place, we continued to paſs over ſome mountains, and plains that were overflowed, and about noon began to aſcend mount *Taurus*, which the inhabitants call *Caſeluſan* I have already given ſome account of it, as likewiſe of the river *Kurp*, and the bridge over which one paſſes at that place. When we had croſſed another, named *Kurpu-koebaeʒ*, we halted in the mountains, after a journey of five leagues

We advanced on the firſt day of *April*, into another mountain, where we ſaw the tombs of the inhabitants of the adjacent villages, and were obliged to ſtop for ſome hours at a track of arable lands, becauſe our horſes were quite fatigued with the journey We there met ſeveral travellers, and a large caravan, well provided with arms In the mean time

1707 time I then advanced, with some others, as far as *Paggesyiek*, but the rest of the company, and all the beasts of burden, continued in the mountains Our caravan passed by us the next day, and we were informed that they had lost some horses We rejoined it about noon at *Ries*, where we continued till the next day, and as we afterward passed by a certain village, we had some dispute with the custom-house officers, whose demands we were obliged to satisfy. Notwithstanding which, we met others of them on horseback, armed with lances, who exacted the same duty from us which we had so lately paid. It was to no purpose for us to tell them, that we had already discharged all dues of that nature, and we were forced to give them some *Mamoedies*, in order to get rid of them. We then passed on by a small lake, whose borders were enamelled with a thousand flowers, and full of small blue hyacinths, which is a very extraordinary circumstance in that quarter, where most of the plants have a withered appearance We arrived about six at the small *Caravanserat* of *Koereten*, where my ague returned

upon me, and obliged me to continue there till the next day, during which time the *Armenians* set out for *Ardevil*. I followed them the day after, and got thither at three in the afternoon. The *Georgian*, who came with us from *Ispahan*, died there in the night, and it created no little surprize, when he was found to be a *Mohammedan*, and circumcised

The author's arrival at Ardevil

Some days after the mourning for *Hussein*, which I have frequently mentioned, was renewed. The weather proved excessive cold, and all the ground was covered with snow. We were obliged to wait in this city for the arrival of a large caravan, which set out from *Ispahan* before us; this quarter being much infested with robbers, and especially the country of *Mogan*: Notwithstanding which several *Armenians* went to *Gilan*, in order to proceed from thence to *Astracan*, by the *Caspian Sea*. I commissioned one of these people to buy me some pieces of silk, which are there made in great perfection This city is six days journey from *Ardevil*, where also they make fine silk, but not comparable to that which is manufactured at *Gilan*.

CHAP. LXXXII.

The author's departure from Ardevil. *The injustice of the officers of the customs A melancholy accident The rivers* Kur *and* Aras *The author's arrival at* Samachi. *Violent proceedings of the* Persians *A fertile country*

The author's departure from Ardevil

WE set out from *Ardevil* the 17th of *April*, in order to proceed to *Mierasiraef*, and at our arrival there went to lodge at the house belonging to the conductor of the caravan. The next day we advanced as far as *Sabbad-daer*, which is but two leagues from *Ardevil* We found the ways very bad, and met a large caravan But nothing is so incommodious, in that quarter, as the smoke, which has no outlet but the door. On the 19th we passed over a great stone bridge on the river *Karassoe*, whose stream is exceeding rapid The custom-house officers came thither, and obliged us to pay a *Mamoedie* for every horse, tho' I had already paid three for mine at the gate of the city, and two for my baggage before I left the *Caravanserai*. We, however, were

T t obliged

1707 obliged to submit to this imposition, notwithstanding they had no right to demand it. When we had travelled the length of three leagues, we stopped by the side of the village of *Koroet-siaey*, where we stayed till the dawn of day, and then proceeded three leagues farther, having no place but the open country for our lodging. The next day we passed over the mountains as far as *Barsand*, a country neither under the jurisdiction of *Ardevil*, nor under that of *Mogan*, for which reason we were obliged to pay three *Mamoedies* there for every beast of burthen. We travelled but two leagues the day following, by reason of the bad weather, and halted on the bark of a little stream, where provisions were brought us from *Baesye-Zaboran*, at the entrance into the territory of *Mogan*. As the peasans of this place pass for great thieves, we always were upon our guard, and the next day we passed over the river of *Balbaroe*, whose current is very rapid, and we proceeded along the bank of it for a considerable time, finding tents and cattle where-ever we came. We also met a caravan coming from *Samachi*, and going to *Ispahan*. Nothing can form a more agreeable prospect than the meadows enamell'd with various flowers on each side of this river. We there fed our horses, which is a convenience rarely found in that country. The next day the *Armenians* solemnized their *Easter*, having provided a lamb for that purpose, after which we continued our journey, and were favoured with very fine weather.

The way full of robbers.

A *Persian* merchant of our caravan fell from his horse, and unhappily broke all his ribs, and the violence of the hurt was so great, that it at once deprived him of speech and reason. We used all possible means to save him, and apply'd *Mummy* to him, (of which I alone was provided) but to no purpose, for he died in the night, and was carry'd to *Ardevil* to be interr'd.

We advanced but two leagues on the 27th, and were obliged to lodge in the open country. As the air was serene, we had the pleasure of viewing the mountains of *Schirwan*, and arrived about eight the next day on the banks of the *Kur* and *Aras*, and where these rivers unite their streams. I there found a great alteration in the banks, all the reeds which formerly rendered them inaccessable, having been cut down. That day was employed in conveying our baggage over to the other side, as we had done when we came that way before. On the 29th we made a considerable progress northward along the river, and then to the east, and again passed the night under a fine star-light, but without any water. The last day of the month we found a good spring, which flowed from the rocks within the mountains, and we arrived about night at *Samachi*. I went to pay my compliments to a *Russian* nobleman, whose name was *Bories Fedowits*, and with whom I became acquainted at *Astracan*, where he had a regiment. He was at present consul in this city, and treated me with great civility, acquainting me at the same time, that he was preparing for his return to *Astracan* by the way of *Niesawaey*, and therefore desired we might travel together.

The authors arrival at Samachi

The *Persians* at that time committed great acts of violence against the jesuits, whose convent they would have demolished, but it happened by good fortune, at that very instant, that one of these fathers, who was a good physician, and well known to the people, had likewise eloquence enough to persuade them to return, without executing their intended design. They, however, came a second time, but without doing any injury. These violent proceedings frequently happen, thro' the indulgence of the governor, who is a man entirely abandoned to his pleasures, and particularly to wine, which he pretends the king has authorised him to drink.

Violences committed by the Persians

Such an example as this, which the inhabitants very readily conform to, occasioned the disorder I have mentioned,

1707 mentioned, and expofes ftrangers to all forts of impofitions, and to fuch a degree, that they cannot pafs the ftreets without having ftones thrown down on their heads This obliged me to keep my chamber during my continuance in that city, but my precaution did not entirely fecure me from infults, which are there practifed with impunity, the laws being altogether difregarded Whereas the preceding governor was an equitable man, who made himfelf feared, and faithfully difcharged all the duties of his office. Another inconvenience which contributes much to thefe licentious proceedings, is, that the troops receive no pay, and fubfift by rapine alone The *Mufcovites* who live here are expofed to the fame injurious treatment, and are yet perpetually reprefenting the eafy manner in which the *Czar* might revenge the injuftice they fuftain, by invading that part of the country, to which the others reply, that fuch a revolution would not be difpleafing to them, fince they fhould be more happy under the government of the *Czar*, than under that of their natural prince. They even make no fcruple to declare, that they would attempt nothing in their own defence, but pray to *Mohammed* that this may be the event, and it is certain, that it would be no difficulty for the *Czar* to accomplifh it. This, however, is a confiderable government, and yields large revenues, on this fide the *Aras*, which divides it from the other territories of the *Perfian* monarchy. Thofe likewife which produce the filks of *Gilan*, together

with the cottons and faffron, are well 1707 known The foil alfo produces excellent wines, red and white, which are ftrong indeed, but exceedingly agreeable when tempered with water, efpecially the white It likewife affords very fine fruits, fuch as apples, pears, chefnuts, &c. to which I may add, that excellent horfes and cattle are bred there In a word, it is a very fine country, and exceed- *The country fruit-* ing fertile on the fide of *Georgia*; but *ful* there are not a fufficient number of inhabitants to cultivate it in a proper manner. It abounds, however, in game, rice, and grain, and the bread which is made there is excellent.

Baggu likewife affords a commodious haven. The governors of this province never fail to enrich themfelves in a fhort time, and it would certainly prove a very commodious acquifition to his *Czarian* majefty, fince it lies contiguous to his dominions, and is very advantageous to thofe of his fubjects who traffic there for any confiderable time. It might likewife be preferved without any difficulty, after it had once been conquered, by erecting forts there.

Before my departure from this city, I wrote to my friends at *Ifpaban*, and gave my letters to the jefuit I have mentioned before, and from whom I received all poffible civilities, nor could I help deploring his hard fate, and that of his brethren, who are obliged to live in a place where they are expofed to the outrages of a populace, who are always infolent and implacable to the *Chriftians*.

CHAP.

CHAP. LXXXIII.

The author's departure from Samachi, *and arrival at* Niefawaey, *from whence he proceeds to* Aftracan

The author's departure from Samachi.

ON the 24th of *May,* I left *Samachi* in the evening, the *Ruffian* conful, and thofe of his retinue, having fet out before us, but I overtook them in the mountains about a league from the city, in company with feveral *Armenians,* and fome *Indians* We began our journey at break of day, and paffed by a demolifh-d building, that refembled an antient monument, being full of tombs. We then croffed a river, together with fome leffer ftreams, and continued our journey over mountains that were covered with fmall wild trees, and a variety of green plants, and at eight in the evening we halted on the brink of a canal. The next day we followed the courfe of the river, which conducted us to the mountains, and there we croffed it a fecond time, and paffed the night on it's bank, after travelling eight leagues From hence we proceeded into a plain, that fronts the *Caffain*

Sea, and where we had a diftant profpect of feveral villages, and arable lands, and likewife of other parts of the country that were overflowed : About feven we difcovered the downs, and the fea itfelf, along the fide of which we continued our journey toward night, and paffed over a fmall gulf which it forms up the country, and where I found feveral touchftones At ten we arrived at *Niefawaey,* where we rejoined the *Ruffians,* who had taken another way. We there found fix *Ruffian* barks, together with a great number of tents along the fhore, and under which feveral mercantile commodities were depofited The *Ruffians,* who were to pafs the winter in that place, had made themfelves barracks of trees, and the others fheltered themfelves under tents. I drew the profpect of this place, which is reprefent- in the following plate.

His arrival at Niefawaey

VUE DE NIESAWAEY

1707 Three days after we advanced to the fhore, which was but a quarter of a league from us, and they then began to embark their goods, which confifted of filks and rice, but we were obliged to continue fome days there, on account of the violent duft which an eaft wind had raifed, and to which this coaft is extremely fubject, as I have formerly obferved I there drew a fketch of the fhore, which is exhibited, together with the tents and barks, &c in plate 240

On the 8th of *June* every thing was embarked, and one of the fmalleft veffels fet fail for *Aftracan*, from whence two were juft then arrived, and one other from *Tarku* or *Tirk* I went in the evening on board the leffer of thefe veffels, with the conful, and fome *Ruffians*, together with three or four *Armenians*. I drew, the next day, another profpect of *Niefawaey*, from our bark, in the manner it appears in plate 241 not omitting the high mountains, which are always covered with fnow. We fet fail at two, with eighty perfons on board, including the failors, and in the evening advanced as far as *Derbent*, five leagues from *Niefawaey*, but without difcovering the city In the night, we fail'd to the northward, and loft fight of land by break of day, but the wind changing, at fun-fet, we came to anchor near the coaft of *Tirk*, in a depth of thirty fathom

On the 14th we continued our courfe with an eafterly wind, which lafted only till evening, when we were obliged to caft anchor a fecond time. The 18th, the wind tacked about to eaft-north-eaft, when we hoifted fail again, and found in the evening from ten to nine and eight fathom water, and from feven to fix toward morning, and four about noon, when the water was whiter and frefher than before We likewife met a bark bound from *Aftracan* to *Niefawaey*, and the conful ordered a gun to be fired as a fignal for the commander to lie by At four we found the water frefh enough

Vol. II.

to be drinkable, and then came 1707 into three fathom and a half The wind, which was frequently changing, obliged us to anchor once more in ten foot water, and as our veffel drew eight, we often ftruck againft the ground In that condition we remained till the 21ft, when the wind fhifted to eaft north-eaft, but varied again in the evening, foon after which we were becalmed It then changed to the north, and continued three days at that point, upon which the conful fent orders to the other fhip, which had not left us, to repair immediately to *Aftracan*, in order to fend out the other veffels, in cafe the weather fhould not alter But the wind veer'd to the weft, and was accompanied with thunder and rain, and the fea was not above eight foot deep in that place The 27th in the afternoon we difcovered three veffels, which we took for pirates, and therefore ftood upon our guard, having two brafs cannons and other fire-arms. As they only rowed, they quickly came up with us, upon which we fired off a gun, and they retired; but when they afterward advanced toward us again, we found them to be the fame that we had ordered from *Aftracan*, which rejoiced us not a little, becaufe they brought us a fupply of provifions, which we greatly needed And yet our firft apprehenfions were not altogether without reafon, it being very ufual to meet pirates in that fea, who never *Pirates* fpare thofe who are fo unfortunate as to fall into their hands They come from the mountains, and are commonly *Samgales*, intermixed with *Ruffian* rebels

On the 30th we weighed anchor, the wind being fouth-weft, and fteered to the fouth, in eight foot water, but the uncertainty of the wind obliged us to anchor again, and we were incommoded to fuch a *Troublefome flies* degree, with flies in the night, that I was forced to make ufe of my net.

On the 2d of *July* I embarked in a fmall veffel, to be more at my eafe, and becaufe my provifions grew

U u fhort,

1707 fhort, and I had no inclination to rely any longer on the wind We employ'd oars and fails, directing our courfe to the north, in feven fix, and five foot water, and toward noon difcovered land, at north-north-weft, with the four red mountains, which I have formerly mentioned, and whofe diftance from each other is almoft equal The coaft is not fo high on this fide, as it is toward *Perfia*

As we approached the gulf, we found feveral veffels that are authorized to fearch the cargoes of fhips the banks likewife of that gulf are entirely covered with reeds We continued there at anchor part of the night, becaufe of the calm

On the 3d we came to a dock, or place made for fifhing, where fhips are fearched a fecond time, and at noon came to another, where there is fo little ground, that it proves very difficult to land there I here ate a plate of good fifh. We came about four to the third dock, where we lay at anchor all night, the wind being contrary, and the fea running very high On the 4th we fet fail again, the bank being all covered *Arrival at* with water, and arrived at *Aftracan* Aftracan about ten I went to pay my refpects to the governor, Peter *Jwan tz Gawanske*, who was the *Knees*, or prince, and a man of generofity and merit, who had been governor of this place above twenty years When he had read the letters I delivered to him, he treated me with abundance of civility, and offered to ferve me to the utmoft of his power, during my continuance in that city, but I returned him my thanks, and only requefted him to favour me with a lodging in a private houfe, where I could live more commodioufly than in a *Caravanferai*, and he immediately obliged me in this particular

Our fhips arrived at the city on the 11th, and the governor ordered my baggage to be fent to me, without fo much as fearching it, but I had the misfortune to hear that all my friends, together with the gover-

nor *Timafe Jwan tz Uffoffkie*, and 1707 colonel *de Wign*, had been maffacred in the rebellion of the *Strelfes*, in 1705, and that no more than three or four perfons were faved, who fet out three days before for *Mofcow*, namely, the governor's fon and his wife, together with the conful I lately mentioned, and likewife captain *Wagenaer*, and a certain chirurgeon, and that all the ftrangers with their wives and children, loft their lives in this fatal maffacre, fince which his *Czarian* majefty fent fome regular troops thither, and caufed moft of the *Strelfes* to be executed, as well as thofe who had joined with them in this inhuman flaughter. For my part, I returned thanks to God that I quitted *Perfia* before this fatal accident The governor's wife, who efcaped the fury of the *Barbarians*, had the misfortune to lofe all fhe had in her voyage to *Mofcow*, the fhip wherein fhe was to fail having taken fire, her grief at this misfortune coft her her life foon after her arrival at *Mofcou*

At my return to *Aftracan*, I was *Veffels loft* informed that fourteen veffels had *by negligence* foundered through the negligence of captain *Meyer*, whom I have often mentioned, and who likewife perifhed in this difafter. But five others arrived three months after, under the conduct of *Laurence Van der Burgh*, a man of merit and capacity, who had entered into the fervice of his *Czarian* majefty, and was then employed in weighing up the fhips that were funk, and refitting them, fo as to be ferviceable on the *Cafpian Sea*

Several *Hollanders*, who had ferved in thofe parts, daily arrived at this place, and I had the affliction to hear, that Mr *Meynard*, an *Englifh* gentleman, with whom I had been acquainted at *Zjie-raes*, had loft his fight, and the ufe of fome of his limbs, and had fet out in that condition for his own country.

One evening, when I had com- *An extra-* pany in my apartment, the miftrefs *ordinary* of the houfe where I lodged was *adventure* brought to bed of a fon, without my knowing

1707

knowing any thing of the affair, tho' her chamber was over mine We indeed had taken notice, that several women came there, but as such visits are very frequent, I thought there could be nothing particular at present, and was therefore the more surprized, when my friends were gone, to hear what had happened When the husband, who was one of the commissioners of the chancery, came home, I made him a present of some pistacho nuts, dates, and almonds, to treat his guests. Toward evening they all began to sing in a tone that seemed to resemble their church service, and, as I had never heard any thing of that nature before, I asked my footman, who understood the language of the country, what could be the meaning of this behaviour? To which he replied, that they were all intoxicated with liquor, as was customary on those occasions: But I was ex-

tremely surprized the next day, to find the woman who had been brought to bed, sitting at the street door, with the child in her arms In the evening she treated the women who had assisted her at her labour, with *Aqua vitæ*, and drank very freely of it herself, as is usual in this country

As I was walking one day through the market, I bought a bird, which the *Russians* call *Babbe*, or the *Water-carrier*, of which I had frequently heard people speak, but could never procure one till now, though I had often inquired for it both in this country, and at *Ispahan*. I offered it fish, which it would not eat, nor any thing else, and I could not make the creature extend its neck, which it kept in a deflected position, and seemed to be half asleep. The reader will find the representation of it in the following plate. The bird was young, though four

A very singular bird

1707.

1707 times as large as a goose, which it partly resembled in shape and plumage, the bill was fifteen inches long, and two in breadth, and ended in a yellow hook, like that of a parrot The bag in which it carries its water contains above four pints, and the legs of the creature are short I cut off the head and part of the neck, on which I left the bag, as it appears in the plate

Fires frequently broke out in this city, during my continuance there, but especially in the suburbs of the *Tartars,* who were very industrious to extinguish the flames As I have already sufficiently spoken of these people, I shall only add a particular concerning them, which did not come to my knowledge before

In the year 1246 they chose for the chief of *Tartary,* a certain *Kaine,* to whom they gave the surname of *Gog Cham,* which signifies king, or emperor, and the people call themselves *Moales,* or *Mongales* This emperor and his successors styled themselves in their writings, *The power of God, and emperors of the universe,* and caused the following words to be engraven around their seals, A GOD IN HEAVEN, A KUINE CHAM ON EARTH, *The power of God, and the emperor of all mankind* These princes always maintain five standing armies, to keep their subjects in awe The first of these emperors was victorious on the frontiers of *Persia,* over prince Ba-

...bu, who had made himself 1707 master of all the *Christian* and *Saracen* territories, as far as the *Mediterranean,* and to an extent of two days journey beyond *Antioch,* and deprived him of fourteen kingdoms, which comprehended all the tract from thence to *Persia* The proper name of this prince was *Bajoth, Noy* being a word expressive of his dignity

The *Tartars* were never governed by a greater prince than *Bathu,* whose army consisted of six hundred thousand men, namely, a hundred and sixty thousand *Tartars,* and four hundred and forty thousand *Christians,* exclusive of all the infidels who ranged themselves under his banners This army was divided into five bodies. *Bathu, an emperor of Tarta-*

This country, which lies to the Mongal east, is called *Mongal,* and has four different nations for its inhabitants, namely, the grand *Mongales,* or *Moals,* the *Saniongals,* or maritim *Mongales,* who are likewise called *Tartars,* from the river *Tartar,* which flows through their country, the *Merkates,* and the *Metrites* These four nations greatly resemble each other, living almost in the same manner, and speaking the same language They, however, are separated from one another, and have different chiefs Mention is also made of certain *Gingis,* who inhabit the country of *Jeka* in *Mongal.*

CHAP.

CHAP. LXXXIV.

The author's departure from Aftracan. *Is ship-wrecked on the* Volga *Tartarian pirates. His ar-rival at* Zenogar, Zaritza, *and* Saratof.

The au-thor's de-parture from A-ftracan

AS I was foon to fet out for *Mofcow*, with a *Georgian* lord, who was going in the quality of am-baffador to *Poland*, we defired the governor to appoint us a veffel, to convey us to *Saratof*, and likewife to furnifh us with paffports and fuch orders as would be neceffary for our being accommodated with chariots and horfes, in order to continue our journey from that place I accord-ingly had three granted for my ufe, and the *Georgian* lord as many as he wanted We received our difpatches on the nineteenth of *Auguft*, and found the veffel ready equipped for failing The next day we embark-ed, after taking leave of the gover-nor, and began our voyage with the towing-line, till the wind, which then fhifted to the eaft, permitted us to ufe our fails. But as the gale was very ftrong, and our fhip rolled from one fide to the other, we be-gan to be apprehenfive of fome di-fafter. Some were for fending for another veffel, others for throwing in more ballaft, but none of them came to any fixed refolution. For my part, when I obferved that our greateft danger proceeded from the ill ftructure of the fhip, I infifted on their making the beft of their way toward land, fince I had reafon to fear our veffel would founder The number of perfons on board amount-ed to above thirty ; the *Georgian* had likewife two horfes, and the fhip was one of the fmalleft. It was therefore foon filled with water, near the powder-mills, which are feven or eight *Werftes* from *Aftracan*, at a place where an ancient city formerly ftood , and we had the utmoft dif-ficulty to fave our felves and our baggage, with the affiftance of fome failors, who threw themfelves into the

water. My greateft care was for my papers, and what I had that was moft curious, and I committed all the reft, together with my provi-fions, to the mercy of the waves. The fhip being thrown on one of her fides, the horfes naturally took to the water, and fwam to fhore. The moment we ourfelves arrived there, we rendered thanks to God for our deliverance, for if the fhip had turn-ed on her fide in the middle of the river, we all muft inevitably have pe-rifhed, the river being very broad, and the ftream exceeding rapid. The *Georgian* minifter immediately fent his interpreter to *Aftracan*, in a floop, to inform the governor of what had happened to us, and to defire a new fhip, but the wind continuing very boifterous, he could not fet out till the next day. I fent my footman with him to buy me a frefh fupply of provifions, and to deliver a letter I had written to the commander *Van der Burgh*, wherein I de-fired him to procure us another vef-fel as foon as poffible, and in cafe he fhould not be able to find one ready for failing, that he would fend me a fkiff, to convey me back to *A-ftracan*, till we could have a more favourable opportunity for continu-ing our voyage. During the time I waited for his anfwer, I drew a fketch of the place where we had fuffered fhipwreck ; the two banks of the river are likewife comprehend-ed in the profpect, and the whole is exhibited in the following plate

The commander *Van der Burgh*, came to me in the evening in his own floop, and affured me that the governor had teftified an extreme concern at the accident that had be-fallen us, and would not fail to fend us a better fhip as foon as poffible,

Is fhip-wreck'd.

NAUFRAGE SUR LA WOLGA

that he, however, wifhed we would endeavour to fet our own a floating, in order to its being fent back to *Aftracan.* This we aecomplifhed toward morning, but it immediately funk to the bottom a fecond time, in a very deep part of the river, and we could fave nothing but the tackling. We were vifited again the next day by the commander, who affured us, that the veffel we expected had already fet fail, and that it was much better and larger than the other we had loft He likewife informed us, that the veffel which the governor had difpatched the day before our departure, and which was laden with fruits, and other refrefhments, for his *Czarian* majefty, had likewife been loft in a ftorm, but that her crew been faved, and were now on their return to *Aftracan,* after having been robbed by the *Tartars* Our new fhip arrived the next day, and we found it much better and more commodious than

the former   Our people were then employed in carrying all things on board, that we might fet fail the next day

The powder-mills, which I mentioned before, are but feldom ufed, and we faw no more than feven or eight workmen there

The *Georgian* ambaffador happen- Robbers. ing to advance a little beyond the reft of the company, about eight or nine in the evening, faw eight or ten perfons, whom he took for robbers, advancing toward him , but they immediately had recourfe to flight, when they heard him call his people to his affiftance , and they were not to be overtaken   The governor of *Aftracan* fent us fifteen Soldiers in the new fhip, with orders for them to tend the tackle, and two of them were to be upon duty in the night   In this manner we continued our voyage, being towed along by ten of our foldiers The river was half a league broad in that place,

1707 place, and little more than a quarter at the diſtance of two leagues from thence, and where we heard that another ſhip had been wrecked in the late ſtorm. She was ornamented with flags and ſtreamers, and belonged to a citizen of *Aſtracan*. Our Veſſel was decorated in the ſame manner, and had two pieces of cannon, with ſeveral fire-arms, and a number of bows and arrows, and we likewiſe found her very commodious. As I have already given a ſufficient deſcription of this river, it will be needleſs for me to add any other particulars. I ſhall only obſerve that it is frequently neceſſary for ſhips to be towed up the ſtream, unleſs the wind ſhould happen to prove very favourable. They are likewiſe obliged to lie at anchor, when the wind is either tempeſtuous, or contrary, the *Calmucks* likewiſe appear from time to time on the banks.

We paſſed on the 28th, by a *Corps de Garde*, ſituated on a point of the river, to the right, where the *Volga* pours itſelf through a canal, into the *Caſpian Sea*. Another guard is likewiſe ſtationed on board a veſſel in the middle of this river, and eſpecially in the night, in order to viſit all ſhips that paſs. We ſaw a conſiderable number of *Calmucks*, who were fiſhing with lines along the bank, and we threw them out ſome bread, which they ſwam for, and then carried it to ſhore. We likewiſe ſaw ſeveral camels with two bunches riſing on their backs, and this place is full of thoſe birds that are called *Water-Carriers*, one of which has been already deſcribed. As we were always obliged to be towed along, the men who were employed in that ſervice, went ſometimes on one ſide of the river, and ſometimes on the other, to avoid the *Tartars* who frequent that quarter. Two days after we croſſed another gulph which is formed by the *Volga*, and as we happened then to go on ſhore, we found ſeveral *Calmucks*, as well men as women, who ſurveyed without ceaſing my manner of dreſs, which appear-

ed very extraordinary to them, as 1707 they had never ſeen any thing like it before. As they go bare-legg'd, and have very ſmall feet, they meaſured them with mine, and likewiſe their legs, which are very ſhort. Their wives are alſo very little, and plump, like the men. I was obliged to uncover my boſom to them, in order to ſatisfy their curioſity; and having then given them to underſtand that I was deſirous to ſee theirs, they immediately laughed, and gave me that ſatisfaction without any difficulty. All the habit worn by theſe people, is a kind of petticoat made of ſheep-ſkins, which they change according to the ſeaſon, and wear no cloathing on any other part of their body in ſummer. Moſt of the young men among them go entirely naked, and have their hair plaited like that of the women. Others of them wear a kind of bonnet, together with a waiſtcoat and a pair of drawers, but no ſhirt. They have all broad and flat faces, ſwoln cheeks, and long eyes. They aſked me for ſome tobacco, which the women as well as the men thruſt up their noſtrils, and likewiſe chew.

We continued our voyage on the eaſt ſide of the river, in order to avoid the *Tartars* on the other ſide, who are great thieves: We frequently met ſeveral veſſels, and were from time to time obliged to croſs ſmall gulphs, where we found companies of fiſhermen, and very good fiſh.

On the 2d of *September* we anchored near the place where the chief, or governor of the *Calmucks*, reſides. This officer had lately cauſed a party conſiſting of eighty men, to croſs the river, in order to purſue a body of *Tartars*, who had newly carried off a great number of his horſes, and ſeveral of his ſubjects, but they had not the good fortune to come up with the *Tartars*. We were likewiſe informed that this quarter was infeſted by *Coſſacks*, who are alſo great robbers, and this intelligence made us think it neceſſary to be upon our guard.

We

The au-
thor's ar-
rival at
Tzenogar

We approached *Tzenogar* on the 7th, and caſt anchor on the hither ſide of this place, the wind being contrary and very tempeſtuous, but we ſent for a ſupply of proviſions A great ſtorm aroſe in the night, and our cable dragged to ſuch a degree, that we were driven back to a conſiderable diſtance by the courſe of the river, before we could faſten our veſſel to the ſhore with ſtrong ropes. Every one then betook himſelf to reſt, but I was unable to cloſe my eyes, having the idea of our late wreck very ſtrong in my remembrance

It had always been my cuſtom to give a glaſs of brandy to each of our ſailors once a-day, but I diſpleaſed the ambaſſador by this proceeding, and he gave me to underſtand by his interpreter, that they were a ſet of wretches altogether undeſerving of any ſuch civility My anſwer was, that I had made a ſufficient proviſion for that purpoſe, and that we might happen to have occaſion for their beſt ſervices, to which I added, that I was ſenſible by frequent experience, that nothing gained upon thoſe people ſo much as civility, and that we ought therefore to make a virtue of neceſſity When we approached the city we diſcharged a ſalvo of our fire-arms, and ſaw a great number of ſhips there

We continued our voyage two days after, but the weather proved ſo exceſſive cold, that we were obliged to cover ourſelves with furs, which was a very extraordinary circumſtance in that ſeaſon of the year. As the *Ruſſians* are very bad ſailors, our ſhip frequently ran a-ground, and we loſt our anchor by their neglect. No manner of order is obſerved among them, and the meaneſt ſoldier had as much to ſay as the pilot, which gave me great uneaſineſs. We were likewiſe obliged to call the ſailors ten or twelve times before they would riſe, and I generally found the centinels aſleep, nor was it without great difficulty that we prevailed upon the men to work the ſhip when the weather proved tempeſtuous I never failed therefore to return thanks

every day to Almighty God, for preſerving us in the night, and eſpecially from the *Corſairs*

His arrival
at Zarit-
ſa

We arrived, on the 16th, at the city of *Zaritſa*, where the church, which is all of white ſtone, had been newly built, as well as the city, which was reduced to aſhes the preceding year, and all the buildings were not then finiſhed We continued here two days in order to change our ſailors In the evening, a veſſel arrived here from *Saratof*, but ſhe had been robbed in her paſſage, by the *Ruſſian Coſſacks*, and her crew informed us that the river ſwarmed with theſe pirates, who ſailed out by hundreds in ſmall veſſels. I hereupon deſired the *Georgian* ambaſſador to apply to the governor for a guard, which would not be refuſed provided the requeſt was accompanied with a preſent, for nothing is to be obtained in this country without money The miniſter, however, was deaf to all I could ſay on this head, though I offered to pay my part of the expence At laſt the owners of two other veſſels, which were to ſail for *Saratof*, as well as ourſelves, came to acquaint us, that they would accompany us in the voyage for our mutual ſecurity, having obtained the governor's permiſſion for ſo doing There was likewiſe a third ſhip, which ſet out before us, and her we found afterward a-ground . due care was however taken to ſet her a-float again, and after her merchandize had been dried, ſhe joined us, as the reſt had done

We paſſed, on the 19th, by two ſluices, in a part where the river was very narrow, and where we were told the greateſt danger was to be apprehended with reſpect to pirates This obliged us to be upon our guard in the night, for the ſoldiers who had towed us along in the day-time, wanted reſt Toward morning we met a veſſel which had been plundered by four pirates, and ſaw three others, which alarmed us at firſt, but when they were near enough to be diſtinguiſhed, we found they belonged to

Sa-

Sai atof and Cafan, and were carrying foldiers to Aftracan We afterward croffed a fmall gulph, which affords a retreat to pirates, and we therefore thought it neceffary to be upon our guard at night, after which we continued our voyage, being towed along as before, and foon ran aground But we were fet a-float again by a gale which fprung up in the eaft, and it likewife wafted us to the other fide of the river, where we caft anchor, and continued till eight in the morning, when we fpread our fails to a favourable wind, and were accompanied only by one veffel, the others having fet fail before us

Toward noon we found another gulph to the weft of the river, and faw feveral merchandizes on fhore, which the pirates, who had taken them out of the fhip already mentioned, had not been able to carry off. We afterward faw two barks which were worked with oars, thefe we at firft took for pirates, but they were only fifhermen.

Toward evening another veffel, which came from Saratof, failed by us fhe fet out before us from Aftracan, and was now returning thither. We afterward met Peter Matfewitz Apraxim, governor of Aftracan, and he was accompanied by thirty fail, feven of which were large fhips

His own was covered with red cloth, and ornamented with ftreamers, together with two white flags on the ftern, and top-maft head There were likewife feveral others, fome blue, others red and white, like ours, and fome with two eagles, which are the arms of his Czarian majefty We kept near the land while this little fleet paffed by us, making a very beautiful effect, and there were likewife feveral women on board The ambaffador fent fome water-melons to the governor, who returned his thanks for that prefent by fome perfons of his retinue who came on board our fhip, in a floop, built after the Dutch manner This fleet is exhibited in plate 242, without fails, becaufe the wind was contrary when the fhips paffed by us.

We in this place had a view of a mountain which ends in a flat fummit, and is called the mountain of robbers, becaufe they formerly made it their retreat The wind having favoured us at laft for fome time, we arrived, on the 28th, at Saratof, where we landed with great pleafure, being extremely fatigued with our voyage, and we took up our lodgings in the quarters which were affigned us by the governors of the place.

CHAP. LXXXV.

The civility of the governor of Saratof The manner in which the Calmucks live The author fets out from Suatof, and arrives at Petroskie, Pinfa, Infera, Troitskie, Dimik, Kasjemo, Wolodimer, and Mofcow.

I WENT, the day after my arrival, to pay my duty to the governor, and prefented him with fome water-melons that I had brought from Aftracan, I likewife delivered to him the letters I had for him, and defired him at the fame time, to order

me thofe things that would be neceffary for me in my journey by land to Mofcow. This requeft he granted, in the moft obliging manner imaginable, and accompanied this inftance of his goodnefs with a number of other civilities. The next day

1707 sent me an invitation to visit him, by his interpreter, and I then intreated his permission to pass over to the other side of the river of the *Calmucks*, to which he immediately consented, and ordered me a vessel for that purpose. I found the bank covered with these people, as well men as women, while that on the city side was bordered in the same manner by *Russians*, who were furnished with all sorts of provisions, such as rice, bread, &c. They had likewise large quantities of cloth, little chests and boxes, and a variety of other things, with which they trafick with the *Calmuck*, for horses, cattle, beer, and other productions of their country. I made a draught of this view, which the reader will find in plate 243, where the *Calmucks* are represented on the bank, and the city on the other side of the river. I advanced half a league into the country, in order to see their tents, which I found in a wretched condition, and saw nothing remarkable among them, their most considerable people had indeed quitted this part of the country three days before. They were encamped in troops, like the *Tartars*, in the parts adjacent to *Astracan*, but in a much poorer condition. When I returned to the city, I received an invitation from the governor to take part of a collation with him at his house, where I found the *Georgian* minister, and we were regaled in a very elegant manner. We continued longer in this city than we at first intended, the governor having sent out most of his people to pursue as well the robbers who infested that quarter, as several persons who had escaped out of prison, we were therefore obliged to wait till the 6th of *October*. We, however, caused the chariots we wanted, to be prepared, and covered like our calashes, to secure us from cold and snow, as well as rain and winds, for they are all open at the top. These coverings must be made so as to be easily removed and placed on other chariots, because they are all changed with the horses.

We caused four to be covered in this manner, out of twenty three that were ordered for our use, and of which the *Georgian* minister had nineteen. We then began our journey, after we had taken leave of the governor, and returned him our thanks for all his civilities.

We found the ways perfectly good in this part of the country, but the weather was exceedingly cold and windy, and we arrived about noon at a * *Cabac*, built of wood, where they made us a good fire, which we greatly needed. We, however, did not continue long in this place, and after we had passed over a mountain and some hills, we came to another *Cabac*, having then travelled thirty *werstes*, and through such steep ways, that three of our chariots were overturned. We renewed our journey before day, and found the earth covered with snow, and were likewise obliged to dine in the open country. We indeed found plenty of wood, of which we made a good fire, and arrived about five at *Petroskie*, where the governor ordered quarters to be assigned us. This city has a considerable extent, and is surrounded with a wall of wood, of which all the houses are likewise built, agreeably to the manner of the country, and there are several churches of the same kind of structure. The city gates are at some distance from it, the streets are likewise spacious, and covered with a very hard clay. We here changed our chariots and horses, and set out the next day at three in the afternoon. A little river flows by the city, and we crossed it by means of a large wooden bridge, which is a league in distance from the city, we likewise passed the night in the open air, after a journey of ten *werstes*. We sheltered ourselves as well as we could with our chariots, kindled a good fire, and continued our journey at two in the morning, in very frosty weather, cross a great marsh, but had afterwards fine roads as far as *Konde*, which is a large town, and we arrived there about

* *A house where liquors are sold*

The author's arrival at Petroskie

1707

1707 bout noon, but ftud no longer than two hours, after which we paffed through fome villages, and particularly that of *Apaneka*, at the fide of which flows the river of *Kaminka*, at the diftance of feven or eight *werftes* from *Pinfa* We found good ftoves in this village, where it is cuftomary to enter into the houfes without fpeaking a word We arrived on the tenth, at *Pinfa*, which is a large city, and where we croffed the little river of that name, over a wooden bridge The river of *Kaminka* difcharges itfelf into this, after which their united ftreams flow crofs the country to the fouth-weft This city is fituated on the fouth-weft fide of the river, under a mountain, as is likewife the caftle, which is very large, and furrounded with a wooden wall. The ftreets are broad, and there are feveral churches built of wood. This city is likewife rendered very agreeable by the large growths of trees which furround it, there is alfo a large fuburb on the other fide of the river, and the diftance of it from *Petrofkie* is computed at fixty *werftes* Our chariots were to be changed at this place, and as they are fent for from the villages that lie round the city, paffengers are frequently obliged to wait for them a confiderable time Several *Swedifh* officers were prifoners at this time in the city, from whence we fet out the next day, and paffed through feveral villages, and tracts of arable land, and arrived on the 30th at *Infera*, where our carriages were to be changed again. We here found provifions very cheap, as they had been in every other place, fince we paid but a penny for a large pullet, and no more for twenty eggs, of which even forty or fifty may be purchafed at fome particular feafons, for the fame price I there bought a good *Turky* for three pence, and paid no more for a pig, I likewife gave but twenty pence for a large hog. A fheep may be had for ten pence, a lamb for five, a goofe for two, and bread in proportion.

At Pinfa

Its fituation

At Infera.

The city itfelf makes but a very ordinary appearance, and the caftle has only one wooden wall, flanked with feveral towers As the governor was not in the city at that time, we could not be fupplied with horfes till the 15th The *Georgian* minifter was in fome meafure the occafion of this delay, becaufe he would not pay what was demanded of him, under a pretext that it ought to be there defrayed, but he at laft confented to pay half the fum required

We then continued our journney as far as *Jemfkoi*, which is a very large town, and has a church built of wood. It lies at the diftance of eight *werftes* from *Infera*, where we paffed over a wooden bridge On the feventeenth by break of day, we paffed the *Mokfa*, which difcharges itfelf into the *Occa*, and then continued our journey through a wood, and feveral villages, after which we croffed the river a fecond time, and arrived about noon at *Troyetfkie*, from whence we went to pafs the night at *Belt-foja-tsjas*, having travelled thirty *werftes*. The next day we proceeded as far as *Miegalofkie*, and on the eighteenth continued our journey through feveral woods, that were watered by the *Mokfa*, which is there very broad, and has a paffage over it on a wooden bridge, at the end of which is a *Corps de Garde* We arrived about nine at *Demnik*, which is a poor village, entirely open, and without any caftle. The ambaffador had a new difpute on the 20th with the inhabitants of the place, who refufed to furnifh him with horfes, without money, and this caufed us to lofe abundance of time, which highly provoked me, I not daring to proceed in my journey without him: But they at laft came to an agreement, and we continued our journey along the river, after which we entered the woods through which it flows, and met feveral *Ruffian* travellers From hence we had very bad ways as far as the village of *Vedenapina*, where we paffed the

1707
The fituation of the city

1707 the night At break of day we ftruck into the woods a fecond time, and croffed the river agan, over a wooden bridge, after which we came into very bad roads among the trees, and feveral axle-trees of our chariots were frequently broken, fo that it required time to mend them with the branches of trees The night then approaching, we were obliged to halt near a fmall chapel, where feveral ecclefiaftics had their refidence We there made a good fire, and kept a ftrict guard till the dawn of day, when we continued our journey by the fide of the river, which we afterward croffed, by means of a little bridge of boats, on which no more than two chariots could proceed at one time, and the river was two hundred paces in breadth We found on the other fide a little plain, before a wood, and travelled as far as *Koelekove*, a village fituated on a rifing ground, from whence we defcended into a hollow way, filled with water, which was then frozen. On

the 23d, and by break of day, we 1707 again croffed the fame river on a bridge of wood, and afterward found the ways extremely bad, and filled with little bridges, under which the waters fiow We then proceeded through the town of *Aloffa*, and paffed the night at *Zawata*, where two of our domeftics, who had intoxicated themfelves with brandy, continued with their chariots, and were treated very ill by the *Ruffians*, who had taken away their cloaths and bonnets When they afterward rejoined us in that condition, we had a long confultation whether we fhould return, but the negative prevailed, and we proceeded on our journey We afterward croffed the *Occa*, on little bridges of boats, like thofe I have already mentioned I there drew the courfe of the river to the fouth, where it forms a very fpacious gulph, which extends from eaft to weft, as far as I could judge by my eye, having loft the needle of my compafs The reprefentation of it is exhibited in the following plate.

VUE DE L'OCCA

Our time was taken up in paffing this river, till two in the afternoon, after which we travelled along the fide of it to *Monfo*, a village fituated on an eminence, and at the diftance of fifteen *werftes* from the place where we had croffed the river. The next day we pro-

1707 proceeded to *Kasiemo*, where we

changed our horses, in order to go to *Zerbalova*, which lay about fifteen *werstes* from it, and where the ways proved so bad, that most of our chariots were overturned, which lost us abundance of time. The *Georgian* minister continued his journey with some persons of his train, but I had no inclination to follow him, during the darkness of the night. I therefore waited for the rising of the sun, and arrived about nine, at *Nova derecpna*, on the other side of the wood, and twenty five miles from *Zerbalova*, and from hence I proceeded as far as *Jikesoway*, where I passed the night. The two next days we made but little progress, the ways proving very bad, and my chariot happening to break. On the 30th we found the roads full of water, and about noon had a view

of the city of *Wolodimer*, which is situated on a mountain, where it makes a very fine appearance, on account of its numerous churches, which are white. We afterward crossed the *Clesma*, which flows by it to the south, and discharges itself

into the *Volga*. The city, which is the capital of the dutchy of that name, is very large, and situated on several hills, separated from each other, along the river. Seven or eight of its churches are built of stone, but there are several others of wood, and the distance of this city from *Moscow* is but 150 *werstes*. We continued there no longer than the first of *November*, and then passed thro' several villages, and crossed the river *Wortsa*, where we found the governor of *Pinsa*, who did us the honour to dine with us, and then set out for *Moscow* before us, being not incumbered with baggage like our-

selves. We followed him about four, and were accompanied by several persons armed with clubs, whose extremities were pointed with iron. We advanced on the third as far as *Sallopokro*, a large town, in which is a fine church built of stone. We there found great plenty of provisions, together with good beer, and white bread, but every thing was much dearer than in other places through which we had passed, a pullet being sold for four pence, and all the rest in proportion. As we proceeded on our journey, we passed through several villages, crossed some rivers on little bridges, and went to lodge that night at *Sjeleva*. The next day we crossed the *Clesma* again, on a float of timber, on which I received a fall that crushed my leg to a violent degree, but when we came to *Razoza*, I rubbed it with mummy, which I had brought from *Persia*, and then continued my journey, tho' I was unable to move my leg. The next

day we arrived at *Moscow*, into which the *Georgian* minister would not make his entrance that day. For my part, I returned to my old quarters in the *Slabode*, where I made use of my mummy a second time, and then finding my leg much easier, and being capable of walking a little with my cane, I caused myself to be conveyed in a sledge to the house of Monsieur *Hulst*, the *Dutch* resident. But my leg was inflamed to such a degree the next day, that I was obliged to keep my chamber above fifteen days, the motion which I had undergone in so unseasonable a manner, having prevented the mummy from producing its effect: I therefore found it necessary to send for a Chirurgeon, and I could not walk as formerly, in less than the space of six weeks.

Vol. II.   Z z   CHAP.

CHAP. LXXXVI.

A punishment inflicted on rebels   The arrival of the Czar *at* Moscow *New buildings. Fire-works   The departure of his* Czarian *majesty*

The author visits prince Bories,

I WENT on the 29th, with our resident, to the country house of the *Knees*, or prince *Bories*, (whom I have frequently mentioned) in order to thank him for his favourable recommendations to the governors of *Casan* and *Astracan* This lord received us in a most obliging manner, and would not suffer us to return till we had dined with him.

And the English envoy

The next day I paid a visit to Mr *Witworth*, the minister of *Great-Britain*, who treated me with the utmost civility, and likewise obliged me to dine with him He even did me the honour to come to my lodgings, to see the curiosities I had brought from *Persia* and the *Indies*

An execution

On the first of *December* thirty persons were beheaded, for being concerned in the massacre at *Astracan* This execution, which was performed about noon, lasted but little more than half an hour, and was accomplished without any disorder, the malefactors laying their heads very quietly on the block, without being bound with cords

Three days after prince *Mensikof* gave a splendid entertainment at the house of the deceased general *le Fort* The company present on this occasion were the princess, his majesty's sister, the *Czarina*, and the princesses her daughters, together with the *Czar* of *Georgia*, who was deposed by his brother, and had taken refuge at the court of *Moscow*, where he is entertained with his son the prince, who entered into the service of his *Czarian* majesty, and was taken prisoner by the *Swedes*, at the siege of *Narva* Several lords and ladies of the court were likewise present at this feast, as were likewise the *English* envoy and consul, together with most of the merchants of that nation, and a great number of *Germans* and *Hollanders* The men and women placed themselves separately in two different apartments, and several healths were drank to a discharge of cannon and some bombs This entertainment was succeeded by a ball, and several curious fire-works were played off in the evening.

The Arrival of the Czar at Moscow

On the 6th the *Czar* arrived at *Moscow* about noon, under a discharge of all the cannon on the ramparts, and was received with universal joy, after an absence of two years Two days after I went to pay my duty to that prince at his palace of *Represenske*, where I found him going out in a sledge He received me very graciously, and assured me he was greatly pleased to see me again in his dominions. He was then going to visit the princess, his sister, and I had the honour to follow him This princess presented with her own hand, to every one of his majesty's retinue, a little vermillion glass of brandy, and then placed herself by the *Czar*, who made a sign to me to approach him, and commanded me to give him a succinct relation of my travels, particularly of the court of *Persia*, and the ladies of the seraglio He likewise expressed the same curiosity with respect to the court of *Bantam*, and explained to the princess, and the ladies of her train, all the particulars I had the honour to relate to him in *Dutch* After which her highness presented another glass of brandy to all the company around, and I entreated the *Czar* to grant me a passport, that I might quit his dominions without any molestation, to which he immediately consented He returned to his palace about four, and

and I to my *Slabode*, with a heart full of gratitude for the goodnefs I had experienced from that prince.

On the 23d a *Polifh* bifhop was exchanged for the *Knees Fenderowitz*, who had been taken prifoner at *Narva* Intelligence was likewife brought of the death of the *Great Mogul*, who had lived above a hundred years.

The death of the Great Mogul

New buildings

It will not be improper for me, before my departure from *Mofcow*, to mention fome buildings that were erected there, fince my journey to *Perfia* The moft confiderable of thefe is a large ftructure of ftone, which was begun feven years ago, and was intended for the officers of the mint, but within the laft year and a half it has been converted into a difpenfatory for medicines It is a very fine and lofty building, with a beautiful tower in the front. Its fituation is to the eaft of the caftle, and on the fpot where formerly was a market for fowls The paffage to it lies through a large bafe court, at the end of which is a great ftaircafe, that conducts to the firft apartment, which is vaulted, and very lofty, and contains fifteen feet in depth, and twenty in breadth People were employed in painting it in diftemper at that time. The fide walls are embellifhed with fine crofs work, and the others are to be decorated with *China* fyrup-pots, and other vafes, on the top of which the arms of his *Czarian* majefty are enamelled There are two doors to this apartment, one of which affords a paffage into the magazine of medicinal herbs, the other opens into the chancery, or office of accounts belonging to the houfe There are alfo very beautiful halls finely vaulted, particularly two, which entirely correfpond in ftructure, one of which ferves for a laboratory, and the other for a library, wherein extraordinary plants and animals are likewife preferved. Befide thefe apartments, there are feveral others, particularly that of the prefident or doctor, and another which belongs to the apothecary and his domeftics The doctor has alfo the direction of the chancery, and has under him a vice-chancellor, and feveral commiffioners, and he has even power to punifh with death thofe who are under his direction, whenever they merit fuch a treatment All the phyficians, chirurgeons, and druggifts, receive their falaries in this office of chancery Eight apothecaries are employed in this difpenfatory, and they have under them five boys, and above forty workmen, and from hence his majefty's troops and navies are fupplied with all the drugs and medicines they want.

The director of this houfe is doctor *Arefkine*, a *Scotchman*, and firft phyfician to his *Czarian* majefty, who allows him a yearly penfion of 1500 ducats He has been four years in the fervice of this prince, who has a great efteem for him, on account of his capacity and perfonal merit, and he has gained the affection of all the court by his polite and obliging conduct His majefty made him a prefent of two thoufand crowns when he engaged in this great and arduous work He feemed to be perfuaded, when I left *Mofcow*, that every thing would be compleated in the fpace of a year, and he was then employed in collecting from all quarters, and difpofing with the utmoft elegancy on paper, all the principal herbs and flowers, which are ufeful in medicine, and of which he had already filled a book He likewife fhewed me a large piece of petrified brown bread, and affured me that he intended to fend into *Siberia* for a collection of fimples, flowers, and plants This difpenfatory has two gardens

I likewife found, at my return from *Perfia*, that an hofpital had been built at *Mofcow* for fick perfons. This ftructure is built of wood, on the bank of the river *Jonfa*, and in the *German Slabode* The hofpital is divided into two parts, in each of which are feven beds on one fide, and ten on the other, each bed being

1707 ing intended for two perfons, and there are nine in the middle range, for fingle perfons There are three ftoves in each of thefe divifions, and the chamber appropriated to anatomy is between them The fecond ftory contains feveral little apartments, where the phyfician, apothecary, and chirurgeon of the hofpital lodge The difpenfatory confifts of three chambers, two for the medicines, and a third for the herbs of which they are compofed

On the fide of this hofpital is a manufactory of cloth, under the direction of a draper, who was fent for from *Holland*, and on the other fide of the river *Mofcua*, is a glafs-houfe, where looking-glaffes are made, among which I faw fome that were above three ells in length. Workmen were likewife employ'd in repairing the caftle, together with the red wall of the city, and efpecially to the eaft and north, nor muft I omit, that the three Jefuits who refide in this city, two of whom are *Germans*, and the other an *Englifhman*, have built a little church in the *Slabode*, and painted the infide of it in diftemper

1708 The firft day of the year 1708, was celebrated with rejoicings, and a fine fire-work, in the great fquare, where his *Czarian* majefty gave an entertainment in the lodge that has been formerly mentioned. Some

days after, this monarch gave another 1708. in the houfe of Monfieur *le Fort*, which at prefent belongs to the prince of *Menfikof*, who has greatly enlarged and embellifhed it His majefty, when the repaft was over, paid his ufual vifits to the foreign merchants, and began with our refident, in the manner that has been formerly defcribed He continued with that minifter for the fpace of two hours, after which he made feveral other vifits, being on the point of fetting out for the army Monfieur *Grundt*, the *Danifh* minifter, arrived at that time, and moft of the merchants of *Archangel*, at the latter end of the month, as is ufual

On the fixth of *February*, feventy more of the principal rebels *Rebels executed* of *Aftracan* were beheaded, five were broken on the wheel, and forty-five were afterward hanged

When I had obtained my fecond paffport, I took leave of our refident, and all my friends, in order to fet out on the tenth, having already fecured all the carriages I had occafion for, as far as *Koningsberg* I then waited on the envoy of *Great Britain*, in whofe apartment I found all the merchants of that nation We paffed the evening in a very agreeable manner, after which I went to prepare for my fetting out that night in a fledge

CHAP.

CHAP. LXXXVII.

The author's departure from Moscow, *and arrival at* Waesma, Dorgoboes, Smolensko, *and* Borisof *Villages burnt by the* Muscovites. *The author's return to* Moscow

The author sets out from Moscow

WE set out at one in the morning, and arrived about eight at *Wesomke*, which is thirty five *werstes* from *Moscow* We were seven in company, namely, four *Englishmen*, two *Germans*, and myself, and each of us had a sledge to ourselves, and two for our servants, beside post-horses, in case any accident should hapen to us on the way, as is very customary We had likewise taken care to send others to *Smolensko*, eight days before we began our journey, that they might rest there till our arrival After we had travelled forty nine *werstes*, to *Modenovo*, we passed through several villages, and over a plain, where we met a great number of sledges, at midnight, and arrived about noon at *Ostrosjok*, a village situated in a wood, at the distance of forty *werstes* from the last place, and there are thirty

His arrival at Waesma

seven from thence to *Waesma*, where we arrived on the thirteenth It is a large city, and has a castle built of wood, and several stone towers. We set out from thence about noon,

At Dorgoboes

and came to *Dorgoboes*, on the fourteenth, having travelled sixty nine *werstes* This is a poor village, around which hemp grows in great perfection We there passed the *Nieper*, as we did a second time at *Phova*, which is forty four *werstes* from thence, and we arrived at *Smolensko*,

At Smolensko

on the 15th, after a journey of thirty six *werstes* We were there obliged to shew our pass-ports to the governor, who received us in a very obliging manner, and not only dispatched others to the frontiers, but appointed us a guard for our security In return for these favours, we presented him with a small cask of wine This city, which is very large,

Vol II.

is a bishop's see, it has likewise several churches built of stone, and many others of wood

We set out about five with post-horses we had sent thither, and found the ways full of water In a short time after we came to an enclosure, with a gate, where a guard was stationed, and from thence we proceeded as far as *Krano-selo*, where we passed the night, after having travelled forty four *werstes* We continued our journey at seven in the morning, the weather being very frosty, and met the baggage of the prince of *Mensikof*, and some coaches, in one of which was the princess, his consort, who was going to *Smolensko* About noon we arrived at the frontiers of *Poland*, and two hours after at *Dobroosna*, after a journey of twenty three *werstes* We

The author's arrival on the frontiers of Poland

continued there till nine in the evening, and came about three in the morning to the city of *Copies*, which

At Copies

is within six leagues of *Germany*, each league containing five *werstes*, as I formerly observed, for the way from *Smolensko* is computed by leagues.

We shewed our passports in the morning to general *Allert*, a *Scotchman*, who received us in the most engaging manner imaginable, and gave us to understand, that it would be difficult for us to proceed by *Koningsberg*, on account of the *Swedish* troops, who were on their march from thence, upon which we resolved to take the road of *Wilda* As all the houses were filled with soldiers, we took up our lodging with doctor *Areskine*, who was then in the city, and we passed a very agreeable evening with him and general *Allert* The *Russians* had thrown up lines round the city, and the *Nieper*,

A a a

which

which flows by the side of it, in order to oppose the *Swedes* who were expected in that quarter

We continued our journey on the 18th, through woods that were full of fir-trees, with which that part of the country abounds, and arrived, about ten, at *Kroepka*, where a body of five hundred men were posted From thence we proceeded to *Borifof*, which is a poor village, the houses of which are scattered up and down without the least regularity It however has a wooden castle, which is surrounded with a wall of earth Monsieur *Keiferling*, the *Pruffian* minister, was there at that time We shewed him our passports, and set out from thence at two in the afternoon, but lost our way for some time in the woods, which are very thick However, we arrived, in the evening, at *Juleſena*, and continued our journey from thence at one in the morning, with a guide, who conducted us to *Belaroes*, where there is a large house, which belongs to a *Polifh* lord We afterward passed through another village seated in a plain, where we saw a regiment of soldiers, and arrived at *Krafnafel*, after travelling twelve leagues

At Bon-fot

We continued our journey on the 21ft, and came about three in the afternoon to the village of *Mollodefna*, from whence prince *Alexander* had set out in the morning The *Ruffians* had lately made great devastations there, and in other places, by fire, to prevent the *Swedes* from finding any subsistence in those parts These ravages presented a horrid spectacle to our view All the woods around were filled with the poor peasants, who fled thither to secure themselves from the rage of the exasperated soldiers, and to conceal the little they had been able to save. We saw several of those unhappy people, who were viewing this dismal scene with eyes drowned in tears, and hearts racked with anguish Others were trembling in expectation of the enemy, from whom they apprehended nothing less than destruction Our conductors were

The cala-mitous state of the peasants

shocked to such a degree, at what they saw, that they intreated us with tears in their eyes, to permit them to return Our compassion for them obliged us to consent to their request, and we determined to continue our journey without them, surrounded as we were with flames We, however, bought two of their horses, to carry us to *Wilda*, which was sixteen leagues from thence, but the moment our guides were gone, we found ourselves in a perplexity that seemed to be inextricable, when we began to consider, that if we proceeded forward, we should be in danger of falling into the hands of the *Walachians*, who were in the service of *Sweden*, and that if we should endeavour to return from whence we came, we should inevitably meet the marauders of the same nation, who were intermixed with the *Muſcovites*, and are a people who treat friends and enemies alike, and never spare even their nearest relations. They are a set of men who receive no pay, and obtain nothing but rapine and depredation There were likewise in this part of the country a great number of *Tartars*, and *Calmucks*, who are altogether as bad as the others We therefore continued where we then were, till noon, not knowing what course to take, since the flames encircled us from all quarters, but we at last resolved to commit ourselves to the providence of God, and continue our journey without guides We had no sooner quitted the village, than we met a party of horse, composed of *Cofacks* and *Walachians*, in the *Muſcovite* service, with an officer at their head They immediately stopped us, upon which we shewed them our passports, which they entirely disregarded, saying we were traitors, who intended to go over to the enemy We were in this condition, when a young *German*, who was among them, advanced forward, and represented to them with great freedom, that they acted a wrong part, and treated us in a very injurious manner, upon which one of them

Tar-tars Calmucks

gave

1708. h m a fevere ftroke with a whip, and the other retuined it with ufury He then defired us to fear nothing, fince a general was advancing to us with great expedition, at the head of a great body of horfe. His companions, who were fenfible this intelligence was true, retired as faft as poffible, and left us to ourfelves We were not furprifed at this proceeding, being very fenfible that thefe people, who appear very refolute when they have an opportun ty to rob, are meer daftards where they meet with the leaft refiftance, and betake themfelves to their heels the moment they fee one of their companions drop The body of horfe, which the young *German* mentioned, came up to us in lefs than a quarter of an hour, and was commanded by two lieutenant-generals, one of whom was an *Englifhman*, and the other a *German* The *Englifh* officer, who knew us, had the goodnefs to treat us with the greateft civility, after which we acquainted him with our late adventure, and defired him to inform us, whether he thought it poffible for us to continue our journey in fafety ? He affured us, that it was altogether impracticable, becaufe the *Ruffian Coffacks* were ftill employed in burning all the remaining villages, and in breaking down the bridges, and that it would likewife be impoffible for us to efcape thofe who were in the fervice of *Sweden*, and plundered where ever they came, not fo much as fparing the lives of thofe who had the misfortune to fall into their hands for which reafons he advifed us to return with him, and we found it neceffary to take that refolution This gentleman likewife difpatched a trooper after our guides, who rejoined us with their horfes, fo that as we had two horfes to each fledge, we foon overtook the party who had treated us with fuch ill language , and the *Englifh* officer gave the commander of it feveral lafhes with his whip, in order to inftruct him in his duty.

We were likewife informed, that 1708. the *Swedifh Coffacks* were within four or five leagues of us, and we arrived foon after at the houfe of a *Polifh* lord, which was fet on fire at nine in the evening. Three leagues from thence we found another, which refembled a fortrefs, and there was likewife a body of troops, commanded by colonel *Geheim*, who advifed us to pafs on without halting, becaufe the *Swedes* were expected there. We then proceeded through feveral places, where troops were ftationed, and arrived about three at the palace of *Lefcova*, where prince *Alexander* of *Menfikof* then was. We were in hopes of waiting on him immediately, and with that view had feparated ourfelves, with a guard of four troopers, from the great body of horfe. This prince received us in a very gracious manner, and we intreated him to inform us, whether there was no other road, through which we might continue our journey in fafety , or whether he would be fo good as to difpatch a trumpet to the *Swedifh* army, in order to procure us a fafe paffage ? His anfwer was, that, with refpect to the firft particular, it would be impoffible to proceed on our journey, the *Swedifh* troops having fpread themfelves over all the country , and that it would be of no effect to fend a trumpet to their army, becaufe they would not admit any fuch perfon to an audience, having already maffacred two or three, and feveral drummers , for which reafons the prince advifed us to return to *Mofcow*, and recommended it to me in particular, fince he knew that I had feveral curiofities which I had brought from *Perfia* and the *Indies*. I returned him my humble acknowledgments for his goodnefs, after which I gave him a fuccinct account of my journey, and he then directed us to follow him, for the fpace of three days, that we might not be expofed to the fury of the *Polifh* peafants, who were fhrowded in the woods through which we were to pafs, and fpared none that came in

their

their way Such was the civility of the prince, which I can never sufficiently praise He likewise informed us, that the advance guard of the *Swedish* troops arrived within three hours after our departure, at the last castle by which we had passed, and that they had massacred above a hundred *Russians*, whom they found there. As soon as we had quitted that where we now were, it was set on fire, and as it was full of Hay, the flames reached us in a moment, and obliged us to double our pace. We pursued our journey the whole night, but halted at particular intervals to wait for the baggage This circumstance, in conjunction with the thickness of the woods, made us lose much time, and exposed us to the danger of being surprised by the enemy. However, we arrived about noon, at *Nilnikof*, after we had travelled four leagues through rain and snow

We endeavoured to alleviate the fatigue of our journey with good cheer, without perceiving that we were almost unprovided with bread, which it would be impossible for us to procure in that road Our only remedy was to address ourselves to the prince, and I was deputed to that office, since I had the honour to be known to him He was at table when I acquitted myself of my commission, which caused all the company to smile, but he had the goodness to desire me to be seated by him, which gave me a sensible pleasure, but was very mortifying to my companions, who waited my return with impatience When we rose from table, he ordered me to be supplied with all the accommodations we wanted, and this he did with such an air of goodness, as is not to be expressed.

We renewed our journey toward evening, and passed through several woods that were filled with peasants About three we halted in a village which was not far from the city of *Siebina*, where the prince had invited us to dine with him that day, but his dinner was over before our arrival

We, however, were well entertained by his officers

We took our leave of him on the 24th, and he had still the goodness to send a detachment of three hundred horse before us, to secure our passage, he likewise ordered us a guard of six dragoons, commanded by a *Polish* officer, and they were to accompany us as far as *Smolensko* We arrived about six, at the little city of *Borissova*, having travelled four leagues, and about ten in the morning we came to *Kroepka*, which is eight leagues from thence We then passed through several villages, in one of which there was not a mortal to be found, and came about noon to *Tollothin*, after a journey of seven leagues We set out again on the 27th, and arrived in the evening at the city of *Copies* Colonel *Aller*, together with the *Prussian* minister, and doctor *Areskine*, who had resided there for some time, were just set out from thence, in order to join the *Czar* at *Soienjo*, which was eight leagues from that place, and we arrived at *Dobroosna*, on the last day of the month, and after a journey of seven leagues Here the *Polish* gentleman and his dragoons, who had conducted us out of our way, quitted us in the night without speaking a word, which reduced us to a great perplexity We, however, proceeded on our journey without a guard, and happily arrived about seven at *Bagova*, which is the last village in this part of the *Polish* territories We took up our lodgings among the *Jews*, and came the next day to *Smolensko*, where we went to pay our respects to the governor, and to acquaint him with the particulars of our journey After which we desired him to allow us fresh horses, but he assured us he had not any; notwithstanding which, we found eight that came the evening before from *Moscow*, with a set of travellers who proceeded farther. This was a very seasonable circumstance, and we harnessed four of the horses to our sledges, adding three of our own, but these were so fatigued, that

they

1708. they could hardly move forward, and we had loft feveral by the way In this manner we continued our journey, and arrived about eight in the morning at *Glowa*, after travelling thirty three *werftes* From thence we proceeded to *Dorgobufh, Weefgna*, and *Mofchatofkie*, and at laft arrived at *Mofcow*, where I returned to my old quarters in the *Slabode*, and furprifed all who were there, with my return

On the 10th of *March*, the *Dutch* merchants, who fet out after us, returned thither in the fame manner, and fhortly after all the reft of the travellers, whom I formerly mentioned, did the fame They had ſtopped for ſome time at the camp of his *Czarian* majefty, in hopes of an opportunity for proceeding on their journey Monfieur *Keiferling*, the *Pruffian* minifter, came hither likewife, and as the commotions of war prevented the receipt of letters from *Holland*, from whence five or fix pofts were then due, our merchants came to a refolution to fend an exprefs at all adventures, and I determined to return by water, by the way of *Archangel*, with Monfieur *Kinfius*, brother to the gentleman with whom I came to *Mofcow*.

CHAP. LXXXVIII.

The author's laft departure from Mofcow; *and his arrival at* Preflaw, Roftof, Jereflaw, *and* Wologda. *The manner of travelling by water.*

I SET out from *Mofcow* in a fledge, on the twenty third of *March*, with feveral other travellers, and proceeded that day as far as *Bratoffina*, a town thirty *werftes* from *Mofcow* The next day about nine, we arrived at *Troytfkie*, which has been already defcribed, as well as the fine monaftery of that name We afterward paffed over mountains covered with trees, which undoubtedly create an admirable effect in fummer We there met a party of fix or feven thoufand foldiers newly raifed, and without arms, their officers were in fledges. On the 25th, we arrived at *Preflaw*, where we made no ftay, but proceeded to *Wafka* The next day we paffed by *Roftof*, on the north-weft of the lake which bears that name, and is furrounded with villages. The inhabitants of this quarter cultivate onions and garlic, and the city has a metropolitan who refides there Half a league from thence is the monaftery of *Peuter Zarewitz*, which is encircled with houfes.

From thence we proceeded to *Nikola*, which is forty five *werftes* in diftance from it, and where in the fummer feafon the river *Oetfie-reka* may be paffed on a float of timber. We arrived on the 26th at *Jereflaw*, and lodged in the fuburb of *Troepenoe*, from whence I caufed myfelf to be conveyed in a fledge to the river *Wologda*, in order to draw a view of the city, as well as the time would allow, we being to continue there but three hours This profpect is exhibited in plate 244 It begins with the letter A to the fouth, where flows the *Kotis*, which difcharges its waters into the *Wologda*. There were five veffels, with three mafts each, in the river at that time, and they came from *Cafan* with the utmoft difficulty, being towed up the *Volga* by main force, in order to arrive at *Peterfburg* Several other veffels were likewife frozen in the river At a little diftance from the city is a village with a church built of ftone, and the fuburbs are on each fide. The city is seated on an eminence, and partly enclosed with a stone wall, which has not been finished, because the earth was not sufficiently compact, for which reason it is in a very bad condition. This city is very large, and almost square, and the great number of stone churches which are there, give it a fine appearance without. There are likewise several houses built of stone, but most of them are of wood, as are also four bridges which slant from the houses to the river. The northern quarter is distinguished by the letter B, beyond which is a prospect of several houses, and a church of stone. The city makes a greater appearance on this side than it does on the other, and indeed it may be justly reputed one of the finest cities in all *Russia.* A great number of merchants live there, and a considerable trade is carried on in leather, tallow, brushes, and linnen cloth; but nothing is so much admired here as the beauty of the women, who in that particular surpass all the rest of their sex in this country.

We set out from hence at two in the afternoon, proceeding always to the north, through woods; after which we pursued our journey through several villages, and passed the night at *Wakfere,* after travelling forty *werfts.* We arrived on the 27th at *Oigaskie-jam,* which is thirty *werftes* from the place where we lodged. From thence we had

At Wo-logda

bad ways as far as *Wologda,* where I was resolved to continue till the rivers were navigable, that I might proceed to *Archangel* by water, and carefully examine the course of the rivers between these two cities, since travellers have said but little of them. Beside the beauty of the rivers, this part of the country affords a variety of delightful prospects. About this time seven thousand families arrived at this city from *Dorpat,* the capital of *Livonia,* with an intention to settle there, and they had quarters assigned to them among the *Russians.* This people made their appearance the next day on the river, in order

to be registered, and intelligence came in a short time after, that the city of *Dorpat* had been destroyed after their departure. The most considerable persons among them repaired to *Petersburg,* by the order of his *Czarian* majesty, and were to be followed by some foreign merchants. Soon after this event seventeen hundred of the inhabitants of *Narva* arrived there, and were likewise to continue in that city till new orders; several other persons likewise came thither, and their number in the whole amounted to two thousand seven hundred.

The weather began to thaw toward the close of *April,* and the wind blew a very strong gale, on the first day of *May,* which cleared the river of all the ice. On the 15th in the evening there was a great tempest, accompanied with thunder and lightening, which beat down several roofs, doors, and chimneys, and damaged most of the houses in the city.

The *English* merchants who had accompanied me in *Poland,* arrived at this city on the 30th, and set out the same night for *Archangel.* They had suffered greatly in the storm, which overthrew several of their carriages.

I drew, from my chamber window, the course of the river *Wologda* to the west, and it is represented in plate 245, as is a branch of cedar in plate 246. It is a very common tree in this country. I drew the leaves and fruit from nature. I have seen one of a prodigious size, that was produced from a seed brought from *Siberia,* a country abounding in trees of this species, and where some are as large as those on mount *Libanus.* There are likewise very considerable growths of them in the country adjacent to *Moscow.*

The course of the Wologda

With respect to the river *Wologda,* which was formerly called *Nisson,* its source is one hundred *werftes* above the city of that name, in a large marsh, between the lake of *Koeben,* and the *White Lake,* and it discharges itself into the *Suchana,* after having

WOLOGDA

BRANCHE DE CEDRE. 246

having received into its channel, the waters of feveral fmall rivers, above *Wologda* And yet thofe of this river are exhaufted to fuch a degree in the fummer, that people fometimes pafs it without wetting their feet, and only by leaping from one part of the fand to another It is about fifty paces broad in this place, where feveral other ftreams are likewife to be feen The diftance of the *White Lake* from hence does not exceed ninety *werftes*, and it abounds with excellent fifh, fuch as *Soedakes*, *Sterlettes*, perch, and fmelts, whofe exceeding whitenefs has given this lake its name. On the contrary, there is another lake, at the diftance of fifty *werftes* from the city to the northweft, and which extends as far as *Kargapol*, and then difcharges itfelf into the *Donega*, which falls into the *White Sea* This lake produces fifh of all kinds, but they are entirely black The *White Lake* flows into the *Volga*, through the *Soxna*, at the diftance of fome leagues from *Pereflaw Refanfke*.

Before I quit the fubject of this city, it may be proper to obferve, that thofe who intend to fet out from hence by water to *Archangel*, muft have little veffels made purpofely on that Occafion, and capable of containing five or fix paffengers, but thofe who have occafion for them, muft fend directions for their being built, before they fet out from *Mof-*

cow, that they may be ready, when the paffengers arrive at this place They are as commodious as poffible, and are furnifhed with wooden beds, tables, feats, and all other neceffaries They are called *Kajoeks*, and feldom coft more than twenty five rubels, which are equal to one hundred and twenty five florins, and they have twelve or fourteen rowers, each of whom may be hired for fix or feven florins There are other veffels fmaller than thefe, and they are called *Karbaffes*, but they contain no more than one or two paffengers, and fix rowers Thefe little barks coft five rubels and a half, each of the rowers will require four florins, and eleven or twelve muft be paid to the pilot; fo that the whole expence will amount to no more then thirteen rubels No more than two rowers work at a time, and they relieve themfelves every ten, fifteen, or twenty *werftes*, as they can agree among themfelves The diftances at which they relieve each other, and which are called *Peremines*, are marked out, either by a church, a village, a river, a tree, or a crofs. *Archangel* is computed to be a thoufand *werftes* from *Wologda* by water, and fix hundred and thirty by land, and this inequality is occafioned by the various windings of the river

C H A P.

CHAP. LXXXIX.

The author's departure from Wologda, *and arrival at*
Todma *A defcription of* Oeft-joega, *or* Ouftiough.
The junction of the river of that name with the
Suchana, *and the* Dwina *Salt-works. Mountains of*
Alabafter. The mountain of Orlees. *The author ar-*
rives at Archangel.

I SET out from *Wologda* on the
17th of *June*, after I had provided myfelf with a bark, and all
other things that were neceffary. We
proceeded at firft to the fouth, and
then to the eaft, through a channel
bordered with little woods on each
fide, and after we had advanced
twenty *werftes*, we came to the river *Soegna*, or *Suchana*, into which
the *Wologda*, which is not fo large
a river, difcharges its ftreams On
the 18th we fet up a fail made of
mats, and fteered to the eaft, and afterward to the fouth, paffing by a
timber-yard, where the fhips that
tranfport mercantile goods from *Wo-*
logda to *Archangel*, are built, and
the bank was covered with fir-trees
On the 19th we kept on to the
eaft, and I landed on a fpot of
ground that was filled with a growth
of wild ftrawberries, and rasberries,
flowers, and rofe-trees This fituation is in the northern latitude of
59 degrees, and 50 minutes, where
the bank of the river rifes to a confiderable height, and is fhaded over
with fir, birch, and alder-trees, and
we there faw tracts of arable land,
together with fome meadows, and
obferved that the river flowed to
the north, and then to the eaft
We faw feveral fifhermen in this
place, and afterward paffed by the
ifland of *Jedo*, in which is a fmall
church, and we arrived in the evening at the city of *Todma*, at the conflux of the rivers *Suchana* and *Todma*
I drew the profpect of this city to the
fouth-weft, as it appears in plate
247 It is fituated on an eminence
near the river, and in the northern

latitude of 60 degrees and 14 minutes. It is fmall, and muft be
ranked among thofe of the meaner
clafs, and all the buildings are of
wood The diftance from hence
to *Ouftiough*, is computed at two
hundred and fifty *werftes* Near this
city is a large mill, built in the
Dutch manner, except only that it
has but two fails, which were partly broken At the diftance of eight
werftes above the city, we faw feveral large ftones in the river, and
they rofe above the furface of the
water, but moft of them are vifible only in the month of *July*,
when the ftream is low, but it
was then two good fathoms in
depth to our right Several green
tracts of land appeared in the middle of the river, but the fouthern
fide is always navigable, and the
channel is a hundred and fifty paces broad in feveral places. On the
twentieth we came about noon to
Stare Todma, which fignifies *Old*
Todma, and this is the fpot where
it was begun to be rebuilt thirty years
ago, but the work was not continued, and it was built in the place
where it now ftands I could eafily read here at midnight, without
a candle, whereas when I left *Wo-*
logda, there was no travelling later
than ten at night. We paffed on
the 21ft by *Apocko*, which is a large
town, fituated on each fide of the
river, and there is a fine church in
it, with a fteeple and domes covered
with tin The foil of the country
around it is fertile, and produces
corn It likewife prefents the eye
with very delightful views. People
were

TODMA

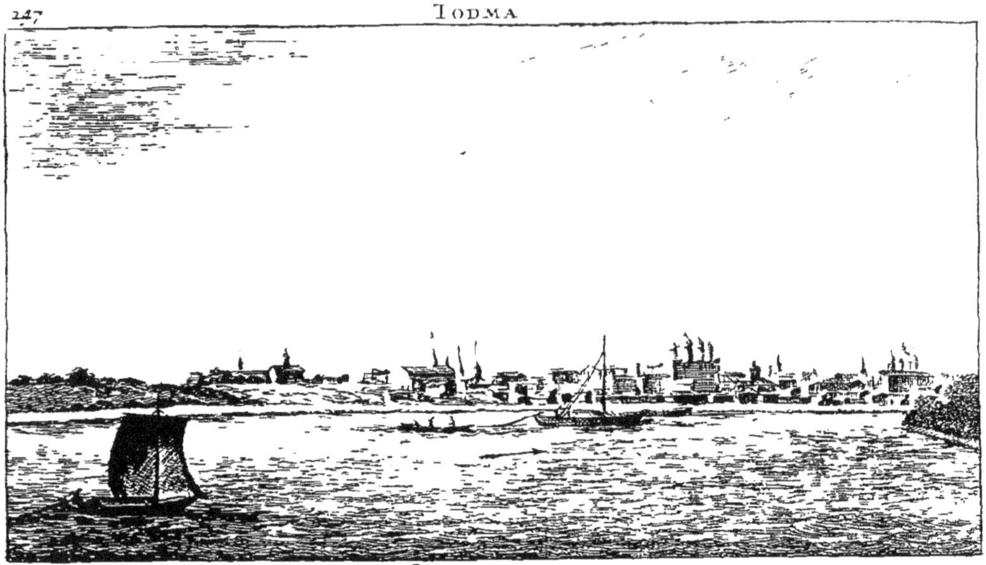

248 OEST-JOEGA

246 VUE SUR LA RIVIERE-DWIENA

LE MONTAGNE ORLEÙS 252

1708

were here employed in conveying wood to the bank, where several lime-kilns are erected This part of the country is full of villages, the land likewise is very low, and abounds with corn The river produces plenty of fish, and is a good werfte in breadth About eight in the evening we paffed by the monaftery of Dereefne, which is built of wood, and inclofed with a wall of the fame fubftance From hence

At Oeft-joega

we could fee the city of Oeft-joega, or Ouftiough, which makes a very confiderable appearance in that quarter, and we arrived thither in the fpace of an hour This city is five hundred werftes from Archangel, and has ten or twelves churches, all built of white ftone, except the domes, two of which are cover'd with tin, as are likewife the little fteeples. All the other churches, together with the houfes, are built of wood, and the archiepifcopal palace, where the archbifhop refides, is a large ftructure The greateft part of the city is feated on the left fide of the river, and there is a ftone church, and two of wood, in that part of it which is on the other fide That on the left extends along the river in the form of a half moon It is a good league in length, and a quarter of a league in breadth, in fome places, and the breadth of the river is equal to a werfte After one has paffed by the city, the river turns to the fouth-eaft, and the land lies low The monaftery of Troyts is not above half a league fouth-eaft from this flexure of the ftream. The river Joeg, or Jugh, flows fouthward into the Niefna-foegna, or Suchana, and their united ftreams are then called the Dwina, which fignifies junction The city therefore is feated at the extremity of the Suchana, the outlet of the Joeg, and the mouth of the Dwina, and in the northern latitude of 61 degrees, and 15 minutes The Joeg flows from the city of Glienooy, which is forty werftes from this place

The merchants in this city are very numerous, and great quantities

Vol II.

of grain are tranfported from hence to all parts I drew at midnight, and on the fide of the monaftery of Troyts, a profpect of the city, which is exhibited in plate 248. The letter A fhews the fift opening of the Dwina, B the outlet of the Joeg, C the courfe of the Suchana, D, the monaftery of Troyts, E, the city, before which is an ifland, and the continent is feen to the right and left. The Dwina is a league in breadth, at the city, and to the diftance of a league beyond it, after which it contracts itfelf into the breadth of a hundred paces, but gradually enlarges its channel half a league lower

On the 22d we continued our voyage to the north-eaft, and paffed by a village called Czar Conftantine, and likewife by feveral others, and alfo fome iflands, and the monaftery of St Nicholas The land is low, and extremely agreable. When we had advanced thirty werftes from the city, we went to fee the falt-works

Salt-works

of the Gooft, or officer of the cuftoms, whofe name was Wafieli Groetin They are not far from the river, and confift of four pits, in each of which are placed feveral trunks of trees hollowed through their whole length, and ftrongly compacted together with cords They rife twelve feet above the furface of the earth, and are likewife funk to the depth of twenty feven fathoms below it The water afcends through them to the furface, from whence it is conveyed by pipes, to places appointed for its reception, and each pit is enclofed with a wooden building I caufed one of them to be opened, in order to tafte the water, which was extremely falt, and thefe four pits afford as much water as would fill twenty falt-pans, though there were but fix in this place, and only one was ufed at that time. Thefe falt-pans are likewife in feparate lodges, in the middle of which is a large ftove, and a great fire is kindled in it, when the falt is worked The pans are fquare, and made of iron, they have likewife a circumference of fixty feet, and are a foot and a half

1708

1708 in depth The water is constantly boiling, for the space of sixty hours, in order to extract the salt, and when the water evaporates too fast in boiling, the pans are from time to time replenished with more Each of them produce four *poet* of salt, which are equal to 1333 pounds The salt-pan is raised over the stove, by means of large poles, and iron hooks, fastened to the beams of the lodge. The usual price for a *poet* of salt is two pence, but they sometimes pay three at *Archangel* The *Czar* has for some time entirely appropriated all the salt works to himself

As we continued our voyage, we passed by several villages, as likewise a large bank of sand, and an island two *werstes* in length, and full of trees. From thence we advanced to the north, and came to the river *Wietsigda*, which is said to have its source in *Siberia*, and it discharges itself into the *Duina*, at a place where they are equal in breadth, the distance from shore to shore, both of the one and the other being a good half league These united rivers form, at the distance of half a league from their conflux, a kind of bason, in the land to the south, and it there receives the name of *O-fer*, or the *Lake* It extends from the north to the west, and to the northwest There is likewise a little island in this part of the river, which is there two fathoms and a half in depth The stream is rapid, and the banks are bordered with villages.

We proceeded, on the 23d, as far as the town of *Peremogora*, which has two small churches, and is seated on an eminence along the river The little river *Levele* flows by it, and extends itself ten *werstes* up the country The eye has here an unbounded view of the *Duina*, which deflects into a number of windings in this place, and forms several gulphs like half-moons, and a *werste* in breadth This prospect is represented in plate 249, and several banks of sand are to be seen in that part of its channel. As we proceeded to the

north-west, we every moment saw villages, situated in a beautiful country full of trees The river is here very broad, it likewise forms some islands, and is two fathoms and a half in depth On the 24th we saw a fine church, with a dome covered with tin, in a little village, about half the way from *Oust, ugh* to *Archangel*, and in the northern latitude of 63 degrees, and 10 minutes We here saw a ship which had run a-ground, and several islands full of trees We likewise had a view to the left of the little river *Pende*, which is very deep, and flows above forty *werstes* up the country

On the 27th we found the shore very high and stony, and approached the mountains of Alabaster, which are to the left of those who advance northward, and we landed, in order to see them The inhabitants of the country call them *Pissertje*, which signifies ovens, and the cavities from whence they derive that name, are so many subterranean grots formed by nature in a surprising manner The principal entrance into them is by columns shaped out of the rock in the form of pilasters, and there are several windings which lead into little grots. I advanced with a candle above a hundred paces, in one of the largest of them, and the natives pretend that it extends above thirty *werstes* in length, though some among them are of a different opinion I was very desirous of proceeding farther, but the ground was too muddy. The openings into these subterranean passages resemble gates, and I drew a part of them, together with a distant view of the river, in the manner they are exhibited in plates 250 and 251, where I have represented two vaulted openings, that one would imagine were supported by pilasters, between which a vessel is seen on the river, and the bank on the other side There are other passages to the right and left, and several small grottos, of no considerable length. The stones which compose them are as white as Alabaster, but

Mountains of Alabaster

not

1708 but not fo hard, and they are employed in very agreeable works I preferved a piece of one, as well as of the rock above it. This place is about 150 werftes from Archangel, and the mountains, which comprehend a league in extent, may be feen for the fpace of two hours, along the river, but there are no grottos beyond this place. The upper part of them is fhaded with a growth of trees, and a large tract of arable land lies all around them.

After we paffed by thefe mountains, a great ftorm drove us to land, but we afterward advanced to the north-weft, and the river through our whole courfe was a werfte in breadth We proceeded on the 26th to the north-eaft, with a contrary wind, and were towed along very flowly Toward the evening we paffed by Stoepina, which is a large town full of houfes, it has likewife a church with a fteeple, and all the adjacent land is admirable. We came foon after to the mountain of Orlees, which rofe to our left, and feveral hundred perfons were employed in hewing out ftones, and preparing them for the caftle of New Dwinko, which is near Archangel, and to which they were to be conveyed in five veffels which were made for that purpofe. At a fmall diftance from this mountain is a little village, and fome houfes on the other fide of the river, where lime is made When we had advanced fo far, we proceeded to the north, but the mountain which is very lofty, and juts out into a point, turns the courfe of the river to the eaft, and from thence to the north-weft The channel is not above fifty paces broad in this part

The mountain I have now mentioned is reprefented in plate 252 The ftones which are rang d on the fide of it refemble a building, its top is covered with trees, and around it lies a tract of arable land The river enlarges its channel, as one advances forward, and feveral other mountains of ftone are there to be feen

The mountain of Orlees

We came, about eight, to a Cabak *, which had been lately robbed by a fhip's crew, whofe veffel lay by it, and they had been very inhuman to the people of the houfe, one of whom, who was a man, we faw breathing his laft The bad weather obliged us to anchor there all night

A public houfe where liquors are fold.

We continued our voyage on the 27th, to the north-eaft, and paffed by a great bank of fand, and a timber-yard which belonged to two Ruffian merchants, who build a great number of veffels there, and have a fine country houfe, ornamented with five little towers beautifully painted. We there faw a large number of villages on our right and left, and fome iflands that are inhabited The nearer we came to Archangel, the longer the werftes proved

We faw the city of Kolmogora, about eleven, at the diftance of a league and a half from us, and beyond the iflands Some time after we had a view of the monaftery of Nowoj-Preloetkey, which is built of ftone, and on one fide of it there are houfes on a mountain The land rifes high, and the river of Kolmogora, which flows behind the ifland, difcharges its ftreams into the Dwina. On the 28th we faw fome fmall rivers, and feveral villages, at the diftance of ten werftes from Archangel, and had afterward a profpect of the monaftery of St. Michael, whofe church is built of ftone From thence we continued our courfe till we arrived at the city

It is fituated in the northern latitude of 64 degrees, and 22 minutes, and there were at that time twenty two veffels in the road, namely thirteen Dutch, three Englifh, five Danifh, and one from Hambourg; but the next day two other Englifh fhips arrived there

The author's arrival at Archangel

On the 9th of July, the feftival which bears the name of his Czarian majefty, was celebrated, and prince Gallitzin, who was then governor of the city, entertained all the foreign merchants, with a number of other perfons,

perfons, at the caftle of *New Duinlo.* Several veffels arrived here in a few days.

I was informed at *Archangel,* that the *Blew-Sea-Horfe,* a *Dutch* fhip, which had fet out from thence on the 8th of *October,* 1707, with a convoy, having fprung a leak, the mafter was obliged to go in his floop on board the *Campen* man of war, which was commanded by captain *Van Buren,* in order to defire affiftance, and that while he was making this application, a ftrong gale happening to rife, the mafter could not return to his own fhip His men therefore defpairing to fee him any more, had taken a refolution to fail in queft of fome port along the coaft, and after they had wandered in this condition, till the 3d of *November,* they approached the ifles of *Swetenoes,* where they caft anchor the next day, having toiled beyond expreffion, to keep the fhip above water, by working continually at the pump, but they at laft dragged the veffel to land, where they paffed the winter feafon, and their provifions having failed them at the end of five weeks, during which time they had not feen any living creature, they had fubfifted for three months on nothing but millet and tallow. While they were reduced to this extremity, they faw fome *Laplanders* arrive in fledges, but could not unfold their condition to them, fince they were unacquainted with their language, and not finding any wood, they were obliged to ufe the planks of their fhips for fewel, and drank nothing in all that time, but fnow water, they, however, had faved what they could of their cargo, which chiefly confifted of leather; but after they had continued in this condition till the twelfth of *May,* ten of them refolved to rifque a voyage to *Archangel* in a skiff, but having advanced as far as the river of *Pennoy,* they were ftopped eight days

by the ice, and did not arrive at *Archangel* till the third of *June,* having loft three of their companions in their voyage It was added, that thefe unhappy perfons, had, however, been fo fortunate as to receive from time to time, frefh fifh from the *Laplanders,* and made their millet ferve for bread, till at laft feven *Dutch* fhips having arrived on the bank of the ifles of *Swetenoes,* the pilot of the veffel which had been wrecked, fent part of the cargo he had faved, and feven failors to *Archangel,* while he himfelf remained in the ifland, with two of the fhip's crew, to wait for new orders, till at laft the men he had fent away, having returned with twenty *Ruffians,* the reft of the cargo was dried, and all of them then came to *Archangel* I had all thefe particulars from the pilot himfelf, whom I invited to my lodgings, in order to be informed of the truth

In this city was a *Ruffian,* fixty-fix years of age, and he paffed for a faint among his countrymen He had been married, but quitted his wife, in order to run naked up and down the country, between this city and *Wologda,* and he frequently came to the market, and even entered the churches He feemed very ignorant, and even deftitute of tolerable fenfe, notwithftanding which, I am perfuaded that his whole intention was to procure himfelf a livelihood by acting the faint, and indeed he did not fucceed amifs He fometimes wore a fmall cincture of net-work round his loins, but frequently went without any covering at all, and in this manner wandered about the country in winter, as well as fummer One of my friends brought him to my lodging, and I painted him juft as he then appeared He promifed to come to me a fecond time, but was not punctual to his word, and all my endeavours to procure another vifit from him were ineffectual, at which I was not a little furprifed, fince I had been very liberal

1708. beral to him. His hair and beard were matted into long twifts, for he never made ufe of a comb The reader will find him reprefented in plate 253

A Ruffian animal

I had feveral little animals, called *Born-doefkie*, brought to me, and I bought them, with an intention to bring them to *Holland*, but could preferve none but the oldeft among them Thefe creatures refemble Squirrels, but they are fmaller, and have a grey fkin marked with brown fpots They are extremely fond of rasberries, and will likewife eat bread, and crack nuts in a very agreeable manner, having long pointed teeth

On the 25th a *Dutch* fhip arrived, with a *French* Pafport, and I was refolved to finifh my voyage on board that veffel.

I went on the 13th of *Auguft*, to congratulate the governor on the good news he had then received of the defeat of fome rebels, who intended to furprife the fortrefs of *Afoph*, but the governor of that city having routed and difperfed them,

they feized *Bolowien*, their own chief, 1708. who flew himfelf, upon which they furrendered at difcretion, and brought his head to the governor

Some days after, I made my application to prince *Gallitzin*, for leave to fhip my baggage without having it fearched, and he was pleafed to grant my requeft in a very obliging manner, giving me at the fame time a writing under his own hand, to prevent my being expofed to that inconvenience at *New Dwinko*

This prince is a gentleman of politenefs and merit, and much efteemed by ftrangers He was formerly ambaffador at the *Imperial* court, and readily came into all the manners of it He likewife underftands *Latin* and *High-Dutch* extremely well

Before I fet out from this place, news came of the victory obtained by the allies over the *French* at *Oudenard*, and it was confirmed by fome tranfport fhips, which occafioned an univerfal joy.

CHAP. XC.

The author's departure from Archangel. *The caftle of* New-Dwinko *The mountain of* Poots-fioert. *The northern cape. The iflands of* Inga *and* Surooy. *The author arrives at* Amfterdam *and the* Hague. *The Conclufion.*

The author fets out from Archangel

ON the twenty third of *Auguft*, I went on board the veffel in which I was to fail to *Holland*, and we came in a fhort time to the caftle of *New Dwinko*, where we caft anchor, while our paffports were examined, and till we had obtained a licence to proceed on our voyage About three the flag was hoifted on the caftle, which is the ufual fignal for veffels to depart. There is a wooden bridge over the river, and

likewife a draw-bridge, under which two fhips may pafs at a time I drew the caftle as it appears in the following plate

We were detained here by contrary winds, till the twenty fixth, and then caft anchor on the fide of three *Ruffian* men of war, of twelve and eighteen guns On the 27th three others came up with us, and the next day we faw a fleet of about 150 merchant-men, with a convoy of

CHATEAU DU NOUVEAU DWINKO

nine men of war, five of which were *English*, three *Dutch*, and one *Hamburgher* The fleet confisted of sixty-eight *English* fhips, fifty *Dutch*, eighteen *Hamburgers*, three *Danish*, and one *Mufcovite*, which laft came from *the Ifle of Bears*, laden with whale blubber She had met with good fuccefs in her voyage, and both the mafter and pilot were *Dutchmen* This fleet employed the whole day in paffing by us in a line, which formed a very agreeable view, and fuch perhaps as had never been feen before in this part of the world What appeared moft furprifing to us was, that this fleet entered the river without taking one pilot to affift them

Among this fleet was a *Danish* fhip of twenty guns, and a flag on her main maft, and it had on board Monfieur *Ifmeyhof*, who had formerly been at the court of *Denmark*, in the quality of ambaffador from *Mufcovy* This minifter immediately landed with all his train, and Madam *de Dolgerocke*, whofe husband had lately fucceeded Monfieur *Ifmeyhof* at the *Danifh* court, embarked in the fame veffel, in order to proceed to *Copenhagen*, where

her fpoufe then was This fhip then lay at anchor in the outlet of the river, that fhe might not be obliged to ftrike her colours, which could not have been avoided if fhe had advanced farther There were fome fhips indeed which attempted to pafs without performing this ceremonial, but the *Czar*'s fhips fired upon them twenty cannon loaded with ball, which obliged them to comply, and they were likewife compelled to pay above fifty florins for each fhot, after which they all anchored before *New Dwinko*.

We advanced on the 30th into the *White Sea*, with a fouth-weft wind, and continued our courfe to the north-weft About noon we doubled the grey cape, but fuch a thick fog arofe, that we loft fight of the fhips that accompanied us But as it happened to grow clear toward the evening, we faw the *Lapman* fhore, which we coafted all night, and the next day, which was the firft of *September*. The weather was then extremely fine, but we could not fee any trees, houfes, or human creatures, on that coaft Our depth of water was then from twenty two to twenty fix fathom, and we again

The White Sea

faw

LES MONTAGNES POOTSHJOERT

CAP DU NORD

257

L ISLE SURGOY

259

1708. faw nine of our fhips behind us We proceeded in our courfe the next day, to the north-weft, the wind being very ftrong, and the waves forming a great fwell, and we once more loft fight of land, and likewife of the fhips which accompanied us We advanced, about noon, to the northern latitude of 60 degrees, and 50 minutes, near the ifland of *Kilduin*, which lay to the north-weft of us, and is about feventy leagues from *Archangel* On the fourth we had another view of the land, which had difappeared It belongs to the crown of *Denmark*, and is inhabited by the *Fin-markers*, *The mountains of Poots-fioert* who keep on the mountains of *Poots-fioert*, which were covered with fnow. They are reprefented in plate 255, in a diftant view of five leagues, and they have a gulph, behind which three or four divifions of thofe mountains are feen This gulph was to the fouth-weft of us, and we continued our courfe to the north-weft In the morning we likewife *The gulph of Tanebay* faw the gulph of *Tanebay*, which advances far up the country, at a point formed by the mountains, and in the manner it appears in plate 256. In a fhort time after we perceived other land beyond it, in the latitude of 70 degrees and 8 minutes The wind proving contrary all that day, we ftood for the *Offing*, and veered about, and the next day had another view of the gulph to fouth-weft and by fouth I believe it is at leaft two leagues in breadth About evening we came into the latitude of 70 degrees and 30 minutes, and as the wind proved more favourable on the 7th, we had a view of the northern cape I drew it as it appeared to the fouth-weft and by fouth of our fhip The largeft and moft projecting rock of this cape, is called *the Mother*, and the leffer, which rife to the right and left of it, have the name of *the Daughters* The cape land is feen behind thefe rocks, together with an opening between them, and the whole is reprefented in plate 257.

About fix in the evening we faw 1708. the iflands of *Inga* on one fide of *The iflands of Inga and Surooy* us, and to the right a fmall rock called *Schips-holm*, with the land beyond it, as the profpect appears in plate 258 We then advanced to the fouth-weft, the wind being foutheaft, and came about feven in the morning within four leagues of the ifland of *Surooy*, which lay to our left, in the form reprefented in plate 259

Amidft a range of mountains is a *A large gulph* large gulph or bay, over which veffels may fail, and find an outlet to the left, between the mountains, which are feparated from one another The gulph is diftinguifhed by the letter A, and another is reprefented at B The weftern point of thefe mountains is marked out by C, and fhips may likewife pafs between the iflands All the inhabitants of this coaft are fifhers, and go to *Bergen*, and *Dronthem*, in order to fell their fifh This country likewife belongs to the crown of *Denmark*.

We advanced next to the rocks or iflands which are called *the North* *Unknown iflands of the North and South Foele* *and South Foele*, or the unknown rocks, and which are not inferted in our maps They are wafhed by the fea on all fides, and fome of them are entirely covered with fnow.

On the 9th we faw a veffel waiting at fome diftance, to fpeak with us, but as we had a fpeaking trumpet, we fpoke firft, without advancing any nearer. She had hoifted her colours, and we faw fhe was an *Englifh* frigate from *London*, and fhe was going with orders to the *Englifh* fhips which were then at *Archangel*.

We came, on the 11th, into the northern latitude of 68 degrees and 8 min. and advanced fouthweft and by weft, with a good northerly wind, being then not far from *Loeffoert*, which *Loeffoert* is about 250 leagues from *Archangel*, and at the fame diftance from *Amfterdam* The wind having changed in the night, we ftood to the *Offing*, and came by day-light into the latitude of 69 degrees 9 minutes, and the next

1708 next day into 67 degrees 8 minutes On the 14th, at half an hour after seven in the morning, there was a

An eclipse of the sun

great eclipse of the sun, which was almost entirely darkened for the space of half an hour, and at last was covered by a cloud We were then in the latitude of 66 degrees 44 minutes, and had a favourable wind The next day we found ourselves in 65 degrees 55 minutes, with a gentle breeze from the north, and we then steered to

An extraordinary phænomenon

south-south-west During the night an extraordinary phænomenon appeared in the air, and shot out long beams of light to such a degree that all the element seemed to be in flames, and one might easily read without a candle, but this appearance did not continue above the space of two or three minutes

The next day we had a contrary wind to south-south-west, and it continued with so much violence all the following day, which was the 17th, that we were obliged to fasten our rudder, and commit the ship to the mercy of God, having only our main-sail and mizzen up, during all that and the next day, but the wind flackened in the night, and veered about to the north, upon which we directed our course to the south, and came on the 19th in the latitude of 65 degrees, having been driven back four or five leagues to the north, but after this we had a contrary wind On the 21st we found ourselves in 64 degrees 14 minutes, and the wind blowing a very strong gale in the evening, we had a violent storm in the night And as the darkness was very great, the extraordinary agitation of the waves made the sea seem all on fire. This weather still continuing on the 22d, we were once more obliged to fasten the rudder, and were driven back almost ten leagues On the 26th, we came into 62 degrees 30 minutes, with rainy weather, and the night was as dark as possible. On the 28th we came into 62 degrees 10 minutes, and the next day into 61 degrees 40 minutes.

An eclipse of the moon.

That night there was an eclipse of the moon, which began at half an

hour after eight The greatest part of 1708. its disk was darkened an hour after, and the eclipse ended about eleven. On the last day of the month, the wind shifted to the west, and we steered south-south-west, after having had a contrary wind for fifteen days

On the first of *October* we came

The northern part of Hitland

into the latitude of 61 degrees 24 minutes, and saw the *Hitland* to south-south-east, and at the distance of seven or eight leagues from our ship, which was then steering south-east and by south The next day we continued our course to the south, with a westerly wind, having always in view the same land to the south-west, in the latitude of 61 degrees 9 minutes, and we were then about six leagues from the cape On the 3d we came into 60 degrees 10 minutes, and the next day into 59 degrees 16 minutes, having the wind to the north, and directing our course south and west, and we then saw four sail of ships at some distance from us We that day caught

A little fish of an extraordinary species

four cods, in one of which we found a small fish, whose length did not exceed two inches · It had two fins on one of its sides, and a third on its back, with very sharp prickles It was likewise thick spotted with yellow and white, that glittered like gold and silver I preserved it, because I had never seen any fish like it We found ourselves at midnight in the latitude of 58 degrees 10 minutes, steering south-south-west, and about noon the next day in 56 degrees and 30 minutes Our depth of water during the night was from seventeen to fourteen fathom

On the 7th in the morning we came to the hether side of the dogger-bank, in thirty fathom water, and favoured with fine weather, and a fair wind We then passed another sand called the *Well*, from whence we saw, about four o'clock, ten or twelve sail, which approached us about eight They consisted of three men of war, accompanied by a victualling pink, and some galliots, from one of which we learnt that they were going to meet the *India* fleet

1708 fleet, which was then arrived, and that they had met a *French* privateer the day before   As we advanced in company, we saw a hundred fail at a diftance, and likewife the privateer, who had hovered about in the night without daring to come up with us

We began to fee land about eleven, after which we paffed by the buoys, and the remains of a fhip which had been wrecked the preceding year, near *Helder*, and the next day we entered the *Texel*, from whence we proceeded to *Amfterdam* in nine hours, to the great fatisfaction of us all

I was informed, at my arrival there, that the curiofities I had fent from *Batavia*, came fave thither the preceding year, and that the burgomafter *Witfen*, to whom I have more obligations than I am able to exprefs, had ordered them to be kept in the *India-Houfe*. I likewife found letters here from the governor of the *Indies*, and my other friends, and was informed that the figure I had fent from *Perfepolis* was fafely arrived   I went from hence to the *Hague*, the place of my nativity, and arrived there the 24th.   I was received with great joy by my relations and friends,

who imagined I had been dead, as they had heard from all quarters   1708.

Nothing remains for me now, but *The con-* to return thanks to Almighty God, *clufion* for preferving me by his good providence through the whole courfe of my travels, in the firft of which I employed nineteen years, and feven and a quarter in the fecond : And for having averted from me the dangers to which travellers are expofed in foreign countries, fo very diftant, and fo little frequented.   I ought to teftify my gratitude in a peculiar manner on this occafion, fince I have experienced all poffible civilities, in my various journeys, and have likewife preferved all the curiofities I had collected with fo much care, and with no little labour and expence, together with all the plans and defigns I have drawn, notwithftanding the oppofitions that were thrown in my way.   I wifh the public may receive this relation of my travels, with as much fatisfaction as I experienced in preparing it for the prefs ; fince I hope it will be found to contain fome particulars worthy of attention, and I may add too, that I have fpared no expence, in order to render it agreeable and inftructive.

REMARKS

O F

CORNELIUS LE BRUYN,

On the PLATES of the Antient

PALACE of PERSEPOLIS.

Publifhed by Sir JOHN CHARDIN and Mr. KEMPFER.

SOME Perfons of diftinction and great learning, having intimated to me, that it would be proper to offer fome light to the public, with refpect to the difference between the plates which exhibit the ftately ruins of the antient palace of *Perfepolis*, in the travels of Sir *John Chardin*, and thofe which I have publifhed on the fame fubject, I thought it incumbent on me to fatisfy the curiofity that has been created on this occafion, and likewife to juftify my own proceeding. In order to accomplifh this defign, I have examined with the utmoft exactnefs whatever has been written and publifhed for a certain time on this fubject, as well with relation to thofe antiquities in general, as to each branch of them in particular, that I might make myfelf fully acquainted with all that has been advanced, either with inconfideration or folidity, and without reflecting in the leaft on the reputation of thofe illuftrious travellers whofe plates and fentiments differ from mine, or pretending to derogate from their merit and learning in any other particular.

It is not eafy to form an accurate judgment of the architecture of thefe ruins in general, fince all the upper part of the edifice is entirely deftroyed, and what remains of that below, are only feparate members, which have no communication or connection with each other. A better conception may indeed be formed, with reference to the nature of the capitals, and their ornaments, by thofe fragments of the columns which are ftill vifible, and I have drawn them in four different points of fight, in order to form a compleat capital As to the pedeftals, they are of three forts, but the difference between them confifts chiefly in their foliage, fince they are all round, and fhaped in the fame manner, as is evident by the plates I have here fubjoined, in one of which an entire cornice is reprefented in the fame manner as feveral others are ftill to be feen, on fome of the portals and windows of thefe celebrated ruins.

I was not inclinable to enlarge on thefe particulars in the account of my travels, becaufe I always hoped to find fome perfon better fkilled in the antient architecture than myfelf, and intended to take that opportunity of inftructing myfelf, fo as to be able to treat of this fubject agreeably to the rules of art, but as yet I have not had the good fortune to fucceed in my defign However, as I find it

has

has been attempted by others, who have acquitted themselves of that province in a very imperfect manner, by reprefenting things otherwife than they really are, either through their unacquaintednefs with fuch antiquities as tnefe, and their unskilfulnefs in defigning, or elfe for want of employing a fufficient time on a fubject of th s nature, or contenting themfelves with making inaccurate sketches, which they afterward were unable to correct, or laftly, becaufe they employed fome mercenary draughtfmen, as was the cafe of Sir *John Chardin,* who could not draw himfelf, as he acknowledges in his writings, and h is likewife affured me in converfation I therefore thought it incumbent on me to point out the miftakes they have committed, and likewife to juftify what I have advanced in my preface, with relation to thofe defigners, who not being wrought upon by that folicitude for reputation, which is neceffary for the difcovery of truth, have committed egregious errors, and likewife with refpect to thofe who pretend they have drawn every thing with their own hand

In the year 1712, a defcription of the *Holy Land* was printed at *Amfterdam,* with the name of *John Balthafar Metfcher* prefixed to it : But this author had fo little regard for truth, that he has inferted the plates of fome cities of *Hungary* into his defcription of *Judea* and *Palestine* The plates I mean, are thofe of *Tokkai* for *Tiberias,* and *Peter Waradin* for *Nazareth,* with feveral others that I could mention, and he has even prefumed to dedicate a work of this nature to no lefs a mafter of polite literature than the elector Palatine.

I fhall now return to my fubject, and begin wi h Sir *John Chardin,* who reprefents the firft profpect of *Perfepolis* in plate 52, almoft like a platform, which may be taken in at one glance, and is nothing but mere imagination, fince the lower part of thofe ruins are vifible only

in the manner I have drawn them The ftair-cafe of the facade ought not to have been elevated higher than the fide-walls, unlefs it be to the right, where there is an afcent to the columns, and the wall of the facade ought to have but half the height he has affigned it, in proportion to its extent To this I may add, that moft of the columns are out of their place, and he has exhibited five of them with only half their fhafts, tho' in reality there is but one that appears in this manner He has likewife mifreprefented one half of the pedeftals, as well as the animals which are carved upon the columns, and as the whole feems to appear in a level, the two royal tombs in the rock muft confequently be lower than mine, though they are certainly much higher than he his reprefented them The mountain likewife flopes abundantly too much in that plate, and thofe ftone coffins which are exhibited on the left, ought to have been difpofed at the end of the facade. Thefe I have reprefented, together with the whole edifice, even to the fmalleft ftone, in plate 117, and exactly in that point of fight in which they appear on the fpot.

The fifty third plate in Sir *John Chardin's* work, is defective in the fore-view, where moft of the confiderable edifices, together with three buildings, and four other ftructures oppofite to thofe, fhould have been exhibited All that appears on the two fides is likewife contrary to truth, and the ftones are drawn without any imitation of real antiquity. I muft add to, that inftead of the four pilafters which are reprefented near thofe edifices, there ought to have been but three, and they are not even difpofed in their proper fituation. One is alfo wanting at a little diftance, and thofe beyond it have no refemblance to the originals The fame may be faid of the laft edifice in the back-view, and the inaccuracy is ftill greater with refpect to the ftructure between that edifice and the columns, not the leaft remains of any

wall

wall being now to be seen   The number of columns likewise in this plate is less by one than it is in the preceding, but he did not forget the five last coloumns, tho' the first of them to the right is undoubtly the highest of all, but it is there exhibited with all the faults I have pointed out in plate 119.

The wall of the facade of the edifice, which is represented between the two flights of stairs, in the fifty-fifth plate of Sir *John Chardin*'s travels, has more stones by one half in its height, than it ought to have, and they all appear equal, directly contrary to the original, and even to his own description of that structure Those of the palliers or perrons, which he has represented like those of the wall, and to the number of 16, ought to have been very different from all the others, this perron being paved with large stones, in the manner I have expressed them in plates 120 and 124, where this stair-case, with its broken steps, and unconnected fragments, are exhibited in their proper appearance, without any addition or diminution

Sir *John Chardin*'s fifty-sixth plate represents two columns in their full dimensions, and they appear with their capitals, as if they had been newly erected, tho' without supporting any architrave ; whereas mine are delineated in a very ruinous condition, as may be seen in plate 121, and a large fragment of shapeless stone rests on the tallest of them, entirely agreeable to the original. Those figures likewise of animals which that gentleman has exhibited in the front of the pilasters that rise on the side of these columns, have no resemblance to the originals, with respect either to the bodies and feet, or those ornaments of the head which he has assigned them, the faces being all impaired to such a degree, that they are hardly to be distinguished, as he himself acknowledges in the fifty-fourth page of Vol IX   The pilasters are likewise represented in their compleat dimensions, tho' they all ought

to appear in the manner I have expressed them in the 122d plate of my travels.

The same figures are seen in the 57th plate, with the head and feet projecting from the front of each pilaster, and the rest of the body extending from the side, which is an absolute impossibility, and the effect of mere invention, as are likewise the ornamented heads of men, which are there added   For my own particular, I have been careful to represent them agreeably to the manner in which I found them, and with the wing which is still entire, and surprisingly beautiful, I have likewise added all the ornaments, together with all that is broken and defaced in those animals, and without omitting the three compartments of characters, as they appear in my 123d plate.   It is certain that human heads seem to have been fixed on these winged animals, but I thought it sufficient to represent them in the manner they then appeared

With respect to the figures in Sir *John Chardin*'s 58th plate, I shall observe in general, that they are too distant from each other,   and that the first of them which appears in the first range, ought to have had neither a collar nor chaplet, with which he has ornamented the breast and shoulders, nor indeed any thing of that nature   The left arm likewise of the second figure ought not to hang down parallel with the body. The fifth figure is represented with a leg in each hand, and the sixth is furnished with two buckets, which are meer invention, and not conformable in the least to the original, where the five figures which follow the first have an entire similitude with each other, and their arms are represented as supporting some particular habit.   The dress and bonnets likewise which he has bestowed upon them, are altogether as imaginary as the rest, and all the heads ought to have been represented in a disfigured appearance   The ornament, in the form of a vase, is expressed with the same inaccuracy, as is evident by my

126th

126th plate The firſt figure in the ſecond diviſion, diſtinguiſhed by the letter Q, holds an unknown machine in its hand, inſtead of a ſtaff, the lower end of which ought to reſt on the earth, behind the legs of that figure The four which follow this are equally defective, and there ought to have been five, all habited in the ſame manner, for they are very viſible, tho' the heads and faces of them are impaired The fifth ſhould have had a large ſtaff in its hand, inſtead of that which it is repreſented as graſping, and the animal that follows it ought to have had a bridle round its muzzle, and not round the horns, as Sir *John Chardin* has been pleaſed to repreſent it. The ſtaff likewiſe which the figure on the ſide of that animal places on its back, ought to have been much larger than it is· In a word, there are but ſix human figures in this range, whereas there ought to have been ſeven

This gentleman has likewiſe exhibited ſeven figures in the third compartment, and the third of thoſe figures is repreſented with buckets, the fourth with a kind of bottles, and the fifth with the legs of a man; all which are mere fancy. And there ought to have been four figures in habits, which, tho' greatly defaced, are ſtill diſtinguiſhable There likewiſe ought to have been eight other figures in this diviſion, five of which have large cinctures folded round the body, and the two laſt, which are on the ſide of the two goats, and are repreſented by Sir *John Chardin* with large ſtaves, ought to have claſped their arms about thoſe animals, which have only one horn riſing on the forehead, and are very different from thoſe deſcribed by him I may add too, that theſe figures ſhould have been exhibited in a bending poſition, and not ſo high as the others

Sir *John Chardin* is altogether as inaccurate with reſpect to the figures of the fourth compartment, where the firſt of them is repreſented with an unknown inſtrument in its hand, inſtead of which it ought to have

had a large ſtaff. The ſecond likewiſe ſhould have raiſed its buckler to the head of the horſe that follows it, and whoſe feet ought to have reſted on the earth I may add too, that the ſide figure ſhould extend the right foot before the left leg of the horſe, whoſe tail ought to have been repreſented in an erect poſition The three following figures are as ill expreſſed, and there ought to have been four, the firſt of which ſhould have held a ring in each hand, and a flow of drapery ought to have been repreſented on the arms of the other three The laſt figure in this diviſion, as exhibited by Sir *John Chardin*, has the legs of a man in its hand, the reaſon of which is incomprehenſible to me, ſince nothing of that nature was ever ſeen in the original ſculpture. The cinctures likewiſe, which are folded round the bodies of theſe figures, are too low, and the ends of them ought to appear

The ſame gentleman has repreſented eight figures in the fifth range, tho' there are but ſeven in reality, and the third is not to be now diſtinguiſhed. The drapery likewiſe is defective, and none but the three laſt figures ought to have had lances, of which the firſt, who has likewiſe a buckler, holds one, and each of the other two graſps three with both hands The halter of the ox, which is there led in proceſſion, ſhould have been fixed round the muzzle, inſtead of being faſtened to the horns, and the tail ought to have flowed down to the earth, cloſe by one of the legs, and the right leg of the two hinder ones ſhould not appear. In a word, the figure of this animal has no reſemblance with the original.

In the ſixth or laſt diviſion, Sir *John Chardin* has repreſented ſix figures, the firſt of which have each of them a quiver ſlung on the back, and an unknown machine in the hand, all which is mere invention: And indeed there ought to have been ſeven figures; the firſt of which,

that

that leads the next in the train, should have been reprefented with a ftaff in its hand, and in a habit very different from that which appears in his plate. It fhould likewife have been drawn with a cincture, the two ends of which appear in the fore part of the body. The five figures which fucceed this ought to have been reprefented with bucklers, and very fhort mantles, together with drawers defcending to the feet. The fourth and fifth figures fhould have been expreffed with rings in their hands, and the fixth ought to have grafped a trident. After this laft, a horfe fhould have followed, led by the bridle by a feventh figure, habited like the reft. The feet likewife of this horfe fhould have refted on the earth, and its mouth ought to have been behind the buckler of the fixth figure.

In the firft divifion of the laft range, Sir *John Chardin* has reprefented a figure which holds the fecond by the hand, the third and fourth have little buckets in their hands, the fifth carries fome other thing, and there are two others on the fide of a horfe harnefs'd to a chariot. This divifion is to be found exactly under the firft compartment of the firft range, and at the foot of the ftaircafe, where fix figures appear habited alike, in long plaited robes, and each of them grafps a lance with both hands. All of them likewife, except the laft, have quivers hanging on their backs. There are fome other figures before thefe, but they are broken and defaced to fuch a degree, that their number is not to be diftinguifhed. We will therefore proceed to the five compartments that follow, and the reader may compare that which I have juft mentioned (and where the horfe appears harnefs'd to a chariot) with the fecond divifion of my twelfth range.

In the fecond divifion, as exhibited by Sir *John Chardin*, are fix figures, and a horfe with one of his feet aloft in the air, which is very different from my reprefentation of

that compartment, the firft figure in which ought to have had long and wide fleeves. The hand likewife of that which leads the horfe fhould have refted on the body, and all the feet of the horfe ought to have been reprefented on the earth. I may add too, that the drapery of thefe figures has no fimilitude to the original fculpture. The three laft figures likewife ought to have had their hands raifed higher, and their heads defaced.

Sir *John*'s third divifion reprefents nine figures, eight of which are in fhagged habits, which are very extraordinary, and no way agreeable to thofe that are to be feen at *Perfepolis*. The middle figure has fomething of a peculiar form in its hand, inftead of the two buckets with which I have reprefented it.

His fourth divifion contains no more than fix figures, all habited in the fame manner, whereas the firft ought to have been different from the others, and fhould be reprefented with large fleeves, and a particular kind of bonnet. The others ought to have plaited drawers, falling down to the middle of the leg. The bunches likewife which rife on the back of the camel that follows, are out of their proper place, and too diftant from each other: To which I may add, that the muzzle of this animal ought to reft on the head of the laft figure.

This gentleman has feven figures in his fifth compartment, but the firft of them ought to have been reprefented with large fleeves, and the fecond and third with other habits. The fcales borne by the third are too flat, and they ought to have hung by no more than two thick cords, inftead of which he has allowed them three flender ftrings. The fourth, which bears a vafe in each hand, ought likewife to have been reprefented with rings. The fixth fhould grafp its lance with both hands, and the mule ought not to have been led by the bridle. The cinctures likewife of thefe figures fhould have been raifed higher

The

The lion and the bull, which are to be seen in the same plate, have no correspondence with the original figures The bull is there represented with its mouth open, and turned toward the lion Three of its feet likewise rest on the earth, the other is reared aloft, and the tail seems to lash the hinder legs of the lion. It has likewise two horns on the head ; whereas there ought to have been no more than one, and that in the middle of the forehead. The mouth of this animal should have rested on its own body It ought likewise to have been represented with a large ear, a bridled head, the two hinder legs fixed strongly on the earth, the right behind the left, the left of the forelegs bent in the air, as preparatory to a leap, and it should also have been exhibited as employing its horn in its defence. The fourth leg ought not to appear, the tail likewise should have been disposed between the hinder legs, and the ornaments on its body ought not to have been forgotten. The right leg of the lion should be placed before the left, the tail likewise ought to descend to the ground, with the tip of it turned up, all which particulars are very different from Sir *John Chardin*'s representation of those figures, and he has succeeded as little, with respect to the talons, and the fore leg of the lion This animal likewise ought to be exhibited, as fixing his fangs on the hinder part of the bull, and not in the middle, the head too, ought to have been represented in a different manner, and he has omitted all the ornaments. The height of the rock which appears behind these animals ought to be less by one half, and as wide again, with a work of foliage on the upper part Beside all these defects, he has not represented the broken figures which are still visible on the rock of the stair-case, in the manner they are expressed in my plate.

I am apt to imagine, that the figures which appear on the stair-case, at the end of that gentleman's

58th plate, are intended to represent those I mentioned in my observations on the six figures comprehended in his first compartment of the last range, but as I am not able to conceive how he came to be furnished with the twenty nine figures which are there represented, I shall not bestow any observations upon them, but proceed to those of his 59th plate He has there exhibited forty two figures, among which 28 are represented with lances, and entire in all parts but the head, whereas it is very certain that the originals are greatly impaired, and there is not one entire figure (even among the twenty eight that have lances) whose drapery is distinguishable as high as the neck, nor have they any little bonnets, like those with which he has represented them. But there is not one whose cincture is not visible on the back part of the body, as is evident by those very figures which I have exhibited, with all their defects in plate 127. The fourth figure of those that follow the lance bearers, has neither hands nor buckler. The drapery of the sixth ought to flow down to the feet, and the eleventh should rest its right hand on the buckler of the figure that follows The fourteenth, and last, of those which Sir *John Chardin* has exhibited, is habited in a different manner from all those that are to be found at *Persepolis*, whereas its dress ought to correspond with that of the twelfth figure. I have likewise represented fifty figures in that range, though at the same time I have omitted ten, because they were too much disfigured.

Sir *John Chardin* has represented on one of the columns of his 60th plate, the heads and upper-part of the bodies of two kneeling horses, which is a meer work of imagination. There is indeed a shapeless mass of stone, which seems to represent in part, the four feet and body of a camel, but very obscurely, as I have drawn it on the same column in plate 152. It is likewise evident, by some pieces
which

which are fallen down, that this animal had ornaments on the breaft. As to the other column, which fupports a fragment of ftone, I have not feen any with a capital of that nature, nor any which refembles that in the 61ft plate of Sir *John Chardin*'s work, and which may be feen in the plate I have here annexed.

With refpect to the three figures he has given us in plate fixty two, it will be found, by comparing them with mine, in plate one hundred forty three, that the two figures which follow the firft, ought not to have the head and fhoulders touching each other They are likewife greatly defaced, and the firft figure ought not to have been reprefented with a ftaff, though it might poffibly have had one in former times, fince other figures which refemble this, are ftill to be found with fuch at *Perfepolis* The beard of this figure fhould defcend no lower than the breaft, which ought to be vifible between it, and the fleeves of the figure, and the feet of thefe figures fhould reft on the earth.

The 63d plate of Sir *John Chardin*'s work, reprefents a pilafter, which feems to be newly made, and the upper part of it is filled with ornaments, and figures of men and animals. The fame pilafter is reprefented in my 152d plate, exactly as it appears on the fpot, and greatly impaired The figure which appears before that which is reprefented as fitting, feems to be fpeaking to it, with a bending pofition of body, and that which follows it feems to be a man, and not a woman. The feated figures likewife ought to reft againft the back of the chair.

His 64th plate reprefents another pilafter, as perfect as the former, tho' in reality it is greatly impaired, in the manner it appears in my 153d plate, and yet his draughtfman has placed on the fide of it, feveral fragments that have fallen from it The feated figure ought likewife to reft againft the back of the chair,

and the draperies of the other figures are not conformable to the original. A judgment may be formed of the reft, by comparing thefe two plates together As I thought this part of the ruins extremely beautiful, I drew one of the largeft and moft perfect of its pillars, as it appears in my 163d plate Sir *John Chardin* has omitted the ornament on the upper part of this pillar, and fupplied the want of it with a work of foliage, that never appeared on the original

This gentleman has likewife reprefented, in his 65th plate, three gladiators encountering as many different animals, and all in the fame pofition, but they have no refemblance to the originals, as any one may judge, who compares them with mine, in plates 130 and 146. Several of thefe gladiators are to be feen at *Perfepolis*, one of them encounters a bull with a fingle horn, and ftabs him with the right hand on one fide of the pilafter, and to the left of another There is likewife another of thefe gladiators engaing a winged or horned lion, which he feizes by the mane The laft are vifible half way down the legs, but the others are buried in the earth up to the knees, in the manner I have defcribed them, together with the animals, and the particular fituations of the combatants, from page 14 to page 21 All which I have performed with the greateft exactnefs.

Sir *John Chardin* has another feated figure in plate 66, which I have likewife reprefented in its proper attitude, together with the true form of a chair, and footftool, in my 156th plate Thofe figures alfo which this gentleman has added, are exhibited in my 145th plate, exactly conformable to the originals

We will now proceed to the royal monuments which he has reprefented in his 67th plate The lower part of thefe tombs, as far as the cornice, is too lofty by more than one half, and the upper part, which refts againft the natural rock, is as much too low The figure and the

altar

altar which appear on these monuments, are too near the corners, where the heads are disposed, and the lions he has placed below, are less than the real number A proper judgment may be formed of the whole, by comparing those plates with my 158th, where I have expressed every particular with all possible exactness, even to the minutest stones, which are much impaired, and the small elevation of the rock above the tomb I have likewise represented in plate 162, the fine head, together with the ornament in form of a column, which appear on the side of this monument, and the supporters of the upper part of the edifice, are exhibited in plate 164 As the second tomb, to the south, is exactly like this, except its being more ruinous, I thought it unnecessary to represent it

Sir *John Chardin*'s 69th plate presents to view the characters impressed on a window, and which are to be seen in my 134th plate, but the first line only of those characters corresponds in part with mine, and indeed they may possibly have been taken from some other window. I am likewise as incapable of refuting those that appear in the middle of that plate, because I am sensible that such characters have been carved in later times, as well as those which I have represented in plates 135, 136.

We will now proceed to the dimensions of the edifice in general, and the particular members of it that are most worthily to be considered Sir *John Chardin* declares, in the 50th page of his ninth volume, that this august structure presents to view an admirable facade of 1200 feet in length, and 1690 in depth, and that the circumference comprehends 1660 paces, to each of which he allows two feet and a half, or thirty inches He then adds, that the wall rises to the height of twenty four feet, but that the altitude is not equal in every part. He likewise affirms, that some of the stones are fifty two feet in length, as well as

around the stair-case as the wall, and that those of the commonest size, are from thirty to fifty feet in length, and from five to six in height He assigns to this stair-case an altitude of twenty two feet and some inches, and to each step a breadth of twenty two feet, and a height of something more than two inches, together with a depth of fifteen He then adds, that this stair-case consists of 103 steps, the lower flight of which contains forty six steps, and the upper fifty seven

I have assigned to the facade which I have described in page 10. an extent of 600 paces from north to south, and a height of forty four feet, each containing eleven inches, but it is lower in some places The southern front contains 390 paces, and the wall on that side rises to the height of eighteen feet and seven inches, but is less by some feet in several places The northern length contains 410 feet, with a height of twenty one, but this is not equal in all parts. Beside these 410 paces, there are thirty more toward the slope of the mountain, and from thence another part of the wall is continued to the mountain itself. If we add to this the extent to the east, along the mountain, which comprehends as many paces as the facade, namely, 600, this edifice will have a circumference of 2030 paces, equal to 5050 feet. And I found, on the upper part of the edifice, that the distance from the middle of the facade to the mountain, was exactly 400 paces.

On the parapet, which extends along the three sides of this structure, is a pavement composed of two stones eight feet in extent : But some of them are from eight to nine, and ten feet in length. Others are six in breadth, and some less The principal stair-case is not placed in the middle of the facade, but toward the northern end, which is 165 paces from thence, and the southern extremity is at the distance of 435 paces from this stair-case. The tract of ground, between the two flights

Vol. II.

of the ſtair-caſe, is but forty two feet in extent, and contains a depth of twenty five feet and ſeven inches to the wall, the ſtair-caſe poſſeſſing all the reſt The inequality in the length of theſe ſteps does not exceed five inches, which are inſerted into the exterior ſtones, which extend to the ſide facade, and are of an equal length Theſe ſteps are but four inches high, and fourteen in depth   The northern flight contains fifty five ſteps , but that which winds off to the ſouth has fifty three, which are more ruinous than the reſt   We may reaſonably ſuppoſe that a length of time has buried ſeveral of thoſe ſteps, with part of the wall, under the earth

When the firſt flight of the ſtaircaſe has been aſcended, one ſees a perron, fifty one feet and four inches in breadth, and paved with very large ſtones , there are likewiſe two other flights, each containing forty eight ſteps , ſo that there are 103 ſteps to the north, and 101 to the ſouth. Here is likewiſe a ſecond perron, which contains twenty five feet in breadth, and is alſo covered with large ſtones, ſome of which are from thirteen to fourteen feet in length, and from ſeven to eight in breadth Some are likewiſe ſquare, others long and narrow, and ſome very ſmall. This pavement extends thirty two feet along the facade, and the ſtones which compoſe it are joined together with exquiſite art   The reſt of the ground in this part of the ſtructure is very compact, and the facade riſes to the height of thirty ſix feet between the flights.

Sir *John Chardin* declares, in the 73d page of the 9th volume, that the columns which are neareſt to each other, are ſeparated by a diſtance of 25 feet , and that a ſpace of fifty feet lies between thoſe which are moſt remote from one another , each foot conſiſting of twelve inches He likewiſe counts twelve ranges of ten columns, and adds, that *Figueroa* imagined there were but ſix ranges, with no more than eight columns in each range , from whence he concludes that there muſt be a miſtake in the figures, ſince he himſelf counted three ranks, with ten columns in each

Theſe columns begin at the diſtance of twenty two feet and two inches from the ſtair-caſe where the figures appear, and they conſiſt of two ranges, each containing ſix columns , of which there is but one remaining Eight pedeſtals, however, are yet to be ſeen, together with the cavities of earth in which three others were inſerted   They were diſpoſed along the wall of the ſtair-caſe, and at the ſame diſtance from one another, as the firſt is from that ſtair-caſe There are likewiſe ſix other ranges of ſix colums each, at the diſtance of ſeventy two feet and eight inches from the former, and their ſpace of intercolumniation is equal to twenty two feet and two inches There are but ſeven of them ſtanding, but all the baſes, tho' ruinous, are ſtill in their places One of theſe ſeven columns is in the firſt, and another in the ſecond range , the third has two , and there is one in each of the others Eaſtward from hence, and at the diſtance of ſeventy one feet, were two other ranks of ſix columns each, toward the mountains , but four are all that are ſtanding at preſent , there are likewiſe five ruinous baſes, and the cavities of the reſt are ſtill viſible It ſeemed evident to me, that theſe, which I frequently meaſured, were oppoſite to the twelve which were diſpoſed along the facade, as I have deſcribed them in page 13 I was likewiſe careful to examine every place where it was viſible that columns had formerly ſtood, and I found that their number amounted in the whole to 205 I was altogether as induſtrious, with regard to the figures, whoſe height I alſo meaſured   The largeſt of theſe appears only in part above the earth. The head is two feet and ſeven inches in height, and the hand, which ho'ds the lance, is ten inches in breadth There are other figures ten feet high, and ſome but ſeven feet five inches Others correſpond with nature in their dimenſions

Some

Some are higher by two feet, and others are not so tall as a human body The figures on the side of the stair-case are but two feet and nine inches high , and those on the stair-case itself have much the same dimensions That which I brought away with me is but one foot nine inches and a half in height There are some which are but two feet high, and others no more than one foot and a half The number of those figures, including human and animal forms, amounts to 1300, as I have already observed page 29

All these columns are fluted in the same manner , the shafts of some consist of three pieces, and others have four, exclusive of the capital, which is composed of five different pieces, and of an unknown order, which differs in every particular from the other five. The greatest dissimilitude between the columns is, that

some have capitals, and others are without them Their height is almost equal, their elevation varying only from seventy to seventy two feet, including the capital, which constitutes about a third part , and they are seventeen feet and seven inches in circumference. Those, however, must be excepted which are on the side of the portals, and are but fifty four feet in height, with a circumference of fourteen feet and two inches All the pedestals are round, and comprehend twenty four feet and five inches in their circumference, but the lower moulding exceeds it by a foot and five inches They are four feet and three inches in height, and have three sorts of ornaments

The four ruinous capitals, which have already been mentioned, are represented, with their ornaments, in the following plate , and they are

marked with the letters A, B, C, D. The laft is that of the column which is moft entire, and is on the fide of the two portals On three of thefe capitals are large fhapelefs ftones, which originally reprefented animals, but no certain judgment can be formed of them at prefent The letter E reprefents a compleat capital, compofed of the other four. The three pedeftals which appear at the letter F, are drawn with the greateft exactnefs from the originals G reprefents the cornice of one of the portals

I likewife found a fragment of a column that was not fluted, and it differed from all the others It was twenty feet in circumference, and twelve feet four inches high, and we may conclude from hence, that there formerly were other columns like this.

It remains that I fpeak of the tombs of *Naxi Ruftan*, which Sir *John Chardin* has reprefented in his 74th plate And I muft obferve, in the firft place, that the difpofition of the whole is very defective, and cannot be all feen at the fame time in that manner, efpecially the two equeftrian figures, with the ring, and that which projects from the middle of the rock He has likewife placed them to the eaft, inftead of the weft, and at the diftance of 330 paces from the tombs, but they are not to be feen fo far off I may add too, that the figures, among which is that which projects from the rock, ought to be much lower than thofe which hold the ring, and inftead of eight of thofe figures there fhould have been but feven Three of them are on the right, and two on the left of the figure which rifes from the rock, but thofe five, which are behind the wall, as I obferved in page 33, ought to be vifible no farther than the breaft The feventh of thefe figures, which has the hands croffed upon the body, is on this fide of the wall, to the right.

The fquare edifice, which Sir *John Chardin* places beyond the laft

tomb, ought to front the firft, and fhould likewife have been exhibited with all the numerous and different apertures, with which I have reprefented it in plate 166 I have expreffed the true ftructure of one of thefe monuments, in plate 167 As to thofe four reprefentations which Sir *John Chardin* has placed below the tombs, they are meer invention, and a judgment may be formed of them, by comparing them with mine, in plates 168, 169, and with my reprefentation of the two equeftrian figures with the ring in plate 170

In the year 1712 another book of travels was publifhed in *Latin* by Monfieur *Engelbert Kempfer*, and this work contains fome plates of *Naxi Ruftan*, and *Perfepolis*, which I have carefully examined, in order to difcover their defects, with the fame liberty as I have taken, and the fame exactnefs I have obferved, with refpect to thofe of Sir *John Chardin* The author of thefe travels declares, indeed, in his preface, that befide the various difficulties he had to furmount, previous to the publication of his book, nothing created him greater uneafinefs than the ignorance of the engravers, who fucceeded very ill in copying in little, thofe original defigns, which he drew on the fpot with all poffible exactnefs, and he adds, that if thofe plates were not abfolutely neceffary for the illuftration of feveral things, he would not have inferted them in his work, to which he declares they are a difgrace

The firft of thofe plates, in page 107, reprefents the royal tombs, but is extremely confufed, and differs from the original in many particulars

The fecond, in page 109, reprefents two equeftrian figures, holding a ring, and under the horfes feet are the heads of two giants, which the author pretends were two conquered princes, and that their bodies are covered with earth. I, for my part, did not difcover any thing of this nature, nor can I comprehend, why the bodies fhould be covered

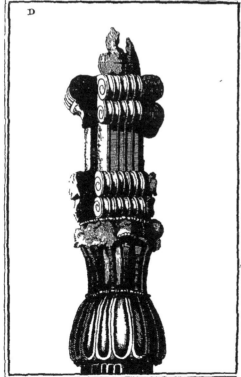

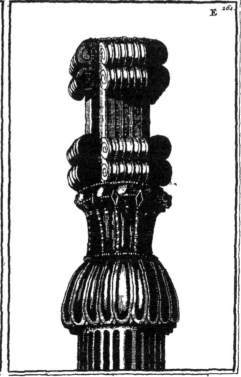

covered with earth, when the horfes which appear in the fame place are altogether entire Monfieur *Kempfer* has likewife given thefe figures a drapery, and head-drefs, which have no conformity with the originals, and the horfes, whofe feet are not feen, are very different from mine in plate 170 To this I may add, that only one of his figures holds the ring, for the others do but touch it

His third plate, page 311, exhibits eleven figures to view, whereas there ought to have been but feven, namely, three on the right, and two on the left of that figure which projects from the rock. the five which are behind the wall ought to appear no farther than the breaft, and the 7th figure fhould have been without the wall, to the right, and it ought not to have had two faces, like a *Janus.* The author imagines, that this 7th figure has been added in later times, by way of derifion, becaufe, fays he, the nofe is of a monftrous length, and there is no true proportion in any part of the figure For my part, I could never obferve any fuch difference between that and the other figures

His fourth plate, page 313, reprefents one of the tombs of *Naxi Ruftan*, ornamented on the two fides with figures from the top to the bottom, but which certainly ought not to be there, as is evident by my 167th plate. The tombs of *Perfepolis* are decorated in this manner, but they are not hewn out fo high in the rock, as appears by my reprefentation of the whole in plate 158 The rock likewife ought to be plain, and not wrought into ornaments like a work of tapeftry

The fifth, fixth, and feventh plates are wanting in Mr. *Kempfer*'s book, but his 8th, page 318, reprefents two figures with lances, altogether undefaced, together with little ornaments in form of a crofs, on their bonnets For my part, I found them in a very ruinous condition, and I have accordingly defcribed them in this manner I, however,

thought I could diftinguifh them to be figures fighting on horfeback

I believe that what this author has reprefented in his 319th page, may be intended for that which is exhibited in my 168th plate But his draught is too defective to deferve a particular enumeration of its errors His tenth plate is alfo unintelligible, and the eleventh, in which three figures are reprefented, is not worth refuting The reader may confult my 169th plate, where the crowned heads, which he has reprefented on the earth, are not to be found, but the real form of thofe figures, together with their habits, and what they wear on their heads, are exhibited with great exactnefs

Mr *Kempfer* reprefents in his 14th plate, page 323, the fquare edifice, which is to be feen, with all its apertures, in my 166th plate But inftead of refuting all the defects he has introduced, I fhall only fay in general, that he has exhibited feveral Things which are not to be found upon the fpot, and has omitted others which are really there.

Having thus taken a furvey of the tombs of *Naxi Ruftan*, with this author, we will now accompany him to *Perfepolis.* He reprefents in page 324, the firft point of view of this palace, which is exhibited in my 117th plate, where all the columns are rightly placed, and thofe that are moft diftant are not fo high as the neareft. The broken column appears diftinctly there, as well as the ftorks nefts, which are to be feen on fome of the columns. The true height and form of the portals are expreffed, as are likewife thofe which are near the two columns The two monuments which he has reprefented are at too great a diftance from one another, and raifed too high in the rock. Their elevation fhould not exceed that of the columns, and the rock itfelf ought not to be fo high as he has fhewn it The earth which feparates the two flights of the ftair-cafe, and the defcent from the wall, are vifible in my plate.

Vol II.

H h h

The

The second point of fight is likewife reprefented in the 334th page of Mr *Kempfer*'s work, but the firft part of the edifices ought to have been larger The portals are too near one another, and the ruins to the left have no refemblance to thofe on the fpot The higheft edifice has too many large portals like one another, and he has omitted the raifed ftone of one of the pilafters, together with feveral other ruins The greateft part of the wall to the right is deftroyed, and the tract of ground which leads to that edifice ought to appear His ftair-cafe agrees as little with the original, and it ought to appear as I have reprefented it in plate 150, but the whole plan of our author is too fmall, and likewife too deep in perfpective The curtain which appears between the facade and the columns, is too fquare, and he has introduced too many entire portals. The columns are at too great a diftance from one another, and likewife too regular, and the number of pedeftals is too great The ftone ciftern is much larger than it ought to appear, and it fhould not be on the fide of the wall next the columns, but nearer to the portals, the two columns of which are reprefented higher than their real elevation For the firft portal ought to be thirty nine feet in height, and the columns are but fifty four The ftorks neft, which he has placed on one of the columns, is abundantly too large The plain ought not to appear in the middle, contracting itfelf to the weft, nor fhould the mountains be fo far to the eaft, but they ought to appear as they are exhibited in my 119th plate, where I have omitted nothing, even to the fmalleft tree

His plate of characters, page 333, has no correfpondence with mine in plate 126, and yet they are intended for the fame, but they are all confufed, and he has inferted fome which ought not to have been there He has reprefented twenty four perfect lines, whereas feveral characters are wanting in mine, and

the three firft lines are entirely defaced But I have reprefented all that are vifible in the other lines, even to the minuteft point

He obferves, in page 336, that there are fifteen paces from the ftaircafe to the firft portals, and thirty from thefe to the others If we allow two feet and a half to each pace, the firft portals will be thirty feven feet and a half from the ftair-cafe, whereas the fpace between them comprehends forty two feet The columns are at the diftance of twenty fix feet from the firft portal, and fifty-fix from the fecond, both which numbers amount to eighty two feet, but he has computed no more than feventy five. He adds, that each pilafter is compofed of two ftones, jointed together with fo much art as to be fcarce vifible And yet the firft portal confifts of eight ftones, and the other of feven, as I have obferved in page 11 where the whole is defcribed with all poffible exactnefs, and as it appears in my 121ft, 122d, and 123d plates, together with the animals and columns He fays, with refpect to the animals, that as the heads are entirely defaced, it is impoffible to judge what fpecies they were intended to reprefent, and adds, that the laft, which are winged, may poffibly have been griffons, and that there really is one, whofe head refembles that of a bearded man, though it be much impaired, which indeed is true He takes the ornaments of thefe animals for rofes or coral I have exhibited two of them in plate 156

He affigns to the columns a circumference of two fathoms, and twice the height of the portals, but this reprefentation has been already confidered He likewife places three or four ftorks nefts on one of thofe columns only, whereas they are to be found upon feveral He has alfo exhibited figures on the ftair-cafe, in page 341, and begins with the upper part, where he has placed, at the head of other figures, a man on horfeback, followed by a chariot
                                                 drawn

drawn by two men, who are succeeded by a winged lion encountering a bull, to which he has added a table of twenty four lines He then represents in his stair-case, several figures habited in different manners, and carrying various forts of things These he has alternately intermixed with mules, oxen, sheep, camels, and cypress-trees planted in fine vases, above the two contending animals. With respect to the other side, which is to the east, he contents himself with saying, that it is full of figures armed with lances The author indeed acknowledges, in page 340, that he has sketched out this procession something slightly, and without entering into a strict examination of the particulars, and then adds, that his engraver has committed many errors in this part of the work, as well with respect to the figures, as the order in which they are disposed, and that these defects were occasioned by his misapprehension of the author's design, and the remarks he has made Upon which he promises to give the publick a set of more correct plates, in some future impression of his work, and it is certain that he may easily succeed in that particular, like several other persons, after having seen my plates In a word, this whole representation is very far from corresponding with the celebrated ruins of *Persepolis*, and a judgment may be formed of it, by what I have exhibited in plate 126 It seems very improbable, therefore, that all these faults should be chargeable on the meer negligence, or unskilfulness of the engravers, who ought naturally to conform to the orders, and trace out the sketches they receive. But indeed his verbal description is altogether as imperfect as the plates, and he himself says, that the first figure which appears on the upper-part of the stair-case, is a man on horseback Whereas it is very certain, that no equestrian figure is to be seen either there, or in any other part of the ruins of *Chelminar*, nor is there the least appearance that

any thing of that nature was ever there. The same may be said of the chariot drawn by two men, as also of those extraordinary animals which he has represented as encountering one another, and also of the cypress planted in the fine vases he has assigned them I may therefore affirm, that these human and animal figures, together with all the rest, are so remote from truth, that I shall not charge my self with the unnecessary trouble of pointing out their defects

He represents, in page 344, a portal, which is the work of meer imagination, since instead of placing the figures within the entrance, he has disposed some on each side without, and others within, descending from a rock with strange animals in their hands, and above the entrance, he has placed a small figure, which indeed is to be seen on the top of the pilasters, but not within the portal Our author adds, that figures are to be seen there habited in long robes, the first of which he imagines is a bishop at the head of his clergy; and he likewise affirms, that in each of the portals, a giant is to be seen, together with a griffon, or a lion, into whose belly the giant plunges a dagger, and he places on the top, an hieroglyphic figure, equally compounded of a man and an eagle, with a variety of ornaments like those at *Naxi Rustan.*

His 347th page represents a window, with small ornaments on the outside, and characters all around it, descending to a considerable depth. These characters are indeed placed there instead of foliage, but they are not continued so far down as he has represented. The reader may see in what manner they are exhibited in my 128th plate

Our author likewise declares in page 340, that he found seventeen of the seventy columns, the traces of which are still visible, and he believes they were distributed into four divisions, separated from each other by a thick wall of black marble, the ruins of which still rise to the
height

height of a fathom, are six paces in length, and one in thickness He pretends, that these columns were placed at the distance of nine paces from each other, and that they were raised on three sorts of pedestals, some square and rude, like a work in the gothic style, others round, and partly ornamented with the leaves of lillies: To which he adds, that in the spaces between these columns, there are some which are fluted, and others entirely plain In a word, that they have a circumference of three fathoms, and are about fifteen in height. As I have already sufficiently specified their dimensions, it is altogether unnecessary to repeat them here; and therefore I shall only say, that neither plain columns, nor square pedestals are to be found there

In the 330th page, our author assigns to this edifice a length of 570 paces, from east to west, tho' their number scarce amounts to 400, as I have already observed, and in the middle, where the greatest extent is from north to south, he allows it no more than 400 paces, tho' the real number is 600, he adds, that the height of the wall is not equal in every part, but that it may be allowed six fathoms for the altitude in general. The reader may consult the particulars of my description He afterward affirms, that the stones of this wall are large, exactly square, and polished on the outside The two former particulars of this description have already been shewn to be false, nor are all the stones polished, as he declares. Some indeed are so, and they appear as smooth as mirrors in the portals and windows, but none of this polish is to be seen on their outside, and I leave the reader to judge what time it would have required to polish every stone both within and without I have indeed declared in my first volume, that the inside of the *Egyptian* pyramids is polished, and that the stones are joined together in a most exquisite manner, but there is no polish to be seen on their outside

Our author represents the first flights of the stair-case in the facade, as consisting of fifty five steps to the right, and fifty eight to the left, and as many in the second flights, the total of which will amount to 110 on one side, and 116 on the other, whereas there are but 103 to the north, and 101 to the south He likewise allows each step a length of eight paces, a breadth of two and a half, and a span for the height All which he has conceived at random, without measuring what he has taken upon him to describe.

As for the stones of the rock, which these two writers, as well as several others, take for black, white, and red marble, it is certain, as I have observed, page 29, that all the edifice is cut out of the natural rock, so that it is altogether ridiculous to suppose the materials were brought from any other quarter It is even obvious to any eye, that the greatest part of the edifice is formed of such materials as were produced by the mountain against which it is situated This is apparent beyond contradiction, with respect to the two royal monuments, the stair-case of the facade, the two sides of the structure, the large stones of the wall, and several other members of the building, particularly to the north The polished stones, indeed, and especially those within the portals, and the windows, together with the large angular stones, which still appear in the earth, have a great resemblance to marble, because they are streaked with white, grey, red, and yellowish veins intermixed with a deep blew, and lines of a black dye But I look upon this variety of colours to be the effect of time, since nothing of that nature is to be seen in the rock itself The greatest part of the edifice is tinged with a light blue, as is evident from several pieces of the rock, and by the figure I brought away from those ruins

I shall here mention two antiquities which are taken notice of by our author, who says, page 354, that

on

on the top of a certain hill, there are several square and ruinous fragments of a wall of marble, together with portals which opened into an apartment fifteen paces square, whose situation is from the north-west to the south-east, and the facade of which fronted the plain He then adds, that there are several figures with lances still visible on some pieces of marble, and likewise three gates of a reddish marble, which are about three fathoms high, two of which front each other, and the third is situated toward the mountain He likewise says, that the outside is smooth and finely polished, and not at all defaced by time, and that no sort of sculpture is to be found on the outward surface, but on the sides within there are some figures a little larger than the life, separate from each other, and habited in very wide and long robes, which flow down to the feet, and that the sleeves of these vestments are plaited like those of the sacerdotal garments That some of these figures seem to shoot out, and others to shrink back, and that they are all clothed in the same manner That the particular figure, which is under the gate, to the north-west, holds an urn in the left hand, and in the right, which is more elevated, a censer, something like a small lantern : That there is such another figure as this under the opposite gate, and which holds the same thing, and that the others have neither heads nor hands, that the figure to the east is likewise defaced, and holds a little packet in its left hand, and a flower, or something like it, in the right

This is the same edifice which I call, in page 50, *Mazyt Madre, Sulemoen,* or the mosque of the mother of *Sulemoen*; and I found that this edifice was between eighteen and twenty paces square One may there see three portals like those of *Persepolis,* represented in plate 161, and whose inward height is equal to eleven feet, and on each of the sides is the figure of a woman as large as the life, and holding something in its hand like those at *Persepolis*. On the

two sides of the rock, out of which the portal to the south-west is formed, are nine small figures much impaired by time, and their bodies are half buried in the earth, and to the north-west is a kind of stone cistern, which is mentioned by our author · All the rest is surrounded with stones separated from one another, and which owe that kind of situation to a length of time Most of the pilasters of these portals are out of their places, and these removals can only be imputed to an earthquake The greatest part of the cornice, belonging to the middle portal, is still visible, and the true form of these portals may be seen in my 178th plate, where only half the figure of the woman that is placed below, appears to view, by reason of the stones which surround it. At the distance of a good league from hence, one may find several figures carved on the rock, and our author says, page 363, that the two first represent *Rustan* and his wife in conversation together, that the head of this hero is covered with a casque; that his beard and hair are short, and that his neck is ornamented with a collar of jewels. To this he adds, that the breast and body of this figure are damaged, and that a plaited vestment hangs down from the waist He then tells us, that the figure which represents the wife of *Rustan,* is beautiful, and as large as the life, and that she has jewels on her forehead, and round her neck, as likewise an upper robe, which is very short, and plaited below. He farther acquaints us, that the Figure of *Rustan* has his left hand on his stomach, and with his right presents a flower to the queen, which she receives with her left, and presents to him with her right hand a fruit which resembles an apple, or a pear. To which he adds, that the two other Figures represent heroes or kings, but that *Rustan* is still the largest of all.

For my part, I found in that place, as I intimated in page 51. three tables, and some other pieces of sculpture carved in a very rude manner on the rock, and that on the firft of thefe tables were two figures, one of which holds his hand on the guard of a large fword   That the fecond table exhibits the figure of a man with a round machine on his head, and on the third, which is equal to the firft, and lower than that in the midole, is a figure with a kind of mitre on his head, and his left hand refting on the guard of his fword, like the former, but that the whole is fo impaired by time, as to be hardly diftinguifhable, as I have reprefented the fame in my 179th plate   Only the large fword of that figure which our author calls king *Ruftan,* is ftill very vifible, but as to the collar, the cafque, and likewife the flower, which he fays this prince holds in his hand, and which the queen receives with her left, I can affirm, that nothing of this nature is there to be found   I am likewife very uncertain whether this latter figure be that of a woman, for it is exceedingly defaced, and yet our author affirms, that it reprefents a very amiable woman, with jewels on her forehead, and round her neck   The middle figure feemed to have fomething in its Hand, much refembling a bowl   In a word, I found that thefe figures, together with what they have on their heads, and in all other particulars relating to them, are not very different from thofe tables which appear below the tombs of *Naxi Ruftan,* and that the former may probably have been the fame with thofe that are there reprefented as holding a ring, in plate 169

It may naturally be concluded from all I have faid, that I have proceeded very differently from other travellers, in the examination of what I faw, and that the only view I propofed in my travels, was to unfold thofe antiquities, which have not been placed in their true light by any perfon before me, and that my defign was to offer to the public a more perfect

work, in this refpect, than any which have been publifhed by others   I undertook it altogether with this defign, and was defirous to fatisfy my natural curiofity for things of this nature, without any thoughts of making my fortune in foreign countries, or engaging myfelf in the fervice of any one   I can likewife affirm, that I drew with my own hand, and have painted in diftemper, on paper, and from the original objects themfelves, thofe reprefentations of them, which are to be found in my travels, and that I have completed the whole in fo orderly and exact a manner, that I could have made ufe of them in the relation of my travels, without giving myfelf the trouble to have them engraved

I brought away an entire figure from the rocks of *Perfepolis,* into my own country, together with feveral other curious pieces, a large collection of characters, and other ornaments, which fufficiently prove what pains I took, during the three months I continued at *Perfepolis* · all which time I devoted my ftricteft attention to thofe illuftrious ruins.   I may therefore take the liberty to reprefent myfelf as the firft perfon who has placed them in the full light, and rendered juftice to them, after an interval of 2000 years, and without deviating from the rules of art, either in the relation I have given of them, or with refpect to the plates which were engraved, under my infpection, with all poffible juftice and accuracy   I therefore flatter myfelf that I have merited the approbation of all thofe who are lovers of art and undifguifed truth   I have likewife taken the pains to paint feveral extraordinary pieces of drapery, both of men and women, which the curious may fee at my houfe, together with a variety of *Indian* fifh, fruits, and birds.

A LET-

A LETTER

Written to the

AUTHOR

ON THE

Subject of his REMARKS,

By a Lover of ANTIQUITY.

SIR,

I HAVE read with pleasure, your remarks on the errors committed by Sir *John Chardin* and Mr *Kempfer*, in the accounts they have g ven us of the celebrated ruins of the ancient palace of *Perjepolis*, but cannot take upon me to d cide any thing concerning them, since I never had an opportunity of viewing them on the spot. I think, however, that the fine plates you have caused to be engraven, and the circumstantial description you have given of those Antiquities, in the course of your travels, as well with respect to the edifice in general, as to each piece in particular, merit the attention and suffrages of learned men, and lovers of antiquity, more than any other relation which I have yet seen When one considers the extent of that superb structure, together with the number of figures, and other curiosities which are there to be found, as is allowed by all who have been upon the spot, it must be confessed that a person ought to have excellent eyes, a masterly hand, and a large share of judgment, to acquit himself well on that subject, and that he must have joined to these, an application and patience that are not to be expressed. And yet Mr. *Kempfer* freely confesses, [a] that he was hardly three days upon the spot · And tho' he endeavours to persuade his readers, in several parts of his work, particularly, *Relat* v. § 3. *p* 331. that he drew with great exactness the principal fragments of those noble ruins; but that his engraver copied his drawings in a very inaccurate manner, the contrary is yet too visible in the disposition of the whole, as you have very justly observed, and all the parts of it are exhibited in so unmasterly and injudicious a manner, that it is impossible to discover any great strokes of art, or the least air of antiquity, or any thing indeed that corresponds with the relations that have been written on this subject by the antient *Greeks*. To which I may add, that tho' a person be really master of all the qualities that are requisite for the proper accomplishment of such an undertaking as this, it will yet be impossible for him to form so long and circumstan-

[a] Fascicul II Amœnit Exotic Relat iv Sect 2 p 20,

stial

ſhal a relation as Mr *Kempfer* has given us, in ſuch a ſhort time as that in which he was converſant with theſe ruins Sir *John Chardin* likewiſe did not allow himſelf a ſufficient time to examine them very ſtrictly, and to give a clear repreſentation of what he there ſaw, ſince he acknowledges, in the 9th Volume, and 175th page of his travels, that he employ'd no more than five days in his ſurvey of *Chelminar*, and in completing his draughts and deſcription of that ſtructure, and adds, that he was obliged to hire a painter for that purpoſe It muſt therefore be allowed, Sir, that tho' ſome figures in his plates may be ſaid to reſemble yours in a few particulars, and it be likewiſe evident that they were drawn on the ſpot, it is yet very apparent, that they were worked off in haſte, and ſome things were touched ſo very ſlightly, that it became neceſſary to finiſh them afterward by mere gueſs This you have very judiciouſly obſerved in your remarks, wherein you have refuted all the errors he has committed, and have proceeded with all the exactneſs of a man who has ſeen things with his own eyes, and examined them in the ſtricteſt manner I am therefore perſuaded that every judicious reader will declare in your favour without the leaſt heſitation, and it muſt be naturally allowed, that the repreſentation of thoſe ruins, made by ſo curious a connoiſſeur as yourſelf, are preferable to thoſe of a hired painter, who continued no more than five days upon the ſpot, and took but a tranſient view of things; whereas you was conſtant in your application there, and proceeded with all imaginable exactneſs for the full ſpace of three months. This is my opinion with reſpect to the work in general, and I think it is not ill founded. But, at the ſame time, I am far from pretending to derogate either from the merit of thoſe gentlemen, or the applauſe they deſerve in every other particular.

Tom. 3
145 de
l Ed in 1

But as you are deſirous, Sir, of knowing my ſentiments of thoſe hiſtorical remarks which thoſe gentlemen have interſperſed in the relation of their travels, with reference to the figures that are to be ſeen at *Chelminar*, I ſhall do myſelf the honour to acquaint you, that Mr *Kempfer* ſeems to me, to have been extremely conciſe in thoſe particulars, and Sir *John Chardin* altogether as ſuperficial, whilſt you have omitted nothing that has been written by the ancients with relation to *Perſepolis*, and the antient *Perſians* This might ſuffice in general, but in order to afford you all the ſatisfaction in my power, I ſhall now examine what theſe gentlemen have advanced on this ſubject, in which I intend to be as brief as poſſible, and as clear as is conſiſtent with that little knowledge Heaven has been pleaſed to afford me

Sir *John Chardin*, ſpeaking of theſe famous ruins in general, which the modern *Perſians* call *Chelminar*, declares, that they are not the remains, either of the palace of the ancient kings of *Perſia*, or of that of *Darius* in particular, but that they are the ruins of a temple in the ancient city of *Perſepolis* See *Vol. ix page* 156 He then alledges ſeveral reaſons in proof of what he advances, the moſt plauſible of which is, that in ancient times palaces in that country were not built on mountains, but on the banks of rivers, for the benefit of a refreſhing air He then endeavours to juſtify his opinion by the order of the figures on the ſtair-caſe, which he would have his readers believe are the proceſſion of a ſacrifice, becauſe each figure carries ſomething that was uſed in ſolemnities of that nature among the Pagans, as he pretends, and he even finds fault with *D. Garcia de Silva de Figueroa*, for calling this proceſſion a triumph, in the 150th page of his embaſſy. He likewiſe adds, in page 63, that this proceſſion is divided into ſeveral bands, ſome containing ſix, and others

Tom 3
p 102 de
l Ed in 4

Tom 3
p 104 de
l Ed in 4 others nine figures, and that they are separated by a tree which refembles a cyprefs. He then tells us, that the general band is led by a man, who holds another by the hand, as if he conducted him in the quality of a victim and that this reprefentation is exhibited in every particular band, except one To this he adds, that five forts of victims feem to be in this proceffion, namely, a dromedary, a bull, a couple of hegoats, an horfe, and a mule And he obferves, that tho' one fees but one dromedary, two he-goats, and one mule, yet there are feveral horfes, which induced him to think that this was intended to reprefent a facrifice to the fun He then cites *Herodotus* and *Strabo*, to prove that the antient *Perfians* offered horfes to the fun, as well as other animals, but has not pointed out the place where this paffage is to be found in thofe famous hiftorians And tho' he acknowledges that he cannot find any exprefs declaration, either in facred or prophane hiftory, that the *Perfians* facrificed human creatures, like fome of their neighbours, and that the *Guebres* abfolutely deny that any fuch immolations were ever made by their anceftors, he yet affirms, that the man who is led by the hand, is a victim, as well as the horfe and the dromedary For he cannot conceive what elfe that figure can be intended for, in this proceffion, all the other human figures of which carry fomething that relates to a facrifice He

Tom 3
p 108 de
l'Ed in 4 likewife maintains in page 77, that the tract of ground where the columns appear in their greateft number, is the choir of this imaginary temple, and the place where the victims were facrificed, to which he

Tom 3
p 114 de
l Ed in 4 adds in the 93d and following pages, that he is perfuaded that the great number of edifices and apartments, which appear to the eaft, and north, and which are fewer toward the north, and toward the fouth, were

the feveral apartments of the facrificers, and other priefts of the temple, fince fuch ftructures were cuftomary among the pagans, and were even fome of the appendages to the temple of *Solomon.*

In order to anfwer this kind of reafoning in a few words, I muft acquaint you, Sir, that feveral palaces are to be found at this day in plains, throughout the eaft, but we are not to conclude from thence, that this was the practice at all times, and in all places I may alledge, as a proof of what I advance, that the antient city of *Jerufalem* was not fituated on the delightful banks of *Jordan,* but on the mountains of *Moriah* and *Sion,* as the facred fcriptures declare The temple of *Solomon* was built on mount *Moriah,* by the order of king *David,* the father of that prince [a] The palace of *David* was alfo on mount *Sion,* as was likewife the fortrefs of that name, and which was a place of fuch ftrength, that the *Jebufites* did not believe that prince could make himfelf mafter of it, even after he had taken *Jerufalem,* as may be feen in the fecond book of *Samuel, chap. v. ver* 6, *&c* [b] The palaces, or fortreffes of the ancient kings of *Egypt,* at *Memphis,* which was once the capital of that kingdom, were likewife fituated on an eminence, or the declivity of a mountain, which floped toward the city, that lay at the bottom, as *Strabo* obferves [c] in his account of the antiquities of that city, which ftill fubfifted in his time In a word, the palace of the Khalifahs of *Egypt,* at *Al Kahira,* or *Cairo,* is alfo fituated on a rock or mountain, as you obferve in your firft account of your travels, chapter 39 And as the climate of *Egypt* and *Judæa* is altogether as hot at leaft as any part of *Perfia,* Sir *John Chardin*'s argument feems therefore to have no weight. I may add too, that the delicious plain in which thefe

[a] Vide Jofeph rer Judaic 1 c 14
[b] Vide etiam Jofeph rer Judaic lib 7 c 2 & Buno in not ad Cluver Introduct Geogr lib 5 c 20 & Chriftoph Heideman Paleftin c 2 n 10
[c] Lib 17 rer Georg in fin & feq pr

famous remains of the grandeur of the ancient monarchy of *Perſia* are ſituated, is watered by a variety of rivers and leſſer ſtreams, which frequently overflow their banks, and temper the glow of the ſun-beams in the ſummer ſeaſon We may likewiſe take it for granted, that there were ſeveral ſprings and ſubterranean cavities, together with a great number of wells in the palace itſelf, and which have been ſince filled up with the fallen fragments of thoſe ſuperb ruins, and deſtroyed by thoſe barbarians, who laid that fine country under water, which is a fate that *Memphis* and *Jeruſalem* have likewiſe ſuſtained But what is ſtill more to our purpoſe, Sir *John Chardin* frankly acknowledges, in the 173d page of the ſame volume, that the inhabitants call *Chelminar The Temple of the Winds*, becauſe a breeze of air perpetually blows in that place Why, therefore, may we not ſuppoſe a palace to have been built there, as well as a temple ? To this we will add the teſtimony of *Athenæus*, [a] who declares, that *Cyrus*, and the kings of *Perſia* who ſucceeded him, reſided at *Ecbatane*, the capital of *Media*, during the exceſſive heats of the ſummer, and paſſed the autumn at *Perſepolis*, the winter at *Suſa*, and the ſpring at *Babylon* Add to this, that the manner in which *Diodorus Siculus* deſcribes the palace of *Perſepolis*, gives us ſufficient reaſon to believe that *Chelminar* is that very palace : For though that author mentions a triple wall, which encompaſſed that palace, and though theſe three incloſures are no longer to be ſeen there, that will not be thought a circumſtance of any conſequence, ſince the *Greek* authors from whom he tranſcribed that deſcription, ſome ages after the deſtruction of that palace, may have taken ſome particular angles, or ſections, of that edifice, or ſome corners or ſides of the rock on which it

Tom ; p 140 Ed in 4

is ſituated, for walls, or thoſe walls, if any ſuch there were, may have been entirely deſtroy'd in a courſe of ſo many ages But what ſeems moſt material to me is, that *Diodorus* adds in the ſame place, That *to the eaſt, and behind the palace, there was a mountain which was called the* Royal Mount, *where the tombs of the* Perſian *kings were built* As thoſe circumſtances, therefore, together with ſeveral others which I may have occaſion to mention, as I proceed, are ſtill to be found at *Chelminar*, the learned *Don Figueroa*, who was a perfect maſter of antiquity, concludes very juſtly, in my opinion, that this place ought to be conſidered as the genuine ruins of the ancient palace of *Peſepolis*, which was deſtroyed by *Alexander the Great* See his embaſſy, pages 160, 161, 162, &c. and page 41. of your own travels into *Perſia* We will now proceed to Sir *John Chardin*'s ſecond argument.

He ſays, that the ornaments on the ſtair-caſe of theſe ſtately ruins, repreſent a proceſſion, and probably one of thoſe which were made at ſolemn ſacrifices, and particularly thoſe to the ſun But the teſtimonies which he cites from *Herodotus* and *Strabo*, to juſtify his conjecture, are altogether inconcluſive. *Herodotus* indeed declares [b] that the ancient *Perſians* made oblations to the ſun ; but he does not ſeem to ſay, that thoſe offerings conſiſted either of horſes, or of any other animals, for he only declares, that the *Maſſagetæ* offered up to him, as the moſt active of all gods, the ſwifteſt of their quadrupeds, namely horſes *Strabo* ſays the ſame [c] when he mentions the *Maſſagetæ*, but, with reſpect to the *Perſians*, he ſays nothing more, than that they honoured the [d] ſun There is more reaſon, in my opinion, to affirm, that the *Perſians* offered horſes to the god *Mars*, from the authority of *Strabo*, [e] who declares, that they

[a] Lib. 12 p. m 513
[b] Lib 1 c. 131
[c] Lib 12 c 131
[d] Lib 15 p m. 732
[e] Cit lib p m. 72

ho-

honoured the god of war above all other deities, and that the people of *Caramania*, a province subject to the *Perfians*, offered mules to him, because they ufed thofe animals in their wars, inftead of horfes However, as *Xenophon* affirms, [a] that *Cyrus* offered horfes to the fun, and [b] *Paufanias*, that the *Perfians* facrificed horfes and other beafts to that luminary, we will not conteft their authority, but we, however, are not to conclude from thence, that the figures on the ftair-cafe of *Chelminar* reprefent the proceffion of a facrifice, nor that the ftructure itfelf was a temple of *Perfepolis*, becaufe it was cuftomary for the *Perfians*, on the birth-day of their kings, which was anciently called *Tycta*, to flaughter a great number of goats, mules, oxen, deer, and fheep, and the fubjects afterward ferved them up at the royal table, as *Athenæus* informs us [c] from ancient *Perfian* authors, whofe works have long ceafed to be extant It is much more probable, therefore, that thefe figures reprefent one of thofe feftivals, rather than a facrifice And what is ftill more to our purpofe, *Herodotus*, who lived in the time of *Xerxes the Great*, when the monarchy of the ancient *Perfians* was in its utmoft glory, declares, that they had no images of gods, nor temples, nor altars, and that they even derided thofe nations who had them, and were contented with offering their facrifices on lofty places free from all impurity [d], which likewife is confirmed by *Strabo* [e] I think this is fufficient to prove, that the ruins of *Chelminar* are not thofe of a temple, fince the ancient *Perfians* had not any, and confequently thefe muft be the remains of a palace, to which the figures and ornaments correfpond much better. For though Sir *John Chardin* endeavours in a very inge-

nious manner to fupport his opinion, by comparing the reprefentations on the ftair-cafe with fome particular cuftoms which prevail among the modern *Perfians* and *Indians*, yet I cannot fee that he can derive much advantage from that proceeding, fince perfons of judgment are fenfible, that modern cuftoms differ there, as well as in other countries, from thofe of the ancients, and efpecially with regard to an antiquity that has fubfifted above two thoufand years For which reafon I am well perfuaded, that if one of thofe *Batavians* who lived a thoufand years ago, was to appear upon earth again, he would be altogether unacquainted with the manners, language, and habits of his modern countrymen The prefent cuftoms and manners of the *Guebres*, and thofe of the pagans of *India*, which Sir *John Chardin* fo frequently alledges in his juftification, are no more in his favour than the other particulars he has mentioned; for the modern *Guebres* differ from the antient *Magi*, as much at leaft as the modern *Jews* deviate from their orthodox anceftors, and as much as the generality of modern Chriftians vary from the primitive church, both in their manners and doctrines The *Guebres* of this age are a fet of poor ignorant creatures, who in confequence of a length of time, and the great changes which have happened in *Perfia*, have loft the true knowledge of their anceftors manner of worfhip, of which they retain nothing but the letter, in the fame manner as the *Samaritans* have preferved that of the pentateuch It may even be prefumed, that the *Greeks*, who adored falfe deities, introduced many novelties in their time, into the *Perfian* religion, and which were very incongruous with the ancient manners of

[a] Lib 8 Cyrop c 24
[b] In Lacon fect lib 3 c 20
[c] Lib 4 p m 145, &c
[d] Vid cit lib 1 p 131 & 132
[e] Lib 15 p m 732

this

the people. The *Parthians* indeed, and another race of *Perfian* kings, reigned in that country for some ages after the *Greeks*, but it is very probable, that the *Saracens*, who afterward made themselves masters of it under the first Khalifahs, and then the *Tartars*, under *Tamerlane*, and after them, the *Turks*, did not fail to introduce several great changes there, either by tyranny, or a series of artful conduct, and we may naturally conclude, that these alterations contributed not a little to obscure and perplex the affairs of the ancient *Perfians* The *Indians* likewise have been no less obnoxious to changes and revolutions of this nature, but as they have no relation to our present subject, I shall not enlarge upon them

I freely acknowledge, for my part, that I think the relations which the ancient *Greek* historians have given us of the manners and customs of the first *Perfians*, in peace and war, and in every other particular, except what relates to their religious worship, deserve much more credit than all the fabulous histories of the modern *Perfians* It is certain, that the *Guebres* of our time are very commendable for entirely rejecting all false gods and idols, and for acknowledging one God alone, in which particulars they render justice to their ancestors, and likewise declare, that they pay an external honour only to the planets, as Dr *Hyde* has observed in his history of the religion of the ancient *Perfians*, and he declares, that he collected that account from their own writings To which I may add, that you yourself received the same account from their own lips, as you observe in the 79th chapter of your travels. I think therefore we need nothing more to refute, or at least to weaken Sir *John Chardin*'s second argument; since, if the ancient *Perfians* were not idolaters, it is cer-

tain that the figures of the stair-case cannot be supposed to be carrying in procession to this pretended temple, those things which real pagans used in their sacrifices And indeed they prove the very contrary, by the manner in which you have represented them, agreeably to history and reason I shall not take any notice of the errors he has committed, with respect to those figures, since you have sufficiently pointed them out, and no one can be a better judge of them than yourself The historians likewise declare in your favour, since they all deny that the ancient *Perfians* ever sacrificed human creatures, as the *Maffagetæ* did, according to *Herodotus* [a] and [b] *Strabo*. And these authors would certainly have said the same of the *Perfians*, if they had acted like the *Maffagetæ*

As to the figures which Sir *John Chardin* represents as bearing human limbs, I think you have sufficiently proved, that it is all mere imagination, and it is impossible it should be otherwise, if the whole be rightly considered It is still less conceivable, that the second figures which are led by the first in each band, should be intended for victims, since some of them have a machine on their left side, which he calls the case of a bow, in his 69th page, but there is much more reason to believe it to be a *Gerra*, or buckler made of cords and leather, which the *Perfians* carried on the left side, as they did a poinard on the right hip, as *Herodotus* observes [c] in his account of the arms of the ancient *Perfians*. This is confirm'd by the 58th and 59th plates in Sir *John Chardin*'s travels, since this buckler is seen in the first of those plates, where the left side of the figures appears, and particularly that which is distinguished by the letter O The poinard likewise is visible on the figures in the second plate, where

Tom 3 p 102 de l'Fd in 4.

[a] Lib 1 c. 216
[b] L 11 pag m 513 2
[c] Lib 7 c. 61

they

they are turned to the right, and are habited like the preceding figures, whose poniards are not seen, but the two ends of the scabbard appear on some others. Now it seems very unnatural to me, to have victims conducted to the altar, with bucklers and poniards on their sides

In the same 58th plate, Sir *John Chardin* has represented a person of rank, distinguished by the letter A, who conducts another with a *Tiara* on his head, and his habit resembles that of a *Magus,* or some priest. And yet, this figure, according to Sir *John Chardin,* must needs be a victim; which is very extraordinary. That which is marked with R in the same plate, together with the four following figures, have an instrument in their hands, which he calls a fleam, in his 69th page This was an ancient instrument, and he says it is still used in several parts of the east, instead of a lancet, which was not known in that country, till the *Europeans* maintained a commerce with it But this manner of reasoning proves nothing in my opinion, for beside that you represent this band of figures very differently from that gentleman, and without any fleams, I am not able to comprehend wherein they could be useful, unless it was to bleed the victims, which would have been something very singular I will not take upon me to decide what the other figures carry, for I would avoid all prolixity, and indeed you have said all that can be offered on that subject, in your fifty third chapter: For which reason, I shall only declare in general, that after a due consideration of the whole, I think this procession resembles a triumph more than any thing else, as *Figueroa* judged, or a birth-day sacrifice The several encounters of animals, likewise, who are engaged in combat either with one an-

other, or with men, correspond much better with a palace and a festival, than with a sacrifice and a temple, and especially as the ancient *Persians* had not any of these latter Sir *John Chardin* has represented one of these combats, in his 70th page, between a lion and a common bull with two horns, and he declares that combats of this nature are still exhibited for the entertainment of the people, at the festivals and public shews of the *Persians* , and that they are managed in such a manner, that the lion is always victorious, because that animal is an emblem of the *Persian* monarchy *Figueroa* only says, page 150, that a lion rending a bull is to be seen, and that the sculptor had represented the combat so well, that nothing can be excepted against it; but he has not said that this animal has horns Monsieur *Thevenot* expresses himself to the same effect in his travels[a]. But as I find that you have represented all, and even the least ornaments, with much more exactness than others, I imagine that these gentlemen, who sketched them out in a slight manner for want of time, have not taken notice that this bull has but one horn, and especially Sir *John Chardin,* who represents this animal without the least air of agreeableness, and in a position which is altogether unnatural, and directly contrary to that of *Figueroa.* If this animal therefore be such as you have represented it, I should not believe it to be a bull, and it seems to me to have more the air of a horse or a mule, and it is likewise bridled and harnessed like a horse Perhaps it may be one of those *Indian* mules which are mentioned by *Ctesias,* [b] who says that they resemble horses, and some of them exceed those animals in size. He adds, that they have a mane of a violet colour, a white body, black eyes, uncloven hoofs, and on their

[a] L. 2. c 7
[b] In Indic juxta, excerpt Phot c 35

forehead a black horn, which is white near the head, and red at the point. He then informs us that this horn is shaped into drinking cups, and that this animal is so exceeding vigorous and swift, that he cannot be taken without great difficulty. *Elian* has given us much the same account [a], and *Aristotle* likewise says, that there are mules in *India* which have one horn, but that their number is very inconsiderable [b]. *Pliny* relates the same thing [c]. And you may likewise consult *Bartholinus* on this subject [d]. But however the fact may be, I think you have represented it much in this manner on the stair-case, and as to those animals which are exhibited in Sir *John Chardin*'s 65th plate, there may possibly have been such, notwithstanding they are unknown to us. You likewise represent, in your 130th plate, a hero encountring a lion with one horn, and it is certain that nature sometimes produces such monstrous births. I must indeed confess, that the combat between the lion and the mule with one horn, does not seem more extraordinary to me, than those between the mules and bears, which you mention in the 39th chapter of your travels.

I can easily agree with Sir *John Chardin*, who says, page 70, that he believes the inscription in characters, which appears at the end of the long basso-relievo of the stair-case, contains an explication of the sculpture there, and yet I am fully persuaded by the reasons I have alledged, that these famous ruins are those of a palace, and cannot possibly be the remains of a temple.

It is also probable that the tract of ground where most of the columns stand, was originally a court before the palace, like that which was before the king's house at *Susa*, mentioned in the book of *Esther*, c. v. and through which a flow of fresh

Tom 3 P 102 de l'Ed. in 4.

air was admitted into the apartments. One may even presume, that these columns did not support any architrave, as Sir *John Chardin* has observed page 76, but we may venture to suppose that a covering of tapestry or linnen was drawn over them, to intercept the perpendicular projection of the sun-beams. The great number of apartments, whose symetry is no longer distinguishable, were undoubtedly appropriated to the prince, and the officers of his court.

Sir *John Chardin* expresses himself as positively, with relation to the drapery of the figures, as he did with respect to the imaginary temple, and the sacrifices he supposed were offered there, because he discovers some similitude between these habits and those that were worn by the ancient worshippers of fire, or of the *Guebres*, who are still to be found in the *Indies*. He adds, page 59, that the under-vestment of these figures is intended to represent a cotton or silken garment, which is wrapped three or four times round the reins, and the end of which is inserted into the cincture, after which he informs us, that the habits which are cut and sewed, were introduced by the *Mohammedans*. He likewise declares, page 61, that the variety which is to be seen in the head-dress and drapery of those figures, proceeds only from the diversity of countries and climes in the vast empire of *Persia*. He represents some of them, in his 58th plate, in shagged habits, while others are naked, and he gives tiaras to some, and to others handkerchiefs wound about the head, instead of bonnets, in his 60th page, all which is the work of his own fancy, and contrary to the testimonials of ancient authors. For my part, I am persuaded, there is no more similitude between the habits of the pagan *Indians* of these days, and those of the ancient *Persians*, than there is between our manner of dress and

Tom 3 p 113 de l'Ed in 4

Tom 3 p 114 de l'Ed in 4.

Tom 3 p 104 de Ed in 4

Tom 3 p 163 Ed in 4

[a] L. 4 de Nat. Animal. c. 52.
[b] L. 2 Hist. Animal. cap. 50.
[c] L. 11 Hist. Nat. cap. 37 & 46.
[d] De Unicornu cap. 17.

that of our anceftors, and indeed I do not find any figures in your plates that are either naked, or covered with furs　Nor has *Herodotus* mentioned any thing of this nature in his account of the arms and habit of the troops of *Xerxes the Great*　And we find that the drapery of thofe figures which are ftill remaining at *Chelmi-nar*, correfponds with the habits of thofe different nations　I likewife think it very extraordinary, that the ancient *Perfians* fhould have learned the ufe of cut and fewed garments from the *Mohammedans*, fince *Athenæus* declares, that thofe ancient *Perfians* were the firft of all nations who addicted themfelves to luxury and pleafure·　If they wore plaited robes of cloth with large fleeves, and folded them twice or thrice over their reins, as they are reprefented by Sir *John Chardin*, there is but little probability that the famous *Paufanias* of *Sparta* would have clothed himfelf in that manner　And yet *Thucydides* and *Cornelius Nepos* declare, that he wore a royal habit in the mode of the *Medes*, that is to fay, a long plaited robe.　It is likewife certain, that if this habit had been made of cloth neither cut nor fewed, and that it was wrapped over the reins, the ancient *Greeks* would undoubtedly have ridiculed him, our modern *Dutchmen* would have taken him for a *Bohemian* fortune-teller, and the people of *Courland* would have faid pofitively that he was a peafant of *Semigall* or *Livonia*

But I think it time to draw to a clofe, Sir, and fhall therefore do my felf the honour to affure you, without ftopping any longer at trifles, that your plates in the 53d and 54th

chapters, agree perfectly with the defcriptions in ancient authors, and I am perfuaded that every reader of tafte and judgment will prefer the account of your travels, in that particular, to that of Sir *John Chardin.* Your remarks likewife on the tombs of *Naxi Ruftan*, are very accurate and judicious.　Permit me, Sir, to add to what you have obferved, that *Abul-Pharagius* declares there was a hero named *Ruftan*, in the time of *Jefdegerd*, before whofe reign *Chelminar* was undoubtedly built, as the modern *Perfian* hiftorians allow. But all the ftories related of this *Ruftan* are not to be credited, and I even believe that the tomb which is faid to be his, is really that of *Darius*, who is mentioned by *Ctefias*　The reft of Sir *John Chardin*'s remarks are not material enough to require an anfwer

As to the explications which are offered by Mr *Kempfer*, they feem to correfpond very well with yours, if we except his plates and remarks: For which reafon you will permit me to pafs over inconfiderable circumftances, which can be agreeable to none but credulous minds.

Thus, Sir, have I endeavoured to comply with your defires, and if there be any other particular wherein you judge me capable of ferving you, I hope you will do me the juftice to believe, that I will undertake it with pleafure, as being

　SIR,

　　Your moft humble Servant,

　　　　H P.

ᵃ Lib 12

F I N I S.

INDEX.

INDEX.

Cal-

INDEX.

INDEX.

INDEX.

INDEX.

INDEX.

INDEX.

INDEX.

INDEX.

INDEX.

FINIS.

CPSIA information can be obtained
at www.ICGtesting.com
Printed in the USA
LVHW061631080722
723065LV00023B/320